SUMTER COUNTY ALABAMA

Index to

Wills and Estate Administrations
1834-1884

Register of Deaths
1881-1892

and

Cemetery Records

Joseph F. Stegall and *Jud K. Arrington*

HERITAGE BOOKS
2007

HERITAGE BOOKS
AN IMPRINT OF HERITAGE BOOKS, INC.

Books, CDs, and more—Worldwide

For our listing of thousands of titles see our website
at
www.HeritageBooks.com

Published 2007 by
HERITAGE BOOKS, INC.
Publishing Division
65 East Main Street
Westminster, Maryland 21157-5026

Copyright © 1997 Joseph F. Stegall and Jud K. Arrington

All rights reserved. No part of this book may be reproduced or transmitted in any form or by any means, electronic or mechanical, including photocopying, recording or by any information storage and retrieval system without written permission from the author, except for the inclusion of brief quotations in a review.

International Standard Book Number: 978-0-7884-0755-0

CONTENTS

	Page
Foreword	iv
Early County History	vi
Index of Wills and Estate Administrations	1
Register of Deaths	47
Cemetery Records	103
Index of Cemeteries	396
Index of Graves	398

FOREWORD

I inherited a great love for genealogy and history from my mother, Elizabeth Bell Stegall, who has spent a good portion of the latter part of her life doing genealogical research for our family and for others. She and her friends, Jud K. Arrington and the late Nelle M. Jenkins, also spent many hours in the 1960s and 1970s plying through bushes and briars throughout Sumter County to locate old cemeteries and to record tombstone inscriptions.

After retiring from the Air Force in 1976 and returning to Alabama, I more seriously pursued genealogy as a hobby. To ensure that I knew where to look for information, Mother, who worked in the Courthouse at the time, introduced me to the Orphans Court Records. In those old records of estate administrations and guardianships of orphans are contained details about our ancestors' lives and deaths that are both exceptionally interesting and genealogically invaluable.

The first court record following the death of an individual often dealt with the appointment of an administrator of the estate. In many cases, there was also a need to appoint a guardian for the minor children of the family in those days when there was no state or federal agency to provide for them. The record of the appointment of a guardian usually identified the children by name and age and by their relationship to the deceased.

Later, an inventory of the real and personal property of the deceased was often submitted to the court by the administrator of the estate, along with names of the heirs to the estate.

During slavery time, the real property inventories included the names of slaves owned by the deceased, and the estimated value of each slave. I will always remember the feeling of depression that overwhelmed me one day when I read one such list of slaves, and their values, and to find at the end of the list the name "Ophelia", her age as "65", and her estimated value as "Worthless". That was a poignant reminder that those of us who have problems finding our ancestors will never have the problems that would be faced by a descendent of Ophelia. She had no recorded surname, and she probably never made the record books again, unless it was to be in a deed for her sale to another master.

The initial objective of this work was to publish a consolidated index of the 33 volumes of the Orphans Court Records and the recorded wills for the same time frame. However, I was also mindful of the need to publish the countywide cemetery records that my mother and her friends, Jud Arrington and Nelle Jenkins, had developed, but never published. Finally, we added the only extant death records for the 1800s. They are particularly significant since there are no cemetery monuments to mark the graves of most of those persons. Most of them were poor black people who had been slaves.

I hope that you will find this compilation of early Sumter County records to be of value in your genealogical research.

Joseph F. Stegall
York, Alabama
1997

EARLY COUNTY HISTORY

Sumter County, Alabama was founded in 1832, following the Treaty of Dancing Rabbit Creek in 1830 between the United States and the Choctaw Indian Nation. By virture of the treaty, the Choctaw Nation ceded to the United States all of its lands west to the Mississippi River in exchange for land in Oklahoma.

Adjacent and nearby counties to the east of Sumter had been settled some 15 years earlier, following General Andrew Jackson's defeat of the Creek Indian Nation at the Battle of Horseshoe Bend. Upon the founding of Sumter, settlers in those counties to the east, as well as persons seeking new land from Virginia, the Carolinas, Georgia and Tennessee rushed to purchase land in the newly founded county and, in many cases, to homestead it.

By 1835, most of the land was privately owned, either through land grants to Choctaw Inddians who chose to remain on the land, or by settlers who purchased land from the federal land office at nearby Demopolis. Thriving settlements were established along the Tombigbee River, the eastern boundary of the county, at Jamestown, Gainsville, Jones Bluff, McKee, Bluffport and Blacks Bluff, and at the inland locations of Gaston, Patton's Hill, Payneville, and the county seat of Livingston.

By 1840, Sumter was one of the wealthiest and most populous counties in the State of Alabama. It had a population of almost 30,000, consisting of approximately 8,000 whites and 22,000 black slaves. Gainesville was the third largest city in the state.

Choctaw County was formed in 1847 from the lower two townships of Sumter and the five northern townships of Washington County. In 1871, the Choctaw County Courthouse at Butler burned, along with almost all of the public records.

Sumter County continued to grow until the Civil War, even though many of the very early settlers, or their children, had moved westward as the frontier expanded and the Texas Territory was opened for settlement.

Today, Sumter County is a sparsely populated region of some 17,000 people. Unlike the early days when there was a great demand for new land on which to grow cotton, there is no cotton grown in Sumter County today. Most of the land is used for growing timber or for pasturing cattle. A few small industries are located at Livingston and at York. Life is slow-paced, with no traffic jams, very little crime and lots of outdoor recreational opportunities.

PART I

INDEX

WILLS AND ESTATE ADMINISTRATIONS

1834 - 1884

EARLY COURT HISTORY

The Orphans' Court was the earliest court-of-record in Alabama for the administration of estates and the guardianship of minor heirs. This court had its roots in the court system of the Mississippi Territory, long before the State of Alabama joined the Union. The name of the court was undoubtedly chosen to reflect one of its primary responsibilities, which was to protect the inheritance rights of minor heirs and to ensure, through guardianships, that these minors would be properly cared for until they reached adulthood.

By an Alabama Legislative Act of 1823, the responsibilities of the Orphans' Court Judge were defined as "to take the probate of wills, grant and repeal letters testamentary and letters of administration, appoint and displace guardians of infants and idiots, lunatics, and persons non compos mentis, and to make all necessary orders for the issuing process and other purposes within his jurisdiction . . ." (Toulmin's Digest, Title 16, Ch. X, Sec. 4 and 5).

In 1850, the Alabama Legislature abolished the Orphans' Court and replaced it with the Probate Court. Sumter County records indicate that this had little or no effect on court functions. In fact, the records of the Probate Court continued to be filed in volumes labled "Orphans' Court Records" until 1884.

The early Sumter County court records have been well-preserved, and they are open to the public in the Probate Office Annex, Monday through Friday, from 8:00 a.m. to 4:00 p.m.

USE OF INDEX OF WILLS AND ESTATE ADMINISTRATIONS

This is a consolidated index of deceased persons whose estates were administered by the Orphans' Court during the 50-year period from 1834 until 1884, the recorded wills of some of those persons, and the names of other deceased persons, both of Sumter County and elsewhere, whose names are not indexed in Sumter County court records, but were found by the author in the guardianship records.

Most of the persons in the latter category appear to have left estates of so little value that court action was not warranted. However, they left minor children who needed guardians. The others in this category lived and died elsewhere, but left minor heirs in Sumter County.

The volume and page number in the Orphans' Court portion of the consolidated index gives the location in the records of the first entry with regard to the person. In most cases, there were multiple entries, some on subsequent pages within that volume, and some in later volumes. The researcher should look for additional entries under both the name of the deceased and the names of persons who may have been appointed guardians of the deceased's minor children.

The handwriting in the old court records is often difficult to interpret and, frequently, the spelling of a name changes from one record to the next. The author used deeds and other records to reconcile difficult cases. However, in those cases in which the correct spelling could not be determined, an alternative spelling is included in parentheses.

This index includes names of a few persons who left recorded wills but, for one of several reasons, there is no record of the administration of their estates. In a few cases, it was because the county was formed in 1832 but the court only dated back to 1834. In other cases, as discussed above, the deceased lived and died elsewhere, but had minor heirs living in Sumter County.

Finally, the index includes the wills of a few people who died during the last year (1884) covered by the Orphans' Court Records. The estate administration actions for those cases are not cited here, but they may be found in later Probate Court Records on file in the Probate Court Annex.

NAME	WILL BOOK VOL.	PAGE	ORPHANS COURT VOL.	PAGE
Abney, Hardy	1	384	6	138
Abrahams, James A.	3	94	33	26
Adams, Benjamin W.			1	362
Adams, James R.	1	288	3	457
Adams, John			11	312
Adams, John Q.			13	660
Adams, Lucy A.	2	565	21	443
Adams, W. F. L.	2	163		
Adkins, John			3	420
Adkins, Martha			21	179
Alexander, James M.			22	563
Allen, James	1	191		
Allen, Joseph	1	393	6	380
Allison, Robert G.	1	523	10	307
Altman, Henry	2	610	27	210
Amason, Asa	3	48	31	309
Amason, Elbert	2	625	28	252
Amason, Eli			1	225
Amason, Emalina			12	340
Amason, John			7	145
Amason, Nathan	3	59	31	397
Amason, Sarah			10	620
Amason, Thomas			3	443
Amason, William			16	249
Anderson, Albert G.			7	410
Anderson, Amanda M. F.			7	513
Anderson, Hannah W.	2	499	19	49
Anderson, James	1	420	8	16
Anderson, Joshua			11	361
Anderson, Leroy H.			21	691
Anderson, Mason L.			1	202
Anderson, Sarah			24	255
Anderson, Vincent			1	31
Amderson, William	1	378	5	704
Anderson, William S.			20	243
Andrews, Elizabeth			14	454
Apperson, Armistead A.			3	496
Arnold, Esek			2	204
Arrington, Anthony L.			1	391
Arrington, Caroline J.			27	612
Arrington, Crawford			10	668
Arrington, Elizabeth			20	530
Arrington, Henry			22	470
Arrington, Henry F.			26	139

NAME	WILL BOOK VOL.	PAGE	ORPHANS COURT VOL.	PAGE
Arrington, John J.			24	633
Arrington, John S.			9	613
Arrington, Joseph J.			29	767
Arrington, Mary J.	2	433	21	623
Arrington, Mary M.	2	417	21	712
Arrington, Robert			24	590
Arrington, Samuel J.	2	469	22	444
Arrington, William			22	439
Bacon, Henry			2	496
Bailey, Isadore			26	563
Bailey, J. M.			27	551
Baird, Felix W.			1	229
Baker, John E.			24	596
Baker, John W.			16	526
Ball, Willis			10	673
Ballard, Edward			5	788
Ballard, James			26	618
Barber, Abraham			5	776
Barbour, Daniel B.			18	101
Bardwell, Hiram	3	89	32	371
Barlee, James H.			24	406
Barnes, Bennett B.			24	356
Barnes, Charles			4	366
Barnes, James G.			25	315
Barnes, John T.	2	603	27	29
Barnett, John W.			15	84
Barret, J. V.			30	586
Barrett, Caroline M.	2	650	29	475
Barrett, Carrie Dewalt			20	157
Barrett, Harrison			8	485
Barron, John			13	662
Barron, Mary			2	499
Barron, Sarah			2	481
Barron, Silas M.			2	38
Barron, William			13	662
Bartee, James H.	2	572	27	374
Bates, Robert A.			1	322
Bates, William	2	75	13	78
Battle, Sallie S.	3	74	32	142
Beal, James			9	565
Beane, Opie			1	485
Beavers, Dixon			3	351
Beavers, James	2	360	20	119

NAME	WILL BOOK VOL.	PAGE	ORPHANS COURT VOL.	PAGE
Beavers, Thomas			11	98
Beazley, Edward			2	267
Beazley, John W.	1	70	1	559
Beazley, Lemuel			1	113
Beazley, Lemuel W.			13	136
Beazley, Micajah			9	248
Beazley, Richard			10	48
Beazley, Thomas			9	822
Beazley, William A.			1	365
Beazley, William N.	1	453	9	75
Beck, Alfred			1	127
Beck, R. M.			2	152
Beebe, Asa	1	264		
Beggs, Martha N.	3	129		
Beggs, Robert M.			24	328
Bell, Edward S.			21	375
Bell, Elizabeth			12	560
Bell, Frederick	2	319	18	62
Bell, Pamillia	1	381	5	401
Bennett, Anthony Sr.	1	386	6	153
Bennett, Charles W.			31	2
Bennett, James C.			25	332
Bennett, Kennard			5	501
Bigham, John			6	389
Billups, James W.			28	316
Billups, Thomas M.			21	756
Bingham, Mary			12	433
Bingham, Samuel			12	341
Binns, Allen P.			7	495
Binns, George F.			1	639
Bird, Jesse J. J.	1	348	4	812
Bird, Lydia Ann			21	358
Bird, William	1	102	2	256
Bishop, Elizabeth	1	409	7	146
Bishop, Robert C.			9	663
Bizzle, Bryant			11	219
Blackburn, William			4	63
Blacksher, David	2	608	26	582
Blackwell, Philemon			10	236
Blackwell, Thomas J.			8	407
Blair, George W.			14	429
Blakeney, James			13	460
Bland, John P.			15	299
Bledsoe, Yancy			2	253

NAME	WILL BOOK VOL.	WILL BOOK PAGE	ORPHANS COURT VOL.	ORPHANS COURT PAGE
Bliss, Jonathan	3	79	32	199
Blount, Rebecca			2	290
Blythe, Samuel			1	193
Bohannan, Young	1	273	3	228
Boling, Henry	1	310	4	331
Boling, William R.	2	330	18	476
Bolton, Ellsworth			21	372
Bolton, Manasieth F.			22	244
Bolton, William	2	6	11	95
Bond, John			1	382
Boney, Nancy	2	109	13	595
Boney, Wimbeck			6	179
Boon, Joseph	1	183		
Boone, John C.			17	187
Bordeaux, Lewis			13	307
Bostick, F. Marion			19	539
Bostick, Garland			20	15
Boutwell, George			5	678
Boyd, John	1	426	7	918
Boyd, John	2	89	13	396
Boyd, Matthew H.			31	379
Boyd, Robert			32	600
Boyd, Samuel B.	2	140		
Boyd, Susan H.			14	273
Boyett, Ellen A.	2	200	15	295
Boyett, Lock	1	136	2	230
Boyett, Missouri	1	499	10	556
Boyett, Robert	1	105	2	99
Boyett, Sarah	1	339	4	508
Brackett, Anson			14	343
Bradford, John J.	1	31	1	497
Bradford, Margaret	1	565	3	372
Bradley, Martha C.			19+	91
Bradley, Wayne A.			14	330
Bradshaw, Robert	2	639	29	207
Bragg, William T.	1	431	8	408
Branch, William S.			6	322
Brantly, James			15	450
Brashears, Ellen S.	1	251	3	455
Brashears, Jesse			3	454
Brashears, William M.			9	684
Brashears, Zadock			3	309
Brewer, Jackson			12	126
Brewer, Mary			18	517

NAME	WILL BOOK VOL.	PAGE	ORPHANS COURT VOL.	PAGE
Brewer, Thomas J.			13	692
Brewer, William	2	35	11	697
Briggs, Henry A.			12	523
Bright, Thomas G.			1	375
Brockway, A. E.			26	166
Broome, Darcus			8	167
Broome, Spyers			8	169
Brown, A. J.			18	256
Brown, Alanson	1	42	1	86
Brown, Bartlett			3	445
Brown, Benjamin			1	383
Brown, Brady M.			8	586
Brown, Charles A.			9	217
Brown, Charles G.			26	571
Brown, Henrietta			22	102
Brown, James M.			12	237
Brown, Jerre H.			26	172
Brown, John			1	473
Brown, John E.	3	62	31	690
Brown, John G.			29	66
Brown, Julana	1	44	1	142
Brown, Lewis S.			7	144
Brown, Robert A.	2	397	21	290
Brown, Robert L.	2	574	25	124
Brown, Sherrod			8	487
Brown, William A.			8	407
Brown, William W.			1	463
Browning, Nancy			21	314
Brownrigg, Alfred			4	637
Brownrigg, Edwin			3	716
Brunson, Leonard C.	2	156	14	198
Bryan, Joseph W.			5	478
Bryant, John A.			9	355
Bryant, John B.			7	695
Bryant, Washington			30	45
Buchanan, May	2	324	18	191
Buckholts, Adeline			2	611
Buckholts, Augustus			3	725
Buckholts, Betsy			1	402
Buckholts, Celestia A.			2	610
Buckholts, Peter			7	501
Buckholts, Rebecca			2	610
Buckholts, William H.	1	65	1	539
Bunn, Alfred			1	97

	WILL BOOK		ORPHANS COURT	
NAME	VOL.	PAGE	VOL.	PAGE
Bunn, William S.			18	636
Buntin, Martha			13	385
Buntin, William			12	371
Burkhart, Peter			5	741
Burns, Andrew			32	228
Burridge, Harriet			10	232
Burton, David S.			21	421
Burton, Drury L.	1	493	9	736
Burton, John L.			1	332
Burton, Nancy J.			26	572
Burton, Thomas			13	693
Busby, John F.			14	323
Cage, Jesse	1	392	7	170
Caldwell, John E.			27	303
Calloway, Amasa			8	501
Calvert, Robert			1	63
Camber, Francis A.			17	128
Camber, Joseph			20	223
Cameron, Angus B.			3	207
Campbell, J. L.			20	204
Campbell, Jane			32	571
Campbell, R. M.			33	403
Campbell, Robert W.	2	212	16	10
Carlton, Warren	1	38	1	237
Carpenter, John			16	537
Carpenter, Jubal			21	107
Carpenter, Thomas			19	52
Carre', Robert			33	294
Carroll, Edmond			5	116
Carroll, George W.			2	247
Carroll, Jacob			2	394
Carson, John			2	188
Cato, William H.			7	732
Chamberlagne, William	1	232		
Chambers, Elizabeth	1	174	2	569
Chandler, Norborne E.			8	510
Chaney, Albert B.			18	578
Chaney, Green B.			19	131
Chaney, Peyton	1	127	2	248
Chapman, Joseph			17	94
Chapman, William C.			18	237
Chapman, William S.			2	90
Cherry, Jared W.	2	634	28	794

NAME	WILL BOOK VOL.	PAGE	ORPHANS COURT VOL.	PAGE
Cherry, Martha	3	115		
Chiles, C.			18	409
Chiles, Elizabeth R.			21	257
Chiles, Hiram			7	66
Chiles, Samuel H.			23	164
Chiles, Walter			1	318
Chiles, Walter L.	1	459	12	240
Chiles, William E.			26	252
Chinn, Benjamin			13	121
Christian, Turner G.			19	41
Christopher, Ralph G.	1	107	2	155
Chunn, Berryman			3	776
Clanton, George C.	1	114	2	157
Clanton, Harriet R.	1	520	10	232
Clanton, Landon	1	87	2	40
Clanton, Solomon W.			16	445
Clark, David W.			16	85
Clark, John P.	1	143	2	314
Clark, William H.			5	604
Clarke, David W.	2	99	13	297
Clary, Samuel H.			15	240
Clayton, Philip			2	185
Clements, Edward			2	303
Clinton, Matthew	1	315	4	315
Coats, Ann			18	33
Coats, J. G.			33	432
Cobb, John B.	1	8	1	56
Cobbs, Thomas	1	204	2	575
Cocke, Amanda E.			14	94
Cocke, William T.			31	736
Cockrell, Emerson			5	44
Cockrell, James			14	618
Cockrell, Martha A. E.			21	108
Cockrell, Milicent			22	238
Cockrell, Nathan E.			21	109
Coffman, Samuel H.	1	94	2	30
Colby, John K.			2	223
Coleman, Reuben			17	203
Coleman, Samuel Cruse	3	108		
Coleman, Spilsby	1	429	8	349
Coleman, William Henry			8	844
Colgin, John			1	562
Colgin, Sarah A. F.	2	115	13	780
Colgin, William R.	1	74	1	675

	WILL BOOK		ORPHANS COURT	
NAME	VOL.	PAGE	VOL.	PAGE
Collier, John			8	86
Conaway, John T.	1	277	3	458
Cone, George B.			11	490
Cook, John F.			1	227
Cooper, Richard			2	36
Covington, Harrison W.			11	208
Cox, Odom			16	292
Craig, John H.			21	717
Craig, Robert	2	350		
Cravy, Elizabeth			15	128
Cravy, Emily			16	548
Cravy, Hugh	1	49	1	166
Cravy, Jacob			8	502
Crawford, Rosannah	1	508	10	116
Crawford, Thomas			12	283
Crawford, William			1	325
Crenshaw, Ruth			10	267
Crews, Thomas R.	2	462	23	102
Crimm, Warren W.			11	421
Crisp, Benjamin A.			1	425
Crisp, Naoma H.			4	217
Criswell, Elijah	1	526	10	313
Cromwell, Charlotte			3	727
Cromwell, Elijah			1	226
Crooks, Malinda			12	273
Croom, Bryan			21	455
Croom, Nicholas P.	2	466	22	402
Crowson, Aaron	1	25		
Cubley, John K.	1	121	3	91
Cummings, James			18	5
Curry, Avery V.			1	133
Curry, David			6	392
Curry, Lucretia			29	530
Curry, Ruth			1	129
Cusack, Corinne D.	2	645	29	408
Cusack, John C.			1	70
Cusack, Thomas	2	630	28	415
Dabbs, S. A. R.			1	167
Dabney, Martin D.			15	486
Dallas, Alexander			21	294
Dalrymple, James			20	782
Dandridge, William H.			25	116
Daney, Albert G.			1	608

| | WILL BOOK | | ORPHANS COURT | |
NAME	VOL.	PAGE	VOL.	PAGE
Daniel, Benjamin T.			11	69
Daniel, Ephraim	2	28	11	543
Daniel, Henry T.			19	343
Daniel, Joseph			8	626
Daniel, Matthew A.			11	68
Daniel, Rufus			11	67
Daniel, Thomas			26	228
Danner, Jacob G.			14	555
Danner, Robert			17	391
Danner, Thomas G.	2	555	20	570
Dansby, Eleanor	1	292	3	744
Darden, Benjamin J.			19	442
Darden, James			4	236
Darden, John			4	423
Darden, John H.			19	442
Darland, John			14	141
Davidson, James D.			10	105
Davis, Brooks H.			2	275
Davis, Darcus			5	149
Davis, Eli			1	514
Davis, Francis			17	227
Davis, James P.			17	149
Davis, Jesse P.			15	227
Davis, Littleberry B.			6	632
Davis, Nehemiah			16	17
Davis, Samuel	2	68	13	33
Davis, Thomas			4	653
Davis, William R.			29	35
Dawkins, John T.			21	396
Dawson, Eliza			12	505
Dean, Alexander	2	419	21	751
Deane, Nathaniel P.			29	652
Dearman, Solomon			1	481
Dearman, William A.			11	731
Decostro, John G.			1	483
Dees, George			3	72
Dees, William M.			7	735B
Dees, Willoughby			2	226
Deloach, Alfred B.			13	308
Deloach, Etheldra C.			16	459
Denton, George			28	525
Dial, David			13	310
Dial, James	2	624	28	237
Dial, James C.			23	192

NAME	WILL BOOK VOL. PAGE		ORPHANS COURT VOL. PAGE	
Dial, Jeremiah			3	205
Dial, Jeremiah S.			18	199
Dill, John			7	737
Dillard, John J.	1	528	10	341
Dillard, John J.	3	102		
Dillard, Nancy J.			30	445
Dillard, William			1	387
Dodson, Elijah J.			7	880
Donald, Arabella A.			6	375
Donald, Simon			2	609
Donald, Thomas	1	259	3	495
Donald, Thomas J.	2	581	25	426
Donald, William J.			14	296
Donald, William S.	2	147	14	143
Donaldson, Hugh H.			1	522
Doty, Peter	(Deed Book 2,		Page	11)
Drake, William	2	507	19	471
Drew, James C.			2	104
Drew, Thomas			31	714
Drinkard, Pleasant L.			20	787
Drinkard, William A.			20	790
Driskell, Jacob			26	179
Driskell, William			13	25
Drummond, Emily A.			7	735
Drummond, William			4	280
Duke, John			10	604
Duke, Sarah J.			17	209
Duke, William			11	600
Duncan, Alexander			1	762
Duncan, John			2	388
Dunning, Wiley			16	329
Duren, Jonathan			10	141
Durfey, Eliza C.			26	44
Earp, William	1	329	3	15
Easley, Warham	1	84	2	17
Eason, Ithiel	2	486	13	151
Eason, J. R. T.			21	773
Eason, John T.	2	421	21	770
Eason, T. H.			21	772
Eason, Thomas			16	309
Easters, Caldwell	1	317		
Eaton, Humphrey F.			17	383
Edmonson, John			4	130

NAME	WILL BOOK VOL.	PAGE	ORPHANS COURT VOL.	PAGE
Edmundson, Thomas	1	294		
Edwards, Achilles			9	778
Edwards, Anna	1	557	11	14
Edwards, Gray H.			8	431
Edwards, Mary C.			15	118
Edwards, Mary E.			15	245
Elliott, Andrew			1	462
Elliott, Anna	1	536	10	453
Elliott, James M.			24	547
Elliott, Richard			3	373
Ellis, Delpha			16	394
Ellis, Edwin	3	39	31	195
Ellis, Freeman			14	350
Ellis, Solomon			7	748
English, William			1	230
Epes, John C.			18	319
Epes, Richard J.	2	570	23	55
Epperson, William J.			10	424
Epps, James			5	64
Eskridge, E. A.			26	143
Eskridge, Lemuel			32	148
Eskridge, S. G.			26	144
Eskridge, Thomas			2	259
Estes, Caldwell			4	408
Estes, Carter	1	303	3	781
Etheridge, David			1	88
Etheridge, James T.	3	23	30	340
Etheridge, William			2	502
Evans, Abner			12	348
Evans, Arabella			22	240
Evans, Ellington	2	586	24	598
Evans, Harrison			4	373
Evans, John P.			27	493
Faires, Rebecca A.	3	102		
Farish, Eliza P.	1	97	2	39
Farmer, James J.			9	629
Farmer, Millicent	1	485	9	699
Faunt, Thomas			7	218
Faust, John E.			33	635
Fawcett, Lyle B.			1	646
Ferrell, James	2	524	18	510
Fincher, Hilliard J.			26	601
Finley, Ann	1	401		

NAME	WILL BOOK VOL.	WILL BOOK PAGE	ORPHANS COURT VOL.	ORPHANS COURT PAGE
Fleming, Robert	1	517	10	253
Fleming, Shemei			5	504
Flora, Nancy			6	67
Flowers, Bennett P.	1	539	10	457
Flowers, Henry B.			7	220
Flowers, Jacob D.			10	406
Flowers, Joel			5	126
Flowers, John	2	358		
Flowers, Perry			13	698
Flowers, Sarah M.	2	627	26	400
Fluker, David			13	805
Fluker, William	2	119	13	766
Foard, Francis	1	513	10	174
Foard, Thomas J.			15	229
Fort, Henry	1	443	8	430
Foster, James J.	1	487	9	628
Foster, John W.	1	341	3	281
Fowler, Newton	1	200	2	566
Fowler, Thomas			12	200
Foy, Edward	1	390	7	219
Foy, Ellen A.	3	112		
Foy, Terry			3	354
Franklin, Abner			2	318
Freeland, George W.			1	55
Freeman, Josiah	1	395	12	482
Frierson, Gideon B.			13	664
Frierson, William V.			20	789
Frost, John			1	676
Fry, John W.			12	55
Fulford, Stephen	1	445	8	748
Fulton, M. F.			24	266
Gage, David			7	923
Gage, Winston			33	139
Gaines, Benjamin	1	99		
Gamble, Martha			2	506
Gamble, Samuel E.			9	534
Gamble, Walter	1	139	2	237
Garland, Winston			10	622
Garrett, William			17	124
Gary, William B.	1	373	5	496
Gasky(Gasque), Thomas	1	159	2	387
Gates, Solan A.			24	355
Gatewood, Armistead			24	503

NAME	WILL BOOK VOL.	WILL BOOK PAGE	ORPHANS COURT VOL.	ORPHANS COURT PAGE
Gatewood, Rebecca			24	502
Gatewood, Thomas	2	386	9	610
Gathings, James			6	83
Gay, Elizabeth			7	698
Gee, George W.			15	94
Gee, John H.			16	595
Gee, Theodric J.			16	11
Gee, Thomas			21	470
Gee, Varner A.			3	443
Geiger, Alexander	2	636	28	82
Geiger, John W.			3	489
Gholson, Greenville	1	132	2	315
Gholson, James H.			21	333
Gibbs, Charles R.	2	648	28	435
Gibbs, Edwin C.	3	26	30	443
Gibbs, Matthew			10	4
Gibson, Samuel	1	22		
Gibson, William A.			12	285
Gilbert, Henry F. D.			21	251
Gilbert, James M.	2	62	10	772
Gilbert, John M.			20	86
Gilbert, Susan			17	344
Gilbert, William	2	617	27	612
Gilbert, William Sr.			10	187
Gill, Jerome	1	553	10	755
Gill, Mary			33	220
Gillespie, Joseph	2	87	13	255
Gillespie, Mary	2	314	17	356
Gillespie, Sarah W.			33	541
Gilmore, Isabella			29	565
Gilmore, Nathaniel	1	439	8	442
Glasscock, Lucy			21	762
Glenn, Berry			12	18
Glenn, Robert	1	170	2	231
Godfrey, Dozier			4	66
Godfrey, William	2	481	13	56
Gordon, Mary			5	51
Gordon, Posey			8	342
Gorman, Elijah			4	387
Gorman, Elizabeth			14	96
Gould, Daniel	1	555	10	769
Gould, John M.			23	1
Grady, Robert	2	57	12	466
Graham, Ann			18	330

17

	WILL BOOK		ORPHANS COURT	
NAME	VOL.	PAGE	VOL.	PAGE
Graham, Archibald			1	357
Graham, Charles	1	511	10	131
Graham, Charles G.			5	494
Graham, Charles W.	2	151	14	200
Graham, Dempsey			27	602
Graham, Dempsey A.	2	111	13	694
Graham, Elijah	2	130	14	53
Graham, Elijah W.			21	335
Graham, James E.			4	355
Graham, Zelina			15	210
Grant, Francis M.			8	71
Graves, Robert	1	171	2	534
Gray, John H.			32	71
Grayson, Ralph W.			15	483
Grayson, Young W.	2	522	19	581
Green, Aba			24	471
Green, Bolling	1	433	8	192
Green, Caster			1	472
Green, Daniel	1	245	3	232
Green, Rolly			16	91
Green, William H.			13	768
Greene, George			10	244
Greene, Mary			10	1
Greene, Susan			12	478
Greenlees, Isabella			17	490
Greenlees, John			14	186
Greenlees, Joseph	3	92	32	408
Greer, Isaac S. O. G.			26	115
Gregory, James G.			13	79
Gregory, Obediah	2	431	22	84
Gregory, Sarah A.	3	76	32	164
Gregory, William J.			26	403
Grice, John			21	183
Grice, Stephen			10	95
Griffin, A. H.			25	288
Griffin, Claiborn	1	275	3	485
Griffin, Eliza Jane			16	591
Griffin, James			11	420
Griffin, James			13	762
Grigsby, Luke M.			5	191
Grigsby, Sarah	1	6		
Grimes, James W.			20	627
Grun, Daniel			8	400
Gulley, Rebecca			26	138

| | WILL BOOK | | ORPHANS COURT | |
NAME	VOL.	PAGE	VOL.	PAGE
Gully, Jesse			12	433
Gully, William			5	751
Gunn, William B.			13	661
Gwinn, Chesly R.			6	13
Hadden, Elizabeth	1	435	8	202
Hadden, Isaac	1	465	9	558
Hadden, Robert W.			11	309
Hadden, William			8	434
Hadley, John L.			24	279
Hainsworth, Amelia	2	587	26	12
Hainsworth, James L.	2	264	16	234
Hair, James	2	560	20	639
Hair, Martha W.			30	661
Hale, Harriet C.	2	317	18	37
Hale, Lemuel B.	3	6	29	730
Hale, Mary A.	2	497		
Hall, Archibald	2	224	16	58
Hall, James W.			18	622
Hall, Kerney C.			30	535
Hall, Robert Clarke			1	83
Hall, Thomas			5	151
Halsell, Gabriel			9	107
Halsell, Nancy			3	248
Halsell, Patience (S.P.)	1	541	9	821
Halsell, Thomas			1	330
Holsomback, John G.			13	652
Hamill, Newton J.			26	567
Hampton, Aba W.			1	54
Hampton, Obediah Woodson	1	27		
Hand, Obediah	1	55	1	233
Handley, Peter			32	101
Harding, Edward D.			1	617
Hardy, James			2	231
Hardy, Martin			13	72
Hardy, Nancy			2	231
Hare, Willis V.			27	608
Harper, Catherine C.			19	45
Harper, James			11	518
Harper, James W.			16	517
Harper, John E.			20	222
Harper, Robert			1	196
Harper, Sophia	2	589	26	184
Harper, Wyatt	2	654	22	399

NAME	WILL BOOK VOL.	PAGE	ORPHANS COURT VOL.	PAGE
Harrell, Abner			9	662
Harrell, Abraham			2	529
Harris, A. H.			28	246
Harris, Alexander H.			21	792
Harris, Charles A.			10	215
Harris, Henry H.			20	227
Harris, Irene			21	559
Harris, John W.			29	218
Harris, Joseph H.			15	461
Harris, Josephine			20	1
Harris, M. A. H.			29	218
Harris, Norflit T.			18	495
Harris, Rebecca B.	2	391	21	150
Harris, Richard	2	1	11	59
Harrison, Simmons	2	537	20	148
Harrison, Simmons Sr.			14	179
Hart, William			4	91
Hartsfield, James M.			33	10
Harwell, Ann			11	23
Harwell, William T.	2	81	12	514
Harwood, Edward T.			15	417
Harwood, Elizabeth D.	2	637	20	110
Harwood, Robert E.			20	115
Harwood, Samuel M.	1	257	3	306
Haskins, Matthew			20	439
Haskins, Thomas			20	439
Hasson, Isaac			5	65
Hatch, Edmond L.			1	1
Hatch, George N.	1	221	3	202
Haupt, Lewis			30	186
Haupt, Sebastian	1	36	1	130
Hawkins, Thomas B.			14	428
Hayes, Willis F.			22	93
Hays, Dumprey S.			16	18
Hays, Martin J.	2	60	12	512
Hays, Mary K.			16	18
Hazlewood, Angelletta			17	385
Heard, Joel			5	808
Heard, John			4	275
Heard, William			3	30
Hearn, Elijah			14	296
Hearn, Elizabeth			17	352
Hearn, James	2	174	14	444
Hearn, Jasper			17	352

| | WILL BOOK | | ORPHANS COURT | |
NAME	VOL.	PAGE	VOL.	PAGE
Hearn, S. N.			16	562
Hearn, William			5	45
Hemphill, J. H.			29	673
Henagan, Christopher			7	697
Henagan, Sarah J.	3	19	30	292
Henderlite, Isaac			3	334
Henderson, Alexander			11	24
Henderson, Thomas O.	1	472	9	567
Hendrix, Jonathan D.	2	315	17	503
Herbert, George P.			3	554
Herring, Joseph	3	45	31	256
Hibbler, Elizabeth			19	492
Hibbler, Martha B.	2	585	24	594
Hibbler, William H.	2	380	20	457
Higgenbothom, E.			16	537
High, William			1	111
Hill, James T.			10	461
Hill, John C.			21	234
Hill, Robert			28	350
Hill, Thomas B.			22	557
Hill, Thomas M.	2	412	21	628
Hillman, Joshua W.			12	298
Hillman, Judson J.			28	746
Hillman, Nimrod W.	2	66	13	73
Hillman, William P.			20	98
Hinchie, Garland			5	670
Hines, Charles A.			7	30
Hines, David			12	443
Hines, Elizabeth			27	394
Hines, Frederick	1	416	7	759
Hines, George K.			5	736
Hines, William			21	86
Hinton, Joseph H.			18	425
Hitt, Austin	2	50	12	394
Hitt, Benjamin B.			10	189
Hitt, Charles B.			24	529
Hitt, Easter	1	387	9	671
Hitt, Henry J.			10	226
Hitt, John			7	201
Hitt, Richard			3	713
Hix, John			1	674
Hoard, Addison			17	366
Hoard, Josephine			19+	79
Hobson, Edmond C.			15	228

NAME	WILL BOOK VOL.	PAGE	ORPHANS COURT VOL.	PAGE
Hodges, Allen			4	358
Hodges, Creed C.			13	456
Hodges, F. M.			21	476
Hodges, Hugh			5	13
Hodges, John			19+	35
Hodges, John W.			19	632
Hodges, Philemon			2	387
Hodges, Robert	1	363	5	63
Hodges, Rosanna(Rozena)			16	589
Holcomb, Alvin H.	2	54	12	434
Holden, William H.			16	34
Holder, Chesley	2	429	22	174
Holland, Emily A.			31	655
Holland, John	1	253	3	310
Hollifield, Daniel	1	561		
Holly, Elizabeth			10	233
Holly, Godfrey			4	105
Holly, Jesse J.	2	399	21	292
Holly, Zachariah			2	314
Holsomback, John G.			15	188
Honeycut, Adam			3	330
Hooks, David			1	58
Hooks, Robert D.			7	28
Hooks, Susan	2	196	15	339
Hooks, Thomas C.			3	710
Hoot, Mary F.			32	83
Hopkins, Martha			14	508
Hopper, James			4	769
Hopper, John			15	432
Hopper, Mary			12	13
Hopper, William			15	133
Hopson, Bluford			22	632
Hopson, Edward C.			15	104
Horn, Harris	1	365	5	493
Horn, Henry			8	433
Horn, Jacob			21	739
Horn, John	1	196	2	606
Horn, John W.	1	279	3	453
Horn, Josiah R.			2	317
Horton, Elizabeth Ann			19	265
Horton, John W. W.			23	218
Horton, Margaret A.			23	225
Hough, Jackson			2	313
Houlditch, Isaiah B.			10	261

NAME	WILL BOOK VOL.	WILL BOOK PAGE	ORPHANS COURT VOL.	ORPHANS COURT PAGE
Houlditch, William	1	111	2	129
House, James H.			2	95
Houston, Erastus L.	2	550	20	509
Houston, Hamilton			18	503
Houston, Henry			7	429
Houston, John	1	489	10	11
Houston, John J.			32	175
Houston, Lewis			16	541
Houston, Martha L.	3	114		
Houston, Nancy E.			30	493
Hovey, William H.	2	643	29	8
Howard, John Jr.			2	229
Howington, Herrod			2	234
Hubbard, James W.			1	115
Hubbard, Matthew			3	105
Hubbard, Woodson			12	250
Hudson, Thomas D.			2	565
Humphries, L. B.	2	621	26	120
Hunt, Absolem			2	137
Hunter, R. S.			15	84
Hutcherson, Washington	2	268	16	118
Hutchings, Jessie			25	303
Hutchings, Jesse H.			3	394
Hutchings, John T.			17	87
Hutchins, James L.	2	641	29	224
Hutchins, John H.			13	655
Hutchins, Richard			2	374
Hutchins, Thomas H.	1	270	3	432
Hutchins, William P.			15	35
Inge, Robert S.			10	186
Inge, William			5	70
Inmon, Joseph C.			20	245
Irby, Adline			28	405
Irby, Elvina			11	470
Irby, James H.			16	15
Irby, Moses	1	497	9	851
Irby, Wesley			28	405
Irons, James H.			2	541
Isbell, James			16	191
Ivy, Benjamin	2	491	16	564
Ivy, Charles	1	377	5	688
Ivy, James B.	3	10	30	159
Ivy, John M.			6	296

NAME	WILL BOOK VOL.	WILL BOOK PAGE	ORPHANS COURT VOL.	ORPHANS COURT PAGE
Jackson, Delila			4	226
Jackson, Elijah			2	142
Jackson, Elizabeth			13	212
Jackson, Ephriam			2	164
Jackson, Jacinth	2	615	26	627
Jackson, James C.			4	15
Jackson, Randall			2	39
Jackson, William R.			2	469
James, John S.			20	213
James, Philip			6	14
James, Thomas E.	2	527	17	8
James, William Dobin	1	10		
James, William H.			1	152
Jarman, Bryant			8	448
Jarman, Emanuel			12	49
Jarman, Thomas	2	618	28	67
Jemison, Francis C.			3	103
Jemison, Francis H.			2	375
Jemison, John S.	1	326	4	267
Jemison, William H.			4	421
Jenkins, Janett			13	157
Jenkins, John T.			19	496
Jenkins, Oliver			21	763
Jenkins, Richard	2	309	17	144
Jeter, Sarah M.	2	12	11	140
Johnson, Asa			30	199
Johnson, Elizabeth	1	473	3	326
Johnson, Henry			2	511
Johnson, Lewis	3	38	31	147
Johnson, Peter W.			15	257
Johnson, Sumner			13	299
Johnson, Thomas H.	2	85	20	661
Johnson, Wiley G.			3	2
Johnston, Charles			2	257
Johnston, Elizabeth			3	326
Johnston, Henry G.			26	86
Johnston, Peter W.			13	39
Joiner, Orrin	3	110	33	561
Jones, Abram			5	747
Jones, Alexander			3	435
Jones, Benjamin A.	2	291	17	307
Jones, Blake B.			3	255
Jones, Daniel			27	440
Jones, Elizabeth			10	235

NAME	WILL BOOK VOL.	PAGE	ORPHANS COURT VOL.	PAGE
Jones, Elizabeth D.			28	655
Jones, Frily	2	526	19	554
Jones, Gabriel	1	247	3	311
Jones, Gaden			9	339
Jones, Henry K.			3	346
Jones, Hull			6	412
Jones, James E.	1	145	2	367
Jones, James G.			10	243
Jones, James J.			15	60
Jones, James W.	2	506	19	342
Jones, Jesse			1	46
Jones, Joel			4	300
Jones, John M.			11	602
Jones, John P.			5	460
Jones, Maria J.			18	408
Jones, Martha			12	510
Jones, Matthew			9	693
Jones, Rosetta			32	37
Jones, Samuel L.			1	176
Jones, Sarah J.			12	272
Jones, Syrena	2	552	20	518
Jones, W. M.			24	616
Jones, William D.	2	193	15	129
Jones, William H.			20	518
Jones, Zachariah			3	783
Jordan, Williamson			24	338
Jowers, George			2	607
Kane, James			17	374
Keane, James			15	455
Keeland, William H.			13	26
Kendrick, Mary J.			21	647
Kendrick, William Thomas			21	646
Kennard, Ingram B.	1	471	9	589
Kennard, James P.			32	265
Kennard, John M.			4	67
Kennard, Smith O.			13	431
Kennard, Thomas A.			30	554
Kennedy, Hardy			13	387
Kennedy, Harriet A.			30	554
Kennedy, Sarah J.			19	458
Kennon, Howard L.	3	31	31	110
Key, Joel M.			29	105
Killen, Emma			7	793

NAME	WILL BOOK VOL.	WILL BOOK PAGE	ORPHANS COURT VOL.	ORPHANS COURT PAGE
Kimbrough, J. A.			8	67
King, Michael A.	2	513	19	245
King, William G.			15	461
Kinnard, M. C.			32	48
Kinnon, Richard			1	606
Kirkland, Robert L.			12	477
Kirkland, William	3	57	31	345
Kirkpatrick, James			5	819
Knight, Arthur			10	714
Knight, Cynthia	2	52	12	413
Knight, James L.			17	45
Knight, Jarrett			1	50
Knight, Joseph			9	286
Knight, Paul S.			3	711
Knight, Peter			10	90
Knight, Thomas J. G.	1	142	2	243
Knight, William			5	497
Knott, William H.			27	139
Knox, Elizabeth			2	166
Knox, John			2	168
Knox, John Clementine			10	520
Knox, Mary Jane			5	395
Kornegay, Daniel			8	439
Lacy, Austin H.			4	456
Lacy, Elisha	2	363	20	135
Lake, Joseph G.			9	566
Lake, Sarah L.	2	629		
Lake, Susan E.			16	485
Lamberson, John			32	313
Lancaster, Benjamin	3	86	32	325
Landrum, John			5	654
Langham, Walker D.			2	164
Lanier,			27	458
Larkin, Abram			28	362
Larkin, James M.	1	441	8	586
Larkin, James R.			19	457
Larkin, John R.			11	375
Larkin, Mary A.			14	243
Larkin, Susan E.	3	7	29	791
Larkin, Thomas			24	385
Larkin, William S.			24	462
Lavalle, John	2	654	12	115
Lavender, Bryan			2	504

NAME	WILL BOOK VOL.	PAGE	ORPHANS COURT VOL.	PAGE
Lavender, Hugh L.			1	109
Lavender, Jane	1	454	9	134
Lavender, Margaret			4	112
Lavender, Robert S.			22	562
Law, George			19	70
Lawler, Eli			21	495
Lawson, Mumford	1	213	3	92
Lawson, Thomas			7	707
Lee, Daniel			10	346
Lee, James M.			33	21
Lee, John R.			19	523
Lee, Susan	2	557	20	582
Lee, William			3	257
Leeman, Hugh	3	29	30	599
Leeman, Nancy A.			31	640
Lewis, A. M.			20	783
Lewis, Arthur			1	532
Lewis, Daniel O.			2	369
Lewis, David K.			33	431
Lewis, George			10	379
Lewis, John C.			18	280
Lewis, Joshua	2	326	18	457
Lewis, Lewellin			31	624
Lewis, Moses			1	157
Lewis, Obedience			21	789
Lewis, Owen			28	615
Lide, Hugh S.	3	72	32	105
Lightfoot, Henry C.			1	535
Lindsey, Ellis			26	466
Linn, Charles W.			1	50
Lipscomb, H. P.			30	189
Litchfield, William			1	475
Little, Amariah	1	324	4	424
Little, B. B. Jr.	2	577	25	538
Little, Ben B.	2	439	22	258
Little, Edwin S.	2	407	21	385
Little, Elizabeth	2	582	24	551
Little, Gray			16	5
Little, Joseph J.			29	144
Little, Patrick H.			28	32
Little, Seth	3	84	32	307
Little, Seth Sr.	2	454	22	601
Little, Susan			26	492
Little, W. G. Jr.	3	78	32	194

NAME	WILL BOOK VOL.	WILL BOOK PAGE	ORPHANS COURT VOL.	ORPHANS COURT PAGE
Little, Will	3	17	30	183
Littrell, Elijah			20	576
Lloyd (See Loyd below)				
Lockard, Thomas			20	660
Lockard, William			29	286
Lockard, William J.			20	156
Lockhart, Joel			2	153
Long, James D.	2	279	17	181
Long, Julia			11	485
Long, Richard B.	2	177	22	260
Long, Simon E.	1	96	2	86
Look, Rebecca			1	482
Love, Edward W.			29	214
Love, Nathan			29	212
Lovelady, Obed			4	282
Lowe, N. G.			19	276
Lowry, George			14	120
Lowry, Joseph J.			12	349
Lowry, Prudence			30	168
Lowry, Vernal	2	22	11	213
Lowry, Vernal Jr.			14	119
Loyd, Elizabeth			16	129
Loyd, William B.			11	11
Lummus, William A.			21	719
Lunny, Peter W.			5	53
Lusk, William J.			32	140
Luttrell, Edward D.			4	125
Lynch, Nicholas			22	117
Lynch, Susan D.			18	123
Lynn, Charles W.			9	136
Lynn, M. W.			24	357
Manley, Hardy B.			9	504
Manning, Elijah L.	1	551	10	724
Manor, Aaron			9	533
Markham, Eliza M.			20	786
Marsh, Bryant			13	199
Marsh, Darius			3	313
Marsh, Edmond			23	155
Martin, Marcus(Marius)			23	210
Martin, Thomas			2	131
Martin, Virginius			4	316
Mason, James T.			15	151
Mason, Thomas			12	339

	WILL BOOK		ORPHANS COURT	
NAME	VOL.	PAGE	VOL.	PAGE
Massa, F. F.	1	446	9	25
Massey, Ann L.			1	400
Massey, Darling L.			1	39
Masters, William B.			24	144
Matthews, William A.			6	306
Maury, Alexander C.	1	134	2	232
May, Asahel			1	37
May, James B.	1	68	1	542
May, Jonathan	2	519	19	480
May, Joseph E.			24	168
May, Lambeth C.			13	301
May, Martha W.	2	564	21	432
May, Mary A.			10	460
May, Pleasant			30	201
May, William A.	2	458	22	157
Mays(Mayes), James M.			29	104
McBride, Alexander	2	553	20	546
McCain, Adam			2	367
McCain, Adam S.			28	139
McCain, Weldon S.			15	190
McCain, William R.			21	339
McCall, John			7	807
McCants, John L.	1	51	1	164
McCartney, Joseph	2	48	12	112
McCartney, Malachiah	2	31	11	636
McCarty, Molsey			5	784
McCauley, George			1	537
McClure, William A.			21	711
McConnell, John A.	2	127	14	13
McConnell, Thomas			2	167
McConnico, Christopher S.			26	417
McCorkle, Joseph	1	479	9	639
McCorkle, Thomas J.			18	273
McCorkle, Violet	2	190	15	100
McCormick, Thomas J.			21	309
McDaniel, Elizabeth			6	86
McDaniel, Henry			33	383
McDaniel, John M.			33	631
McDaniel, William			1	151
McDonald, Daniel A.	2	277	16	594
McDonald, Drew M.			22	440
McDonald, Hugh L.	2	395	21	262
McDonald, Malcomb			11	310
McDonald, Samuel			18	2

NAME	WILL BOOK VOL.	PAGE	ORPHANS COURT VOL.	PAGE
McDow, William L.			28	82
McElroy, Darcus			25	299
McElroy, Henry	2	64	13	76
McElroy, Isaac	1	533	10	322
McGehee, Louisa			11	705
McGhee, Thomas	1	261		
McGlone, Patrick			11	666
McGowen, James R.			22	487
McGowen, Thomas R.			22	488
McGowen, William			16	131
McGregor, John			2	376
McGregor, William			10	519
McGrew, John Sr.			4	49
McGrew, John C.			14	299
McInnis, Malcomb			13	431
McJimsey, Robert			13	306
McKay, William L. D.	1	410	7	361
McKenzie, William			29	57
McKeowan, John			23	449
McKerrall, Mary E.			30	68
McKinley, Daniel	2	113	13	715
McLaughlin, Moses			27	447
McLendon, Ezekial			15	36
McLendon, William			5	704
McLeod, Norman			5	131
McMillan, Archibald			8	517
McMillan, Catherine			31	199
McMillan, Clarinda M.	2	344	19	81
McMillan, Daniel			18	636
McMillan, Drury	2	355	18	632
McMillan, Elizabeth	3	41	31	212
McMillan, Hugh			29	135
McMillan, James			1	380
McMillan, John			6	461
McNab, James C.			4	30
McPherson, Cyrus	2	77	20	261
McPherson, William			31	638
McRae, William P.			12	240
McSween, Catherine	1	457	9	412
McSween, Daniel D.			13	651
McTurk, William J.			2	503
McWorther, James			1	517
Meador, James			6	91
Meador, Job			24	282

NAME	WILL BOOK VOL.	PAGE	ORPHANS COURT VOL.	PAGE
Meador, Joel			7	833
Meador, John			9	822
Meador, Lavincy	2	33	9	659
Meador, Reason			21	593
Meador, Reuben			10	106
Meek, J. T.			24	638
Meek, William B.			7	348
Melton, Andrew J.			20	113
Melton, Sheperd L.			20	112
Merrell, Moses G.			2	312
Merriman, Salmon S.			3	461
Merriwether, Lucinda			14	415
Metcalf, Jacob R.			21	534
Miles, F. J.			27	167
Miller, Charles	1	217/239	3	180
Miller, John A.			9	414
Miller, John C.			19	482
Miller, William E.	1	450	9	59
Mims, Seaborn			3	371
Mitchell, Benjamin J.			17	324
Mitchell, James	2	170	14	415
Mitchell, Yancy	2	575	24	393
Mobley, G. B.			32	45
Moffett, Elihu			2	289
Moncrief, Francis M.			13	580
Moncrief, S. B.	2	210	16	61
Moncrief, Sampson			14	559
Moncrief, Sophia			14	484
Monett, Samuel			1	223
Monette, J. Wesley			31	180
Moore, Aaron			2	571
Moore, Arthur			2	609
Moore, James			24	281
Moore, Jemima			14	415
Moore, Josiah	2	302	17	302
Moore, Lodawick	1	208	2	612
Moore, Marcus D.			21	648
Moore, Matthew			18	409
Moore, Robert			1	35
Moore, Robert H.			20	427
Moore, Sarah S.			5	562
Moore, Thomas	2	44	12	105
Moore, William A.			17	80
Moore, William F.			5	833

NAME	WILL BOOK VOL.	WILL BOOK PAGE	ORPHANS COURT VOL.	ORPHANS COURT PAGE
Mooring, James A.	3	27	30	526
Morgan, John	2	632		
Morris, George	3	59	31	342
Morris, George W.			15	165
Morris, Landon J.			11	22
Morris, Richard H.			1	332
Mosby, Hezekiah	1	236		
Mosely, Jerome B.			2	376
Moulton, C. M.	2	236	16	282
Mulvee, Anthony G.			13	664
Murley, Ann			18	283
Murley, Stephen W.			26	489
Murphy, Moses	1	151	2	389
Murphy, Thomas	1	178	2	510
Murrell, William H.			3	345
Myers, Asbury	1	296	3	721
Myers, James			2	142
Myers, Kesiah			1	377
Nagle, George J.			19	556
Nance, Benjamin D.			24	536
Nance, Sarah			17	384
Nance, William T.			22	229
Nash, Mariah J.			21	671
Naugle, John S.			20	209
Neal(Neill), William			4	66
Neale(Neal), Wallace S.			19	540
Nelson, Amasa			2	500
Nelson, Francis J. W.			13	122
Nettles, Zachariah			10	352
Nevill, Samuel L.			17	281
Newton, Richard			33	171
Nichols, James R.			2	251
Nichols, William J.			26	566
Nicholson, Charles			13	530
Nicholson, R. S.			27	142
Noble, Jeremiah			17	81
Noble, Stephen			5	749
Noble, Stephen P.			14	558
Norwood, David L.	1	218	3	41
Norwood, Elias W.	1	61	1	371
Null, James			1	32
Oats, Henry D.			19	475

	WILL BOOK		ORPHANS COURT	
NAME	VOL.	PAGE	VOL.	PAGE
O'Bannon, James	2	622	28	100
Oliver, Elizabeth	1	411	7	898
O'Neal, Alvin	1	308	4	153
O'Neal, Cherry L.			13	93
O'Neal, E. A. B.			33	267
O'Neal, Eli	2	451	22	564
O'Neal, Gaston			3	349
O'Neal, Patience			5	719
O'Neal, Thomas			5	720
O'Neal, William			7	370
Ormond, Thomas	2	601	26	435
Owen, John M.			5	796
Pack, Joseph	1	153		
Pack, William			2	571
Parham, Matthew			17	257
Parham, Nancy			17	536
Park, Robert			3	776
Park, Conaquie	2	503	19	468
Parker, James	2	165/204	14	342
Parker, James V.	2	334	18	459
Parker, Martha T.	2	533	19+	80
Parker, Parley			1	432
Parker, Sherod H.			1	134
Parker, T. V.			20	315
Pate, Samuel R.	2	97	13	461
Patton, Arthur			1	94
Patton, Joseph	3	53	31	319
Patton, Joseph E.			21	284
Patton, Wayne C.			14	198
Patton, William	1	72	1	603
Paylor, Richard T.	2	613	26	590
Payne, Daniel			4	638
Payne, Dilliard S.			5	500
Payne, James			6	46
Payne, John G.			12	272
Payne, Ransom			4	387
Payne, Richard			2	9
Payne, Susan W.	2	136	14	71
Payne, W. W.	2	490	15	451
Pearce, E. J.			26	121
Pearson, Isaac F.			31	268
Pearson, Joel E.			26	576
Pearson, Nancy			9	717

NAME	WILL BOOK VOL.	PAGE	ORPHANS COURT VOL.	PAGE
Peck, Edwin			1	392
Peevy, Emeline			27	63
Perrin, Abner			13	389
Perry, Ann	1	150		
Perry, John			7	851
Perry, John C.	1	346	4	735
Perry, Sidney S.			8	683
Perry, Winney			1	533
Persons, William	1	24		
Peteet, John T.			21	366
Peteet, Thomas			1	36
Peteet, William			20	164
Peyton, James C.			19	409
Peyton, Josephine			24	287
Peyton, Moses			14	219
Phares, John C.	2	605	26	499
Phillips, Benjamin			5	664
Phillips, Duncan B.			7	370
Phillips, Francis			16	67
Phillips, John	1	405	7	96
Phillips, John W.			28	461
Phillips, Martha G.			12	282
Phipps, John			3	42
Pinkard, John M.			13	297
Pipkin, Archelaus			19	494
Pipkin, Harriet S.	3	4	29	601
Pippin, R. C.			33	197
Pollard, John			11	155
Poloney, Alexander			2	539
Pool, James			17	289
Pool, John			2	539
Pool, Mary			24	28
Pool, William			2	308
Porter, Frederick	2	241	16	117
Porter, L. T.			33	393
Posey, Jesse H.	1	122	2	239
Posey, Pleasant M.			2	276
Posey, Sarah	1	124	2	254
Posey, William P.			3	229
Potts, Henry	1	289	5	540
Potts, Henry Sr.	1	88	2	38
Potts, Nancy			7	641
Potts, Stephen S.			9	155
Powe, Alexander C.			24	456

NAME	WILL BOOK VOL.	WILL BOOK PAGE	ORPHANS COURT VOL.	ORPHANS COURT PAGE
Powe, Julius A.			12	271
Powell, James A.			30	335
Powell, John			13	140
Powell, Penelope	2	79	19	55
Poythress, Joshua L.			14	96
Praytor, B. F.			25	256
Praytor, James T.			24	412
Praytor, Middleton A.			13	41
Preston, Washington			11	269
Prestwood, John			20	108
Prince, Richard			9	676
Prince, Susan E.			13	86
Pruitt(Prewitt), John	2	19	11	181
Pyle, Jeremiah			6	89
Pyle, Samuel			2	615
Quemby, Matthew			23	455
Ragsdale, Hiram C.			12	507
Rambo, Joseph B.			17	414
Ratican, Michael			4	125
Rea, H. W.			18	11
Rea, Robert R.	2	410	21	549
Rea, Tabitha			14	47
Reavis, John	1	193		
Reavis, Turner			29	288
Reed, George W.			22	474
Reed, Henry C.			20	785
Reed(Reid), John A.			13	131
Reed, Mary			3	454
Reed, Reuben			10	237
Register, Stephen			3	36
Reid, Elizabeth			29	550
Reid, George W.			23	226
Reilly, James S.	1	161	2	394
Rencher, Daniel G.	2	592	26	402
Rhodes, Elizabeth			2	533
Rhodes, James A.			8	741
Rhodes, James S.			8	478
Rhodes, John	1	400/414	7	450
Rich, Reuben			2	388
Richardson, A. W.			21	359
Richardson, Augustus			6	125
Richardson, Bryant			1	48

NAME	WILL BOOK VOL.	PAGE	ORPHANS COURT VOL.	PAGE
Richardson, Bryant Jr.			27	579
Richardson, Furny W.			18	250
Richardson, George A.			5	737
Richardson, Uny			4	356
Riggins, Eli			2	36
Riley, Zennice			11	312
Ritter, John			29	454
Rivers, John W.			13	774
Rix, Charles			10	720
Roan, Jesse L.			1	30
Roan, Mary			1	514
Roan, Sarah			1	43
Robbins, William R.	2	221	15	551
Robertson, H. C.			33	99
Robertson, John H.			32	93
Robertson, Joseph A.			3	345
Robertson, Samuel W.			25	535
Robinson, David			21	678
Robinson, John			10	588
Robinson, Thornton	1	147	2	368
Roby, W. W.			19	437
Roddy, John			3	738
Rogers, A. A.	2	238	16	463
Rogers, A. E.			30	513
Rogers, Asa D.	2	529	20	8
Rogers, Joseph	3	1	29	526
Rogers, Nelson A.			16	130
Rogers, S. J.			24	541
Rory, James			9	420
Ruffin, Joseph			17	343
Rush, James			5	114
Rush, William			1	49
Rush, William L.			1	140
Rushing, Elijah D.			13	298
Rushing, Enoch D.			10	455
Rushing, James M.	3	99	33	505
Rushing, Mary	1	67/101	1	228
Rushing, Stephen	1	337	4	408
Rushing, Susan			33	505
Rushing, William			10	260
Russell, David M.	2	403	21	371
Russell, W. W.	3	69	32	41
Saddler, Felix F.			11	488

NAME	WILL BOOK VOL.	WILL BOOK PAGE	ORPHANS COURT VOL.	ORPHANS COURT PAGE
Sample, Robert T.			15	406
Sanders, David			15	164
Sanders, E. C.			32	219
Sanders, Elias			1	540
Sanders, Hannah			10	230
Sanders, Moses M.			15	455
Sanders, Rosa			9	850
Sanders, Thomas A.	1	91	2	16
Sanderson, Agnes S.			8	739
Sanderson, Daniel			2	270
Saunders, Elizabeth			23	27
Saunders, William B.	2	541	20	358
Savage, James			1	384
Scales, John			13	78
Scales, Peter P.	1	46	1	399
Scott, John			4	226
Scott, John B.			15	145
Scott, Lewis M.			26	145
Scott, Robert			14	18
Scurlock, Napolean B.	1	375	5	502
Scurlock, William H.			5	72
Seale, Bluford			29	34
Shackleford, Alexander	2	583	24	561
Shackleford, James			1	602
Shackleford, James T.	2	37		
Shackleford, Joseph S.			17	550
Shackleford, Richard D.			9	240
Shamburger, Joshua			6	130
Shates, Francis A.	1	35		
Shea, John	3	83	32	214
Sheid, Jesse J.	2	511	19	590
Shelby, Winfield M.	3	96	33	111
Shelton, Samuel J.			7	67
Sherard, John H.			14	98
Sherard, Napolean B.			18	346
Shilburn, William A.			2	379
Shine, James B.			15	406
Short, Jordon H.			19	456
Sibley, Samuel B.	3	43	31	253
Silliman, Thomas N.			13	531
Simmons, James			1	451
Simmons, Robert	2	159	14	273
Simmons, William M.			19	479
Simpson, James	2	441	22	287

NAME	WILL BOOK VOL.	PAGE	ORPHANS COURT VOL.	PAGE
Simpson, James Conroe			31	389
Sims, Amanda			3	711
Sims, James			2	298
Sims, Josephine	3	15	30	176
Sims, Leroy			9	616
Sims, Morton	1	438	8	298
Sims, Reddick			1	41
Sims, Wilkins J.	2	646	29	433
Sinclair, Amelia A.			7	397
Sledge, Mary L.	3	67	32	31
Sledge, Sallie Alberta			31	558
Sledge, W. H.			32	157
Sloan, James			7	672
Sloan, Thomas B.			11	286
Smart, Susannah			12	443
Smith, Delia	1	321		
Smith, Edward W.			31	325
Smith, Henry	1	21	1	53
Smith, James H.			14	59
Smith, John J.			22	257
Smith, John M. N.			9	657
Smith, John W.	2	215	16	25
Smith, Joseph A.	3	21	30	329
Smith, Joshua T.	1	131	2	258
Smith, Joshua T.	2	388	21	164
Smith, Robert B.			23	216
Smith, Solomon	1	383	5	632
Smith, Stephen			3	10
Smith, Susan J.			17	48
Smith, William			3	777
Snedecor, Lucy C.	3	109	33	559
Somers, George	2	523	19	478
Soule, John M.			18	637
Soule, Virginia R.			30	325
Southerland, Samuel M.	1	163	2	497
Sparkman, Lewis			17	390
Sparks, Charles A.			8	478
Speed, Celia Thurman			12	476
Speed, Elizabeth			2	566
Speight, Edwin G.	2	383	21	55
Speight, Samuel			2	233
Sprott, James			27	603
Sprott, Robert			20	243
Stallings, Burrel			2	558

NAME	WILL BOOK VOL.	PAGE	ORPHANS COURT VOL.	PAGE
Standifer, Abraham H.	1	280	3	490
Stanton, Elizabeth	1	284		
Stanton, Henry T.	1	368	5	134
Stanton, James D.			3	722
Stanton, Louisa J.			18	309
Stanton, Matilda			29	162
Stanton, Sommerville			29	124
Steele, Abner A.			3	434
Steele, Augustus D.			1	444
Stephens, Frederick			11	269
Stephens, John H.	2	182	14	564
Stephens, Penelope			18	409
Stevenson, Humphrey			9	180
Stevenson, Mary Ann			7	914
Stewart, Charles S.			21	151
Stewart, Joseph K.			13	298
Stewart, Richard E.			16	97
Stewart, Susan E.			11	249
Stillings, James N.			9	179
Stocker, William J.			2	225
Story, Samuel W.			5	782
Stratton, Robert J.			24	572
Strickland, John W.			19+	20
Stringfellow, Robert R.			3	471
Strother, Edward H.	1	350	5	361
Strother, P. S. C.			13	297
Stuart, A. J.			26	295
Stuart, R. F.			24	463
Sturdivant, Wheelus			1	320
Summerlin, Alfred F.			13	653
Summerlin, Pheistor			16	260
Summerlin, Serena			13	587
Summerlin, Wiley			1	544
Summers, George			25	514
Swann, Isaac	2	260	16	234
Swann, Tincy	1	545	10	642
Sweeney, Bryant			10	185
Swilley, Jarred O.			8	683
Swilley, John W.			28	98
Swilley, Samuel			20	12
Tagart, Jacob			1	548
Talbot, Rhoda	2	460		
Talbot, William H.	2	654	20	632

	WILL BOOK		ORPHANS COURT	
NAME	VOL.	PAGE	VOL.	PAGE
Tankersly, Felix			25	609
Tankersly, George G.	2	546	20	491
Tarleton, John R.			2	246
Tartt, Archelaus B.			15	67
Tartt, Elnathan	1	59	1	360
Tartt, Enos			18	466
Tartt, James B.			28	263
Tartt, Jonathan			13	753
Tartt, Margaret			24	342
Tartt, Thomas E.			3	375
Tate, John			21	476
Tate, William			20	116
Taylor, Clarinda M.			19	53
Taylor, Doc M.	2	580	24	441
Taylor, Elizabeth Jane			8	287
Taylor, John			1	422
Taylor, Madison B.	2	514	19	511
Taylor, Samuel	2	103	13	526
Taylor, Sins			7	401
Terrell, Sarah	1	549	10	671
Terrill, Susan	1	211		
Thetford, Anderson			19	212
Thetford, William			15	226
Thom, Margaret			16	472
Thomas, Edmond			30	89
Thomas, Hymerick H.			2	58
Thomas, Ichabod			1	536
Thomas, John R.			2	58
Thomason, J. F.	2	447	25	472
Thompson, Asa W.			1	407
Thompson, Bryan(Bryant)			3	726
Thompson, Daniel			5	562
Thompson, Edwin N.			17	50
Thompson, Isaac			1	488
Thompson, James	1	503	10	87
Thompson, James	1	543		
Thompson, James F.			24	181
Thompson, James H.			13	701
Thompson, John	1	285	3	641
Thompson, Mary			27	63
Thompson, Nancy M.			17	50
Thompson, Prolate			11	684
Thompson, Samuel			30	481
Thompson, Sarah			27	601

	WILL BOOK		ORPHANS COURT	
NAME	VOL.	PAGE	VOL.	PAGE
Thompson, Sarah A.			26	567
Thorn, James			5	261
Thorn, Margaret A.			13	459
Thorne, Jesse			2	33
Thorne, Willis			11	216
Thornton, Henry R.	2	376	20	452
Thornton, Seth B.			12	155
Thornton, William G.	1	64	1	504
Threadgill, William			18	574
Thurman, William			11	669
Tidmore, Mark	2	488	14	575
Tippin, John W.			15	99
Tisdale, Adelia			15	63
Tisdale, William D.			15	68
Todd, Elizabeth			12	242
Todd, Frances			11	432
Todd, John P.			7	916
Todd, Mrs.			5	395
Todd, Thomas			12	242
Tolbert, Hugh			7	672
Tom, Moses			2	567
Tom, Ohoyo	1	301	3	716
Tompkins, Bennet			5	657
Tool, Joseph			5	69
Torbert, Hugh			2	559
Torry, Phalby	2	510		
Townsend, Frances Y.			5	501
Trahan, Wesley B.			1	467
Trammel, Thomas			8	522
Travis, Amos C.			9	535
Travis, Caesar			27	201
Travis, Enoch	1	167	2	471
Travis, Philip G.			4	324
Truelove, Ransom			9	570
Truitt, Samuel J.			21	505
Tubb, James			3	32
Tureman, Sarah E.			22	88
Turner, Axum			1	333
Turner, D. L.			15	459
Turner, John S.	3	90	32	389
Turner, Mary			9	472
Turner, Patience	1	559	11	27
Turner, William D.			2	269
Turner, William F.			31	618

| | WILL BOOK | | ORPHANS COURT | |
NAME	VOL.	PAGE	VOL.	PAGE
Tutt, Artelia			19	493
Tutt, James B.			6	614
Underwood, George R.			15	419
Underwood, James			1	75
Underwood, L. V.			30	233
Underwood, Thomas R.			20	298
Underwood, W. D.			17	387
Upchurch, Burwell			8	589
Vandegraff, Juliette			30	672
Vandegraff, William J.	1	223	8	20
Vandegraff, William J.	2	566	23	3
Vann, Joseph	2	93	13	390
Vary, Elbert M.			10	130
Vaughan, Isaac S.	1	495	10	4
Verner, George W.			1	450
Verrell, Mary(May)			5	499
Verrell, William F.			6	484
Voss, Henry Otto	3	8	29	796
Walker, C. D.			32	190
Walker, Harry			17	482
Walker, Henry			17	482
Walker, James M.			10	423
Walker, James W.			19	229
Walker, Thomas			17	482
Walker, William			2	259
Wall, Hugh			4	418
Wallace, David			1	146
Wallace, James	2	184	14	402
Wallace, John H.			12	515
Wallace, Joseph A. J.			3	369
Wallace, Louisa			14	401
Wallace, W. A. J.			6	531
Wallace, William			2	625
Wallace, William B.			15	201
Waller, John W.			24	625
Waller, William			3	62
Walton, James F.	1	343	4	498
Walton, Richard G.	2	556	20	581
Ward, Thomas B.			14	336
Ware, Susan	2	611	27	213
Warner, Sarah J.			23	400

NAME	WILL BOOK VOL.	PAGE	ORPHANS COURT VOL.	PAGE
Warren, James S.			7	785
Washington, Elizabeth A.	2	179		
Washington, Robert	2	249	18	17
Washington, Robert W.	2	15	11	144
Washington, William E.	3	30	30	657
Watkins, Charles H.			2	154
Watson, Albert G.	1	407	7	410
Watson, Emily	2	253	16	131
Watson, Jarred			20	330
Watson, John	1	181	2	504
Watson, John F.			22	146
Watson, John F. Sr.			23	254
Watson, Mary Ann			12	509
Watson, Patrick E.			10	191
Watson, Rebecca			3	206
Watson, Thomas F.			22	191
Watt, D. C.			29	680
Watt, George L.			13	138
Watt, Joel			20	338
Watt, John			6	306
Watt, Mary M.			16	283
Webb, Henley B.	2	178	22	301
Webb, Richard			1	374
Wedgeworth, James			6	611
Weeks, Bythal			4	69
Weir, Peter			24	499
Welch, William			1	329
Westbrook, Moses			21	46
Weston, John M.			28	193
Weston, Robert H.	1	388	4	31
Weston, W. K.			31	307
Wheat, Bird			21	203
Whitaker, J. J.			21	533
White, Adam			9	39
White, Andrew J.			3	488
White, Ben			32	131
White, James H.			19	477
White, John W.			21	272
White, Pleasant	2	471	22	278
White, Robert			1	214
White, William P.			23	247
Whitehead, Jonathan			8	72
Whitfield, George W.	1	241	3	448
Whiting, Peter B.			5	666

NAME	WILL BOOK VOL.	WILL BOOK PAGE	ORPHANS COURT VOL.	ORPHANS COURT PAGE
Whitney, David S.	1	116	2	166
Whitney, Manning S.			2	564
Whitsett, Laura			20	281
Whitsett, Joel C.			18	114
Whitsitt, John C.	2	495	18	633
Whittle, James			11	201
Whittle, Reuben			11	201
Wideman, Henry			2	254
Wiggins, A. J.			19	506
Wiggins, Eli			4	785
Wiggins, Elisha			13	71
Wiggins, Francis D.			3	355
Wiggins, Lemuel A.			1	541
Wiggins, Sarah	2	39	12	141
Wiggins, Stephen			20	573
Wilbourn, Peter B.			1	45
Wilbourne, Peter H.			13	548
Wiley, Robert P.	2	590	26	384
Wilkinson, Alexander			11	128
Wilkinson, Charles			1	673
Williams, Edward	1	352	5	267
Williams, Edward J.	1	482	9	608
Williams, Humphrey			4	474
Williams, J. C.			15	320
Williams, James O.			12	437
Williams, Johnson C.	1	463	9	481
Williams, Robert M.			1	449
Williams, William J.			4	132
Williams, William O.			7	87
Williamson, Alexander	2	372	20	269
Williamson, Edwin			2	224
Williamson, George	1	1	1	26
Williamson, Mary B.	1	360	5	412
Williamson, Susan D.			14	427
Williamson, William E.	2	604	27	123
Willingham, Phillip	3	46	31	263
Willis, Asa B.			13	310
Wilson, Boyd H.	1	120	2	205
Wilson, John C.			16	582
Wilson, Joseph			4	323
Wilson, Martha O.			30	110
Wilson, Samuel			1	581
Wilson, Samuel R.			1	480
Wilson, Simon M.			22	62

| | WILL BOOK | | ORPHANS COURT | |
NAME	VOL.	PAGE	VOL.	PAGE
Wilson, Woodman	1	477	9	504
Wimberly, James A.			10	481
Wimberly, Jesse P.			19	580
Wince, James			8	482
Windham, James J.	3	3	29	522
Windham, Willie(Wiley)			3	3
Wingate, John M.	1	403	7	475
Winston, Anthony	1	567	2	576
Winston, Joel W.			4	93
Winston, John(?) W.			2	246
Winston, Sally Ann	1	306	4	68
Winston, William			16	51
Womack, Daniel			1	99
Wood, Sarah			3	32
Wood, William	1	422		
Woodall, James M.			26	382
Woodall, Sith			14	142
Woodard, Sarah			9	64
Woodard, William			5	10
Woods, Andrew M.			31	31
Woods, David H.			5	562
Wooten, John W.			21	338
Wooten, Melvina M.	2	530	20	68
Wooten, Richard			21	457
Wooten, Sallie			26	576
Wrenn, Arthur M.			17	5
Wrenn, James			4	414
Wrenn, Margaret J.			15	209
Wrenn, Samantha A.	2	562	21	403
Wrenn, Sarah	1	299	4	19
Wright, George P.			7	661
Wright, James			3	149
Wyatt, Ivy			13	9
Wyatt, Zachariah			9	508
Wylie, R. P.			28	251
Yarbrough, Alfred	2	257	15	433
Yarbrough, George			9	508
Yarbrough, Neil S.			19	231
Yarbrough, William			2	252
Yarbrough, William C.	1	563		
Yates, Luke			1	612
York, Shubal			6	139
Young, William Jr.			3	203

PART II

REGISTER OF DEATHS

1881 - 1892

REGISTER OF DEATHS
1881 - 1892

In 1881, the Alabama Legislature enacted a law that required the County Health Officer to "keep two books, styled respectively, The Register of Births, and The Register of Deaths; in which he shall register all the births and deaths that may occur in the County." The County Health Department continues, today, to maintain such records, but, of the very old records, only the Register of Deaths, 1881 - 1892 is extant.

This record is significant because it is the only public record of the existence of many people within the county during the 1800s, particulary the former slaves who constituted the majority of the county's population and, thus, the majority of the citizens who died during this time. This record also provides interesting insights into the medical problems faced by Sumter Countians approximately 100 years ago.

Correctly transcribing some of the medical diagnoses was challenging. Except to correct obvious errors in spelling, an attempt was made to transcribe the document as written, even though some of the medical terms could not be found in today's dictionaries.

As is the case with the cemetery inscriptions that follow in Part III, persons included in this index were born during or before 1865. Information about persons who were born after 1865, and who died between 1881 and 1892, can be furnished by the author upon individual requests.

NAME	RACE	BORN	AGE	DEATH
CAUSE OF DEATH		PLACE OF BURIAL		
Abbott, Alice	W	AL	31	9/22/89
Chronic diarrhea		Jones Bluff		
Adams, John	B		67	8/11/87
Heart disease		Warsaw		
Adams, Thomas	B	GA	25	10//86
Concussion of brain		York Station		
Agord, Mack	B	AL	20	11/23/84
Pneumonia		Near Warsaw		
Aimes, Winslow	B	AL	35	11/25/83
Gunshot wound		Jones Bluff		
Alexander, E. A.	W	AL	35	3/1/83
Consumption		Chestnut Grove		
Alexander, Elizabeth	B	AL	26	6/10/90
Septicaemia		Jones Bluff		
Alexander, Isabella	W	NC	71	9/13/89
Heart disease		Beat 4		
Alexander, John	W	AL	38	3/18/89
Typhoid fever		Curls		
Altman, Maj. J. W.	W	SC	66	2/8/85
Heart disease		Unknown		
Altman, Roxanna	W	AL	37	2/5/90
Pneumonia		York Station		
Alves, Ashley	W	VA	94	10/20/83
Old age		Cokes Chapel		
Alves, Elijah Simson	W	AL	57	6/24/82
Heart disease		Cokes Chapel		
Amason, Elizabeth	W	NC	73	2/20/86
Cerebral hemorrhage		Sumterville		
Amason, Emma	B	AL	18	5/25/81
Pulmonalis phthisis		Sumterville		
Amason, Hannah	B	AL	40	11/20/89
Rheumatism		Sumterville		
Amason, Hatty	B	AL	25	4/29/82
Consumption		Sumterville Beat		
Amason, Lucy	B	NC	80	1/14/86
Burn		Livingston		
Amason, Sam	B	NC	70	11/26/87
Cerebral apoplexy		Sumterville		
Amason, Sam Asa	B	AL	35	8/29/85
Strangulated hernia		Sumterville Beat		
Amason, Simon	B	NC	55	10/20/87
Cirrhosis of liver		Sumterville		
Anderson, Martha	B	AL	34	2/3/84
Consumption		Pickens Co. Ala.		

NAME / CAUSE OF DEATH	RACE	BORN	AGE	DEATH / PLACE OF BURIAL		
Anthony, Gideon	B	NC	75	1/25/82		
Pneumonia		Unknown				
Armstrong, Kenny	B		30	7/7/82		
Injury from cars (RR)		Livingston				
Armstrong, Margaret	B	NC	63	1/21/89		
Paralysis		Unknown				
Armstrong, William	W	AL	48	12/3/89		
Apoplexy		Unknown				
Arnold, Esther	W	CT	58	8/19/82		
Malarial fever		Gainesville				
Arrington, Allen	B	MS	22	12/9/81		
Typhoid fever		York				
Arrington, Hal	B		28	9/27/87		
Neglected fever		Belmont				
Arrington, Henry	B	AL	24	8/31/88		
Brain inflammation		Brewersville Beat				
Arrington, Sam	B	AL	28	1/9/92		
Tonsillitis		Livingston				
Artis, Drid	B	AL	82	12/25/89		
Alcoholic poisoning		Unknown				
Autry, H. R.	W	NC	73	8/14/88		
Old age		Jones Bluff				
Avery, William	B	AL	25	1/19/84		
Pneumonia		Greene County				
Baker, Suky	B	NC	46	8/18/81		
Stomach cancer		Gainesville				
Baker, Tempe S.	W	AL	27	12/30/85		
Typhoid fever		Pleasant Grove				
Baldwin, Helen V.	W	AL	22	2/4/83		
Pneumonia		Livingston				
Ballard, M. J.	W	AL	26	7/12/89		
Congestion		Cokes Chapel				
Ballard, Winter	B	AL	20	9/1/82		
Bowel inflammation		Wilder's Place				
Banks, Jesse H.	W	AL	57	1/26/87		
Pneumonia		Siloam Church				
Banks, Mary	W	AL	53	4/21/91		
Measles		Siloam				
Barker, Claiborn	B	AL	85	9/19/87		
Unknown		Belmont				
Barnes, Samuel W.	W		51	9/10/82		
Opium habit		Warsaw Beat				
Baron, Jane	B		70	2/1/86		
Consumption		York Beat				

NAME / CAUSE OF DEATH	RACE	BORN AGE DEATH / PLACE OF BURIAL
Battle, Susan / General debility	B	AL 54 6/2/90 / Gainesville
Bates, Burrel / Remittent fever	B	AL 35 9/12/83 / Brewersville
Bates, Nancy / Consumption	B	AL 38 11/23/86 / New Prospect Ch.
Baxter, Polly / Congestion of brain	B	AL 40 1/25/86 / Jones Bluff Beat
Beasley, Bettie / Congestion of bowels	W	NC 72 7/10/85 / Livingston Beat
Beasley, William H. / Hemorrhage of bowels	W	SC 73 1/7/83 / New Prospect Ch.
Beavers, Lewis / Wound by saw	B	AL 22 7/28/81 / Beat 3
Beavers, Mrs. / Apoplexy	W	NC 60 12/20/83 / Mt Moriah Church
Bedwell, Albert M. / Consumption	W	AL 24 4/8/82 / Livingston
Beggs, Martha / Heart disease	W	NC 57 11/8/83 / Livingston
Bell, Ambrose / Inanition	W	34 2/23/88 / Bethel
Bell, Bennet B. / Debility of age	W	NC 80 9/19/84 / Warsaw Beat
Bell, Betsy / Kerosene burn	B	35 7/3/83 / Gainesville
Bell, James H. / Ulceration of bowels	W	NC 71 10/17/87 / Warsaw
Bell, Jerry / Typho-malarial fever	B	VA 45 6/21/87 / Sumterville
Bell, Robert / Pneumonia	W	MS 40 12/26/89 / Salem Church
Bell, Seny / Debility of age	B	NC 80 4/11/84 / Bell's Place
Bester, Emma / Unknown	B	AL 53 8/9/90 / Gainesville
Billups, Emily / Paralysis	W	AL 83 12/16/86 / Siloam Church
Billups, Henry / Pneumonia	B	SC 65 1/26/84 / Intercourse
Bimms, Lucy / Pulmonalis phthisis	B	AL 45 7/12/81 / Belmont
Binns, Eliza / Old age	W	VA 87 12/3/81 / Near Jones Bluff

NAME	RACE	BORN	AGE	DEATH
CAUSE OF DEATH		PLACE OF BURIAL		
Bird, Francis	B	AL	32	2/24/86
Bright's disease		Gainesville Beat		
Bird, Good	B	AL	25	2/15/89
Killed		Unknown		
Birdsong, Eliza	B	SC	75	6/10/88
Heart disease		Jones Bluff		
Bishop, Jim	B	AL	30	2/8/87
Consumption		Elizabeth Church		
Blackman, George	B		35	1/29/84
Pneumonia		Marengo Co. Ala.		
Bliss, James	B	VA	74	4/17/91
Paralysis		Gainesville		
Blocker, Martha	B		55	9/13/88
Pneumonia		Gainesville		
Blocker, Violet	B		71	8/30/87
Heart disease		Warsaw		
Bloodworth, J. R.	W	GA	73	1/15/84
Congestion of lungs		York		
Bloushard, Edward	B		65	12/29/89
Congestion		Hares Beat		
Boling, Kim	B	NC	73	11/29/84
Colitis		Near Livingston		
Boller, Allie	B	AL		4/14/86
Consumption		Matthews' Place		
Bonner, Rody	B	AL	35	8/23/85
Remittent fever		Pickens Co. Ala.		
Bostwart, E. M.	W		71	11/19/89
Breast cancer		Unknown		
Bourber, Morris	B	AL	40	1/1/86
Consumption		Livingston		
Bowden, Mary Ann	B	AL	40	11/1/87
Labor		New Prospect Ch.		
Bowers, William E.	W	SC	53	8/24/83
Malarial fever		Shawn Church		
Bowling, Ceny	B	TN	80	8/9/82
Colitis		New Prospect Ch.		
Bowling, Harrison	B		70	5/27/81
Typho-malarial fever		Livingston		
Bowman, Kittie	B	AL	24	7/10/89
Consumption		Beat Three		
Boyd, Jennie	W	MS	39	2/3/86
Acute bronchitis		Payneville		
Boyd, Sarah	B	AL	48	7/17/89
Uterine cancer		York		

NAME	RACE	BORN	AGE	DEATH
CAUSE OF DEATH		PLACE OF BURIAL		
Bradley, Albert	B		25	8/4/83
Gunshot wound		Unknown		
Bradley, Dan	B		85	3/21/85
Paralysis of bladder		Unknown		
Branch, Rebecca	W		60	6/10/87
Dysentery		Livingston		
Branen, Rebecca	B	SC	98	7/23/85
Debility of age		Elizabeth Church		
Brassfield, Neal	B	AL	27	6/13/85
Epilepsy		Poorhouse Cemetery		
Braswell, Hannah	B	AL	37	10/6/88
Heart disease		Jones Bluff		
Brewer, Anderson	B	AL	16	11/14/81
Dysentery		Unknown		
Brewer, Mariah	B	AL	39	5/9/81
Heart disease		New Prospect Ch.		
Brewer, Sim	B	AL	25	2/2/87
Pneumonia		Livingston Beat		
Brewster, Nancy	W		54	3/4/83
Pneumonia		Siloam Church		
Broadnax, Louisa	B	AL	63	11/26/85
Dropsy		Jones Bluff Beat		
Brooks, John	B	AL	23	2/8/83
Pneumonia		Brewersville		
Brooks, Mandy	B	AL	35	1/10/92
Influenza		Livingston		
Brown, Alexander	B	AL	45	8/15/81
Consumption		Livingston		
Brown, Alfred	B		45	1/16/84
Strychnine poisoning		Marengo Co. Ala.		
Brown, Anarky	B	AL	55	3/7/85
Heart disease		Poorhouse Cemetery		
Brown, Aus	B	AL	50	1/31/86
Pneumonia		Brewersville		
Brown, Austin	B	SC	75	10/15/84
Debility of age		Livingston		
Brown, Caroline	B	AL	30	12/7/81
Typhoid fever		Near Jones Bluff		
Brown, Cinda	B	AL	37	4/27/90
Post partum hemorrhage		Sumterville Beat		
Brown, Clarissa	B	SC	84	11/16/83
Old age		Jones Bluff Beat		
Brown, Delia	B	AL	20	9/20/85
Dropsy of heart		Sumterville Beat		

| NAME | RACE | BORN | AGE | DEATH |
CAUSE OF DEATH		PLACE OF BURIAL		
Brown, Eliza	B	AL	35	11/27/87
Typhoid fever		Jones Creek		
Brown, George	B	SC	80	1/13/88
Bowel obstruction		Jones Creek		
Brown, Hardy	B	AL	60	4/29/86
Rheumatism of heart		Jack Tim's Place		
Brown, Henry	B	VA	33	8/21/82
Typho-malarial fever		Parker Place		
Brown, J. T.	W	MS	35	6/10/84
Dropsy		Siloam Church		
Brown, Jane	B	AL	30	8/23/88
Malarial fever		Jones Bluff		
Brown, Laura	B	AL	35	6/10/81
Pulmonalis phthisis		Sumterville		
Brown, Laura	B		28	7/30/86
Septicaemia (labor)		Livingston Beat		
Brown, Lex	B	NC	75	1/10/86
Pneumonia		Poorhouse Cemetery		
Brown, Mary	B	VA	87	1/5/83
Debility of age		Poorhouse Cemetery		
Brown, Mary J.	W	SC	67	3/6/83
Pneumonia		Jones Bluff Beat		
Brown, Nancy	B		45	12/22/81
Paralysis		Gainesville		
Brown, Phillis	B	AL	65	1/29/86
Heart disease		York Beat		
Brown, Prine	B	AL	49	2/7/90
Heart disease		Jones Bluff Beat		
Brown, Simon	B	SC	80	9/24/86
Debility of age		Puereus Graveyard		
Brown, Sophia	B		65	2/5/82
Pneumonia		Livingston Beat		
Brown, Tennessee	B	AL	30	7/18/86
Carcinoma		Livingston		
Brownrigg, Audie	B	AL	50	5/14/90
Spinal meningitis		Livingston Beat		
Brownrigg, Lidie	B	VA	77	12/27/89
Unknown		Livingston		
Brownrigg, Lyttleton	B		80	9/18/81
Ascites		Near Livingston		
Brownrigg, Sophie	B	AL	50	4/3/87
Bright's disease		Brownrigg Place		
Brownrigg, Spot	B		45	12/18/88
Typhoid fever		Gainesville		

NAME CAUSE OF DEATH	RACE	BORN	AGE	DEATH PLACE OF BURIAL		
Brunson, George Lawrence Typhoid fever	W	AL Zion Church	33	5/1/82		
Bryant, Bob Pneumonia	B	NC Sumterville Beat	65	11/9/82		
Bryant, Charles Pneumonia	B	AL Near Warsaw	50	1/27/84		
Bryant, Harriett Puerperal fever	B	AL Sumterville	40	10/21/87		
Bryant, Lizzie W. Puerperal convulsions	W	AL Sumterville Beat	26	3/2/82		
Bryant, Rose Consumption	B	AL Parham Place	29	11/7/82		
Bullock, Pink Pneumonia	W	MS Sumterville Beat	40	2/10/85		
Burks, Sarah Consumption	B	AL Unknown	32	3/25/89		
Burroughs, Henrietta Consumption	W	AL Gainesville	22	2/9/82		
Butler, Daniel Pneumonia	B	AL Brewersville	60	1/31/86		
Byrd, (Male) Debility of age	B	GA Poorhouse Cemetery	85	10/14/86		
Cahoon, David Malarial fever	W	NC Cokes Chapel	72	11/10/83		
Cahoon, J. C. Consumption	W	AL Cokes Chapel	35	5/ /87		
Cahoon, Mrs. Face cancer	W	AL Cokes Chapel	45	6/27/83		
Caldwell, Della Malarial fever	W	AL Belmont	23	10/2/84		
Caldwell, Johnnie Inez Dysentery	W	AL Belmont	26	8/31/87		
Calhoun, Lacy Old age	B	NC G. M. Wrenn Place	90	12/14/89		
Cambers, Mrs. Chronic bronchitis	W	NC Poorhouse Cemetery	71	4/18/89		
Cameron, Harriet Malarial fever	B	AL Near Warsaw	35	9/10/85		
Campbell, Harriett Heart disease	B	VA Livingston Beat	78	5/7/90		
Campbell, Sallie Consumption	B	Cokes Chapel	38	2/28/91		
Campbell, Sam Pericarditis	W	York	68	6/4/88		

NAME	RACE	BORN	AGE	DEATH
CAUSE OF DEATH		PLACE OF BURIAL		
Campbell, Squire	B	AL	22	11/10/87
Typho-malarial fever		Sumterville		
Canebreak, Sukie	B	SC	80	10/3/84
Debility of age		Jones Bluff Beat		
Cannady, Needham Ward	W	NC	53	1/2/87
Pneumonia		Cokes Chapel		
Cannon, Jerry	B	AL	47	4/7/86
Abscess of liver		Cannon's Farm		
Carr, Ann Jane	W	NC	49	6/5/81
Pneumonia		Cokes Chapel		
Carraway, Needam	B	NC	75	8/17/82
Dropsy		Unknown		
Carroll, Jacob	W		68	12/28/87
Dysentery		Brewersville		
Carter, Lucy	B	AL	25	4/3/88
Pelvic cellulitis		Unknown		
Casey, J. T.	W	AL	44	1/21/92
Consumption		Jones Bluff		
Chaney, Albert	B	AL	78	12/5/83
Injury from gin		Livingston Beat		
Chaney, Amy	B	AL	43	11/14/88
Unknown		Unknown		
Chaney, Corry	B	AL	35	4/16/87
Burn		Black Bluff Beat		
Chaney, Harry	B	AL	64	1/17/84
Pneumonia		Black Bluff Beat		
Chaney, Jerry	B	AL	61	5/17/89
Alcoholism		Unknown		
Chany, (Female)	B	AL	65	4/2/85
Heart disease		Choctaw Co. Ala.		
Chapman, Clara	B	AL	85	2/14/90
Asthenia		Livingston Beat		
Chapman, Lewis	B		25	8/12/87
Malarial fever		Unknown		
Chapman, Robert	B		85	8/17/88
Malarial fever		Livingston Beat		
Childe, Agnes	B	AL	65	2/22/92
Heart disease		Gainesville		
Childs, George	B	AL	35	10/25/84
Malarial fever		Belmont		
Chiles, Elizabeth	B		81	4/25/90
Paralysis		Unknown		
Chiles, Hardy	B	MD	68	8/11/89
Pericarditis		Unknown		

| NAME | RACE | BORN | AGE | DEATH |
CAUSE OF DEATH		PLACE OF BURIAL		
Christian, Julia Ann	B	AL	18	11/ /81
Consumption		Jones Creek Church		
Clark, Cherry	B	SC	80	6/2/86
Breast cancer		Livingston		
Clark, T. J.	W		28	12/21/84
Cardiac dropsy		Livingston		
Clarke, Jane	B	AL	40	12/5/88
Metro-peritonitis		Jones Bluff		
Clay, Ella	W	AL		8/10/83
Consumption		Cokes Chapel		
Clay, Rose	B	NC	70	9/27/84
Paralysis		Belmont		
Cobb, Martha N.	W	AL	30	11/15/84
Pneumonia		Mt Herman		
Cobb, Teresa	W	GA	22	11/15/85
Strychnine poisoning		Unknown		
Cochrane, Mrs. Siner	W	AL	50	12/11/88
Cancer		Black Bluff		
Cockrell, Dan	B	AL	26	7/8/85
Consumption		Livingston Beat		
Cockrell, Dempsey	W	NC	77	5/3/86
Apoplexy		Old Baptist Church		
Cockrell, James A.	W	AL	35	2/2/84
Typho-malarial fever		Livingston Beat		
Cockrell, Mrs. Leonidas A.	W	MS	26	4/9/90
Post partum hemorrhage		Livingston		
Cockrell, M. N.	W	AL	57	10/6/87
Malarial fever		Brewersville		
Cockrell, Minna	W	AL	38	6/11/83
Heart disease		Livingston		
Cole, Elva	B	AL	38	9/12/87
Carbuncle		Brewersville		
Cole, John	B	VA	80	4/12/84
Bladder hemorrhage		Gainesville		
Cole, Mary	W	VA	80	9/9/82
Congestion		York Station		
Coleman, Emeline	B		60	1/10/88
Dropsy		Poorhouse Cemetery		
Coleman, Fannie	B	AL	33	5/4/90
Lung consumption		Livingston		
Coleman, Ophelia	B	AL	30	3/25/90
Pneumonia		Livingston		
Coleman, R. E.	W	NC	69	10/16/85
Congestive chill		Meridian, Miss.		

NAME CAUSE OF DEATH	RACE	BORN	AGE	DEATH PLACE OF BURIAL	
Collier, Edmond Dropsy	B		60 Unknown	4/25/82	
Collins, Lizzie Malarial fever	B		40 Unknown	2/8/91	
Collins, Martha Dropsy	B	AL	22 McDow's Cemetery	9/12/84	
Conley, Margaret Unknown	W	AL	38 Beat 7	11/20/90	
Connelly, John Pneumonia	B		70 John T. Smith's	1/19/84	
Conner, Lucy Unknown	B	AL	27 Belmont	2/3/82	
Cook, Carolina Dropsy	B	SC	70 Parker Place	7/14/86	
Cook, Isaac Malarial fever	B	VA	70 Arrington Place	10/5/82	
Cook, Jack Old age	B		80 Bluff Port	11/10/87	
Cook, James M. Measles & meningitis	W	AL	35 Livingston	4/23/82	
Cook, Jane Pneumonia	B	AL	19 Belmont	1/27/84	
Cook, Thomas L. Measles	W	AL	24 Livingston	4/5/82	
Cotton, Zella Heart disease	B	AL	43 Jones Bluff	2/11/84	
Crabbe, Julius Pneumonia	B	AL	22 Darden's Ferry	2/7/84	
Crady, Betsy Unknown	B		50 Mt Zion	10/15/85	
Craig, Jerry Malarial fever	B	NC	65 Brewersville	5/10/83	
Cravens, Mary Consumption	W	VA	70 Gainesville	1/2/82	
Creagh, Elijah Congestion	B	AL	56 Beat 9	7/4/90	
Crews, Abraham Old age	B	AL	98 Grants Chapel	1/4/90	
Crocket, Carie Unknown	B	AL	45 Jones Graveyard	1/6/88	
Crockett, William Ascites	B		63 W.A.C. Jones Place	7/11/81	
Culpepper, George C. Typho-malarial fever	W	AL	24 Thornville	10/27/83	

NAME CAUSE OF DEATH	RACE	BORN	AGE	DEATH PLACE OF BURIAL
Cunningham, Eva Apoplexy	W	MD	73	3/21/82 Livingston
Curry, Fannie Congestion of brain	W		AL 38	12/17/84 Gainesville Beat
Curry, Martha Angina pectoris	W		VA 81	7/8/84 Hatch Graveyard
Dabbs, Thomas Old age	B		VA 100	5/23/87 Gainesville
Dailey, Josephine Consumption	B		AL 29	2/16/87 Kornegay's Place
Dailey, Violet Dawson Puerperal septicaemia	B		AL 28	3/20/85 Chapman Graveyard
Daily, Jacob Brain congestion	B		VA 65	8/17/85 Near Livingston
Daly, Sampson Double pneumonia	B		AL 25	2/15/83 Brewersville
Daniel, Alex Tuberculosis	B		AL 33	4/14/90 Sumterville Beat
Daniel, Phares Pneumonia	B		AL 25	1/13/84 Near Warsaw
Davenport, Cora Malarial fever	W		AL 29	9/25/82 Boyd Graveyard
Davis, Ann Pneumonia	W		AL 35	4/8/85 York
Davis, Benjamin Gunshot wound	W		23	7/20/81 Rocky Mount
Davis, Delly Heart disease	B		SC 85	12/3/90 Gainesville
Davis, H. W. Lung congestion	W		OH 73	2/18/90 Jones Bluff Beat
Davis, Lou Typhoid fever	W		AL 49	9/5/89 Choctaw Co. Ala.
Davis, Lucinda Brain congestion	B		AL 21	9/10/84 Mt Zion Church
Davis, Lury Consumption	B		AL 25	4/26/83 Greene Co. Ala.
Davis, M. V. Congestion	W		42	12/ /82 York
Dawson, Joseph Cancer	B		NC 50	12/26/82 Preston Beat
Deane, Louisa Womb cancer	B		VA 75	9/15/85 Black Bluff Beat
Deason, Felix G. Spinal injury	W		AL 70	2/12/87 Near Belmont

NAME / CAUSE OF DEATH	RACE	BORN	AGE	DEATH / PLACE OF BURIAL
DeGraffenreid, Margaret	B	AL	20	1/9/84
Puerperal septicaemia				Livingston
Dennis, Abon	B	AL	40	8/3/89
Dropsy				Brewersville
Derby, Elizabeth P.	W	AL	43	8/3/86
Myelitis				Derby Cemetery
Dew, David	B	MS	50	10/14/90
Angina pectoris				Greene Co. Ala.
Dial, Brady	B	AL	48	4/28/90
Tuberculosis				Sumterville Beat
Dial, Maggie B.	W	AL	27	12/29/86
Malarial fever				Payneville Beat
Dial, Sarah	B	AL	60	1/16/92
Peritonitis				Sumterville Beat
Diggs, Pompey	B	NC	68	7/12/81
Heart lesions				Gainesville
Dinsimore, Lincoln	B		24	10/2/87
Malarial fever				Hares
Dixon, Dicey	B	AL	26	8/14/85
Unknown				Black Bluff
Dobbs, Cynthia	B	NC	84	4/27/83
Debility of age				Gainesville
Dodson, Kate	B	AL	20	11/7/84
Gunshot wound				McCainville
Dorough, George	W	MS	30	10/18/83
Typho-malarial fever				Beat 5
Dowing, Amy	B	AL	70	10/29/87
Operation shock				Bennett Place
Drake, Amanda Doland	B	AL	35	7/25/81
Childbirth				Drake Plantation
Drake, Jackson	B	AL	44	2/6/84
Pneumonia				Black Bluff
Drake, Rutha	B	AL	56	1/22/84
Pneumonia				Drake Graveyard
Drayden, George	B	AL	26	7/21/85
Malarial fever				Gaston
Draydon, Sopha	B	SC	100	12/16/83
Old age				Gaston Beat
Drinkard, Nancy G.	W	SC	77	8/6/84
Peritonitis				Bethlehem Church
Drinkard, Washington	W	AL	73	1/11/84
Chronic cystitis				Bethlehem Church
Drinkard, William M.	W	AL	55	10/6/84
Cardiac dropsy				Cuba Beat

| NAME | RACE | BORN | AGE | DEATH |
CAUSE OF DEATH		PLACE OF BURIAL		
Drummond, Pheby	B	AL	50	7/20/87
Brain trouble		York		
Dun, Henry	B	AL	30	4/30/91
Brain congestion		Unknown		
Dunn, Cheny	B	AL	84	7/20/88
Dropsy		Unknown		
Dyles, Obediah	B	TN	80	2/18/82
Pneumonia		R. Hibler's Place		
Eason, Charity	B	AL	36	5/21/87
Unknown		Sumterville Beat		
Eason, Joseph Addison	W	AL	21	9/20/81
Dysentery		Livingston		
Eason, Landon	B	NC	90	9/29/82
Debility of age		Poorhouse Cemetery		
Edwards, Adeline	B	VA	45	3/27/85
Pneumonia		Livingston		
Edwards, Harriet	B	AL	30	5/20/86
Unknown		Sumterville Beat		
Edwards, Savannah	B	AL	50	3/25/91
Pneumonia		Jones Bluff Beat		
Edwards, Turner	B	AL	25	10/8/87
Dysentery		Brewersville		
Edwards, Wesley	B	LA	40	12/10/87
Blood poison		Poorhouse Cemetery		
Elliott, Jim	B	AL	45	5/30/84
Pharyngeal abscess		Payneville Beat		
Ellis, Mima	W		76	10/9/85
Malarial fever		Warsaw Beat		
Epes, Amy	B	VA	75	7/22/88
Hydrothorax		Unknown		
Epes, Lizzie	B	AL	50	5/19/88
Typhoid fever		Jones Bluff		
Eppes, Sallie	B	AL	43	2/9/83
Dyspepsia		Gainesville		
Estelle, Amelia	B	AL	18	7/1/83
Typhoid fever		Unknown		
Estelle, Hannah	B		42	10/27/82
Pneumonia		Unknown		
Estelle, Jim	B	NC	60	1/22/83
Pneumonia		Unknown		
Etheridge, Caroline	W	AL	75	5/4/90
Paralysis		Cotahaga Beat		
Ethridge, Martha	W	AL	63	1/21/86
Paralysis of brain		Bluff Port Beat		

NAME	RACE	BORN	AGE	DEATH
CAUSE OF DEATH		PLACE OF BURIAL		
Eubanks, Minnie	W	AL	20	3/31/82
Measles		New Prospect Ch.		
Evans, Polly	B	VA	76	12/28/82
Paralysis		Gainesville		
Ezell, Lou	B	AL	31	8/30/89
Died from operation		Unknown		
Falkner, Isaac	B	AL	20	9/30/81
Pneumonia		Chandler Place		
Farmer, Eliza	B	AL	27	5/1/89
Dropsy		Bluff Port		
Faust, Rev. J. E.	W	AL	47	6/7/82
Heart disease		Livingston		
Fearce, Mark	B		76	1/31/85
Heart disease		Poorhouse Cemetery		
Fellow, Delphine	W	AL	46	9/24/86
Heart failure		Livingston		
Fellows, H. D.	W		49	7/25/84
Heart disease		Livingston		
Fields, Henry	B		45	7/27/81
Dropsy		Unknown		
Fields, Jackson	B	AL	31	8/5/89
Unknown		Unknown		
Fincher, Jim	B	Africa	80	2/16/85
Debility of age		Livingston		
Flagg, Rhoda	B		50	12/12/89
Typhoid fever		Gainesville Beat		
Flowers, Samuel	W	SC	84	12/13/82
Pneumonia		York Station		
Flowers, Sophronia	W	NC	45	9/20/89
Chronic diarrhea		Cokes Chapel		
Floyd, Sam	B	AL	25	5/1/86
Pneumonia		Lee's Station		
Fluker, Amanda	B	AL	29	1/29/84
Pneumonia		Black Bluff		
Fluker, Lily	B	MD	90	12/3/85
Debility of age		Poorhouse Cemetery		
Fluker, Mollie	B		50	8/23/84
Womb cancer		Unknown		
Fluker, Nathan	B	PA	100	4/22/85
Debility of age		Poorhouse Cemetery		
Ford, Susan	W	AL	60	3/20/84
Congestive chill		Belmont		
Foster, Adeline	B		87	11/6/82
Debility of age		Gainesville		

NAME CAUSE OF DEATH	RACE	BORN AGE DEATH PLACE OF BURIAL
Foster, Thomas	B	75 10/15/81
Debility of age		Gainesville
Fowler, Wesley	B	AL 45 4/29/86
Consumption		Belmont Beat
Foy, Luke	B	AL 50 1/6/85
Pneumonia		Gainesville
Foy, Margaret	B	AL 35 7/3/85
Consumption		Sumterville Beat
Frankle, Mrs.	W	81 8/19/83
Malarial fever		Livingston
Franklin, Mary	B	SC 80 9/3/82
Debility of age		Gainesville
Frazier, Agnes	B	AL 25 12/11/81
Cachexia Africana		Preston Beat
Frazier, Cage	B	AL 25 10/25/82
Pneumonia		Preston Beat
Frazier, George	B	NC 42 2/22/85
Pneumonia		Lacy's Beat
Frazier, Lewis	B	72 3/26/91
Unknown		Unknown
Friend, Nellie	B	AL 60 4/11/87
Ascites		Unknown
Fulford, Ann	B	AL 28 1/25/85
Pneumonia		Grants Church
Fuller, George	B	27 1/27/87
Congestion of brain		York Beat
Fulton, Green	B	AL 35 12/26/81
Stabbed		Mt Zion
Fulton, Lea	B	TN 101 7/27/90
Old age		Gainesville
Fulton, William F.	W	TN 81 10/4/86
Old age		Bethel
Gandy, Jarman	B	28 9/25/85
Lung abscess		Warsaw Beat
Gandy, Matilda S.	W	81 8/14/87
Old age		Gainesville
Garrett, Ann	B	AL 35 1/12/84
Pernicious fever		Jones Bluff
Garrett, Kesiah	B	AL 70 3/22/91
Paralysis of brain		Jones Bluff
Gary, Martha	B	AL 18 4/16/82
Typhoid fever		Gainesville
Gay, Benjamin	W	NC 73 3/13/89
Kidney degeneration		Warsaw

NAME	RACE	BORN	AGE	DEATH
CAUSE OF DEATH		PLACE OF BURIAL		
Gee, Crecy	B	AL	20	6/17/81
Dropsy		Jones Bluff		
Gee, Sidney	B	AL	31	11/16/89
Consumption		Sumterville		
Gibbs, Jesse A.	W		76	6/4/85
Paralysis		Gainesville Beat		
Gilbert, Elizabeth	B	AL	41	2/7/91
Unknown		Belmont		
Gilbert, J. W.	W	AL	22	8/23/87
Typhoid fever		Souls Chapel		
Gilbert, William Buckner	W	AL	19	2/26/82
Typhoid fever		Souls Chapel		
Giles, Sallie	W	AL	65	3/16/84
Rheumatism		Giles Graveyard		
Gillespie, Harriet	B	VA	80	4/7/91
Pneumonia		Brewersville		
Gillespie, Minerva	B	MS	60	8/14/85
Bowel inflammation		Wilder Plantation		
Gillespie, Minnie	W	AL	24	3/26/88
Nephritis		Belmont		
Gilmore, Barbara	B	AL	50	1/15/83
Pneumonia		Black Bluff Beat		
Gilmore, Ottaway	B	AL	60	3/2/83
Pneumonia		Black Bluff Beat		
Gilmore, Willie Ann	W	AL	48	2/8/82
Heart disease		Gaston		
Gilmore, Mrs. Willis	B	AL	38	3/1/85
Pneumonia		Lee's Station		
Ginn, M. G.	W	AL	67	4/14/89
Dropsy		Poorhouse Cemetery		
Glass, Millie	B		80	8/10/82
Dropsy		Wiat Hill Cemetery		
Glass, Peter	B		86	6/11/81
Old age		Near Coatopa		
Godfrey, Charley	B	AL	62	12/13/83
Hydrothorax		Jones Bluff		
Godfrey, Cornelia O.	W	AL	28	12/13/86
Pneumonia		Sumterville		
Godfrey, Dr. James M.	W	AL	58	1/20/90
Bright's disease		Sumterville		
Godfrey, Jane	B	AL	45	6/9/88
Consumption		Jones Bluff		
Goode, H. D.	B	AL	34	3/22/91
Heart disease		Tuscaloosa		

NAME CAUSE OF DEATH	RACE	BORN AGE DEATH PLACE OF BURIAL
Goodloe, M. C. Uremia	W	TN 68 3/1/82 Gainesville
Goodloe, Robert Acute diarrhea	W	AL 33 7/25/89 Gainesville
Goodwin, M. A. Liver abscess	W	AL 34 3/8/88 Shorts Church
Gordon, Harriett Anaemia	B	AL 67 12/4/88 Hares Beat
Gordon, Millie Pneumonia	B	AL 35 4/5/90 Hares Beat
Gordon, Stella Neurasthenia	B	AL 24 4/26/87 Gainesville
Gowdey, Ben Congestive fever	B	AL 21 9/25/84 York Beat
Gowdey, Fayette Chronic nephritis	B	AL 65 5/26/86 Livingston
Gowdy, Alice Consumption	B	AL 45 1/1/92 Livingston
Gowdy, James Broken spine	B	AL 58 7/15/89 York
Graham, Harriett Heart disease	B	NC 65 9/7/87 Gaston
Graham, Joseph Consumption	W	AL 50 10/27/85 Chestnut Grove
Graham, Peggy Congestion	B	NC 80 9/26/84 Warsaw
Grand, Laura Pneumonia	B	18 1/5/83 Unknown
Grant, Eliza Influenza	B	AL 30 4/10/91 York
Gray, Henry Spinal meningitis	B	AL 23 3/21/87 Gainesville
Gray, Julia Convulsions	B	AL 23 6/16/85 Chapman Place
Grayson, Caesar Typhoid fever	B	AL 31 1/16/84 McDowell's Station
Grayson, R. W. Malarial fever	W	AL 44 11/22/86 Belmont
Grayson, Susan Pneumonia	B	AL 39 12/10/84 McDowell's
Green, Andrew Consumption	B	VA 68 11/15/88 Unknown
Green, Mrs. M. Pneumonia	W	NC 72 1/25/85 Livingston

NAME CAUSE OF DEATH	RACE	BORN	AGE	DEATH PLACE OF BURIAL		
Green, Sallie	B	AL	25	9/9/86		
Remittent fever		Livingston Beat				
Greenlee, J. M.	W	AL	51	6/29/89		
Inanition		Jones Bluff				
Greenlee, M. E.	W	AL	47	5/26/89		
Heart disease		Jones Bluff				
Greenlees, Leah	W	AL	60	12/18/84		
Heart disease		Jones Bluff Beat				
Gregory, Sylvanna	B	AL	35	12/24/86		
Consumption		Zion Hill				
Grice, Cornelius	B		19	8/27/82		
Congestive fever		Hares Beat				
Grice, Henry	B		75	2/23/91		
Influenza		Unknown				
Griffin, Willis	B	AL	30	11/19/87		
Enteritis		Sumterville				
Griggs, Isabel	W	AL	25	11/18/82		
Consumption		Gainesville				
Grove, Zorbie B.	W	AL	26	1/23/89		
Stomach congestion		Warsaw				
Groves, Dr. A. G.	W	MD	72	10/31/86		
Heart disease		Warsaw Beat				
Gully, Nancy	W	AL	35	12/29/84		
Pneumonia		Brewersville				
Gunn, Mary Jane	B		25	6/27/82		
Rectum cancer		Mt Zion				
Guy, William	B	AL	31	5/15/83		
Typhoid fever		York				
Hagan, Lucy	B		65	8/17/84		
Pernicious fever		Jones Bluff				
Hagan, Olivia Jane	W	AL	40	7/12/83		
Dropsy		Swan Burial Ground				
Haggards, George	W	NC	75	12/22/83		
Locomotor ataxy		Cokes Chapel				
Hainsworth, Jack	B	AL	69	5/24/85		
Paralysis		Black Bluff Beat				
Hair, Adison	B	AL	21	6/13/84		
Consumption		Livingston				
Hale, Deely	W	NC	58	4/28/83		
Heart disease		Gainesville				
Hale, Mrs. E. C.	W	GA	27	9/16/88		
Typhoid fever		York				
Hale, Joseph Wilson	W	SC	69	11/22/86		
Necrosis of maxilla		Elizabeth Church				

NAME CAUSE OF DEATH	RACE	BORN PLACE OF BURIAL	AGE	DEATH
Hale, Margarett Pneumonia	B	AL Intercourse	50	5/30/87
Hale, Mary Consumption	W	AL Elizabeth Church	24	8/6/84
Hale, Mary Isabella Puerperal septicaemia	W	AL Cokes Chapel	22	2/26/84
Hale, Rose Peritonitis	B	AL Beat 4	24	9/1/89
Hale, Samuel A. Unknown	W	NH Unknown	73	3/9/83
Hall, Jim Gunshot wound	B	AL Unknown	32	8/31/87
Hall, Susan Unknown	B	VA Unknown	56	5/17/89
Hall, Winnie Consumption	B	VA McElroy's Cemetery	75	3/1/84
Halsell, Martha A. Congestion of lungs	W	TN Warsaw	44	1/28/85
Hancock, Elizabeth Malarial fever	W	NC Belmont	48	10/15/84
Hand, William Malarial fever	B	AL Jones Creek	65	8/4/89
Handy, Dinah General dropsy	B	AL Preston Beat	22	7/25/86
Handy, Thomas Typhoid fever	B	AL Wilder Place	25	8/25/82
Hare, Martha B. Congestion of lungs	W	AL Warsaw Beat	66	1/18/87
Harper, Gastin Typhoid fever	B	AL Gainesville Beat	30	8/29/88
Harper, Phebe Unknown	B	AL Bethel Church	51	12/30/81
Harral, Bryant Dysentery	W	MS Mississippi	69	8/2/82
Harrington, Maggie Hemorrhagica purpura	W	Brewersville	23	12/1/81
Harris, Boliver Strangulated hernia	B	NC Gainesville	76	8/17/83
Harris, Burwell Typho-malarial fever	B	VA Sumterville	50	1/22/88
Harris, Caroline Old age	W	SC Unknown	76	2/22/90
Harris, Gideon Pneumonia	B	AL York	29	3/25/89

NAME / CAUSE OF DEATH	RACE	BORN	AGE	DEATH / PLACE OF BURIAL
Harris, Jim	B		24	6/1/82
Hepatitis				Unknown
Harris, Maddie S.	W	AL	20	9/19/81
Uremia (childbirth)				Siloam
Harris, Marinda	B		60	6/21/83
Heart disease				Gainesville
Harris, Mary	B	AL	35	11/8/83
Consumption				Gainesville Beat
Harris, Mattie	W	MS	40	10/28/83
Stomach cancer				Gainesville
Harris, Mollie	B	SC	47	2/3/90
Influenza				Gainesville
Harris, Park McLellan	W	AL	35	3/1/82
Consumption				Livingston
Harrison, Baalam	B	AL	46	4/27/91
Gunshot wound				Brewersville Beat
Harrison, Hannah	B	NC	65	10/26/88
Unknown				Zion Church
Harrison, Joseph	B	NC	64	10/28/85
Unknown				Mt Zion
Harrison, Julius	B	AL	30	6/3/87
Dysentery				Jones Bluff
Harrison, Phoebe	B	AL	50	9/27/84
Congestion				Jones Bluff Beat
Harrison, Randall	B		80	9/28/83
Congestive chill				Black Bluff
Hart, Drewsy	B		22	6/ /86
Unknown				Unknown
Hart, Elizabeth	B	AL	36	6/26/85
Malarial fever				Gainesville Beat
Hart, Zane Moses	W	AL	36	9/19/82
Congestive chill				Unknown
Harwood, R. G.	W	AL	25	10/13/86
Malarial fever				Gainesville
Haupt, May	B	TN	50	6/4/87
Unknown				Belmont
Haygood, Mrs.	W	VA	63	5/13/85
Apoplexy				Mt Hebron
Henagan, Ann	W	SC	82	1/10/84
Debility of old age				Jones Bluff
Henagan, Effie M.	W	SC	47	10/1/86
Malarial fever				Jones Bluff Beat
Henderson, Aggie	B	MS	24	4/27/85
Puerperal septicaemia				Livingston

| NAME | RACE | BORN | AGE | DEATH |
CAUSE OF DEATH		PLACE OF BURIAL		
Henderson, Lewis	W		77	12/2/84
Heart disease		Belmont		
Henderson, Obedience	W		71	9/13/81
Heart disease		Belmont		
Herd, Eleanor	W	NC	80	4/25/87
Old age		Elizabeth Church		
Hibbler, Austin	B		43	6/10/81
Gunshot wound		Warsaw Beat		
Hibler, Dudley	B	AL	26	3/4/88
Dysentery		Preston		
Hickinbotham, Milly	B	AL	65	11/7/83
Marasmus		Near Gainesville		
Hicks, Crecy	B	AL	22	9/7/81
Pulmonalis phthisis		Near Warsaw		
Hicks, Lilly	B	AL	27	3/11/83
Pneumonia		Johnston Place		
Higgins, Sam	B		55	11/5/84
Pneumonia		Unknown		
High, Clarissa	B	AL	60	9/2/83
Ovarian tumor		Sumterville		
High, Lawrence	B	AL	27	9/5/85
Dysentery		Jones Bluff		
High, Temperance J.	W		65	2/26/86
Heart disease		Sumterville Beat		
Hildreth, Hal	B	AL	67	3/12/82
Pneumonia		Black Bluff		
Hildreth, Jane	B	AL	70	11/8/88
Burn		Unknown		
Hill, Ben	B	GA	37	4/7/86
Consumption		Poorhouse Cemetery		
Hill, John	B	AL	20	3/9/83
Consumption		Nobles Cemetery		
Hill, Mrs. Sam	W	AL	40	9/16/89
Typhoid fever		Gainesville		
Hillman, Emery	B	AL	74	6/28/90
General debility		Jones Bluff		
Hillman, Margaret	B	VA	65	5/2/87
Typhoid fever		Gainesville		
Hillman, Mary Jane	W	AL	64	3/23/90
Laryngeal phthisis		Jones Bluff Beat		
Hines, Elias	B	SC	67	10/27/86
Injury from fall		Jones Bluff		
Hines, Nancy	B		75	12/1/89
Old age		Gainesville		

| NAME | RACE | BORN | AGE | DEATH |
CAUSE OF DEATH		PLACE OF BURIAL		
Hines, Poosa	B	Africa	100	5/22/83
Debility of age		Jones Bluff		
Hines, Sarah	W	NC	83	3/3/82
Old age		Cokes Chapel		
Hite, Lucinda	W		47	3/16/83
Pneumonia		Siloam Church		
Hitt, Mrs.	W		70	6/25/85
Consumption		Siloam Church		
Hodges, Francis M.	W	AL	37	12/18/89
Liver malignancy		Sumterville		
Hoit, Elizabeth	W	VA	71	1/6/90
Paralysis		Livingston		
Hollabaugh, William	W	PA	35	10/18/87
Fever & hemorrhage		Poorhouse Cemetery		
Hopkins, Elizabeth W.	W		62	3/2/84
Pneumonia		Livingston		
Hopkins, Mallissa	B	AL	48	1/13/92
Pneumonia		Warsaw		
Hopkins, Tamar	B	AL	34	5/4/82
Hemorrhage		Black Bluff Beat		
Hopson, Tilda	B	AL	61	7/1/90
Unknown		Beat 6		
Horde, Harriet	B	AL	22	6/25/81
Leucocythemia		Brewersville		
Horde, Lu	B	AL	32	1/14/90
Gunshot wound		Belmont Beat		
Horn, Daniel	B	NC	63	4/12/91
Congestion of lungs		Unknown		
Horn, Iredell H.	W		68	7/5/86
Nervous system exhaust.		Gainesville		
Horn, Mary M.	W	NC	78	3/15/86
Bronchitis		Cokes Chapel		
Horn, Thomas	W	AL	21	2/16/84
Pneumonia		Brewersville		
Horton, Doss	B	VA	89	4/5/87
Influenza		Belmont Beat		
Houston, Emily	B	AL	65	3/18/87
Heart disease		Warsaw Beat		
Houston, Ephriam	B		50	6/14/81
Neuralgia of heart		Near Warsaw		
Houston, Fannie	B	AL	60	9/8/86
Brain inflammation		Livingston		
Houston, Harry	B	AL	65	3/21/83
Pneumonia		Black Bluff		

NAME	RACE	BORN	AGE	DEATH
CAUSE OF DEATH		PLACE OF BURIAL		
Houston, Martha	W	TN	75	6/11/84
Consumption		Livingston		
Houston, Phillis	B		70	6/12/86
Heart disease		Hares Beat		
Houston, Sock	B	AL	40	9/5/88
Consumption		Unknown		
Houston, Vinah	B		71	12/29/89
Hydrothovery		Jones Bluff Beat		
Howell, Monroe	B	AL	35	12/27/88
Pneumonia		Lacy		
Huff, Mary Ann	W	AL	31	12/28/83
Convulsions		Huff Plantation		
Hunt, Sallie	B	AL	24	2/10/89
Paralysis		Gainesville		
Hunter, Annie J.	W	AL	41	11/16/89
Heart failure		Livingston		
Hunter, Charlie	B	AL	26	4/4/89
Consumption		Unknown		
Hunter, Eliza	W	AL	25	9/3/87
Metro-peritonitis		Curls Chapel		
Hunter, Elizabeth	W	KY		10/1/85
Dysentery		Curls Chapel		
Hunter, Harry	B	AL	26	1/24/83
Pneumonia		Jones Bluff		
Hutchings, King	B	AL	38	9/24/85
Consumption		Lacy's Beat		
Hutchings, May	B	AL	51	8/24/89
Heart disease		Unknown		
Hutchings, Robert	B	VA	73	12/14/88
Unknown		Sumterville		
Hutchins, Amanda	B	AL	45	7/24/83
Unknown		Sumterville Beat		
Hutchins, Eliza	B	VA	35	1/27/87
Hemorrhage		Sumterville Beat		
Hutchins, Harriet	B	AL	25	9/15/81
Consumption		Lacy's Beat		
Hutchins, Israel	B	NC	45	2/19/86
General dropsy		Lacy's Beat		
Hutchins, Nancy	B		45	6/21/87
Malarial fever		Sumterville		
Hutchins, Peter	B	VA	80	7/13/87
Heart disease		Sumterville		
Hutchins, Stephen	B	NC	64	3/24/86
Pneumonia		Sumterville Beat		

NAME	RACE	BORN	AGE	DEATH
CAUSE OF DEATH		PLACE OF BURIAL		
Hutchins, Sylvia	B		56	5/31/82
Apoplexy		Sumterville Beat		
Hutchins, Thomas	B	AL	21	2/24/82
Hydrothorax		Sumterville Beat		
Hutchins, Thomas	B	AL	22	2/25/82
Typhoid pneumonia		Sumterville		
Hutton, Ben	B	AL	38	10/17/89
Consumption		Jones Bluff		
Inge, Henry	B	AL	28	7/6/87
Meningitis		Unknown		
Iridell, John	B	NC	70	5/10/84
Pneumonia		Near Jones Bluff		
Jackson, John	B	AL	33	2/27/83
Crushed by wagon		Preston Beat		
James, Alice	B	AL	24	11/9/82
Consumption		Gainesville		
James, Eliza	W	AL		4/8/86
Post partum bleeding		Intercourse Beat		
James, Jane	B		39	11/6/85
Bowels inflammation		Livingston		
James, Judy	B	AL	26	5/15/85
Unknown		Gainesville		
Jarman, Amanda	W	AL	35	1/8/84
Chronic diarrhea		Jones Bluff Beat		
Jarman, Wyley	B		95	10/20/83
Old age		Grants Church		
Jemison, Isaac	B		101	8/20/83
Old age		Grants Chapel		
Jemison, John	B	AL	19	1/17/84
Consumption		Belmont		
Jenkins, Mariah	B	AL	35	4/15/91
Consumption		Beat 5		
Jerry, Mariah	B	AL	48	7/9/86
Sunstroke		Lacy's Beat		
Johnson, Flanders Sr.	B	NC	83	8/27/87
Dropsy		Black Bluff		
Johnson, Frances	B	AL	41	1/28/87
Heart disease		Black Bluff		
Johnson, Green	B	VA	69	12/24/88
Pneumonia		Lacy's		
Johnson, Henry	B	AL	30	8/14/82
Epilepsy		Black Bluff		

NAME / CAUSE OF DEATH	RACE	BORN	AGE	DEATH / PLACE OF BURIAL
Johnson, James / Peritonitis	B	AL	35	4/31/83 / Gainesville
Johnson, Jane / Bowel congestion	B	AL	45	9/3/82 / Jones Bluff Beat
Johnson, Oliver / Pneumonia	B	VA	55	3/10/83 / Brewersville
Johnson, Polly / Consumption	B	AL	30	11/4/84 / Sumterville Beat
Johnson, Sam / Dyspepsia	B	AL	61	7/13/90 / Beat 11
Johnson, Silvy / Burn	B	NC	78	9/8/83 / Black Bluff Beat
Johnson, William / Dropsy	B	AL	50	10/31/83 / Near McDowell's
Johnston, Virginia / Consumption	B	AL	25	8/5/89 / York
Joiner, G. B. / Pneumonia	B	AL	55	12/29/83 / York
Joiner, O. R. / Dysentery	W	NC	66	12/15/83 / Unknown
Joiner, Rebecca / Double pneumonia	B	AL	50	2/15/88 / York
Jolly, Salina / Acute phthisis	B	VA	55	7/16/88 / Unknown
Jolly, Sam / Consumption	B	AL	50	3/7/87 / Bluff Port Beat
Jones, Aaron / Old age	B	VA	92	7/9/81 / Dr. Jones Place
Jones, Amy / Dropsy	B	AL	50	6/14/86 / Warsaw Beat
Jones, Amy Ann / Puerperal eclampsia	B	AL	23	7/7/83 / Near Sherman
Jones, Ben / Cystoflegia	B		75	10/16/87 / Jones Bluff
Jones, Butler / Pneumonia	B	AL	50	3/26/85 / Near Warsaw
Jones, Cephus / Knife wound	B	AL	30	4/4/90 / Jones Bluff
Jones, Daniel / Pneumonia	B		55	4/15/85 / Warsaw Beat
Jones, Edmond / Heart disease	B		65	1/11/88 / Lacy
Jones, Jack / Debility of age	B	NC	84	1/27/85 / Lea Plantation

NAME / CAUSE OF DEATH	RACE	BORN	AGE	DEATH / PLACE OF BURIAL
Jones, Jack	B	AL	32	3/27/90
Measles				York Beat
Jones, Jim	B	AL	50	2/10/92
Pneumonia				Warsaw
Jones, Kim	B	VA	78	12/27/84
Bowel congestion				Bennett's Station
Jones, Mary	B	AL	30	8/2/86
Uterus hemorrhage				York Beat
Jones, Mary	B	AL	41	3/1/90
Tubercular nephritis				Livingston Beat
Jones, Rachel	B	AL	60	3/15/85
Burn				Near Warsaw
Jones, Riley	W		76	5/8/82
Typhoid fever				Siloam Church
Jones, Sally	B		55	7/26/82
Uterus cancer				Warsaw Beat
Jones, William	B			11/25/84
Pneumonia				Gainesville
Jowers, Fanny	W	AL	28	1/17/84
Pneumonia				Livingston
Kaufman, Millie	B		55	11/18/83
Pneumonia				Near Belmont
Kelsie, Nellie C.	W	NY	29	3/5/84
Consumption				Manchester, Iowa
Kendrick, Owen	B	NC	75	7/14/86
Dysentery				Moore's Place
Kendrick, Warwick	B	NC	20	8/28/85
Remittent fever				N. W. Primbles's
Kennard, Jim	B	VA	71	11/13/89
Heart disease				Livingston
Kennard, Nellie	B	AL	16	8/14/81
Typhoid fever				Kennard Place
Kennard, Sofa	B	AL	25	10/2/81
Remittent fever				Unknown
Kennen, Isaac	B	AL	40	12/29/88
Heart disease				Jones Bluff
Kerr, Sarah	W	SC	71	4/10/86
Abscess of liver				Bethel
Key, Elizabeth	W	AL	47	11/9/84
Consumption				Payneville
Key, George	W	AL	64	9/28/85
Bright's disease				Payneville
Keys, Martha	B	AL	24	7/12/84
Bowel congestion				Payneville

NAME	RACE	BORN	AGE	DEATH
CAUSE OF DEATH		PLACE OF BURIAL		
Kimbral, John	B	AL	38	4/2/90
Double pneumonia		Livingston		
King, Alfred	B		70	11/21/90
Dropsy of heart		Curl Station		
King, Gus	B	AL	30	1/9/90
Peritonitis		Livingston		
King, Mack	B	AL	28	1/2/84
Consumption		Poorhouse Cemetery		
King, William	B	AL	33	1/28/90
Pneumonia		Gainesville Beat		
Kinnard, Green	B	AL	35	8/19/84
Dysentery		Livingston		
Kirkland, William	B	AL	50	8/9/85
Typho-malarial fever		Pleasant Grove		
Knott, John	W	AL	30	4/26/84
Spinal meningitis		Salmon Church		
Knox, Alexander		NC	68	8/14/87
Malarial fever		Gaston		
Knox, John	B	AL	50	1/8/86
Stricture of uretha		Elizabeth Church		
Kynard, C. B.	W	MS	23	8/14/84
Consumption		Marion, Miss.		
Lacitor, Caroline	B	NC	64	3/4/90
Consumption		Unknown		
Lambert, William	W	VA	84	8/3/90
Debility of age		Gainesville		
Land, Marbella	W	AL	52	5/26/82
Consumption		Siloam Church		
Landon, Alfred	B	VA	65	1/4/82
Ascites		Poorhouse Cemetery		
Lanier, William	W	AL	54	1/9/90
Gland inflammation		Scooba, Miss.		
Lard, Louis	B	AL	21	9/25/85
Continued fever		Unknown		
Larkin, Annie	B	VA	83	10/10/89
Old age		Beat 7		
Larkin, Cindy	B	AL	27	8/17/84
Malarial fever		Livingston		
Larkin, Irene	W	AL	50	12/3/86
Consumption		Brewersville		
Larkin, Josephine	B	AL	35	11/25/85
Malarial fever		Grants Chapel		
Larkin, Julia	B	AL	29	7/18/87
Metritis, etc.		Jones Bluff		

NAME CAUSE OF DEATH	RACE	BORN	AGE	DEATH PLACE OF BURIAL		
Latimore, Isaac	B	AL	30	9/23/81		
Scrofula		York				
Lawler, Robert W.	W	AL	23	4/7/82		
Consumption		Brewersville				
Lawrence, Lizzie	B	VA	30	4/19/82		
Unknown		Gainesville				
Lawson, Betty	B	AL	30	7/5/83		
Remittent fever		Rencher Place				
Lawson, Norman	B	VA	65	2/7/84		
Pneumonia		Black Bluff				
Lawson, Winnie	B	AL	60	5/14/87		
Heart disease		Belmont				
Lee, Jack	B	AL	22	9/22/81		
Heart disease		Unknown				
Lee, Lewis	B	AL	60	8/23/88		
Dysentery		Brewersville				
Lee, Linda	B		95	5/10/88		
Heart disease		Brewersville				
Lee, M. E.	W	AL	57	2/7/88		
Nephritis		Brewersville				
Lee, Mamie	W	AL	28	11/16/87		
Tuberculosis		Brewersville				
Lee, William	B	NC	71	3/3/84		
Intussusception		Near Livingston				
Legres, Harriet	B		43	8/27/82		
Peritonitis		W. L. McDow's				
Lewis, Adeline	B	AL	46	4/30/88		
Nephritis		Unknown				
Lewis, Becky	B	AL	51	7/9/90		
Typho-malarial fever		Beat 11				
Lewis, Betsy	B	AL	71	6/6/89		
Heart disease		Unknown				
Lewis, Calvin	B	AL	51	4/5/89		
Unknown		Jones Creek				
Lewis, Charles	B		40	1/15/84		
Pneumonia		York				
Lewis, David	W	CT	60	8/4/82		
Pulmonary apoplexy		Gainesville				
Lewis, Dick	B	AL	70	2/18/90		
La Grippe		Gainesville Beat				
Lewis, Eliza Ann	B	AL	30	5/18/82		
Congestion of lungs		Sumterville Beat				
Lewis, Julia	B	VA	29	4/21/89		
Heart disease		Unknown				

NAME	CAUSE OF DEATH	RACE	BORN	AGE	DEATH
			PLACE OF BURIAL		
Lewis, Laura	Puerperal fever	W	MS	35	6/17/87
			Siloam Church		
Lewis, Lu	Congestive fever	B	AL	31	5/29/84
			Unknown		
Lewis, Martha Ann	Consumption	B	AL	25	12/18/83
			Jones Bluff		
Lewis, Sallie	Puerperal fever	B	AL	25	5/20/84
			Unknown		
Lewis, Thornton	Malarial rheumatism	B		71	8/17/89
			Unknown		
Lewis, Tilda	Dropsy	B	AL	50	3/30/87
			Black Bluff		
Lide, Eliza	Consumption	B	AL	42	5/24/89
			Unknown		
Lindsay, Sally	Pneumonia	B		47	3/18/84
			York Beat		
Lindsey, Mariah	Uterine hemorrhage	B	AL	45	3/9/89
			Cuba		
Lipscomb, Elijah	Debility of age	B		80	7/2/82
			Poorhouse Cemetery		
Little, Ritter	Puerperal fever	B		34	12/13/83
			Warsaw		
Little, Violet	Pneumonia	B	AL	35	1/22/84
			Unknown		
Little, Whit	Pneumonia	B	AL	24	3/28/87
			Hares Beat		
Little, William	Consumption	B	AL	22	8/14/84
			Hares Beat		
Lockard, Amanda	Rheumatism of heart	W		67	7/1/82
			Livingston		
Loftin, Mitchell	Pneumonia	B	AL	19	1/28/84
			Black Bluff		
Long, Frank	Typhoid fever	B	AL	23	9/12/83
			Greene Co. Ala.		
Long, Perry	Chronic diarrhea	B	AL	30	9/21/90
			Long's Cemetery		
Long, William	Heart disease	B	TN	65	8/2/81
			Gainesville Beat		
Looney, Serena	Brain congestion	B	AL	24	11/17/87
			Warsaw		
Love, Mrs. James H.	Puerperal septicaemia	W	AL	25	10/14/81
			Livingston		
Lovelace, Jane	Abortion	B		30	12/2/83
			Unknown		

NAME	RACE	BORN	AGE	DEATH
CAUSE OF DEATH		PLACE OF BURIAL		
Loving, Keziah	B	VA	60	10/16/81
Remittent fever		Gainesville		
Low, Polly	B		65	4/26/82
Ascites		Unknown		
Lowery, Billie	B	NC	85	1/28/89
Lung hemorrhage		Jones Bluff		
Lucus, Adeline	B	AL	27	8/29/89
Consumption		Livingston		
Lummus, Louisa	W	MS	41	4/30/91
Puerperal septicaemia		Beat 5		
Lyon, Green	B	AL	40	12/22/88
Pneumonia		Warsaw		
Mabry, Joseph	B	AL	27	9/3/81
Drowned		Gainesville		
Manly, J. Harrison	W	AL	42	9/5/82
Syphilis		Jones Bluff Beat		
Mannice, Broody	B		55	5/26/82
Congestive chill		Unknown		
Manning, Battle	B		22	11/18/84
Malarial fever		Unknown		
Marshall, Edy	B	AL	28	5/3/81
Typho-malarial fever		Livingston		
Marshall, Harvey	B		60	7/17/83
Bronchitis		New Prospect Ch.		
Martin, (Female)	B		70	1/15/86
Froze to death		Gainesville Beat		
Martin, Mary Ann	W	AL	58	11/10/83
Congestion of lungs		Gainesville		
Martin, Matilda	B		60	2/21/82
Ascites		Livingston Beat		
Mason, George W.	W	AL	35	1/15/83
Consumption		Livingston		
Mason, Rhodes	B	AL	22	6/2/83
Pernicious fever		Belmont		
Masten, Ruckless	B	AL	55	9/20/82
Congestive chill		Unknown		
Mathes, Silla	B	AL	30	12/25/83
Pneumonia		Grants Church		
Matthews, Mary	B	AL	35	11/16/90
Typhoid fever		Gainesville		
Matthews, Penny	W	AL	17	8/30/82
Puerperal hemorrhage		Brewersville		
Matthews, William B.	W	AL	43	7/22/84
Consumption		Thornville		

NAME / CAUSE OF DEATH	RACE	BORN AGE DEATH / PLACE OF BURIAL		
Mawhiny ?, Anna	W	AL	31	2/4/90
Perotenalis		York Beat		
May, Andrew	B	AL	24	2/15/83
Pneumonia		Brewersville		
McAlpin, Melinda	B	AL	55	2/8/91
Congestion of lungs		Beat 9		
McAlpin, William S.	W	MS	55	1/21/85
Pulmonary erysipelas		York		
McBride, Alexander	W	AL	32	5/4/83
Consumption		Siloam		
McCann, William J.	W	NC	44	8/10/81
Dropsy		Choctaw Co. Ala.		
McCarty, Kizzie	B	AL	30	2/ /82
Unknown		Belmont		
McConnell, Martha	W	AL	65	1/23/92
Influenza		York		
McCorkle, Sam	B	AL	24	12/1/85
Consumption .		Livingston		
McDaniel, Hamp	B	AL	51	8/5/89
Malarial fever		Unknown		
McDaniel, Hannah	B	AL	46	6/2/89
Blood poison		Unknown		
McDaniel, Henry	W	NC	84	10/12/81
Cancer & erysipelas		Sumterville		
McDaniel, John M.	W	AL	48	7/7/82
Consumption		Sumterville		
McDaniel, Lucy	B	NC	60	3/5/83
Heart disease		Sumterville Beat		
McDaniel, Miranda	B	AL	65	2/27/84
Entero colitis		Sumterville		
McDaniel, Rena	B	AL	75	9/17/81
Typho-malarial fever		Unknown		
McDaniel, Sallie	B	AL	25	7/13/85
Meningitis		Sumterville Beat		
McDonald, Ann	W	SC	58	11/10/84
Albuminuria		Chestnut Grove		
McDonald, Bigham M.	W	AL	27	5/22/85
Consumption		Elizabeth Church		
McDonald, Jane	W	AL	59	7/6/90
Unknown		Beat 4		
McDonald, John	W	AL	64	12/24/88
Paralysis		Curls Chapel		
McDonald, M. A.	W	AL	34	2/2/82
Angina pectoris		Livingston		

NAME	RACE	BORN	AGE	DEATH
CAUSE OF DEATH		PLACE OF BURIAL		
McDonald, M. B.	W		45	11/5/90
Pulmonalis phthisis		Livingston		
McDow, Jack	B		95	8/20/86
Debility of age		Unknown		
McDowel, Henry	B	AL	30	9/13/85
Consumption		Gainesville		
McDowell, Lucy	W	AL	52	10/24/89
Congestion of brain		Jones Bluff		
McElroy, Frank	W	AL	34	9/19/81
Heart disease		McElroy Graveyard		
McElroy, J. R.	W	NC	81	7/12/85
Debility of age		McElroy Graveyard		
McElroy, James R.	W	AL	50	1/12/87
Pneumonia		McElroy Graveyard		
McElroy, Matilda	W	AL	68	9/6/85
Apoplexy		McElroy Graveyard		
McElroy, Mrs.	W	AL	29	2/27/84
Spinal meningitis		Mt Moriah		
McGowan, Peggy	B		45	10/3/83
Pneumonia		McGowan Place		
McGowan, R.J.	W	AL	45	10/23/86
Malarial fever		Mt Herman		
McGrew, John	B	AL	35	1/15/85
Pneumonia		Unknown		
McInnis, Victoria	B	AL	16	5/16/81
Peritonitis		New Prospect Ch.		
McIntyre, Isam	B		80	12/25/81
Congestion of brain		Unknown		
McKenzie, Mr.	W	GA	65	1/20/84
Stomach inflammation		Hale Graveyard		
McKerrell, Ned	B		70	1/29/86
Pneumonia		Jones Bluff		
McKinney, George	W			5/9/81
Pulmonalis phthisis		Binnsville, Miss.		
McKnight, Susan	W	AL	67	7/1/89
Apoplexy		Livingston		
McLean, Peter	W	NC	76	2/18/85
Softening of brain		New Prospect Ch.		
McMahon, Charles	W	VA	70	10/23/85
Old age		Gainesville		
McMahon, Mrs. E. C. R. S.	W	VA	74	10/2/83
Fracture of pelvis		Gainesville		
McMillan, Dora	W	AL	34	6/27/83
Consumption		Brewersville		

NAME CAUSE OF DEATH	RACE	BORN	AGE	DEATH PLACE OF BURIAL	
McMillon, Squire Old age	B		VA Unknown	93	8/25/89
McNamara, John Dropsy of heart	W	Ireland	Warsaw Beat	30	4/19/85
McPherson, Syrus Typhoid fever	W		AL Belmont	25	9/24/87
McRee, Robert Gunshot wound	W		AL Belmont	23	7/9/84
McSwain, Rosa Old age	B		Grants Chapel	84	6/20/84
McSwain, Willis Bright's disease	B		NC Unknown	64	2/22/90
Meador, Sally Childbirth	B		AL Belmont	20	5/28/83
Mellown, Julia Cirrhosis of liver	W		AL Cokes Chapel	35	1/19/82
Melton, Bart Sr. Malarial fever	W		SC Belmont	76	10/24/86
Melton, Mary Pneumonia	W		SC Belmont	72	3/21/83
Merriwether, Mariah Embolism	B		NC Gainesville	56	5/12/82
Miles, Cindy Dropsy	B		Livingston Beat	40	7/30/86
Miller, Anderson Unknown	B		Belmont	29	6/14/83
Miller, Jim Pneumonia	B		AL Spring Bluff	35	3/4/87
Miller, Millie Consumption	B		A.C. Rogers Place	55	8/18/84
Miller, Selina Unknown	B		AL Belmont	30	1/23/84
Millon, Esther Spasms	B		Belmont	60	1/10/87
Mitchell, Annie Consumption	B		MS Grants Church	30	8/28/85
Mitchell, Daniel Carbuncle	W		Gainesville	62	3/11/90
Mitchell, Jesse Meningitis	B		AL Sumterville Beat	35	6/21/85
Mitchell, Penny Hemoptysis	B		NC Poorhouse Cemetery	62	3/4/87
Mitchell, Prudence Annie Paralysis of heart	W		AL Livingston	35	2/15/84

NAME	RACE	BORN	AGE	DEATH
CAUSE OF DEATH		PLACE OF BURIAL		
Mitchell, Sophy	B		67	2/3/82
Pneumonia		Jones Bluff Beat		
Mobley, Washington	B		35	12/27/81
Pneumonia		Hares Beat		
Monette, Jim	W		24	4/15/87
Malarial fever		Livingston		
Moody, Duckie	B	AL	24	8/30/89
Bright's disease		Unknown		
Moody, Henry	W	MS	60	9/20/84
Chronic diarrhea		Toomsuba, Miss.		
Moore, Ellen	B	AL	30	12/12/83
Apoplexy		Payneville Beat		
Moore, James A.	W	SC	56	5/7/81
Pulmonalis phthisis		Bethel Church		
Moore, Jane	B	AL	40	6/15/86
Paralysis		Poorhouse Cemetery		
Moore, Margaret Jane	W	AL	47	7/12/84
Dysentery		Bethel Church		
Moore, Melissa	B	GA	50	9/30/83
Change of life		Tankersley Place		
Moore, Mollie	B	AL	36	12/10/89
Consumption		Unknown		
Moore, Rachel	B		60	4/11/82
Pulmonary oedema		Livingston		
Moore, Richard	B		60	1/20/85
Malarial fever		Unknown		
Morgan, Warren	W	MS	28	2/2/84
Heart disease		Cuba		
Morris, Alfred	B	NC	60	2/14/84
Pneumonia		Gainesville		
Morris, Gus	B	AL	19	5/13/82
Pneumonia		Gainesville		
Mosely, Hannah	B		65	3/10/86
Unknown		Warsaw Beat		
Mosely, Holland	B		106	3/10/86
Debility of age		Preston Beat		
Myer, John	B	AL	27	1/17/82
Typho-malarial fever		Belmont		
Myer, Mrs. W. P.	W	NC	41	9/26/85
Acute tuberculosis		Augusta, Ga.		
Myers, Wilson	B		45	5/3/87
Congestion of brain		Livingston		
Nance, Mary	W	AL	37	3/9/84
Consumption		Gainesville		

NAME / CAUSE OF DEATH	RACE	BORN	AGE	DEATH / PLACE OF BURIAL
Nash, James H.	W		40	1/31/90
Morphine narcosis				Warsaw Beat
Nash, Rachel	B	AL	38	4/15/87
Measles				Hares Beat
Neill, Elizabeth	W	AL	81	11/6/89
Pneumonia				Watts Grove
Neilson, Eugenia Amason	W	AL	23	10/19/83
Vomiting (pregnancy)				Livingston
Nelson, Ella	B	NC	47	11/28/84
Consumption				Cokes Chapel
Nelson, Scott	B	AL	30	12/15/83
Pneumonia				Unknown
Nevill, W. H.	W	SC	76	7/25/87
Heart disease				Mississippi
Nixon, Hiram	B	AL	27	1/15/84
Pneumonia				Jones Bluff
Noble, Caroline Lee	W	AL	67	7/21/88
Dysentery				Black Bluff
Noble, Sarah	B	AL	54	6/21/88
Dysentery				Black Bluff
Noonan, A.	B	Ireland		7/14/90
Hydrothorax				Beat 11
Norfleet, Henry	B	AL	30	12/1/88
Epilepsy				Black Bluff
North, Fannie	W	AL	29	3/7/84
Spinal meningitis				Mt Moriah
Norvill, Jordon	W	AL	26	9/8/87
Malarial fever				Livingston
Norville, Mary	W	AL	71	7/11/90
Heart disease				Livingston
Norville, Rose	B		75	11/25/82
Debility of age				Livingston
Norwood, Cela	B	AL	30	3/12/84
Pneumonia				Drake Graveyard
Nucum, (Male)	W	MS	30	11/20/88
Malarial fever				Unknown
Oakes, William Ervin	W	AL	22	7/16/82
Remittent fever				Jones Bluff
Odom, (Female)	W	AL	31	7/22/90
Measles				Beat 18
Oliver, Emma	B	AL	51	10/9/89
Malarial fever				Beat 13
Oliver, Lewellyn	W	SC	79	1/22/85
Consumption				Warsaw Beat

NAME	RACE	BORN	AGE	DEATH
CAUSE OF DEATH		PLACE OF BURIAL		
Ormond, Kate	B	AL	32	7/25/86
Rheumatism		Pickens Co. Ala.		
Owens, S. W.	W	NC	50	3/29/84
Pneumonia		Unknown		
Pack, Ann	B	AL	43	8/7/85
Pelvic peritonitis		Siloam Church		
Palmer, Susan	B	AL	23	7/5/87
Malarial fever		Sumterville		
Parker, Fannie	B	AL	50	1/25/88
Uterus cancer		Unknown		
Parker, (Female)	B	AL	55	7/19/86
Dysentery		Unknown		
Parker, Harriett	B	AL	61	7/20/90
Consumption		Beat 6		
Parker, Mark	W	AL	66	7/25/90
Apoplexy		Beat 6		
Parker, Socrates	W	AL	60	5/6/81
Pneumonia		Livingston		
Parkman, (Female)	W	AL	42	4/15/91
Multiple neuritis		Livingston		
Parrent, Katie	W	AL	30	4/4/82
Breast cancer		Livingston		
Patrick, Chess	B	AL	45	1/25/86
Pneumonia		Mt Zion Graveyard		
Patton, D. U.	W	AL	34	7/3/90
Malarial fever		Beat 8		
Patton, Eliza	W		81	7/28/83
Bronchial pneumonia		Brewersville		
Patton, Harriett	B	AL	34	8/29/87
Malarial fever		Warsaw		
Patton, Mrs. J. B.	W	AL	30	1/30/90
Uremia		Brewersville		
Pea, Daniel	B		80	12/29/84
Congestion of brain		Jones Bluff Beat		
Pea, Lou	B	VA	76	2/3/84
Paralysis		Gainesville		
Pearce, Thomas	W	MS	60	1/26/90
Rheumatism		Choctaw Co. Ala.		
Pearson, Frank	B	AL	20	4/13/85
Pneumonia		Warsaw Beat		
Peoples, William B.	W	NC	60	9/1/84
Dysentery		4 miles N. Moscow		
Perkins, Ben	B		32	8/26/81
Hanged by sheriff		Gainesville		

| NAME | RACE | BORN | AGE | DEATH |
CAUSE OF DEATH		PLACE OF BURIAL		
Perkins, Jake	B		40	9/9/87
Uremic poison		Gainesville		
Perria, Stewart	B	AL	78	6/29/89
Senility		Gainesville		
Person, Winnie	B	AL	26	9/20/85
Typhoid fever		Mt Zion		
Peterson, Suky	B	TN	63	2/7/83
Pneumonia		Gainesville Beat		
Petway, L. M.	W		30	1/25/88
Pneumonia		Mississippi		
Phares, Isaac	B	AL	75	8/30/86
Pneumonia		Belmont Beat		
Phillips, Jane	B	AL	48	5/27/81
Dropsy		Belmont		
Phillips, Lettuce	B	AL	22	2/7/84
Pneumonia		Belmont		
Phillips, Martha	W	AL	51	10/20/81
Ovarian cancer		Cuba		
Pinson, Eliza	B	AL	52	3/30/83
Pneumonia		Gainesville		
Pipkin, Fannie	B	AL	23	8/31/86
Typhoid fever		Black Bluff		
Pollard, Ella	B	AL	26	11/20/82
Consumption		Gainesville		
Pollard, John	B	VA	62	7/15/86
Bright's disease		Gainesville		
Pool, Six	B		60	8/5/81
Stomach inflammation		Jones Place		
Porter, Jerre	B	AL	70	1/14/92
Heart disease		Livingston		
Porter, Lemuel F.	W	NC	51	6/3/82
Gastritis		Gainesville		
Porter, Margaret	W	AL	51	1/6/82
Paralysis		Gainesville		
Porter, Vinah	B	AL	66	2/15/90
Pneumonia		Livingston Beat		
Porter, Walker	B	VA	75	1/12/92
Heart disease		Bluff Port Beat		
Porter, William	B	AL	35	11/6/84
Pneumonia		Unknown		
Porter, Willis	B	GA	60	11/20/88
Apoplexy		Unknown		
Portice, Boland	B	AL	76	7/14/88
Typhoid fever		Thornville		

NAME CAUSE OF DEATH	RACE	BORN	AGE	DEATH PLACE OF BURIAL	
Portis, Nancy Consumption	B			4/ /84 Mt Zion Church	
Portis, William Howard Locomotor ataxia	W	AL Reeds Chapel	28	9/28/81	
Posey Henry Chronic nephritis	B	AL Livingston	65	6/20/85	
Potts, Catherine Pneumonia	B	 Sumterville Beat	70	1/31/82	
Powell, C. L. Stomach congestion	W	TX York	26	6/30/89	
Powell, Charles Heart disease	B	 Brewersville	60	5/21/87	
Powell, E. A. Remittent fever	W	AL Livingston	28	8/17/83	
Poythress, Catherine Apoplexy	W	VA Sumterville	84	10/18/84	
Praytor, Mary Pneumonia	W	NC Chestnut Grove	70	2/7/91	
Praytor, Mrs. Accidental poisoning	W	AL Livingston	55	5/5/83	
Prestage, Caezar Typhoid pneumonia	B	AL Choctaw Co. Ala.	55	4/23/85	
Prestwood, William Typhoid fever	B	AL Unknown	41	5/11/89	
Prewit, W. A. Chronic dysentery	W	AL Livingston	31	8/10/89	
Price, John Old age	B	GA Livingston	103	9/20/83	
Price, Sallie Heart failure	B	AL Sumterville	41	4/6/89	
Prince, Charley Meningitis	B	 Epes Station	28	2/15/85	
Prince, Henrietta Hydrothorax	B	VA Jones Bluff	65	3/16/83	
Pringle, Andrew J. Congestive fever	W	MS Mississippi	30	7/12/85	
Pritchett, Francis Marion Pneumonia	W	AL Pine Grove Church	28	2/15/91	
Pyers, Robert Drowned	B	AL Bethel Church	30	12/6/82	
Ramsey, Rebecca Puerperal fever	B	AL Lacy's Beat	18	4/19/82	
Ramsey, Sicily Pneumonia	B	AL Gainesville Beat	50	8/28/85	

NAME	CAUSE OF DEATH	RACE	BORN	AGE	DEATH	PLACE OF BURIAL
Rancher, Matthew	Pneumonia	B	NC	80	1/23/83	Preston
Ray, Easter	Typhoid fever	B	AL	17	9/29/82	Gainesville
Reavis, Adline	Pulmonalis phthisia	B	AL	25	12/19/89	Sumterville
Redmond, Edmond	Pneumonia	B		28	6/21/82	Gainesville
Reed, Lucy F.	Anaemia	W	NC	33	8/7/84	Meridian, Miss.
Reed, Mrs.	Typhoid fever	W	AL	36	9/11/84	Mt Moriah Church
Reid, Charles	Bowel inflammation	B	VA	100	4/6/84	Belmont Beat
Reid, Rebecca	Congestion of brain	B	AL	45	3/15/86	Belmont
Rencher, Emma	Typhoid fever	B	AL	18	3/11/82	Rencher Place
Rencher, Hunts	Consumption	B	AL	35	7/7/85	Woodruff Place
Rew, Margaret	Asthma	W	NC	69	5/3/85	Cokes Chapel
Reynolds, Virginia	Pneumonia	W	AL	36	10/29/85	Souls Chapel
Rice, Walton	Unknown	B	AL	25	3/16/88	Belmont
Rich, Dennis	Dysentery	B	AL	50	7/8/85	Jones Bluff
Richards, Ann	Unknown	B		60	12/20/81	Near Sumterville
Richardson, Anthony	Consumption	B	AL	28	5/25/88	Sumterville
Richardson, John	Typhoid fever	B		19	10/10/83	Warsaw Beat
Richardson, Pat	Congestive fever	B	AL	40	6/8/85	Gainesville
Richardson, Rose	Apoplexy	B	NC	60	9/17/82	Sumterville
Richardson, Rose	Congestive chill	B	VA	70	9/17/82	Lacy's Beat
Ricks, Willis	Influenza	B	AL	40	1/22/92	Gainesville
Roads, Michael	Unknown	W	MS	20	1/24/84	Cuba

NAME CAUSE OF DEATH	RACE	BORN	AGE	DEATH PLACE OF BURIAL	
Roberson, Eliza	B		78	8/5/90	
Debility of age			Gainesville		
Roberts, Bill	B	VA	64	6/18/87	
Typhoid fever			Belmont Beat		
Roberts, Ritter	B		50	7/7/87	
Asthma & Uremia			Belmont		
Roberts, Robert Mitchell	W	AL	67	6/16/84	
Chronic diarrhea			Scott Co. Miss.		
Robertson, Susan	B	SC	61	5/10/82	
Unknown			Lacy's Beat		
Robinson, Fanny	B	AL	18	10/4/83	
Pyaemia			G. S. Wilder's		
Robinson, Manda	B		38	8/8/83	
Hypertrophy of heart			Sumterville Beat		
Robinson, Maria	B	NC	55	9/10/82	
Groin abscess			May's Graveyard		
Robinson, Mary	B		80+	2/2/91	
Heart disease			Livingston		
Robnett, J. M.	W	KY	54	9/28/81	
Consumption			York		
Robnett, John Wilson	W	KY	30	9/4/81	
Intemperance			York		
Rogers, Eliza Jane	W	AL	32	8/8/85	
Puerperal fever			Pleasant Grove		
Rogers, Kate	B	AL	20	2/24/85	
Pneumonia			Belmont Beat		
Ross, Anderson	B	AL	36	2/7/84	
Unknown			Belmont		
Ross, Fannie	B	MS	24	11/22/83	
Typhoid fever			York Beat		
Ross, Mary	B	NC	85	3/23/87	
Apoplexy			Belmont Beat		
Rowe, Emaline	B	AL	45	3/25/89	
Womb cancer			Cokes Chapel		
Royall, M. A.	W	GA	71	2/20/88	
Malarial fever			York		
Rumley, Elizabeth	W	NC	70	1/5/85	
Paralysis of heart			Cokes Chapel		
Rushing, America E.	W	AL	46	11/9/81	
Typho-malarial fever			Belmont		
Rushing, Bryant	W	AL	41	11/4/89	
p hition penis			Brewersville		
Rushing, James M.	W	SC	77	6/24/81	
Apoplexy			Belmont		

NAME	RACE	BORN	AGE	DEATH
CAUSE OF DEATH		PLACE OF BURIAL		
Rushing, Susannah	W	NC	73	8/22/83
Stomach cancer		Belmont		
Rushing, William	W	AL	58	7/5/90
Measles		Beat 4		
Russel, Rachel	B	AL	39	10/18/82
Puerperal peritonitis		Belmont		
Sample, Elizabeth	W	AL	58	5/26/82
Paralysis		Rocky Mount Church		
Sanders, Lizzie	W	AL	20	11/20/83
Typhoid fever		Beulah Church		
Sanders, William H.	W	TN	70	12/11/86
Apoplexy		New Prospect Ch.		
Sandy, Martha	B	VA	46	4/20/82
Typhoid fever		Gainesville Beat		
Sandy, Riley	B	AL	18	11/28/81
Erysipelas		Gainesville		
Saulter, Kit	B	AL	37	8/30/86
Typhoid fever		Belmont Beat		
Saunders, Mrs.	B		30	6/5/82
Consumption		Unknown		
Saxon, Richmond	B		75	10/26/82
Debility of age		Unknown		
Scales, William	B	AL	50	7/21/88
Meningitis		Unknown		
Scarborough, A. R.	W	NC	73	7/10/88
Cardiac paralysis		Bluff Port		
Schiffman, Dora	W	Germany	28	7/5/90
Acute congestion		Gainesville		
Scott, George	B	VA	70	4/20/90
Hydrothorax		Jones Bluff Beat		
Scott, Gracie	B	AL	33	7/5/90
Consumption of lungs		Livingston		
Scott, James	B		47	5/18/82
Congestion of liver		Gainesville		
Scott, Jennie	B	AL	24	9/29/82
Congestive chill		Drake Graveyard		
Scott, Lula D.	B	MS	18	1/26/83
Quinsy		Black Bluff		
Scott, Seaborn	B		60	12/27/84
Pneumonia		Black Bluff		
Scruggs, Josiah L.	W	NC	74	3/18/91
Heart disease		Livingston		
Scruggs, Mr.	W		78	7/3/84
Congestion of brain		Hares Beat		

NAME	RACE	BORN	AGE	DEATH
CAUSE OF DEATH		PLACE OF BURIAL		
Seale, Melinda	W	AL	36	1/1/84
Puerperal septicaemia		Brewersville		
Sewell, Sue	W	NC	82	12/11/89
Old age		Old Side Church		
Shackleford, Tony	B	AL	70	6/20/83
Dropsy		Brewersville		
Shed, Allen	B	TN	61	7/18/89
Intussusception bowel		Unknown		
Sheffield, Mary	W	NC	90	10/2/88
Debility of age		Cuba		
Shelby, W. M.	W	NC	72	6/19/81
General dropsy		Sandtuck		
Shelton, Andrew	W		60	12/23/81
Consumption		Chestnut Grove		
Sherrod, Catherine	B	AL	26	10/3/83
Puerperal fever		Jones Bluff		
Sherrod, Edna	B	AL	45	1/26/86
Entero-colitis		York		
Shilly, Martha J.	W	AL	37	1/3/83
Stomach ulcer		Elizabeth Church		
Shirley, Molly	B	NC	80	6/23/85
Debility of age		Poorhouse Cemetery		
Short, Clara	B	AL	30	1/19/90
Consumption		Gaston		
Sibley, J. K.	W	AL	70	1/12/88
Paralysis		Preston		
Siebert, Elizabeth	W	Germany	51	5/8/81
Asthmatic bronchitis		Belmont		
Siebert, William	W	AL	31	11/16/89
Killed by accident		Belmont		
Simmons, Caroline	B	AL	50	11/30/84
Pneumonia		Belmont		
Simms, Solomon	B	KY	90	8/16/82
Paralysis		Wilder's Place		
Simms, William Thomas	W	NC	83	3/1/90
Pneumonia		Sumterville Beat		
Sims, Joseph	B	AL	40	9/14/86
Congestive fever		Near Livingston		
Sims, May	B	AL	36	5/28/88
Consumption		Sledge Place		
Sims, Sarah Ann	W	SC	54	12/14/81
Typhoid fever		Siloam Church		
Sims, William	B	MS	40	9/24/82
Remittent fever		Mabry Plantation		

NAME	RACE	BORN	AGE	DEATH
CAUSE OF DEATH		PLACE OF BURIAL		
Skinner, Laura Ann	B	AL	40	1/27/90
Puerperal peritonitis		Preston Beat		
Sledge, Fannie	B		113	4/27/90
Senility		Sumterville		
Smaw, Jerre	B	AL	50	1/5/86
Pneumonia		Jones Bluff Beat		
Smith, Cinda	B	SC	91	8/28/89
Old age		Unknown		
Smith, Henry	B	NC	70	4/3/88
Bronchitis		Unknown		
Smith, Louis	W	NC	88	1/26/92
Paralysis		Poorhouse Cemetery		
Smith, Minnie Harris	W	AL	23	11/13/83
Malarial fever		Mobile, Ala.		
Smith, Mrs.	W	GA	40	8/15/81
Typhoid fever		Salem Church		
Smith, Nelson	B	AL	23	2/12/84
Pneumonia		Black Bluff		
Smith, Robert	B	AL	18	7/9/82
Chronic bronchitis		Bob May Place		
Smith, Sallie	B	NC	80	6/7/88
Gangrene (senile)		Unknown		
Smith, Thomas H.	W	VA	30	9/3/84
Malarial fever		Gainesville		
Snedecor, Frank P.	W	AL	55	3/4/84
Apoplexy		Mt Hebron		
Snedecor, Lucy A.	W	AL	46	10/27/88
Malarial fever		Gainesville		
Sparkman, Charlotte	B	NC	55	3/6/85
Dropsy		Livingston		
Sparks, Debby	B	SC	85	2/12/85
Debility of age		Bluff Port Beat		
Speight, Edmond	B		53	6/2/82
Malarial fever		Unknown		
Speight, Rose	B		55	6/13/81
Pulmonalis phthisis		Near Sumterville		
Speight, Simon	B	AL	41	6/21/90
Septicaemia		Sumterville		
Speight, Smithie	B		75	9/3/81
General debility		Near Warsaw		
Speight, Susan	B	NC	64	9/20/83
Cardiac dropsy		Hares Beat		
Speight, W. Rick	B		30	10/7/87
Malarial fever		Hares Beat		

| NAME | RACE | BORN | AGE | DEATH |
CAUSE OF DEATH		PLACE OF BURIAL		
Speight, Wright	B	NC	60	2/8/85
Pneumonia		Jones Bluff Beat		
Spidle, Jacob	W	AL	51	9/18/85
Dysentery		Belmont		
Spratt, Ike	B	AL	35	10/24/87
Syphilis		Poorhouse Cemetery		
Sprott, Mary	W	Ireland	75	11/21/82
Pneumonia		Livingston		
Stallings, Sallie	W	AL	26	8/9/86
Puerperal eclampsia		Siloam Church		
Stancel, Allan	B		42	4/17/85
Pneumonia		Warsaw Beat		
Stansell, Mary	B		39	2/18/82
Puerperal fever		Hargrove Place		
Stanton, Maria	B	AL	28	7/28/90
Gastritis		Beat 17		
Stanton, Warren G.	W	NC	74	4/21/86
Pneumonia		Shady Grove Church		
Stanton, William V.	W	NC	71	10/1/87
Heart disease		Warsaw		
Staunton, Lizzie	B	AL	30	12/29/89
Puerperal fever		Warsaw Beat		
Steele, William	B	NC	49	6/28/82
Congestive fever		Gainesville		
Steinwinder, Claburn	W	AL	26	8/19/89
Typhoid fever		Unknown		
Steinwinder, J. C.	W	AL	33	8/28/89
Typhoid fever		Unknown		
Stephens, Mrs. C. M.	W		49	1/8/91
Pneumonia		Siloam		
Stephens, Nancy	W	AL	29	3/28/85
Meningitis		Siloam Church		
Stephens, Rose	B	NC	38	9/3/86
Anasorca		Elizabeth Church		
Stewart, Betty	B	NC	77	8/21/83
Dropsy		W.H. Hawkins Place		
Stewart, George	B	NC	70	3/4/82
Rheumatism		Brewersville Beat		
Stewart, W. H.	W	SC	77	3/31/84
Pneumonia		Binnsville, Miss.		
Stewart, William C.	W	AL	38	1/9/86
Pneumonia		Binnsville, Miss.		
Straight, Daniel	B		36	11/26/84
Spinal meningitis		Warsaw Beat		

NAME CAUSE OF DEATH	RACE	BORN AGE DEATH PLACE OF BURIAL
Strickland, Margaret Remittent fever	W	60 10/1/84 Belmont
Stubb, Matilda Chronic dysentery	B	32 11/21/90 York
Summager, Amanda Pneumonia	B	NC 76 1/30/83 Black Bluff Beat
Summerlyn, Daniel Fever	B	AL 44 1/16/85 Black Bluff Beat
Swain, Jennie Continued fever	W	AL 24 4/15/85 Salem Church
Swann, Matthew Peyton Pneumonia	W	AL 25 5/10/83 Pipkin Place
Swilley, Junie Unknown	B	MD 92 5/12/90 Sumterville Beat
Sydney, Rass Pneumonia	B	AL 40 4/7/82 Lacy's Beat
Talbert, Ellen Liver disease	B	AL 68 5/31/89 Unknown
Talbot, Mack Old age	B	GA 89 1/5/82 New Prospect Ch.
Tankersley, Fanny Paralysis	B	GA 60 2/19/83 Jones Creek Church
Tanner, R. E. Inanition	W	VA 68 7/2/89 Belmont
Tart, Ann Remittent fever	B	AL 25 8/25/85 Wilder's Place
Tartt, Gray Dropsy	B	NC 60 10/12/83 Edwin Tartt's
Tartt, Lizzie Old age	B	NC 80 5/8/88 Unknown
Tartt, Martha Nephritis	B	AL 30 7/31/85 Sumterville Beat
Tartt, Matt Dropsy	B	AL 24 10/10/87 Payneville Beat
Tartt, Thomas Morrison Apoplexy	W	NC 64 8/9/85 Livingston
Tarvin, Frank Consumption	B	70 9/23/82 Gaston
Taylor, Adam Hydrothorax	B	AL 64 8/23/81 Jones Creek
Taylor, Emanuel Pneumonia	B	85 4/19/86 Hares Beat
Taylor, Jennie Uterus hemorrhage	B	AL 31 3/29/87 Payneville Beat

NAME	RACE	BORN	AGE	DEATH
CAUSE OF DEATH		PLACE OF BURIAL		
Taylor, Lucy	B	AL	25	11/29/82
Pneumonia		Lacy's Beat		
Taylor, Matthew B.	W	AL	20	1/14/84
Meningitis		Belmont		
Taylor, Millie	B	VA	100+	12/1/81
Old age		Weeden's Bend		
Taylor, Octavia Levert	W	AL	25	10/4/84
Congestive fever		Belmont		
Terrill, Ann	W	SC	80	12/29/85
Debility of age		New Prospect Ch.		
Thedford, Emily	W	AL	66	8/16/87
Heart disease		Greene Co. Ala.		
Thetford, Cely	B	VA	58	10/3/83
Pneumonia		Jones Bluff		
Thomas, Adeline	B	AL	26	6/22/82
Gunshot wound		Near Horn's Bridge		
Thomas, Albert	B	VA	50	11/5/84
Stomach cancer		Sumterville Beat		
Thomas, Amanda	B	AL	40	6/7/87
Unknown		Sumterville Beat		
Thomas, Ann	B	NC	75	8/27/85
Malarial fever		York		
Thomas, Arthur	B			6/23/82
Typhoid fever		Unknown		
Thomas, Mrs. C. R. B.	W	AL	60	7/23/85
Peritonitis		Gainesville		
Thomas, Hampt	B	AL	40	10/24/85
Heart disease		Unknown		
Thomas, James D.	W	NC	62	12/11/81
Alcoholism		Unknown		
Thomas, Joseph J.	W	NC	74	1/20/85
Apoplexy		Livingston		
Thomas, Julia	B	AL	24	10/14/85
Typho-malarial fever		Gainesville Beat		
Thomas, Julia	B	AL	34	7/17/86
Consumption		Gainesville		
Thomas, William	B	AL	38	3/28/89
Pneumonia		Gainsesville		
Thomson, Louis	B		70	9/29/84
Dropsy		Unknown		
Thompson, John	W	AL	17	2/15/82
Paralysis		Salem Church		
Thompson, Martha	B			8/10/84
Puerperal septicaemia		Mt Zion Church		

NAME	RACE	BORN	AGE	DEATH
CAUSE OF DEATH		PLACE OF BURIAL		
Thompson, Mrs.	B	AL	36	9/28/89
Dropsy		Cuba		
Thompson, Patsy	B	NC	85	6/23/81
Mammary gland cancer		Sumteville Beat		
Thornton, George	W	AL	46	12/5/81
Consumption		Cokes Chapel		
Thornton, Lucinda	B	AL	40	7/29/81
Pulmonalis phthisis		Drake Plantation		
Thrash, Mattie	W	AL	27	9/18/87
Spinal fever		Cokes Chapel		
Tilage, Ki	B	AL	55	2/15/92
Pneumonia		York		
Tillidys, Henry	B	AL	66	5/10/90
Dysentery		York Beat		
Tisdale, Alice	W	KY	25	8/31/81
Membraneous croup		Livingston		
Tolbert, Mary	B	TN	56	6/22/81
Uterus cancer		New Prospect Ch.		
Travis, Amos	B	GA	81	8/2/86
Heart disease		Payneville Beat		
Travis, Fereby	B	GA	80	12/8/82
Pneumonia		Payneville		
Travis, Mary	B	AL	80	9/3/87
Old age		Travis Place		
Travis, Mat	B	AL	30	3/26/87
Aedema of lungs		Gainesville		
Travis, Phillip	B	SC	81	11/14/89
Unknown		Jones Bluff		
Travis, Tom	B	AL	38	2/4/86
Abscess of brain		Unknown		
Trim, (Female)	B		20	8/2/82
Puerperal septicaemia		Gainesville		
Trott, David H.	W	NC	74	6/21/86
Cystitis		Livingston		
Tucker, Dave	B		70	4/8/88
Heart disease		Coatopa		
Tutt, George W.	W	AL	48	9/17/83
Malarial fever		Belmont		
Tutt, J. Z.	W	NC	57	10/14/89
Malarial fever		Belmont		
Tyson, Sarah	B	AL	43	4/10/91
Heart failure		Brewersville		
Underwood, Daniel L.	W	AL	30	9/27/87
Pulmonalis phthisis		Livingston		

NAME CAUSE OF DEATH	RACE	BORN	AGE	DEATH PLACE OF BURIAL		
(Unknown), Cassie Dropsy	B		85	8/31/82 Caldwell Place		
(Unknown), Laura Bowel inflammation	B	AL	22	7/30/85 Livingston		
(Unknown), Lettie Burn	B	AL	40	12/17/86 Poorhouse Cemetery		
(Unknown), Lutisha Septicaemia (abortion)	B	AL	34	7/5/83 Jones Bluff Beat		
(Unknown), William Old age	B	VA	85	8/18/81 Poorhouse Cemetery		
Upchurch, Frank Pneumonia	B	AL	26	1/10/85 Unknown		
Ustick, Jordon Congestive fever	B	VA	80	7/14/86 Livingston		
Vann, Alexander Remittent fever	B	MS	30	10/10/82 Unknown		
Vaughn, Annie Burned to death	W	AL	25	9/25/81 Cuba		
Vaughn, Vinie Cholera	B	SC	73	8/22/89 Unknown		
Wabington, Anne Phlegmaria dolens	B		39	3/31/88 Brewersville		
Wadkins, John Pneumonia	B	AL	30	3/31/88 Warsaw		
Wadkins, Lucy Pneumonia	B	VA	60	1/16/86 Mt Zion Graveyard		
Wadkins, Mary Uterine cellulitis	B	AL	28	8/9/85 Gainesville		
Waits, Ellen Dysentery	W	MS	42	6/23/88 Gaston		
Walker, Antonette Brain fever	B	AL	28	6/9/81 York		
Walker, Charley Pneumonia	B	AL	28	1/20/84 Black Bluff		
Walker, Hench Pneumonia	B	AL	19	3/10/82 Belmont		
Wallace, Jane Congestive fever	B	AL	41	7/20/90 Beat 6		
Waller, Bettie B. Typhoid pneumonia	W	AL	30	11/20/87 Black Bluff		
Walston, Mrs. Dropsy	W	AL	35	7/26/89 Brewersville		

NAME CAUSE OF DEATH	RACE	BORN AGE DEATH PLACE OF BURIAL
Walton, Lucy Consumption	B	45 1/26/84 Intercourse
Walton, Mrs. Cholera	W	AL 67 6/24/87 Zion Church
Walton, Stacy J. Bright's disease	W	MS 30 1/26/85 Belmont
Waltress, William Debility of age	W	NC 79 11/9/84 Pleasant Grove
Wankins, Jesse Typhoid fever	B	11/28/84 Gainesville Beat
Ward, A. F. Heart disease	W	AL 55 5/20/83 Cokes Chapel
Ward, C. C. Measles relapse	W	AL 28 2/28/84 Beulah Church
Ward, Ephraim Erysipelas	B	SC 66 9/15/81 Near Jones Bluff
Ward, Jane Pneumonia	B	AL 60 1/30/86 Walnut Grove
Ward, Jesse Pneumonia	B	AL 31 11/28/84 Near Livingston
Ward, Laura R. Spinal meningitis	W	AL 26 3/30/84 Cokes Chapel
Ward, Primus Malarial fever	B	AL 45 5/19/86 Brewersville
Washington, Crecy Congestive fever	B	50 9/20/84 Near Belmont
Washington, George Consumption	B	AL 40 1/1/87 Jones Bluff
Washington, George Influenza	B	AL 73 1/15/92 Sumterville
Washington, Hetty Heart disease	B	VA 77 8/15/82 Gainesville
Washington, Lettie Pneumonia	B	AL 45 12/19/85 Belmont
Washington, Lucy Consumption	W	NC 53 1/1/83 Gainesville
Washington, Minerva Consumption	B	AL 29 8/16/81 Hickory Flat Ch.
Washington, Mrs. W. B. Consumption	W	NC 52 12/30/82 Gainesville
Washington, Dr. W. B. Gastritis	W	VA 69 12/15/87 Gainesville
Watkins, Mrs. Consumption	W	AL 50 1/12/90 Siloam

NAME / CAUSE OF DEATH	RACE	BORN	AGE	DEATH	PLACE OF BURIAL
Watkins, Ruse / Malarial fever	B	AL	32	2/11/89	Hares Beat
Watson, Co_ad_y / Anasarca ?	B	AL	44	11/28/86	Thomas Watson's
Watson, Embo / Gunshot wound	B	AL	51	5/4/89	Livingston
Watson, Jim / Heart disease	B	NC	70	8/10/84	Gainesville
Watson, Mr. / Malarial anemia	W	GA	55	10/21/82	Poorhouse Cemetery
Watt, Judah / Typhoid fever	B		60	8/23/87	Preston Beat
Watts, Florence G. / Cerebral embolism	W	AL	27	12/29/89	Sumterville
Webb, C. H. / Pneumonia	W	AL	30	3/6/89	Cuba
Webb, Job / Cirrhosis of liver	B		70	1/8/86	Van Graveyard
Webb, Nancy / Cardiac dropsy	B		86	4/6/90	Sumterville Beat
Weir, Becky / Pulmonalis phthisis	B	AL	20	5/26/81	Warsaw Beat
Weir, Betty / Unknown	B		65	8/ /86	Gainesville
Welch, Fannie / Pneumonia	W	MS	40	1/24/84	Mississippi
Wesley, Caesar / Pneumonia	B		57	5/13/81	Haupt's Plantation
Wesley, Noah / Apoplexy	B	AL	19	9/29/82	Near Belmont
Weston, Emma / Paralysis	B	AL	34	5/22/84	Warsaw Beat
Weston, Red / Gastritis	B	AL	68	3/26/87	Warsaw Beat
Weston, William / Pneumonia	B	AL	34	2/5/85	Warsaw Beat
White, D. C. / Bright's disease	W	KY	44	2/10/88	Sumterville
White, Daniel O. / Consumption	W	NC	56	8/13/82	Livingston
White, Davis / Stone in bladder	B	AL	71	8/13/89	Unknown
White, Harmon / Pneumonia	B		73	12/4/84	White Place

NAME CAUSE OF DEATH	RACE	BORN AGE DEATH PLACE OF BURIAL		
White, Joel Dysentery	B		30	10/9/85 Gainesville Beat
White, Peter Pneumonia	B	AL	65	11/18/83 Unknown
White, Sam Dropsy	B		70	6/21/83 Unknown
White, Sarah Congestive fever	W		20	7/15/83 Unknown
Whitehead, Jane Consumption	B	AL	28	12/ /84 Brewersville
Whitehead, Maria Heart disease	B	NC	70	1/28/89 Livingston
Whitfield, Henrietta Debility (insanity)	B	AL	53	7/10/84 Belmont
Whitfield, Jerre Consumption	B	AL	24	3/25/89 Unknown
Whitlow, Stancel Dysentery	B	KY	30	7/6/86 York Station
Wideman, Edward Heart disease	W	SC	74	11/28/81 Near Gaston
Wiggins, Caroline Puerperal fever	B		65	9/22/87 Belmont
Wiley, (Female) Measles	B	AL	31	7/3/90 Beat 5
Wilkerson, Harrison Dropsy	B	AL	38	9/15/87 Siloam Church
Williams, A. B. R. Paralysis	W	SC	75	3/27/85 Siloam Church
Williams, Adline Dropsy		AL	44	2/5/92 Bluff Port
Williams, Edie Debility of age	B	VA	100	10/26/84 Chapman Place
Williams, Elbert Hanged by sheriff	B		45	6/3/81 Livingston
Williams, Ellen Consumption	B	AL	35	5/30/85 Belmont Beat
Williams, Frances V. Pneumonia	W	GA	27	1/31/85 Mt Herman Church
Williams, Frank Erysipelas	B	AL	50	7/1/86 Warsaw Beat
Williams, Fuller Debility of age	B	VA	76	6/20/89 Jones Bluff
Williams, Haywood Typhoid fever	B	AL	19	6/14/82 Wilder Place

NAME	RACE	BORN	AGE	DEATH
CAUSE OF DEATH		PLACE OF BURIAL		
Williams, James	B	AL	38	8/30/89
Consumption		Unknown		
Williams, Jenneta	B	AL	23	9/18/86
Pneumonia		Livingston		
Williams, Kitty	B			12/26/81
Typho-malarial fever		Unknown		
Williams, Lot	B	AL	25	10/12/87
Pneumonia		Preston		
Williams, Phillip	B	AL	30	12/30/88
Haemophtetis		Thornville		
Williams, Polly	B	AL	22	2/26/84
Consumption		Grant Place		
Williams, Sarah	B		22	7/20/81
Scrofula		Gainesville		
Williams, Shotwood G.	W	AL	27	10/10/84
Typhoid fever		Pushmataha		
Williams, Susan	B		65	9/23/87
Uterus cancer		Brewersville		
Williams, Susie	B	AL	28	2/17/85
Pneumonia		Jones Bluff		
Williams, Zacanias	W	AL	22	6/30/81
Measles		Mt Gilead		
Wills, Fanny	B		45	6/18/82
Stomach cancer		Gainesville		
Wills, Isaac	B	AL	38	7/7/90
Uremic poison		Gainesville		
Wilson, Anna	W		44	10/5/85
Compression of brain		Livingston		
Wilson, Harriet	B	AL	28	7/20/83
Consumption		Elizabeth Church		
Wilson, Henry	B	AL	45	6/17/86
Lung injury		Boligee		
Wilson, Mrs.	W		40	4/27/83
Paralysis (syphilis)		Livingston		
Wimberly, Felix G.	W	AL	30	9/15/82
Apparent fall		Bluff Port Beat		
Windham, Frank	B		45	7/23/86
Gunshot wound		Warsaw Beat		
Winston, Adeline	B	AL	21	8/23/86
Puerperal fever		Sumterville Beat		
Winston, Daphne	B	VA	25	3/15/83
Puerperal fever		Sumterville Beat		
Winston, (Male)	B		25	7/31/85
Congestive chill		Livingston		

NAME CAUSE OF DEATH	RACE	BORN AGE DEATH PLACE OF BURIAL
Winston, Orry Typhoid fever	B	AL 36 6/30/84 Lacy's Beat
Witt, Mary D. Congestive fever	W	AL 41 7/15/89 York
Woodall, Mary Softening of brain	B	NC 76 12/20/80 Beat 3
Woods, A. L. Malarial fever	W	GA 31 10/17/89 York
Woods, Jim Old age	B	VA 93 11/27/90 Gainesville
Woodson, Dr. B. B. Fibroid cancer	W	VA 78 5/18/84 Gainesville
Wrenn, Henry Old age	W	80 12/20/89 Sumterville Beat
Wrenn, Jenny Consumption	B	AL 40 12/31/86 Sumterville
Wrenn, Margaret Heart disease	W	AL 70 5/3/85 Cokes Chapel
Wrenn, Maria Acute cystitis	B	AL 55 2/17/88 Sumterville
Wright, Larkin Malarial fever	B	VA 81 10/28/89 Beat 7
Wright, Tom Heart disease	B	IL 35 12/5/84 Livingston
Wyatt, Elizabeth Typho malarial fever	W	AL 25 9/5/82 Choctaw Co. Ala.
Yarbrough, Sarah Puerperal nephritis	B	AL 35 8/1/82 Belmont

PART III

CEMETERY RECORDS

Compiled by

Jud K. Arrington
Nelle M. Jenkins
Elizabeth B. Stegall
Joseph F. Stegall

SUMTER COUNTY CEMETERIES

Most of the cemetery tombstone inscriptions included in this document were compiled by Jud K. Arrington, Nelle M. Jenkins and Elizabeth B. Stegall during the 1960s and 1970s.

This publication is limited to the graves of persons who were born by the end of the Civil War in 1865. Information on graves of persons born after 1865 is available and can be provided upon individual requests.

There are no tombstones to mark the graves of most of the early settlers of Sumter County. In the very early days, tombstones had to be cut and inscribed at distant places and transported by riverboat to a Sumter County port. This was a costly undertaking that few families could afford.

Most of the early settlers were buried in family cemeteries near their homes. The ravages of man and of nature have destroyed many of those cemeteries. Some of them were destroyed after they were surveyed by Arrington, Jenkins and Stegall in the 1960s and 1970s.

The church and municipal cemeteries have been somewhat better preserved than the family cemeteries. However, some of them are in danger of being lost because of neglect and the closure of some churches. At the urging of Jud Arrington, the Sumter County Historical Society placed a fence around the old Gaston Cemetery several years ago. Efforts are now being made through the Sumter County Historical Society to reclaim from nature the Methodist Church Cemetery at Sumterville, which is overgrown with trees, bushes and briars.

ARRINGTON CEMETERY

From State Highway 28, approximately 10 miles southeast of Livingston, turn east on County Road 23. The cemetery is approximately 4 2/10 miles down this road, on the north side, approximately 100 yards from the road.

Arrington

Carter -------- Son of Gen Joseph and Mary Arrington
B Jun 29, 1823
D Oct 3, 1841

Gen. Joseph --- Born in Nash Co. N. Carolina on the 2nd of August 1789 and departed this life Feb 28, 1864

Mary Jackson -- Wife of Gen Joseph Arrington who was born in Nash Co. N. Carolina on the 20th of August 1790 and departed this life Jan 12, 1864

Daughter of
Joseph & M.G.
Arrington ----- B Jul 5, 1851
D Sep 6, 1854

BALLARD CEMETERY
(Destroyed)

Located approximately 3/10 mile south of County Road 32, approximately 1 1/2 miles west of Geiger.

Ballard

Hannah -------- Wife of Lott Ballard
Dau of Hill Williams
Native of Richlands, Onslo Co. N. Carolina Died 1837

BELMONT CHURCH CEMETERY

At approximately 10 miles southeast of Livingston on State Highway 28, turn east on County Road 23. The church and cemetery are approximately 9 1/2 miles down this road on the north side.

Arrington
  Martha S. ----- Dau West & Mary S.
                  Sep 25, 1834 - Jan 16, 1842

Bates
  Annie L. ------ Oct 6, 1818 - Mar 31, 1865

  Mary Speed ---- Wife of O. W.
                  1864 - 1935

  Origin W. ----- 1853 - 1933

Blacksher
  David --------- Feb 26, 1795 - Oct 17, 1868

  Francis W. ---- Died Sep 10, 1840
                  4 yrs 20 days

  Mary Bettie --- Dau U. T. & E. K.
                  Dec 28, 1852 - Jan 27, 1857

  Nancy --------- Consort of David
                  Died Jan 19, 1851
                  55 yrs 10 mo 23 days

  Sius ---------- Mar 1828 - Nov 2, 1845

  Uriah E. ------ Son U. T. & E. K.
                  Aug 10, 1861 - Sep 14, 1861

  William ------- Died Sep 6, 1834
                  3 yrs 11 mo 20 days

Blakeney
  Temperance ---- Wife of Hugh
                  Jun 23, 1816 - Oct 5, 1841

Boyd
  Miss. Sallie
  E. ------------ 1862 - 1931

Coats
    Susan B. ------ Jul 14, 1862 - Aug 30, 1873
    Tempie B. ----- Dau J. M. & Susan
                    Jan 11, 1842 - Aug 9, 1866
Colgin
    Margaret A. --- Dau E. B. & Caroline
                    Dec 15, 1837 - Aug 26, 1848
Collins
    Hiram C. ------ Died Jul 31, 1870   Age Abt 23
Cooper
    Agnes --------- 1841 - 1928
    John ---------- 1848 - 1934
Dallas
    Eliza --------- Wife of Alexander Dallas Sr.
                    Born in Chesterfield Dist. S.C.
                    Jan 14, 1808
                    Died in Sumter Co. Ala.
                    Jun 30, 1837
Estis
    Caldwell ------ Died Oct 12, 1842 Age 80
Evans
    Abner --------- Oct 11, 1807 - Jul 26, 1853
Flowers
    Annie Cadwell - Wife of Robert B.
                    Jan 10, 1855 - Apr 15, 1921
    Robert B. ----- Jan 11, 1848 - May 5, 1913
Gaston
    William H. ---- Son Hugh & Elizabeth R.
                    Jan 16, 1832 - Sep 20, 1836
Gillespie
    Adele --------- Jan 1, 1851 - Jul 22, 1852
    Marian -------- Oct 29, 1846 - Jun 13, 1847
    Mrs. Mary
    McRee --------- Died Feb 19, 1859 Age 74

Grayson
J. Y. ---------- Son R. W. & S. E.
Sep 13, 1865 - Nov 26, 1871

Ralph W. ------ Aug 4, 1840 - Nov 22, 1886

Hadden
David Louis --- Son L. & M. A. Hadden
Jan 23, 1855 Age 18 mo

Sophia
Elizabeth ----- Dau L. & M. A. Hadden
Oct 11, 1845 - Oct 22, 1848

Stella -------- Dau L. & M. A. Hadden
Jul 14, 1857 - Jan 22, 1863

Harper
C. C. --------- Wife of R. S.
Sep 28, 1838 - May 26, 1860

J. W. --------- Oct 14, 1830 - Mar 5, 1858

R. S. --------- Oct 28, 1832 - Aug 24, 1895

Sophia -------- Mar 1, 1806 - Feb 7, 1868

William J. ---- Apr 24, 1860 - Apr 17, 1911

Wyatt --------- Oct 15, 1799 - Nov 6, 1864

Wyatt Judson -- Feb 9, 1835 - Jul 8, 1858

Z. C. --------- Dec 6, 1848 - Dec 14, 1899

Hartsfield
James M. ------ Jun 15, 1830 - Jun 17, 1878

Henderson
Charlotte C. -- Dau Elijah & Sarah Curtis
Wife of Lewis Henderson
Sep 15, 1806 - Apr 19, 1845

Lewis --------- Nov 21, 1807 - Dec 2, 1884

Lewis W. ------ Son Lewis & Charlotte
Apr 11, 1832 - Feb 19, 1861

Henderson (contd)
Obedience ----- Second wife of Lewis Henderson
Mar 10, 1810 - Sep 13, 1881

Sarah J. ------ Dau Lewis & Charlotte
Oct 24, 1829 - Sep 17, 1848

William E. ---- Son Lewis & Charlotte
Sep 24, 1834 - Jun 1, 1864

Hilman
Judson J. ----- Son N. & S. A. Hilman
Feb 22, 1849 - Apr 3, 1871

Holyfield
Daniel -------- Died 1834 Age 78

Horton
Elizabeth ----- Second Wife of Stephen Horton
Oct 8, 1811 - Aug 25, 1886

Frances S. A. - Dau S. & E. A.
May 1836? - Jun 3, 1867

Margaret Ann -- Dau S. & E. A.
Oct 6, 1844 - Aug 22, 1863

Stephen ------- Jul 18, 1809 - Oct 13, 1888

Lawler
Mrs. Sarah J. - Wife of R. W. Lawler
Dau Joseph Patton
Feb 23, 1835 - Nov 20, 1865

May
Elizabeth ----- Died May 17, 1844 Age 25

McAllister
William ------- Jun 24, 1784 - Oct 14, 1853

McCurdy
Oliver Moore -- Dec 14, 1807 - May 11, 1844

McRee
Eliza G. ------ Died Feb 13, 1877 Age 57

William ------- Died Apr 18, 1879 Age 71

Meador
 Job ----------- Born in Anson Co. N.C.
  Aug 1806 - Feb 28, 1867

Melton
 Rev. Bartlett - Jul 11, 1811 - Oct 24, 1886

 Bascomb ------- May 13, 1849 - Nov 29, 1857

 C. C. --------- Jun 7, 1845 - Nov 27, 1900

 Ella Thomas --- Born in Butler, Ala.
  Aug 24, 1861 - May 23, 1917

 Mary ---------- Wife of Bartlett
  Died Mar 22, 1883 Age 72

 William ------- Nov 1, 1835 - May 18, 1854

Morgan
 Isabel -------- Wife of Dr. W. W. Morgan
  Oct 6, 1832 - Jul 31, 1860

Muncrief
 Frances M. ---- Died Dec 18, 1852 Age 16

 Sampson B. ---- Jul 3, 1831 - Mar 31, 1857

 Sophia -------- Feb 7, 1802 - Oct 21, 1852

Nuffer
 C. B. --------- Mar 29, 1846 - Aug 7, 1894

Parker
 Mrs. Mary Ann - Jan 21, 1836 - Aug 9, 1886

Patton
 Wayne C. ------ Sep 29, 1826 - Aug 14, 1855

Perry
 John C. ------- Born in N. Carolina in 1794
  Died Dec 26, 1845 Age 52

Phares
 Mary G. ------- Wife of J. W. Phares
  Nov 23, 1843 - Aug 6, 1892

Phillips
  Henry Jackson - Oct 17, 1839 - Aug 29, 1912

  Martha
  Elizabeth ----- Wife of H. J. Phillips
                  Dec 12, 1844 - Sep 6, 1903

Powell
  Penelope ------ Aug 6, 1840 - Sep 2, 1860

  Temperence ---- Jul 29, 1814 - Mar 18, 1857

Rencher
  Elizabeth
  Jane ---------- Dau of Dan G. Rencher
                  Died Sep 10, 1843
                  10 yr 11 mo 20 d

Rushing
  America E. ---- Aug 21, 1834 - Nov 9, 1881

  Anzo Taylor --- 1857 - 1948

  Christopher
  C. ------------ Son of James & Susan
                  Feb 3, 1840 - May 27, 1862

  Elizabeth ----- Dau of James & Susan
                  Feb 17, 1833 - Nov 2, 1836

  Franklin
  Pierce -------- 1854 - 1933

  George C. ----- Son of Leonidas & America E.
                  Nov 7, 1860 - Jul 14, 1863

  J. M. --------- Apr 16, 1804 - Jun 24, 1881

  James M. ------ Son of James & Susan
                  Nov 8, 1846 - Apr 28, 1855

  Leonidas ------ Dec 15, 1827 - Oct 30, 1869

  Leonidas ------ Son of Leonidas & America E.
                  Nov 14, 1864 - Sep 22, 1865

  Lorenzo ------- Son of James & Susan
                  Jul 11, 1838 - Sep 20, 1846

Rushing (contd)
Lorenzo ------- Jun 26, 1853 - Sep 15, 1887

Marshall B. --- Son of James & Susan
Dec 25, 1848 - Jan 27, 1864

Mary ---------- Born in S. Carolina 1758
Died in Alabama Aug 27, 1837

Mary ---------- Dau of James & Susan
Aug 27, 1835 - Jun 11, 1886

Mary Lee ------ Dau of Leonidas & America E.
Mar 19, 1863 - Sep 2, 1863

Shepherd ------ Mar 4, 1806 - Feb 17, 1885

Susan --------- Dau of James & Susan
Jul 25, 1844 - Jun 11, 1849

Susannah ------ Wife of J. M.
Born in N. Carolina
Jun 9, 1810 - Aug 22, 1883

Winston ------- Son of Leonidas & America E.
Feb 6, 1859 - Aug 22, 1859

Scales
Constantine
Perkins ------- Son of T. A. & N. E. Scales
Died Aug 29, 1863

Seibert
Elizabeth ----- Wife of Nickel
May 13, 1831 - May 8, 1881

J. Nickel ----- Feb 21, 1813 - Feb 23, 1893

John ---------- Son of N. & E. Seibert
Apr 29, 1860 - Aug 20, 1878

William ------- Aug 18, 1857 - Nov 16, 1889

Smith
Adella M. ----- Dau of O. E. & M. T. Smith
Mar 20, 1863 - Sep 20, 1881

Smith (contd)
  Charlie B. ---- Son of O. E. & M. T. Smith
                  Oct 19, 1861 - ___?___

  Capt. John W. - Jul 31, 1792 - Jun 8, 1857

  John W. Jr. --- (No dates)

  Josephine ----- (No dates)

  Margaret
  Scott --------- Oct 16, 1814 - Sep 6, 1840

  Martha T. ----- Wife of O. E. Smith
                  Feb 10, 1840 - Jun 28, 1866

Speed
  Mrs.
  Elizabeth ----- Wife of James S.
                  May 10, 1831 - Jun 3, 1911

  James B. ------ Jul 18, 1851 - Sep 10, 1909

  James R. ------ Jan 23, 1864 - Jul 20, 1940

Spidle
  Elizabeth ----- Wife of Jacob Spidle
                  Mar 18, 1833 - Jul 27, 1909

  John M. ------- Mar 11, 1855 - Jun 9, 1938

  Robert L. ----- Apr 15, 1863 - Mar 30, 1911

  Sallie E. ----- Wife of John M. Spidle
                  May 8, 1857 - Jun 19, 1921

Taylor
  Dock Mills ---- Oct 22, 1865 - Jun 10, 1938

  Madison B. ---- May 28, 1863 - Jan 15, 1884

  Octavia L. ---- Oct 26, 1858 - Oct 4, 1884

Tutt
  Ada V. -------- Wife of James B. Tutt
                  Apr 5, 1861 - Nov 11, 1911

Tutt (contd)
Artelia ------- Wife of John Z. Tutt
           Apr 29, 1829 - May 13, 1861

   Clara B. ------ Dau J. Z. & C. M. Tutt
           (No dates) Age 8 yr 6 mo 6 days

James Beazley - Apr 14, 1849 - Mar 27, 1913

James S. ------ Son James V. & Sarah P. Tutt
           Nov 21, 1851 - Sep 28, 1855

Capt. James
V. ------------ Co. C, 8th Ala. Cav., CSA
           (No dates)

Laurie L. ----- Dau J. Z. & C. M. Tutt
           (No dates) Age 4 yrs 7 mo 19 da

Vise
Jane Flowers -- Mar 1, 1850 - Jul 2, 1915

Wimberly
Andrew
Jackson ------- Feb 26, 1860 - Jan 29, 1913

Cora Landrum -- Jul 5, 1856 - Mar 18, 1916

BETHEL CHAPEL CEMETERY

From State Highway 17 at Emelle, turn east on County Road 24. The chapel and cemetery are 1 8/10 miles down this road on the north side of the road, at its intersection with County Road 74.

Burwell
Margaret J. --- 2nd wife William T. Burwell
           Sep 25, 1857 - Aug 30, 1895

   Mary Ann
   Frierson ------ 1st wife William T. Burwell
           Died July 1845 Age 25

Burwell (contd)
William
Turnbull ------ Sep 13, 1849 - Nov 25, 1909

Daniel
James T. ------ Pvt., Co. B, 56 Regt., Ala.
Vol., CSA
1824 - 1875

Dial
Emma ---------- Eldest Dau J. R. & A. E. Dial
Sep 13, 1846 - Sep 24, 1851

William
Woodward ------ Son J. R. & A. E. Dial
Aug 19, 1848 - Apr, 18, 1849

Dozier
Mrs. Mollie --- Died 1876

Slater -------- Died 1876

Drummond
Amanda E. ----- Wife of David Drummond
Dau Joseph & Violet McCorkle
Oct 12, 1824 - Oct 10, 1853

Fleming
Emma J. ------- Dau R. H. & J. R. Fleming
Oct 29, 1848 - Nov 25, 1849

Infant -------- R. H. & J. R. Fleming
(No dates)

James H. ------ Mar 4, 1823 - May 15, 1847

Margaret C. --- Mar 24, 1827 - Aug 25, 1843

Mary ---------- Wife of William Fleming
Died Nov 4, 1849 Age 89

Mary B. ------- Consort of Pliny R. Fleming
Jan 26, 1792 - Nov 25, 1841

Robert H. ----- Dec 16, 1818 - Mar 28, 1850

William ------- Died Nov 14, 1849 Age 89

Fleming (contd)
  William H. ---- Sep 23, 1820 - Jul 4, 1841

Fulton
  Annie G. ------ Died Mar 31, 1904 Age 85

  Edwin Kerr ---- Jan 30, 1839 - Sep 30, 1904

  Elizabeth
  Dial ---------- Wife of William F. Fulton
                  Sep 14, 1809 - Sep 26, 1842

  Elizabeth K. -- Wife of William F. Fulton
                  Died Jan 1, 1855
                  37 yr 1 mo 23 da

  Franklin W. --- Son W. F. & E. K. Fulton
                  May 28, 1850 - Jun 27, 1851

  Infant -------- Son W. F. & E. K. Fulton
                  Died Aug 14, 1847

  James Harvey -- May 12, 1829 - Mar 31, 1853

  James Harvey -- Jan 22, 1860 - Nov 18, 1860

  James Henry --- Son W. F. & E. K. Fulton
                  Died Jul 15, 1854 1 yr 12 days

  Mary
  Elizabeth ----- Dau W. F. & Mary M. Fulton
                  Died Sep 24, 1846 Age 14 mo

  Mary M. ------- Wife of William F. Fulton
                  Died Mar 24, 1846
                  31 yr 3 mo 25 da

  Nena
  Montgomery ---- May 20, 1849 - Mar 8, 1899

  William
  Frierson ------ Born Aug 25, 1805
                  Near Franklin, Tenn.
                  Died Oct 3, 1886
                  At Gainesville, Ala.

Grice
  Charity ------- Former Wife F. H. Woodward
                  Died Jul 5, 1865   Age 63

Hadden
  Rev. Isaac ---- Born in Abbeville Dist. S.C.
                  Aug 15, 1799 - Aug 27, 1849

  Martha B. ----- Relict Rev. Isaac Hadden
                  She was born Oct 17, 1792 and
                  departed this life Sep 5, 1849

  Rev. Robert
  Wilson -------- Who departed this life on the
                  5th day of January 1852 in the
                  29th year of his age and the
                  4th year of his ministry

Hale
  David M. ------ Son J. P. & J. Hale
                  Nov 21, 1822 - Jan 25, 1844

Hodges
  C. C. --------- Jan 26, 1809 - Oct 31, 1854

  Infant -------- May 23, 1847 - Oct 21, 1847

Holt
  LeRoy --------- Born in Columbus, Ga.
                  Jul 12, 1858 - Sep 19, 1899

Kendall
  Abigail W. ---- Dau Thaddeus R. & Mary Kendall
                  Died Sep 19, 1844   4 yrs 5 mo

Kerr
  Edward Taylor - Son of James & Sinthy Kerr
                  Feb 12, 1846 - Jan 31, 1852

  Frances
  Elizabeth ----- Jan 29, 1839 - Feb 22, 1926

  James D. ------ Jan 12, 1841 - Oct 19, 1876

  John L. ------- 1863 - 1937

  Laura D. ------ Dau William & Sarah Kerr
                  Died Oct 5, 1851   3 yrs 16 days

Kerr (contd)
Mary Elizabeth
  Williams ------ Mar 25, 1834 - Feb 18, 1852

Mary J. D. ---- Dau J. W. & Margaret Kerr
    Died Jul 31, 1842
    7 yrs 1 mo 19 da

Sarah D. ------ Mar 4, 1815 - Apr 10, 1886

Telemachus ---- 1833 - 1911

W. W. --------- 1852 - 1927

William ------- Jun 6, 1803 - Dec 15, 1866

Lavender
Infant -------- Dau R. S. & S. A. Lavender
    Born Jan 4, 1853

Jane ---------- Apr 17, 1799 - Dec 6, 1846

Sarah A. ------ Wife of Robert Lavender
    Mar 5, 1819 - May 3, 1854

London
Laura --------- 1855 - 1892?

McConnell
Dr. John A. --- Oct 8, 1825 - May 24, 1855

McCorkle
Joseph -------- Aug 17, 1775 - Sep 14, 1849

Thomas J. ----- Sep 20, 1830 - Dec 21, 1859

Violet -------- Wife of Joseph McCorkle
    Oct 12, 1790 - Jul 25, 1856

W. F. --------- Apr 13, 1820 - Aug 11, 1840

McDow
Jane ---------- Jul 29, 1792 - Apr 26, 1873

Martha C. ----- May 29, 1833 - Oct 13, 1898

McDow (contd)
```
Mary A.    -------  Wife of Alexander McDow
                    Dau P. R. & M. Fleming
                    Mar 24, 1827 - Nov 2, 1847

W. L.     ---------  Oct 15, 1794 - Mar 31, 1870

W. L.     ---------  Oct 23, 1831 - Aug 30, 1910
```

Mitchell
```
B. F.     ---------  In Memory of
                     Born Apr 16, 1840
                     Died Charlottsville, Va.
                     Aug 4, 1861

Benjamin
James     ---------  Born Abbeville Dist. of S.C.
                     Feb 25, 1809 - Apr 1, 1859
```

Moore
```
Eliza     ---------  Sep 1873  Age 8

Elizabeth C.  --  Wife of Thomas Moore
                  Nov 10, 1796 - Jun 10, 1847

James A.   ------  Dec 28, 1824 - May 9, 1881

S. Evlyn   ------  Wife of J. A. Moore
                   Dau J. A. & E. A. Minniece
                   Died Aug 24, 1869
                   30 yr 6 mo 18 da

Thomas    --------  Jul 23, 1789 - Dec 8, 1852

Thomas J. H.  --  Nov 5, 1836 - Jun 21, 1850

William H.  ----  Apr 9, 1831 - Dec 16, 1858
```

Myers
```
Bettie L.  -----  Wife of T. W. Myers
                  Mar 3, 1840 - Jun 6, 1886
```

Nevill
```
Lizzie L.  -----  Dau Andrew & Mary Nevill
                  Apr 2, 1846 - May 8, 1847
```

Nevill (contd)
  Mary ---------- Consort of Andrew Nevill
                      Dau William & Jane McDow
                      May 1, 1820 - Oct 2, 1852

Parker
  Armsted Burt -- Third Child of Edwin & Eugenia Parker
                      Nov 22, 1851 - Jul 3, 1852

Ramsay
  Alexander H. -- Son J. R. & S. I. Ramsay
                      Nov 7, 1859 - Apr 11, 1880

  J. Reid ------- Dec 14, 1827 - Jun 27, 1899

  James Wrenn --- Sep 27, 1864 - Apr 1, 1946

  Sarah I. ------ Wife of J. Reid Ramsay
                      Jun 29, 1834 - Jan 15, 1900

Riley
  William ------- Died Apr 8, 1871 Age 28

Rix
  Charles ------- Born in Royalton Vt.
                      Aug 10, 1808 - May 13, 1851

  Eleanor
  Porter -------- Wife of George Rix
                      Dau Calvin & Sally Skinner
                      Oct 30, 1813 - Jun 16, 1841

  Frank
  Underwood ----- Son George & Rebecca Rix
                      Aug 18, 1861 - Aug 26, 1861

  Frederick
  Dial ---------- Son George & Rebecca Rix
                      Died Feb 6, 1852 Age 17 mo

  Harry Spence -- Son George & Rebecca Rix
                      Aug 25, 1858 - Sep 9, 1861

  Rebecca ------- Dau George & Rebecca Rix
                      Died Nov 20, 1855 Age 10 days

Robertson
   A. Mc.   -------- Died Oct 26, 1853   Age 12

Sanders
   Moses M. ------ Aug 14, 1815 - May 8, 1857

Silliman
   Dr. C. U. ----- Apr 7, 1833 - Nov 8, 1913

   Jennie
   Mitchell ------ Oct 21, 1845 - Dec 21, 1926

Smith
   Lucy B. ------- Aug 19, 1839 - Mar 23, 1857

   Sterling S. --- Jul 6, 1841 - Sep 18, 1856

Tartt
   Martha Lela --- Dau Enos & Mary Tartt
                    Sep 26, 1856 - Feb 23, 1857

Thomas
   Pollie
   Fulton -------- 1838 - Mar 17, 1923

Underwood
   Adelaide
   Randolph ------ Dau L. V. & E. Underwood
                    Died Sep 10, 1859   Age 11 days

   Emma ---------- Died Jan 1880

   Infant -------- Son L. V. & E. Underwood
                    Born Jun 16, 1862

   Col. L. V. ---- Died Sep 1874

Wheeling
   Esther -------- Wife of William Wheeling
                    Died Feb 3, 1849   Age 57

   William ------- Died Jul 29, 1852   Age 60

Woodard
   Felix
   Hamilton ------ Died Jan 20, 1849
                    42 yr 3 mo 19 d

Wrenn
   Arthur McD. --- May 11, 1832 - Sep 2, 1858

   Elias N. ------ Jan 31, 1829 - Apr 17, 1903

   Eliza P. ------ Born in Pendleton Dist. S. C.
                 Sep 2, 1804 - Oct 24, 1862

   George M. ----- Apr 29, 1825 - Jun 5, 1893

   J. Walter ----- Feb 2, 1863 - Nov 10, 1894

   James --------- Jun 2, 1800 - Oct 18, 1843

   Josiah -------- Mar 3, 1813 - Jun 28, 1885

   Margaret J. --- Dau James & Eliza P. Wrenn
                Jun 6, 1830 - Jun 3, 1854

   Mary E. ------- Sep 9, 1836 - Aug 10, 1862

   Mary Frances
   Templeton ----- Wife of George M. Wrenn
                Jul 16, 1842 - Jun 4, 1909

BETHLEHEM CHURCH CEMETERY
(Choctaw County)

At approximately 17 miles south of York on State Highway 17, turn east on Choctaw County 42. The cemetery is approximately 6 miles down this road on the north side of the road.

Bevill
   Fannie L. ----- Wife of W. G. Bevill
              Nov 6, 1856 - Oct 15, 1892

Burnett
   Dr. W. E. ----- Died Dec 9, 1858
              27 yrs 4 mo

Christopher
   Kate Young ---- Dec 17, 1861 - Jan 18, 1922

   William R. ---- Mar 6, 1861 - May 13, 1921

Clarke
Dr. F. P. ----- Feb 14, 1848 - Nov 17, 1900

Dawson
John A. ------- Jan 25, 1859 - Oct 29, 1937

Drinkard
Alice E. ------ Wife of H. A.
1850 - 1928

Emma A. ------- Wife of F. M.
Mar 11, 1858 - Jun 9, 1913

F. M. --------- Mar 26, 1847 - Feb 19, 1903

H. A. --------- 1846 - 1925

Nancy --------- Wife of Washington
Mar 3, 1808 - Aug 1, 1884

Washington ---- Feb 11, 1811 - Jan 18, 1884

DuBose
Mary V. ------- Died May 27, 1850
Age 36 yr 2 mo 7 days

Fontaine
Infant -------- Dau of S. A. & L.
Jul 17, 1857 - Sep 8, 1857

J. H. L. ------ Mar 23, 1826 - Mar 29, 1857

Sarah A. ------ Aug 24, 1837 - Jul 24, 1857

Foushee
J. M. --------- Dec 15, 1821 - Aug 13, 1906

Harrington
Elbert -------- Hus of S. A.
Apr 26, 1824 - Jan 4, 1895

Horn
Miss Mary S. -- Apr 22, 1832 - Jan 5, 1852

Johnson
John M. ------- Nov 20, 1842 - Jul 27, 1912

Johnston
Eliza A. ------ Wife of J. Wesley
             Sep 19, 1838 - Nov 25, 1879

  Nathan -------- Born in Randolph Co. N.C.
             Mar 3, 1810 Died in Choctaw
             Co. Alabama Jan 18, 1873

  Persis M. ----- Born in Jasper Co. Georgia
             Jan 12, 1813 Died in Choctaw
             Co. Ala. Jan 18, 1873

Kelley
Phamie B. ----- May 27, 1847 - Oct 23, 1930

Marks
Levi ---------- Aug 26, 1828 - Mar 4, 1887

Selena -------- Nov 26, 1818 - Sep 28, 1897

McDaniel
C. C. --------- Nov 29, 1845 - Feb 9, 1924

  Carrie C. ----- Wife of C. C.
             Oct 17, 1845 - Jan 11, 1904

Pennington
A. ------------ Oct 14, 1801 - Mar 13, 1857

E. J. --------- Jul 4, 1840 - Aug 20, 1844

Margaret ------ Mar 27, 1802 - Dec 17, 1885

R. A. --------- Apr 9, 1832 - Oct 8, 1841

Robinson
James D. ------ Hus of M. E.
             Sep 9, 1837 - Jul 2, 1903

James L. ------ Nov 8, 1863 - Nov 20, 1900

Mary E. ------- Wife of J. D.
             May 2, 1840 - Dec 19, 1899

Rodgers
Mossie C. ----- Died Jun 12, 1939

W. E. --------- Died May 10, 1931 Age 69

Steiner
    Kate ---------- Wife of K. S. Steiner
                    Died Jan 31, 1894
Taylor
    John W. ------- Aug 2, 1840 - Oct 22, 1883
Tillman
    William H. ---- Jan 18, 1837 - Jul 19, 1918
Tymes
    W. H. ---------- Dec 19, 1849 - Mar 16, 1913
Webb
    Sarah A. ------ Dec 25, 1841 - Jul 7, 1924
Whitehead
    Jonathan ------ Born in Nash Co. N.C.
                    Sep 14, 1763
                    Died in Sumter Co. Alabama
                    Apr 10, 1846

    Tempee -------- Wife of Jonathan
                    Born in Nash Co. N.C. in 1773
                    Died in Sumter Co. Alabama
                    Sep 14, 1840
Wideman
    Infant -------- Dau of W. E. & Zeola Age 21 da

    Zeola Yeager -- Oct 20, 1859 - Oct 4, 1895
Wilkerson
    Amanda Thrash - Feb 4, 1858 - Jun 26, 1945

    G. N. ---------- May 18, 1851 - Sep 21, 1918
Woodward
    Mrs. Martha --- Nov 29, 1826 - Aug 27, 1847
Yeager
    John C. ------- Aug 1, 1831 - Jun 15, 1876

    M. B. ---------- Apr 8, 1847 - Apr 1, 1936

    Mary E.
    Johnston ------ Wife of John C.
                    Jan 12, 1841 - Jul 3, 1896

Yeager (contd)
  Medora D. ----- Mar 31, 1858 - Aug 2, 1895

Young
  Allen A. ------ Oct 28, 1824 - Mar 30, 1900

  Alzira -------- Dau of R. & M. Young
                    Feb 29, 1832 - Sep 22, 1875

  F. J. --------- Oct 19, 1833 - Mar 24, 1857

  Fannie W. ----- Wife of Dr. O. G. Young
                    Jan 1, 1859 - Dec 1, 1877

  J. M. --------- Apr 3, 1856 - Apr 17, 1943

  Lizzie G. ----- Wife J. M.
                    Mar 31, 1861 - Feb 11, 1928

  Margaret ------ Born 1805 Feb 28, 1846

  Narcisa P. ---- Wife of Allen A.
                    Born in Marengo Co. Ala.
                    Sep 2, 1830 Died May 1, 1882

  Robert -------- Born in Lawrence Co. S.C.
                    Oct 18, 1799 - May 9, 1882

  Robert A. ----- Dec 21, 1855 - Mar 6, 1904

  W. W. --------- Apr 16, 1859 - Oct 30, 1902

  William
  Robert -------- Son J. R. & C. M.
                    Oct 3, 1853 - May 18, 1854

BEULAH BAPTIST CHURCH CEMETERY

At approximately 3 miles south of Ward on County Road 10, turn south on the Charles Spur Road. The church and cemetery are approximately 1/10 mile down the road on the north side of the road.

Allen
  Benjamin J. --- Nov 4, 1847 - Sep 26, 1928

Allen (contd)
Frances S. ---- Feb 15, 1834 - Oct 21, 1924

Baskin
Annie M. ------ Wife of W. S.
Sep 6, 1845 - Jan 19, 1918

W. S. --------- Dec 25, 1844 - Mar 1, 1920

Dill
J. F. --------- Apr 15, 1836 - Dec 24, 1922

Martha -------- Mar 18, 1847 - Feb 5, 1935

Grimes
George -------- Aug 25, 1847 - Jun 26, 1914

Martha Ann ---- 1851 - 1947

Harrington
Rosa ---------- Jun 28, 1847 - Jan 21, 1894

Pond
Annie --------- Wife J. B.
Feb 27, 1848 - Sep 25, 1892

Sanders
John T. ------- Jun 23, 1851 - Oct 4, 1931

Tate
Anne E. ------- Wife G. W.
Jan 12, 1847 - Nov 14, 1907

George W. ----- Dec 16, 1840 - Jun 4, 1916

Mattie J.
Sanders ------- Wife R. H.
Aug 23, 1853 - Feb 7, 1918

R. H. --------- Sep 11, 1847 - Nov 20, 1924

Townsend
Mary ---------- Aug 18, 1826 - May 24, 1898

BLANN CEMETERY

At approximately 3 3/10 miles south of Cuba on County Road 10, turn south on County Road 5. Proceed for approximately 3 1/2 miles and turn northwest on the Jarman Road. The cemetery is 6/10 mile down this road on the east side of the road.

Blann
Eunice -------- Died 1854 Age 3 yrs

Georgia ------- Died 1854 Age 6 mo

J. P. --------- Died 1855 Age 52 years

Culpepper
Asenath ------- 1837 - 1880

George
Clarence ------ Apr 8, 1861 - Oct 29, 1883

Dorough
Fannie Blann -- Wife of G. F. Dorough
              Apr 30, 1842 - Jul 6, 1926

George F. ----- Apr 3, 1853 - Oct 10, 1883

Martin
Mary E. ------- Dau of S. P. & S. Martin
              Born Jun 6, 1859
              Died May 4, 1864

Simeon P. ----- Hus of Sallie Martin
              Died Dec 2, 1899
              Age 62 yrs 6 mos 29 dys

Mathews
Lou ----------- Wife of W. B. Matthews
              Born in 1827
              Died Oct 3, 1904

William B. ---- Born Jan 13, 1841
              Died Jul 21, 1884

BONEY OR OLD LIBERTY CHURCH CEMETERY

From State Highway 17 at Emelle, turn west on County Road 24. At approximately 2 6/10 miles, turn right on the Pete Willingham Road. Follow this road for approximately 7/10 mile to the cemetery on the north side of the road.

Anderson
Ann ----------- Wife of C. Anderson
                Mar 27, 1812 - Jan 12, 1887

Mag ----------- 1835 - Sep 7, 1910

Margaret
Daniels ------- Wife William Louis Anderson
                Jun 12, 1847 - Aug 15, 1910

Sarah --------- Wife of Vincent Anderson
                Jul 15, 1801 - Dec 24, 1880

Vincent ------- (Unmarked grave)
                Died Apr 7, 1833

William S. ---- Son Vincent & Sarah Anderson
                May 22, 1830 - Sep 23, 1862

Boney
Wimberk ------- Died Jun 25, 1845 Age 56

Campbell
Caroline ------ Wife of W. J. Campbell
                Dau Jared & Susan Cherry
                Died Apr 3, 1852
                23 yr 5 mo 13 das

Cherry
Emma Eliza ---- Wife of Henry F. Cherry
                Aug 8, 1837 - May 8, 1929

Rev. Jared W. - May 26, 1796 - Jul 23, 1871

Susan --------- Consort of Jarrard Cherry
                Dau J. & S. Jenkins
                Mar 23, 1797 - May 8,   ?

Choutteau
   M. J.
      Gertrude ------ Dau G. & S. N. Choutteau
                     Jan 22, 1858 - Oct 6, 1865

      Martha E. ----- Dau G. & S. N. Choutteau
                     Nov 10, 1862 - Aug 12, 1863

Clark
   A. V. --------- Son Col. D. A. & R. J. Clark
                     May 12, 1846 - Mar 5, 1880

Cobb
   Louisa C. ----- Wife of J. J. Cobb
                     Jul 15, 1837 - Mar 29, 1880

Folsom
   Squire -------- Oct 18, 1819 - Sep 21, 1904

Fortner
   Gilford J. ---- Jul 4, 1829 - Nov 15, 1876

   Lucinda B. ---- Wife G. J. Fortner Jr.
                     Apr 10, 1831 - Feb 12, 1892

   Richard N. ---- Son Gilford Jr. & Lucinda
                     Fortner
                     Jan 29, 1856 - Apr 30, 1879

Harper
   Daniel Y. ----- May 18, 1829 - Jan 4, 1850

Jenkins
   Annie Andrews - Wife T. L. Jenkins
                     Jan 22, 1856 - Feb 23, 1926

   Susan --------- (Unmarked grave)
                     Died Dec 25, 1850

   Thomas
   Leonidas ------ Husband of Annie A. Jenkins
                     Nov 7, 1852 - Dec 19, 1936

Joyner
   Mary Etta
   Cherry -------- Wife Wm. Bert Joyner
                     Dau Henry & Eliza Parker Cherry
                     Jan 8, 1862 - Aug 11, 1945

Joyner (contd)
William Bert -- Feb 13, 1857 - Dec 29, 1945

Kennon
Marielou ------ Dec 29, 1853 - Nov 13, 1858
Age 4 yrs 10 mos & 15 days

S. Evans ------ Son John & Martha Lacy Kennon
Feb 27, 1856 - Oct 22, 1858

Kent
E. H. --------- Born Oct 11, 1850
Died Jan 5, 1912

Martha
Anderson ------ Wife of E. H. Kent
Jul 22, 1854 - Aug 13, 1929

Kirkland
Elizabeth ----- Wife of D. L. Kirkland
Dau Richard Newton, Butler,
Ala. Died Sep 19, 1868
Age 33 yrs 5 mo & 8 da

Lacy
Caroline M. --- Consort of Elisha Lacy
Feb 28, 1792 - Jul 29, 1847

Capt. Elisha -- Died Jul 9, 1862
70 yrs 1 mo & 23 days

Mrs. Martha --- Consort of W. A. Lacy
Died Jul 1, 1846
21 yrs 7 mo 6 das

W. A. --------- (No dates)

Lunceford
Benjamin F. --- May 11, 1849 - Jan 6, 1923

Harriett
Caroline ------ Wife of J. W. Lunceford
1823 - Sep 3, 1907

Herbert Lee --- Died Oct 10, 1902

J. W. --------- May 7, 1826 - Dec 25, 1910

Lunceford (contd)
  Muhulda J. ---- Aug 25, 1843 - Nov 27, 1913

  S. C. --------- Dec 2, 1852 - Nov 8, 1913

Massangale
  Robert Allen -- Nov 20, 1859 - Jan 25, 1860

McCrory
  Ida Frances
  Folsom -------- Jan 7, 1860 Died May 7, 1922
                      Age 62 yrs 4 months
                      Marr J. B. McCrory Aug 26, 1878
                      Dau Squire & Annie Folsom

  James Bird ---- Sep 14, 1853 - Nov 17, 1939

Meador
  Mary V. ------- Dau P. & T. A. Meador
                    Died Jan 16, 1863

  Rebecca M. ---- Dau P. & T. A. Meador
                    Died Jan 13, 1862
                    3 yrs 5 mo 1 day

Neelly
  Mary
  Elizabeth ----- Wife Henry Franklin Neelly
                     Nov 19, 1841 - Apr 22, 1918

Newton
  Mary C. ------- Born in Edgefield Dist. S.C.
                    Nov 2, 1803 - Jul 5, 1877
                    Wife of Richard Newton
                    Married March 16, 1822

  Richard ------- Born in Duplin Co. N.C.
                    May 11, 1790 - Jul 27, 1878

Owens
  Mary Lavina --- Oct 22, 1837 - Mar 1, 1914

Parker
  Annie --------- Jan 29, 1863 - Jun 1, 1925

  James H. ------ Jun 15, 1854 - May 11, 1909

Parrish
    Elizabeth ----- Wife of S. P. Parrish
                    Dec 4, 1839 - May 6, 1871

    S. P. --------- Apr 4, 1832 - Mar 26, 1894

Ramsey
    Ella D. ------- Wife of J. M. Ramsey
                    Sep 5, 1838 - Jul 28, 1873

    Nancy Graves
    Yancy --------- Wife A. K. Ramsey
                    Born Caswell Co. N.C.
                    Aug 19, 1798 - Jan 18, 1859

    William R. ---- May 16, 1838 - Jun 26, 1874

Richardson
    W. H. --------- Of Rusk Co. Texas
                    Soldier 10th Texas Regt.
                    Died May 24, 1862
                    in Kemper Co. Miss.

Thomas
    Catina A. ----- Wife William Maurice Thomas
                    Sister of Narcissa Anderson
                    Apr 25, 1832 - Jan 22, 1913

    Narcissa F. --- Wife William M. Thomas
                    Dau Vincent & Sara Anderson
                    Sep 19, 1821 - Dec 25, 1885

    William
    Maurice ------- Born Charlotte Co. Va.
                    Jul 13, 1814 - Nov 12, __?__

Treadaway
    Ann Elizabeth - Wife of W. T. Treadaway
                    1851 - 1932

White
    James --------- Died Mar 10, 1865 Age 50

Willingham
    Carrie Powers - Wife of Phillip Willingham
                    Jul 3, 1836 - Jun 8, 1902

    Phillip ------- May 2, 1809 - Apr 3, 1876

Wrenn
  Samantha A. --- Wife George M. Wrenn
                     Dau Alfred & Mary Yarbrough
                     Mar 24, 1836 - Oct 26, 1863
                     Aged 27 yrs 7 mos & 2 days

Yarbrough
  Alfred -------- Dec 13, 1792 - Feb 26, 1857

  Mary ---------- Wife Alfred Yarbrough
                  Nov 3, 1798 - Jun 27, 1853

  Mary Ann ------ Wife James Q. Yarbrough
                  Dau Matthew & Elizabeth
                  Parham
                  Jun 18, 1832 - Jun 3, 1852

  Neil Smith ---- Son Alfred & Mary Yarbrough
                  Mar 6, 1835 - Jan 17, 1861

BOYD CEMETERY

From State Highway 17, approximately 9 miles north of York, turn west on County Road 12. Turn north after approximately 1/2 mile onto a dirt road. After approximately 1/4 mile, turn east on a dirt drive to the cemetery.

Boyd
  Austin G. ----- Son Jefferson & Sara M. Boyd
                 Oct 23, 1850 - Jan 19, 1932

  C. Virginia --- Wife of Jefferson Boyd
                 Jun 15, 1846 - Feb 10, 1885

  Clara Jane
  Powe ---------- Wife of Robert Clay Boyd
                 Jul 14, 1860 - Apr 4, 1940

  Harriett
  Cadmus Moore -- Wife Austin Gambrel Boyd
                 1854 - 1938

Boyd (contd)
Jefferson ----- Born in Newberry Dist. S. C.
Dec 18, 1817 - Jan 19, 1894
Son of John and Jane Boyd

Jennett ------- Wife of John Boyd
Born in Newberry, S. C.
Apr 8, 1781 - Mar 31, 1844

John ---------- Born in Chester, S.C.
Nov 1, 1776 - Sep 4, 1854

John James ---- Son Matthew H. Boyd
Co. A-7, Ala. Cav., CSA
Apr 3, 1837 - Oct 19, 1915

Robert Clay --- Son James Marion & Susan
Simmons Boyd
Jul 25, 1845 - Dec 8, 1920

Robert
Jefferson ----- Dec 29, 1856 - Nov 5, 1928

Sara M.
Hudson -------- Wife of Jefferson Boyd
Jul 17, 1822 - Oct 7, 1865

Susan Davis --- Wife Robert Jefferson Boyd
Sep 17, 1858 - Jun 2, 1946

William
Ellery -------- Son Robert & Rebecca Hopper
Boyd
Feb 4, 1853 - Mar 30, 1877

Danner
E. G. --------- Aug 15, 1842 - May 24, 1895

Elizabeth
Boyd ---------- Wife of Jacob G. Danner
Dau John & Jennett Boyd
1810 - 1873

Hugh G. ------- Son Jacob & Elizabeth Danner
May 27, 1834 - Apr 26, 1927

Jacob Getson -- Born in Union Dist. S.C.
Dec 11, 1798 - Mar 1, 1856

Danner (contd)
  Robert Getson - Son Jacob & Elizabeth Danner
                  Died Feb 6, 1858 Age 15

  Thomas G. ----- Son J. & E. Danner
                  Consort of E. J. Danner
                  Oct 1, 1829 - Nov 15, 1862

Davenport
  Cora ---------- Dau Jefferson & S. M. Boyd
                  Jul 21, 1853 - Sep 23, 1882

  Thomas -------- Feb 19, 1856 - Apr 20, 1881

Davis
  Headley ------- Jun 30, 1834 - Jul 14, 1907

  Mary A. ------- Dau Jacob & Elizabeth Danner
                  Aug 3, 1835 - Jan 27, 1861

  Mary J. Dial -- Wife of Hedley Davis
                  Apr 16, 1848 - Jul 13, 1930

Dial
  Catherine G. -- Wife of James P. Dial
                  Dau Jacob & Mary Boyd Danner
                  Jan 15, 1826 - Jun 16, 1905

  Ella Campbell - 2nd wife of James Dial
                  Mother of Kelly & Coleman Dial
                  Dec 6, 1862 - Nov 21, 1908

  George H. ----- Brother of Robt. Jeff. Dial
                  May 14, 1858 - Feb 9, 1883
                  Tyler, Texas

  Jacobus
  Jeremiah ------ Nov 13, 1850 - Sep 25, 1928

  James --------- Son James P. and Catherine
                  Danner Dial
                  May 14, 1858 - Jan 17, 1935

  James P. ------ Son of Jeremiah Dial III
                  Aug 8, 1820 - Mar 5, 1870

  Miss Jo ------- Jan 11, 1853 - Feb 20, 1930
                  Dau J. J. Dial

Dial (contd)
  Maggie Eakins - 1st wife of James Dial
                  Oct 3, 1859 - Dec 29, 1882

  Mary Etta ----- Wife of J. J. Dial
                  Dau John & Mary Dabney
                  Prestwood
                  Nov 21, 1854 - Nov 1, 1927

  Robert
  Jefferson ----- Feb 10, 1855 - May 14, 1930

Hopper
  Eli Hugh ------ Oct 8, 1858 - Aug 24, 1928

  J. D. M. ------ Husband of S. E. Hopper
                  Dec 16, 1835 - Dec 21, 1885

  James A. ------ Dec 9, 1833 - Dec 25, 1869

  "Uncle Jim" --- Died 1897 Age 80

  John ---------- Died Jan 22, 1857
                  47 yrs 7 mo & 14 days

  Maggie Dial --- Mar 5, 1863 - Aug 21, 1941

  Sarah
  Elizabeth ----- Wife of J. D. M. Hopper
                  Dec 9, 1839 - Jan 9, 1897

  Sarah P. ------ Consort of William Hopper
                  Born in Elbert Co. Ga.
                  Apr 20, 1814 - Aug 8, 1870

  William T. ---- Oct 1, 1845 - May 17, 1869

  Willie Ann ---- Feb 14, 1865 - Jun 15, 1902

Key
  Parks Oliver -- Jan 25, 1852 - Oct 26, 1927

McCain
  Ella Key ------ 1854 - 1926

  George W. ----- 1849 - 1932

Nixon
   Alice Boyd ---- Wife of J. W. Nixon
                   May 11, 1859 - Oct 1939

   J. W. --------- Nov 16, 1856 - Oct 31, 1934

Powe
   Allen C. ------ Co. C, Jeff Davis Legion, Miss.
                   Cav., CSA (No dates)

Prestwood
   Austin -------- Mar 9, 1797 - Dec 9, 1873

   John ---------- Son Austin & Mary Boyd
                   Prestwood
                   Jan 15, 1827 - Jun 1, 1862

   Mary ---------- Consort of Austin Prestwood
                   Dau of John & Jennett Boyd
                   Aug 23, 1802 - Oct 10, 1867

   Mary Eleanor
   Powe ---------- Consort of Newton Prestwood
                   Dau W. & S. Powe
                   Sep 25, 1832 - Oct 15, 1868

Rigdon
   Lexena
   Elizabeth ----- Dau Jacobus J. Dial
                   Jan 27, 1846 - Jun 5, 1916

Thompson
   Dr. Harvey P. - Nov 6, 1858 - Oct 11, 1909

Turner
   Elizabeth ----- Consort James R. Turner
                   Dau A. & M. Prestwood
                   Jul 21, 1825 - _?_ ?, 1870

BRASHIERS - WALL CEMETERY
(Destroyed)

Located approximately 2/10 mile south of Max Larkin's hunting lodge, which is about 1 mile west of old Highway 80 and 1 mile north of old Rooster Bridge.

Brashiers
  H. Tobitha ---- D Sep 17, 1836
                  Age 18 yrs 8 mo
                  Dau of Jesse Brashiers

Wall
  Elizaann ------ D Sep 26, 1836
                Age 2 yrs 10 mo
                Dau D. W. Wall

BREWERSVILLE CEMETERY

Located at the Christian Valley Church, approximately 7 1/2 miles southeast of Livingston on the south side of State Highway 28.

Beville
  John Woodlif -- Jan 6, 1852 - Mar 17, 1914

Blakeney
  J. W. --------- Jun 21, 1847 - Jul 11, 1910

  Roberta E. ---- Sep 16, 1850 - Dec 21, 1925

Boling
  William
  Ransom -------- Born in Wilkes Co. Ga.
                Nov 27, 1799 - Mar 1, 1860

Bolton
  Sarah E. ------ Jul 18, 1833 - Apr 1, 1918

Brockway
  Sallie M. ----- Wife of Dr. D. S. Brockway
               Jan 3, 1862 - Sep 25, 1887

Coleman
  Allison ------- Aug 15, 1852 - Oct 10, 1854

  Robert -------- Oct 26, 1847 - Aug 29, 1851

  Samuel Cruse -- Died Monterey, Mexico
                  Mar 6, 1883 in his 39th year
  Susadele
  McCary -------- Wife Samuel Cruse Coleman
                  Aug 27, 1854 - Jun 25, 1905

  Dr. William
  H. ------------ Aug 28, 1810 - Oct 26, 1883

Crocker
  Jane T. ------- Wife of Dr. J. W. Crocker
                  Jan 3, 1833 - Aug 26, 1896

  Dr. John W. --- Feb 20, 1830 - Mar 23, 1885

Cusack
  Martha L. ----- Mother of S. P. Hand
                  May 16, 1802 - Nov 27, 1876

Davidson
  Ida Sanders --- Jun 7, 1863 - Dec 23, 1947

Estill
  Samuel H. ----- Feb 27, 1864 - Feb 10, 1944

Falconer
  Mary H. ------- Apr 27, 1811 - May 5, 1877

Garland
  Narcissus
  Jane ---------- Wife of W. W. Garland
                  Oct 9, 1853 - May 22, 1945

Gatewood
  G. H. --------- Apr 4, 1859 - Nov 4, 1926

Gibson
  Abbie --------- Wife of William Gibson
                  Aug 23, 1811 - Nov 6, 1884

  Sarah Ella ---- Apr 4, 1848 - Aug 21, 1901

  William ------- Dec 10, 1801 - Apr 13, 1871

Grady
  James Robert -- Nov 15, 1862 - Oct 6, 1894

  M. A. --------- Aug 6, 1849 - Mar 22, 1925

  M. L. --------- Feb 12, 1835 - Feb 19, 1904

  Mollie Ann
  Rushing ------- Wife of Phillip Mae Grady
                  Mar 17, 1857 - Oct 7, 1908

  P. M. --------- May 4, 1851 - Dec 24, 1912

  Rebecca ------- Wife of M. L. Grady
                  Dec 19, 1838 - Jun 26, 1914

Graham
  Joseph -------- Pvt, Co K, 40th Reg., Ala. Inf.
                  Nov 25, 1840 - Feb 16, 1919

Gulley
  Cemantha C. --- Wife of E. S. Gulley
                  Dec 25, 1848 - Dec 29, 1884

  Ellen Bell
  Lee ----------- Wife Woodson Slocum Gulley
                  Jan 15, 1860 - Apr 29, 1948

  Ezekiel
  Slocum -------- Col of 40th Reg., Ala. Inf.
                  Born in Wayne Co. N. C.
                  Sep 26, 1831 - Sep 17, 1896

  Woodson
  Slocum -------- Jun 14, 1857 - Oct 16, 1913

Hand
  Martha Ann ---- Wife of Samuel P. Hand
                  Nov 19, 1839 - Oct 29, 1914

  Prof. O. C. --- Jul 21, 1864 - Aug 9, 1897

  Sallie J. ----- Dau S. P. & M. A. Hand
                  Oct 24, 1856 - Sep 13, 1858

  Samuel Patton - Jan 5, 1835 - Sep 5, 1903

Hand (contd)
  Wayne Thomas -- Son S. P. & M. A. Hand
                       May 3, 1858 - Oct 26, 1860

Henson
  Lida Patton --- Wife of J. W. Henson
                   Sep 21, 1862 - Mar 21, 1893

  Lyda P. ------- Feb 1863 - Mar 1893

Horn
  Curtis Drury -- Apr 16, 1859 - Jul 23, 1920

  E. M. J. ------ Wife of I. W. Horn
                May 3, 1842 - Jul 26, 1900

  Isaac Mc. ----- Oct 20, 1860 - Dec 11, 1866

  Isaac W. ------ Jan 25, 1825 - Sep 22, 1913

  John Lee ------ Apr 6, 1864 - Feb 5, 1940

  Thomas A. ----- Son I. W. & E. M. Horn
                 Nov 21, 1861 - Feb 16, 1884

Johnson
  Lewis --------- Feb 7, 1807 - Jun 26, 1875

Larkin
  Abram --------- (No dates)

  Irene --------- Wife of Abram Larkin
                Sep 17, 1841 - Dec 3, 1886

  Mary S.
  Elliott ------- Mar 12, 1859 - Apr 29, 1938

  Sophie Henson - Oct 11, 1860 - Dec 12, 1944

  William ------- Aug 22, 1845 - Sep 9, 1920

  William
  Robert -------- May 18, 1861 - Apr 3, 1925

Lee
  Catherine
  Rebecca ------- Wife of James M. Lee
                Feb 7, 1830 - May 8, 1862

Lee (contd)
  Catherine
    Rebecca ------- Dau James & Catherine Lee
                    Jun 18, 1854 - Sep 23, 1855

  Daniel W. ----- Son William and Susan Lee
                  Aug 21, 1834 - Jul 26, 1849

  Elizabeth
    Helen --------- Dau James & Catherine Lee
                    Feb 22, 1853 - May 19, 1855

  Ida John
    Corine -------- Dau J. M. & Catherine R. Lee
                    Jan 21, 1862 - May 4, 1948

  James M. ------ Dec 29, 1820 - Jan 22, 1881

  John R. ------- Jan 14, 1831 - Dec 6, 1861

  Mamie E. ------ Wife of W. R. Lee
                  Nov 18, 1859 - Nov 17, 1887

  Mary Eliza ---- Dau James & Catherine Lee
                  Jan 10, 1858 - Oct 30, 1861

  Mary
    Elizabeth ----- Wife of John R. Lee
                    Sep 2, 1839 - Feb 7, 1888

  Susan --------- Wife of William Lee
                  May 29, 1798 - Dec 26, 1862

  William ------- 1795 - 14 Jun 1842
                  Age 46 yrs 11 mos 2 days

  William ------- Son William & Susan Lee
                  Oct 1, 1825 - Mar 19, 1850

Martin
  Ann E. -------- Jul 24, 1847 - Sep 3, 1922

  William H. ---- Jul 3, 1846 - Apr 1, 1919

Matthews
  Irene Torry --- 1859 - 1936

Matthews (contd)
 Penelope V. --- Dau J. M. & E. A. Matthews
                 Dec 13, 1864 - Aug 30, 1882

McCarroll
 Belle --------- Nov 24, 1858 - Feb 3, 1889

McCarty
 Joseph W. ----- Sep 10, 1865 - Sep 3, 1927

McDonald
 James H. ------ Feb 8, 1832 - Mar 14, 1867

McMillan
 A. G. --------- Apr 4, 1854 - Nov 15, 1911

 Dora ---------- Wife of F. G. McMillan
                 Feb 10, 1851 - Jun 28, 1883

 F. G. --------- Oct 29, 1849 - Jun 26, 1894

 Kate G. ------- Wife of F. G. McMillan
                 Apr 20, 1859 - May 28, 1937

McMillon
 Anna B. ------- Mar 9, 1859 - Aug 16, 1867

 Daniel -------- Born 1790 - Oct 25, 1860

 Drury --------- Jan 11, 1796 - Sep 23, 1860

 Elizabeth ----- Nov 11, 1824 - Dec 31, 1875

 Isaac N. ------ Oct 4, 18?5 - Nov 13, 1873

 Preston N. ---- Feb 11, 1852 - Jul 20, 1869

Morris
 George -------- Died Oct 6, 1876 Age Abt 75

 Harriet ------- Died Aug 3, 1896 Age 78

Murray
 Belle Lee ----- Wife of R. L. Murray
                 Jan 11, 1857 - Nov 3, 1880

Patton
 Alice B. ------ Sep 4, 1855 - Dec 28, 1932

Patton (contd)
D. U. --------- Nov 7, 1854 - Jul 3, 1890

Eliza --------- Wife of Joseph Patton
                Mar 19, 1802 - Jul 28, 1883

Ella McMillan - Wife of J. B. Patton
                Feb 14, 1857 - Jan 29, 1890

Joseph -------- Dec 20, 1796 - Oct 20, 1876

Joseph B. ----- Jul 5, 1853 - Oct 16, 1915

Willie A.
Beville ------- Wife of B. B. Patton
                Apr 8, 1860 - May 17, 1865

Powers
Julia T. ------ Wife of Rev. W. I. Powers
                Died Dec 20, 1886 Age 54

Rushing
J. K. P. ------ Nov 1, 1844 - Mar 28, 1918

J. P. --------- Jul 4, 1859 - May 8, 1940

John P. ------- Oct 22, 1808 - Jun 7, 1892

W. R. --------- Dec 11, 1833 - Jul 5, 1890

Mrs. W. R. ---- Oct 1844 - Nov 1926

Scales
Harden L.------ May 13, 1859 - May 1, 1918

Joseph P. ----- Dec 16, 1856 - Jun 9, 1897

Laura C. ------ Dec 29, 1849 - Mar 17, 1936

Nancy Patton -- Wife of T. A. Scales
                Apr 10, 1833 - Apr 7, 1918

Thomas A. ----- Aug 12, 1827 - Feb 11, 1894

Uriah E. ------ Sep 1861 - Feb 1912

William A. ---- 1865 - 1937

Seale
A. L. ---------- Aug 28, 1827 - Oct 2, 1896

Dr. B. B. ------ Aug 23, 1838 - Aug 23, 1909

Bettie Currie
Thetford ------ 1849 - 1924

Malinda F.
McMillan ------ Sep 23, 1847 - Jan 1, 1884

Speed
Dixie T. ------ Wife of S. E. Speed
1862 - 1938

S. E. --------- 1855 - 1942

Torry
G. W. ---------- Mar 31, 1828 - Aug 1, 1895

Kate M. -------- May 4, 1865 - Nov 28, 1926

M. Hadden ----- Jun 2, 1857 - Dec 2, 1919

Turner
Alice ---------- Dau W. F. & A. M. Turner
Mar 16, 1857 - Sep 28, 1857

Ann M. --------- Wife of W. F. Turner
Dec 31, 1827 - Mar 8, 1896

D. L. ---------- Son W. F. & A. M. Turner
Apr 12, 1851 - Mar 23, 1868

Elizabeth
Gillespie ----- Wife of John S. Turner
1856 - 1905

John S. -------- Sep 30, 1849 - Mar 18, 1880

Mattie A. ----- Dau W. F. & A. M. Turner
Jul 4, 1864 - Mar 31, 1868

W. F. ---------- Jun 29, 1821 - Apr 27, 1877

__?__ ---------- Jun 6, 1852 - Aug 29, 1855

Walston
  Maggie T. ----- Jan 15, 1853 - Jul 26, 1883
Wiatt
  Henry H. ------ 1840 - 1863 Son
  Mary C. ------- 1812 - 1884 Mother
  William C. ---- 1813 - 1878 Father
Williamson
  James F. ------ 1822 - 1904
  Molly P. ------ 1849 - 1929
  S. E. --------- Aug 13, 1856 - Oct 10, 1936
Wimberly
  Emma J. ------- Jul 25, 1851 - Dec 12, 1934
  S. A. --------- Aug 16, 1849 - May 10, 1903
Wrenn
  Nancy
  Elizabeth ----- Nov 2, 1830 - Jun 20, 1902

BROWN CEMETERY

From State Highway 17, 2 miles south of Emelle, turn east on County Road 20. After approximately 4 1/2 miles, at Sumterville, turn south on a dirt road. The cemetery is 1 1/10 miles down this road and several hundred feet west of the road, across the road from the antebellum home, "The Cedars".

Brown
  Arthur
  Godfrey ------- Died Oct 9, 1866
                  Age 12 yr 10 mo 6 days
  John E. Jr. --- Died Mar 3, 1866
                  Age 22 yr 8 mo
  John Evander -- Sep 5, 1809 - Mar 17, 1868

Brown (contd)
  Mary Jane ----- Wife of John Evander Brown
                  Jan 12, 1816 - Mar 6, 1883

Harris
  Ella F. ------- Dau R. M. & E. D. Harris
                  Died Feb 19, 1864
                  Age 2 yrs 10 mo

  Infant -------- Child of R. M. & E. D. Harris

  Infant -------- Child of R. M. & E. D. Harris

Praytor
  Hugh Boyd ----- Son of Middleton Praytor
                  Apr 1, 1855 - May 15, 1942

  Mary Jane
  Stewart ------- Wife of Hugh Boyd Praytor
                  Dau Lt. Col. C. S. & Julia
                  Brown Stewart
                  Apr 17, 1857 - Mar 17, 1929

Stewart
  Julia Brown --- Wife of Lt. Col. C. S. Stewart,
                  CSA
                  Dau John E. & Mary Jane Brown
                  Dec 11, 1836 - Mar 1, 1928

BROWN CEMETERY

From State Highway 39, approximately 8 miles
north of Livingston, turn west on County Road 20.
The cemetery is at "Louden", the Brown home, on
the south side of this road, approximately 2
miles west of the intersection.

Brown
  Edwin J. ------ Nov 16, 1843 - ___?___

  Jere H. ------- Sep 6, 1801 - Feb 10, 1868

  Julia A. ------ Mar 14, 1814 - Mar 18, 1850

Lide
   Hugh James ---- May 29, 1858 - Sep 10, 1859

   Infant -------- (No name or dates)

   Infant -------- (No name or dates)

   Jere Brown ---- Oct 4, 1857 - Jul 26, 1859

   Lillian ------- Sep 26, 1862 - Aug 4, 1863

   Sumter -------- Mar 26, 1864 - Nov 27, 1866

Reed
   John Harvey --- Apr 7, 1865 - Sep 19, 1933

White
   Addie Brown --- Oct 9, 1846 - Mar 3, 1931

   David
   Campbell ------ Born Versailles, Woodford
                   County, Kentucky
                   Oct 16, 1842 - Feb 10, 1888

BROWN CEMETERY

From State Highway 17, 2 miles south of Emelle, turn east on County Road 20. After approximately 4 1/2 miles, at Sumterville, turn south on a dirt road. The cemetery is approximately 6/10 mile down this road on the west side of the road.

Brown
   Ann ----------- Born 1839 Died Feb 19, 1909

   Emma ---------- Jan 18, 1863 - Oct 1, 1949

   Jim ----------- May 18, 1856 - Sep 5, 1946

   Lemon --------- Died Dec 13, 1907 Age 91 yrs

Durr
   Ida ----------- Jun 10, 1864 - Nov 14, 1947

Mason
    Matilda ------- Born Nov 17, 1813
                    Died Apr 29, 1897

Reid
    Amanda -------- Founder Livingston Baptist
                    Industrial School
                    Oct 1, 1836 - May 16, 1915

BROWNING CEMETERY

From State Highway 17, approximately 2 2/10 miles north of Emelle, turn east on the Dan Mitchell Road. After 1/2 mile, turn into the driveway of the George Mason home on the south side of the road. The cemetery is approximately 1/3 mile west of this home in a woods.

Browning
    Elizabeth C. -- Born 1829 Died 1853

    John Bailey --- Son John & Clary Browning
                    Nov 21, 1831 - Aug 12, 1869

Handley
    J. H. --------- Nov 24, 1846 - Sep 3, 1853

    Schararrissa
    Browning ------ Wife of Peter Handley
                    (Dates unreadable)

BURTON CEMETERY
(Destroyed)

From State Highway 17, approximately 9 miles north of York, turn west on County Road 12 and go approximately 2 1/4 miles to the Hadden Church. The cemetery is approximately 1 mile across the road from the church in deep woods.

Burton
    Absolem ------- Mar 19, 1823 - Oct 22, 1903

Burton (contd)
Absolem
Farrah Jr. ---- Feb 16, 1858 - May 11, 1868

Margaret Ann -- Died May 25, 1906

(Bullocks, Hodges, Campbells and Calverts are reported to be buried in this cemetery.)

CAGUS CEMETERY

From County Road 10, approximately 2 1/4 miles south of Cuba, turn west on the Cagus Cemetery Road. The cemetery is 1/10 mile down this road.

Bell
Jane ---------- Wife of Joe Bell
        May 15, 1830 - Mar 18, 1906

Joe ----------- Apr 8, 1838 - Sep 30, 1921

Maurice ------- Feb 23, 1861 - Nov 25, 1936

Boone
Ann ----------- Wife of David Boone
        Mar 10, 1848 - Died ___ 8, 1918

David --------- Born ___, 1845
        Died Dec 5, 1909

Bronson
Nancy --------- Died Sep 24, 1925 Age 65

Brown
Harrison ------ Apr 1838 - Apr 8, 1908

Katie --------- Wife of Harrison Brown
        Nov 10, 1844 - Jan 6, 1909

Campbell
Lucy ---------- May 10, 1864 - Oct 20, 1925

Conner
Aggie --------- Wife of Sim Conner
        Jun 19, 1864 - Oct 11, 1915

Cooper
  __?__ ---------- Wife of Demus Cooper
                Mar 7, 1855 - Nov 7, 1895

Core
  Rev. A. C. ---- 1863 - 1931

Dank
  Gregory ------- Jun 1853 - May 13, 1918
                Age 65

Drake
  Josephene ----- 1846 - 1931

Fulford
  Channie ------- Mar 27, 1863 - Oct 23, 1943

Grant
  Alice E. ------ Dec 5, 1860 - Oct 26, 1950

  F. Virginia --- Wife of Silas Grant
                Died Dec 8, 1912

  Silas ---------- Aug 6, 1855 - Dec 31, 1927

McAboy
  Milalia ------- Nov 9, 1851 - Apr 14, 1922

McElroy
  Annie --------- Wife of Spate McElroy
                Jun 15, 1852 - Jan 31, 1911

  Spate --------- Apr 20, 1852 - Jun 9, 1917

White
  Ben ----------- Age 78 years

  Manervie ------ Wife of Ben White
                Jul 5, 1852 - Jul 11, 1907

  Mary ---------- Wife of Ben White
                Born in 1861
                Died Aug 24, 1915

Wilson
  Louiza -------- Mother of Rina Wilson
                Feb 18, 1834 - Jun 15, 1886

CAMPBELL - DERBY CEMETERY

From State Highway 17, approximately 11 1/2 miles south of York, turn east on County Road 42. At 1 mile, turn south on a dirt road. The cemetery is on the west side of the road at a distance of approximately 1/4 mile.

Campbell
John Smith ---- (No dates)

    Justina L. ---- Wife of William Campbell
                     Dec 27, 1820 - Nov 30, 1886

    Mattie -------- Jul 12, 1853 - Apr 13, 1937

    Capt. Robert
    M. ------------ Born Cumberland Co. N.C.
                    Apr 21, 1822
                    Died in Sumter Co. Ala.
                    Oct 29, 1881
                    59 yr 6 mo 8 days

    Robert M. ----- Feb 28, 1855 - Mar 5, 1913

Derby
    Capt. A. J. --- Mar 11, 1837 - Jun 2, 1898

    Elizabeth
    Campbell ------ Jul 23, 1844 - Aug 2, 1886

CENTER RIDGE CHURCH CEMETERY
(Lauderdale County, Mississippi)

From York, take County Road 19 for approximately 10 miles into Lauderdale County, Mississippi. The church and cemetery are on the right side of the road.

Bailey
    Adelia -------- Jan 2, 1852 - Jul 19, 1912

    Amanda -------- Born 1835 Died Jul 1886

    H. L. --------- Mar 27, 1821 - Feb 17, 1904

Bailey (contd)
J. W. --------- Husband of Sarah
                 Mar 27, 1821 - Mar 22, 1900

Robert C. ----- Aug 16, 1860 - Jun 18, 1896

Cobb
Joysey S. ----- May 24, 1828 - May 30, 1918

Ezelle
Calvin -------- Born Jan 8, 1836
               Married Feb 12, 1860
               Died Jul 28, 1907

Johnnie ------- (No dates)

Sammie -------- (No dates)

Sarah F. ------ 1841 - 1926

Frazier
A. E. --------- Born in Wake Co. N.C.
               Aug 2, 1838 - Nov 24, 1905

Theodore ------ Sep 17, 1854 - Mar 21, 1932

Gaines
F. ------------ Sep 11, 1818 - May 6, 1900

Gordon
Cornelius ----- Jan 8, 1865 - Mar 14, 1939

Grantham
Fannie -------- Wife of B. M. Grantham
               Jun 13, 1847 - Oct 16, 1920

Nicholson
G. T. --------- Dec 13, 1847 - Dec 24, 1910

Rutherford
James S. ------ Jan 13, 1857 - Aug 5, 1935

Mary Ann ------ May 14, 1854 - Oct 27, 1925

Shelby
Nancy Jane ---- Apr 24, 1850 - Jan 20, 1929

William L. ---- Jul 11, 1848 - Dec 16, 1920

Simmons
  James A. ------ Feb 24, 1849 - May 6, 1923

  Susan A. ------ Wife of James A. Simmons
                  Jun 11, 1856 - Aug 29, 1900

White
  Rev. D. P. ---- Hus of Mary E. White
                  Mar 4, 1821 - Feb 19, 1880

  Drucilla C. --- Wife of Alfred White
                  Sep 7, 1857 - Apr 12, 1890

  Luther L. ----- Dec 9, 1860 - Aug 18, 1917

Williams
  Henry J. ------ Apr 17, 1846 - Jun 12, 1918

  Margaret A. --- Nov 30, 1848 - Sep 14, 1916

  N. A. --------- Born in Wake Co. N.C.
                  Mar 29, 1815 - Nov 9, 1902

  R. J. --------- Born in Wake Co. N.C.
                  Apr 12, 1840 - Jun 7, 1903

  W. P. --------- Born in Wake Co. N.C.
                  Jul 3, 1843 - Jan 1, 1891

Wright
  Angeline ------ Jul 15, 1847 - Jun 6, 1939

  Armelia ------- Jan 16, 1841 - Jan 6, 1917

  Daniel L. ----- Co. A, 4th Calif. Inf.
                  Feb 28, 1830 - Apr 24, 1914

  James W. ------ Oct 10, 1833 - Mar 2, 1914

  John L. ------- Jun 26, 1805 - Nov 10, 1876

CENTRAL CEMETERY

From State Highway 17, approximately 15 miles north of York, turn east on County Road 20. After approximately 3/4 mile, turn south on a paved road. The cemetery is 1/2 mile down this road on the east side of the road.

Baker
   John Elmore --- Aug 8, 1863 - Feb 9, 1944

Burton
   Rev. John
   Wesley -------- Sep 18, 1851 - Nov 8, 1926

Daniel
   Alice A. ------ Wife of J. T. Daniel
                     Aug 25, 1840 - Sep 19, 1919

Elliott
   Calvin Andrew - Jun 8, 1865 - Dec 18, 1936

Murray
   William L. ---- May 19, 1864 - Aug 20, 1949

CHARCONE CEMETERY

Located about 200 yards east of County Road 85, approximately 5 miles north of its intersection with State Road 116 and approximately 4/10 mile south of St. Johns Church.

Gholson
   Mary
   Elizabeth ----- Consort of James H. Gholson
                    Jun 28, 1838 - May 12, 1862

Hare
   Josephine ----- Nov 2, 1849 - Sep 9, 1861

   Mary J. ------- Nov 11, 1818 - Nov 22, 1866

   Sarah Ellen --- Dau W. V. & M. J. Hare
                   Jul 27, 1846 - Jan 14, 1861

Knight
  L. A. ---------- Nov 4, 1844 - Mar 10, 1902

Shea
  Eliza Jane ---- Wife of John Shea
                  Dau Thomas & Elizabeth Shea
                  Died Nov 20, 1863
                  Age 29 yr 4 mo 25 days

  John ---------- Husband of Bettie
                  Died Aug 18, 1879 Age 60

CHESTNUT GROVE CEMETERY

Located approximately 7 miles south of York on the east side of State Highway 17.

Alexander
  E. A. ---------- Mar 27, 1847 - Mar 9, 1883

  J. M. ---------- Sep 19, 1847 - Mar 18, 1889

Ashley
  Daniel --------- Sep 28, 1820 - Apr 21, 1908

  Joe Lowe ------ Wife of W. R.
                  Apr 12, 1852 - Apr 2, 1927

  Milton -------- Son Daniel & Ollie
                  Mar 4, 1852 - Dec 13, 1871

  Ollie ---------- Wife of Daniel
                  Sep 5, 1818 - Apr 29, 1891

  W. R. ---------- Dec 4, 1847 - May 23, 1914

Barnard
  John ----------- Mar 20, 1833 - Jul 27, 1896

Bartlett
  Emily Woolf --- 1860 - 1925

Brown
  Ann J. -------- Wife of B. F. Jr.
                  Sep 8, 1848 - Jun 25, 1891

Brown (contd)
```
B. F. Jr.    ----- Aug 7, 1846 - Jul 15, 1914

B. F. Sr.    ----- Apr 13, 1821 - Nov 17, 1919

Hiram        --------- Died Nov 20, 1876  Age 72

Melissa      ------- Wife of B. F.
                     Mar 28, 1830 - May 4, 1908

Nancy I.     ------ Dau B. F. & Malissa Brown
                    Oct 15, 1851 - Dec 9, 1931

Narsis       -------- Dec 5, 1853 - Oct 16, 1935

Patience     ------ Oct 12, 1848 - Dec 2, 1934

T. F.        --------- Sep 6, 1861 - Apr 19, 1897

W. S.        --------- Feb 28, 1860 - Dec 2, 1929
```

Curry
```
Theodore     ------ 1850 - 1922
```

Davis
```
Mrs. A. C.   ---- Nov 6, 1855 - Mar 23, 1895
```

Hunster
```
Eliza A.     ------ Wife of J. C.
                    Apr 14, 1861 - Sep 9, 1887

Mary E.      ------- Died Oct 7, 1885
                    Aged about 50 years
```

McAlpin
```
John F.      ------- Jun 13, 1863 - Jun 17, 1933

Robert A.    ----- Mar 6, 1832 - Nov 15, 1900

Sarah B.     ------ May 26, 1841 - Nov 20, 1892
```

McDonald
```
Ann M.       -------- Wife J. H.
                     May 18, 1822 - Nov 8, 1884

George W.    ----- Mar 15, 1856 - Mar 9, 1932

John H.      ------- Sep 1820 - Dec 24, 1888
```

McDonald (contd)
Mattie -------- Wife S. C.
              Dec 10, 1855 - Nov 11, 1909

S. C. --------- Nov 11, 1852 - May 28, 1921

William ------- Mar 1, 1817 - Oct 18, 1885

Mundy
H. J. --------- Wife of W. A.
              Dec 5, 1833 - Sep 9, 1910

J. A. --------- Nov 26, 1855 - Mar 8, 1932

Mary E. ------- Wife of J. A.
              Jan 4, 1860 - Dec 12, 1903

W. A. --------- Husband of H. J.
              Apr 26, 1826 - Sep 16, 1897

Owens
Emily Permilla
Ashley -------- Wife of Albert
              Apr 6, 1846 - Oct 5, 1873

Francis ------- Wife of S. W.
              Dec 12, 1832 - Mar 29, 1884

Pendergrass
A. H. --------- Sep 14, 1839 - Nov 3, 1913

Hattie O. ----- Aug 30, 1840 - Nov 6, 1917

Shelby
J. T. --------- Aug 16, 1850 - Jun 30, 1914

Shelton
Rev. A. J. ---- Dec 26, 1821 - Dec 23, 1881

Elizabeth ----- Wife of A. J.
              Mar 19, 1824 - Oct 13, 1906

Huston Taylor - Aug 30, 1846 - Jul 4, 1927

J. K. P.------- Jul 19, 1845 - May 18, 1916

Rachel C. ----- Jul 28, 1810 - Apr 9, 1891

Shelton (contd)
  Robert R. ----- May 23, 1796 - Jan 8, 1870
Tate
  Emma J. ------- Apr 4, 1860 - Oct 15, 1890
  James T. ------ 1859 - 1924
Williams
  J. J. --------- Aug 3, 1847 - Feb 7, 1917
Woolf
  Sarah --------- Jan 6, 1851 - Feb 25, 1943

CLAY MEMORIAL CEMETERY

Located on U. S. Highway 11 south in Cuba.

Andrews
  H. H. --------- Feb 10, 1843 - Jun 17, 1915
Barrow
  Mrs. F. E. ---- Wife of John Barrow
                  Dec 27, 1840 - May 30, 1906
  John ---------- Jan 27, 1841 - Feb 22, 1911
Bell
  William
  Murphy -------- Mar 14, 1831 - Mar 27, 1886
Bishop
  Sarah F. ------ Sep 10, 1840 - Mar 7, 1908
Brewer
  Eliza --------- May 9, 1820 - Oct 8, 1890
  John R. ------- Jul 4, 1848 - Jun 8, 1935
  Laura --------- 1855 - Jul 18, 1927
  Louise -------- Oct 12, 1853 - Feb 3, 1924
  Mathew E. ----- Apr 3, 1846 - Aug 23, 1915

Clay
    R. A. --------- Feb 22, 1822 - Aug 8, 1890
    Robert P. ----- Jul 19. 1853 - Dec 23, 1888
    Thadeus ------- Oct 1, 1858 - Jul 25, 1888

Daniels
    Asenath
    Florentine ---- Apr 10, 1847 - Feb 10, 1895
    William Seth -- Sep 19, 1846 - Jan 22, 1931

Darden
    John P. ------- Aug 19, 1859 - Feb 19, 1909

Davidson
    Grandmother --- 1840 - 1921
    J. D. --------- Jun 1, 1861 - Mar 14, 1936

Garrison
    James V. ------ Sep 30, 1837 - Sep 1, 1912
    L. Catherine -- Apr 20, 1850 - Nov 23, 1913

Goodin
    Lucy A. ------- Wife of J. J. Goodin
                    Born Mar 6, 1834
                    Married Nov 16, 1866
                    Died Apr 12, 1891

Grimes
    I. C. --------- Nov 30, 1859 - Nov 8, 1916
    Martha -------- 1848 - 1929

Hall
    Beatrice ------ 1862 - 1949
    Edward -------- Feb 27, 1850 - Sep 4, 1930
    Elnora -------- Jul 24, 1854 - Jul 4, 1929
    Grandma ------- Died Jul 28, 1908
    Marcellis ----- 1858 - 1892

Harris
  John Ellis ---- 1859 - 1925

Hearne
  Henry
  Alexander ----- Sep 8, 1861 - Jun 28, 1932

  Mattie Martha - Nov 19, 1864 - Dec 8, 1945

Holmes
  Fannie M. ----- Wife of James H. Holmes
                  May 27, 1845 - Nov 23, 1905

Honeycutt
  Emma P. ------- Apr 23, 1854 - Aug 21, 1944

  Z. W. --------- Jul 6, 1855 - Oct 1, 1917

Huff
  Mrs. Sue ------ May 5, 1857 - Aug 8, 1946

Hurlbert
  Emma F. ------- Sep 10, 1848 - Jul 23, 1928

Husband
  Louis --------- Jan 12, 1838 - Jun 12, 1923

  Mary E. ------- Nov 25, 1822 - Feb 25, 1920

Idle
  Almeda -------- 1855 - 1935

James
  Lytle E. ------ 1854 - 1937

Jarman
  William
  Thomas -------- Oct 2, 1860 - Mar 23, 1938

Lancaster
  Nancy
  Caroline ------ Wife of J. E. Lancaster
                  Feb 4, 1844 - Nov 11, 1927

Lewis
  Martha C. ----- Wife of John Lewis
                  Mar 12, 1833 - Mar 23, 1900

Lewis (contd)
S. A. --------- 1858 - 1918

    Warner H. ----- Born Raleigh N. Carolina
                                    Apr 8, 1822 - Oct 3, 1899

Liggett
Annie
Crutcher ------ Jul 26, 1847 - Jul 26, 1927

Love
Marion V. ----- Jun 28, 1849 - Sep 13, 1910

Mary A. ------- Apr 4, 1849 - Aug 18, 1890

Lummus
James Wesley -- Apr 23, 1847 - Feb 26, 1918

Lula S. ------- Jan 4, 1861 - Jul 30, 1928

Lynn
Agnes
Lancaster ----- 1821 - 1909

Mager
Emile --------- 1853 - 1909

Lottie
Brewster ------ 1861 - 1930

May
Benjamin A. --- 1864 - 1931

McAlpine
Jennie -------- Jan 29, 1854 - Sep 12, 1928

McClamroch
Rev. Albert
S. ------------ Nov 14, 1863 - Apr 30, 1945

McDaniel
Cynthia Ann --- Sep 20, 1820 - Oct 19, 1898

Eli ----------- Jan 1, 1817 - Nov 29, 1889

Maggie A.
Baskin -------- Wife of W. G. McDaniel
                       Oct 19, 1858 - Oct 17, 1914

McDaniel (contd)
  William Gray -- Mar 2, 1858 - Nov 7, 1927

McGowen
  Annie Ward ---- 1864 - 1933

  Thomas
  Pinckney ----- Apr 18, 1864 - Mar 9, 1926

  Virginia N. --- Wife of W. R. McGowen
                Mar 10, 1838 - Jan 19, 1904

  William E. ---- 1858 - 1937

  William R. ---- Sep 24, 1830 - May 6, 1904

Meador
  R. A. --------- Oct 19, 1855 - Mar 1, 1913

Miller
  Ezekiel ------- Apr 12, 1845 - Jun 16, 1922

  Gilbert L. ---- Apr 8, 1841 - Nov 3, 1929

  Louisa J. ----- Jan 4, 1850 - Jan 4, 1929

  Malissa ------- Wife of E. Miller
                Apr 22, 1848 - Sep 9, 1921

Mitchell
  Arbrette ------ Dec 12, 1845 - Jun 16, 1933

  Benjamin L. --- Oct 5, 1842 - Mar 18, 1928

Pettigrew
  Sarah Isadors - Sep 5, 1859 - Jun 23, 1945

  Wallace H. ---- Oct 6, 1857 - Apr 1, 1937

Phillips
  Alice J. ------ Wife of J. T. Phillips
                Jul 10, 1864 - Jan 23, 1891

  L. W. --------- Nov 9, 1864 - Nov 11, 1906

  Mrs. Mary E. -- Nov 22, 1838 - Nov 7, 1919

Pierce
Eliza Ann ----- Feb 1856 - Sep 28, 1913

H. C. --------- Mar 14, 1845 - Oct 17, 1924

Miss Joe ------ Apr 4, 1855 -Oct 18, 1932

Rosie L. ------ Oct 26, 1851 - Jan 21, 1937

William F. ---- Aug 5, 1862 - Apr 5, 1939

Poole
Catherine J. -- Jan 15, 1847 - Feb 4, 1917

Theodoria ----- Oct 26, 1857 - Jun 14, 1938

Viola --------- Oct 31, 1959 - May 24, 1931

Rainer
George W. ----- Dec 23, 1843 - May 2, 1943

Margaret A. --- Dec 21, 1853 - Jan 1, 1929

Rew
Elizabeth W. -- Jan 7, 1858 - Feb 4, 1937

Robert Y. ----- Dec 24, 1850 - Sep 11, 1920

Russell
"Grandma" ----- Nov 2, 1834 - Jan 13, 1914

Shamburger
Emma R. ------- Wife of Dr. W. B. Shamburger
Jul 24, 1865 - Mar 8, 1909

William B. ---- Nov 8, 1857 - Aug 6, 1917

Shaw
Annie T.
Glass --------- Wife of W. O. Shaw
Oct 6, 1857 - Aug 9, 1935

Cynthia Alice
Lewis --------- Wife of W. M. Shaw
Jul 26, 1854 - May 21, 1915

William Uriah - Mar 3, 1863 - Jun 28, 1950

Shelton
  Mary L.
  McDaniel ------ Apr 18, 1853 - Apr 6, 1906

Stallworth
  Mattie Lynn --- 1859 - 1951

  ___?___ ------- 1855 - 1911

Stephens
  Angeline ------ Wife of D. C. Stephens
               Apr 17, 1851 - Aug 21, 1930

  Daniel Calvin - Aug 24, 1849 - Feb 15, 1922

  Eliza Jane ---- Aug 1, 1865 - Jul 21, 1957

  W. H. --------- Oct 29, 1857 - Jun 5, 1941

Sturdivant
  Mary Ann ------ Wife of Dempsey Sturdivant
               1840 - 1919

Swain
  J. T. --------- May 24, 1838 - Jan 14, 1904

  N. E. J. ------ Wife of J. T. Swain
               Dec 26, 1837 - Jun 2, 1908

Tate
  Elizabeth ----- Feb 17, 1853 - Sep 21, 1915

  J. E. --------- Aug 10, 1852 - May 2, 1912

Thompson
  Bassett Henry - 1861 - 1944

  Mack ---------- Oct 7, 1861 - May 26, 1937

Treadaway
  Hollam A. ----- 1851 - 1930

  Virginia M. --- Wife of Hollam
               1850 - 1928

Truelove
  Elijah L. ----- Dec 17, 1864 - Nov 17, 1945

Upchurch
  Abel James ---- Aug 6, 1854 - Jul 9, 1929

Vaughn
  Dr. A. L. ----- Feb 12, 1864 - Aug 31, 1923

  Rev. C. C. ---- Born in Union Co. S. C.
                  Apr 29, 1827 - Jan 14, 1904

  Elizabeth ----- Wife of Rev C. C. Vaughn
                  Born in South Carolina
                  May 5, 1832 - May 23, 1905

  M. A. --------- Wife of W. C. Vaughn
                  Feb 5, 1856 - Sep 24, 1881

Waddell
  Frances Ann --- Wife of J. A. Waddell
                  Nov 1, 1841 - Jun 28, 1900

  James A. ------ Hus of F. A. Waddell
                  Jan 29, 1837 - May 23, 1892

Walker
  Lewis --------- Apr 14, 1864 - Nov 30, 1906

  Matilda ------- Apr 3, 1844 - Dec 23, 1902

Wallace
  Emmer L. ------ Wife of T. B. Wallace
                  Born May 11, 1859

  T. B. --------- May 26, 1864 - Feb 28, 1916

Ward
  David S. ------ Jul 31, 1842 - Nov 7, 1913

  Mollie D. ----- Wife of Dr. H. B. Ward
                  Nov 26, 1865 - Mar 5, 1930

Webb
  Sallie V. ----- 1864 - 1942

Westbrook
  C. F. --------- Wife of J. C. Westbrook
                  Sep 7, 1848 - May 29, 1893

  J. C. --------- Aug 29, 1849 - Aug 11, 1922

Westbrook (contd)
  Mary E. ------- Wife of J. C. Westbrook
                   Died Nov 2, 1912 Age 56

Wiatt
  John F. ------- May 17, 1838 - Jan 6, 1917

  Josephine
  Mason --------- May 10, 1848 - Jan 29, 1936

COATS CEMETERY

Located deep in the woods, approximately 3/4 mile north of County Road 10, approximately 1 mile west of its intersection with State Highway 17.

Matthews
  John ---------- (No dates)

Seale
  Martha -------- Born in Sumter Co. Ala.
                  Feb 25, 1844
                  Departed this life on
                  Nov 27, 1852

Wideman
  Henry --------- Who was born in the Newbury
                  District of South Carolina in
                  July 1792 Died Jul 19, 1839

COKES CHAPEL CEMETERY

From State Highway 17, approximately 4 7/10 miles south of York, turn south on County Road 9. The cemetery is on the east side of the road at a distance of approximately 4 3/4 miles.

Allen
  David C. ------ Jan 13, 1853 - Mar 24, 1930

  Emiline C. ---- Aug 8, 1860 - Sep 25, 1960

Boone
  John C. ------- 1834 - 1914

  M. E. --------- Wife of J. C. Boone
                  Oct 20, 1840 - Jan 20, 1912

Boyett
  Nancy --------- Oct 4, 1855 - Sep 15, 1898

Bragg
  Mary E. ------- Wife of S. P. Bragg
                  Dau Dr. J. N. Gilmore
                  Jul 6, 1863 - Sep 3, 1900

  Nancy --------- Oct 4, 1855 - Sep 15, 1898

  Robert
  Braxton ------- 1863 - 1934

  Sterling
  Parker -------- Feb 11, 1860 - Nov 16, 1931

Brockway
  Dr. A. E. ----- May 2, 1817 - Feb 15, 1868

Brown
  B. T. --------- Jan 25, 1829 - Mar 27, 1910

  Kate ---------- Wife of B. T. Brown
                  Dau M. & E. Rumley
                  Apr 24, 1842 - Dec 9, 1975

Cahoon
  Abigail ------- Mar 11, 1821 - Jun 13, 1911

  Abisha N. ----- Jul 20, 1850 - Oct 1867

  Charlie B. ---- 1862 - 1926

  David --------- Nov 23, 1810 - Nov 10, 1882

  Edgar C. ------ Apr 26, 1860 - Sep 22, 1917

  Fannie E. ----- Aug 6, 1838 - Mar 24, 1927

  H. ------------ A Native of Hyde Co. N.C.
                  Apr 6, 1812 - Nov 26, 1855

Cahoon (contd)
J. F. --------- Mar 9, 1853 - Sep 25, 1932

James H. ------ Aug 26, 1857 - Sep 17, 1870

Joseph C. ----- Sep 5, 1851 - May 18, 1887

Julia E. ------ Dec 27, 1825 - Jun 28, 1883

M. L. --------- Dec 26, 1846 - Feb 23, 1930

Meantha M. ---- Apr 7, 1860 - Feb 2, 1955

Mittie -------- Feb 21, 1844 - Jun 3, 1918

Thomas W. ----- May 18, 1855 - Jan 22, 1936

W. A. J. ------ Mar 18, 1819 - Nov 29, 1898

W. H. --------- Mar 3, 1840 - May 28, 1918

Cannady
Jimmie -------- Son N. W. & S. E. Cannady
Oct 26, 1861 - Jun 29, 1864

Maggie -------- Dau N. W. & S. E. Cannady
Aug 7, 1863 - Jul 12, 1864

N. W. --------- Born Newbern, N. C.
Jul 14, 1834 - Jan 2, 1887

Naomi W. ------ Mar 18, 1802 - Apr 9, 1874

Siddie E. ----- Wife of N. W. Cannady
Apr 6, 1836 - Feb 7, 1911

Cannon
S. A. --------- 1817 - 1899

T. B. --------- 1810 - 1894

Carr
A. J. --------- Wife of J. P. Carr
Oct 12, 1831 - Jun 5, 1881

James P. ------ Co. B, 56th Ala. Cav., CSA
(No dates)

Clay
    Ella K. ------- Wife of R. P. Clay
                   Dau Simon & Susan Hall
                   May 7, 1853 - Aug 3, 1883

Crews
    Clara M.
    Cahoon -------- Dec 20, 1841 - Dec 11, 1921

    Dr. O. L. ----- Nov 7, 1837 - Jul 5, 1871

Dean
    Catherine ----- 1836 - 1916

Dukes
    J. S. --------- Oct 12, 1862 - May 23, 1941

Ezell
    Anna ---------- 1860 - 1939

    J. C. --------- Mar 2, 1849 - Apr 26, 1912

    Viola Shurley - Wife of J. C. Ezell
                    Oct 3, 1855 - Jan 13, 1897

Flowers
    E. M. --------- Wife of H. G. Flowers
                    Died Jul 28, 1906 Age 67

    H. G.---------- Died Feb 6, 1892 Age 58

    Joseph E. ----- Oct 18, 1862 - Jul 3, 1865

    Sophronia ----- Wife of J. B. Flowers
                    Mar 27, 1844 - Sep 20, 1889

Gere
    Augusta
    Marshall
    Croom --------- Jul 14, 1838 - Jul 13, 1918

Gilmore
    Dr. J. N. ----- Dec 15, 1927 - Sep 17, 1906

Hale
    Mary Isabella - Wife of J. A. Hale
                    Sep 1, 1861 - Feb 26, 1884

Hall
  Mrs. Archa ---- Jan 4, 1795 - Jul 1, 1856

  Archibald ----- A native of North Carolina
                  Mar 5, 1793 - Jun 10, 1857

  Dr. Evan P. --- 1839 - 1910

  Jimmie -------- Son of Simon & Susan Hall
                  Apr 22, 1861 - Oct 20, 1866

  Simon --------- Aug 19, 1821 - Sep 15, 1892

  Susan --------- Wife of Simon Hall
                  Oct 29, 1823 - Oct 27, 1892

Harris
  Mary
  Katherine ----- Wife of Dr. E. P. Harris
                  Jan 2, 1841 - Sep 26, 1901

Hillyer
  Agnes Carr ---- Wife of J. M. Hillyer
                  Feb 17, 1865 - Jun 16, 1889

Holmes
  Capt. James
  H. ------------ Jan 15, 1838 - Mar 1, 1889

  Thomas N. ----- A native of North Carolina
                  (No dates)

  Tommie -------- (No dates)

Jones
  John D. ------- Mar 6, 1846 - Oct 26, 1920

  Redding H. ---- Mar 4, 1810 - Jan 16, 1897

  Sarah J. ------ Jul 7, 1849 - __?__

Jowers
  Ellen --------- Wife of W. M. Jowers
                  Jul 11, 1844 - May 7, 1924

  W. M. --------- 1833 - 1915

Lummus
  William A. ---- Born Abbeville Dist. S.C.
                  Apr 5, 1812 - Jan 16, 1864

Marshall
  Elizabeth
  Brooks -------- Wife of M. A. Marshall
                  Nov 3, 1807 in Georgia
                  Sep 27, 1857 Gaston, Ala.

  Matthew A. ---- Feb 20, 1804 Jones Co. Ga.
                  Jan 21, 1881 Gaston, Ala.

Martin
  J. A. --------- 1860 - 1932

Mason
  Elder Ben ----- Jan 21, 1789 - Feb 18, 1848

  Mary H. ------- Dec 27, 1831 - Dec 19, 1903

  Thomas -------- (No dates)

Masters
  Jennie -------- Jan 11, 1858 - Aug 19, 1931

  Joseph B. ----- Sep 25, 1844 - Jan 13, 1918

May
  Sarah A. ------ Wife of Thomas B. May
                  Died Oct 12, 1852
                  22 yrs 11 mos 2 days

Mellown
  Julia Hagins -- Jun 28, 1842 - Jan 18, 1882

Mitchell
  David A. ------ Aug 1, 1854 - Dec 24, 1925

  Mary E. ------- 1857 - 1937

  William H. ---- 1850 - 1937

Modawell
  Alice Eloise -- Dau S. D. & Sallie Fulford
                  Nov 5, 1849 - Aug 5, 1906

Mosley
  Susan ---------- 1852 - 1928

Mundy
  Emma Tate ----- Wife of P. L. Mundy
                  Apr 11, 1855 - May 8, 1893

Nelson
  _?_ --------- Father of Abigail Cahoon
                Born 1700s Died 1800s

Pate
  Ida ----------- Sep 16, 1857 - Mar 16, 1889

Powell
  Elizabeth Ann - Born Jul 5, 1832
                  Died at home of J. C. Ezell
                  Jan 9, 1911

Pratt
  Derius Edward - Jul 4, 1861 - Nov 1, 1955

  Elizabeth P. -- May 2, 1843 - Dec 3, 1920

  George A.------ May 13, 1843 - Apr 19, 1897

  Sallie Boland - Wife of D. E. Pratt
                  Aug 31, 1864 - Feb 9, 1891

Purser
  Charles ------- Aug 26, 1802 - Apr 30, 1884

  Sarah Ann ----- Wife of Charles Purser
                  Sep 14, 1812 - Feb 1, 1873

Radcliffe
  Frank --------- Oct 5, 1844 - Feb 24, 1929

  Minnie A. ----- Aug 24, 1861 - Dec 28, 1941

Rew
  Margaret ------ Wife of William B. Rew
                  Sep 19, 1816 - May 3, 1885

  Mattie K. ----- Oct 23, 1859 - Nov 21, 1949

  R. H. --------- Jun 9, 1858 - Aug 15, 1935

Rew (contd)
W. B. --------- Jul 22, 1819 - Jul 17, 1906

Roberts
Jack ----------- Aug 2, 1821 - Jan 30, 1909

Nancy Ann ----- Wife of Jack Roberts
Apr 15, 1833 - Oct 2, 1903

Rumley
Elizabeth
Tolson -------- Nov 12, 1815 - Jan 5, 1885

Martin -------- Jan 19, 1807 - Mar 10, 1873

Scott
Rebecca ------- Born in Edgecombe Co. N.C.
Died in Sumter Co. Ala.
Aug 18, 1896 Age 101

Sheldon
Mary W. ------- Wife of Israel Sheldon
Jun 27, 1811 - Oct 7, 1841

Shurley
America ------- Wife of Thomas Shurley
Dec 24, 1833 - Sep 7, 1905

Mariah E. ----- Feb 7, 1847 - Dec 10, 1848

Richard D. ---- Mar 5, 1851 - Oct 3, 1852

Sarah A. ------ Dec 8, 1844 - Nov 28, 1845

Thomas -------- Jan 17, 1816 - Jul 2, 1898

Speed
James
Franklin ------ Apr 21, 1834 - Jan 7, 1893

John B. ------- Oct 13, 1858 - Aug 28, 1900

Margaret Jane - Apr 18, 1832 - Sep 14, 1914

Martha Ann ---- Jul 21, 1842 - Jun 6, 1924

Martha Carr --- Sep 20, 1850 - Jun 10, 1930

Speed (contd)
  Wager O. ------ Aug 5, 1803 - Nov 6, 1865

Stevenson
  Drucilla
  Elizabeth ----- Dau H. & Mary Stevenson
                 Oct 28, 1833 - Jun 12, 1844

  Humphrey ------ Jan 27, 1799 - Oct 2, 1848

Tate
  Sarah Gray ---- 1823 - Jul 24, 1905

Tew
  James A. ------ Jun 26, 1860 - Feb 18, 1942

Thorn
  Rebecca -------- Jan 1, 1862 - Sep 22, 1942

Vail
  Dade Portis --- Son R. P. & S. D. Vail
                 Oct 18, 1857 - Jan 17, 1869

  Sarah H. D. --- Dau R. P. & S. D. Vail
                 Mar 4, 1851 - Oct 24, 1852

  Sarah Olivia -- Wife of R. P. Vail
                 Nov 25, 1824 - Mar 15, 1863

Wallace
  Eliza R. ------ Wife of Josephus Wallace
                 Mar 13, 1838 - Feb 25, 1912

  Josephus ------ Born in Newbern, N.C.
                 Died in York Station, Ala.
                 Aug 16, 1835 - Mar 30, 1903

Walton
  J. T. --------- Aug 4, 1849 - Aug 23, 1905

  Louise H. ----- Wife of J. P. Walton
                 Jan 18, 1857 - Aug 12, 1912

  R. J. --------- Jun 12, 1859 - Feb 13, 1904

  Rachel Laura -- Jul 21, 1821 - Jun 23, 1887

Ward

A. Tommie ----- Wife of D. S. Ward
 Apra 26, 1840 - May 21, 1883

Ann M. -------- Wife of Solomon Ward
 Jul 22, 1821 - Oct 4, 1895

Dr. H. B. ----- Oct 7, 1852 - Dec 31, 1917

Hattie C. ----- May 22, 1858 - Dec 15, 1909

James W. ------ Oct 4, 1848 - Sep 2, 1913

Laura R. ------ Wife of Dr. H. B. Ward
 Jan 31, 1857 - Mar 30, 1884

Mollie H. ----- Wife of D. S. Ward
 Jun 27, 1848 - Jul 17, 1895

Solomon ------- Sep 10, 1810 - Nov 4, 1874

Wallace M. ---- Son Solomon & Ann Ward
 Jul 29, 1860 - Aug 18, 1861

Welch

Sgt. L. S. ---- (No dates) CSA

Westcott

Georgie E. ---- Son J. E. & G. E. Westcott
 Dec 3, 1857 - Jun 9, 1863

Georgie E.
Preston ------- Wife of J. E. Westcott
 Born Knoxville, Ga.
 Sep 29, 1836
 Died Lisman, Ala.
 Aug 28, 1921

Joseph Edwin -- Born in Pawtuxet, R. I.
 Died in Opelika, Ala.
 May 2, 1910 CSA

Mollie E. ----- Dau J. E. & G. E. Westcott
 Apr 12, 1860 - Jun 5, 1863

Winningham

J. H. --------- Nov 19, 1839 - Nov 6, 1927

Winningham (contd)
  Nancy E. ------ Jul 6, 1851 - Jul 19, 1931

Young
  Dr. O. C. ----- Jun 17, 1852 - May 4, 1893

COODY CEMETERY

From County Road 10, approximately 3 3/10 miles south of Cuba, turn south on County Road 5. After 5 miles, turn southeast on County Road 6. At 1 1/10 miles, turn south on an unnamed dirt road. The cemetery is approximately 1/2 mile up this road, about 50 yards west, in the woods.

Baskin
  B. J. --------- Sep 7, 1839 - Sep 12, 1855

  C. A. --------- Aug 10, 1834 - Jan 9, 1872

  John ---------- Jan 20, 1813 - Jan 28, 1901

  John T. ------- Sep 13, 1849 - Oct 24, 1850

  Margaret M. --- Jun 4, 1847 - Jun 9, 1847

  Mary S. ------- Jan 21, 1838 - Dec 21, 1841

  Nancy --------- Wife of John
                  Born in Lancaster Dist. S. C.
                  May 26, 1813 - Apr 18, 1873

  Nancy E. ------ May 2, 1842 - Sep 24, 1855

CROOM CEMETERY

Located about 1/2 mile north of County Road 42, 2 3/10 miles east of State Highway 17.

Croom
  Bryan --------- Jan 10, 1839 - Nov 12, 1863

Croom (contd)
  Evelyn -------- (No dates)

  James Bryan --- (No dates)

  James Richard - (No dates)

  Nicholas P. --- Jul 30, 1833 - Mar 20, 1866

  Richard ------- Sep 20, 1805 - Feb 2, 1859

  Richard Bryan - (No dates)

  Winifred B. --- Born at Spring Hill, Lenoir Co.
                N. C. Oct 17, 1812
                Died Sumter Co. Ala.
                Oct 1, 1848

Whitfield
  James George -- Mar 18, 1840 - May 5, 1923

  Susan Croom --- Aug 2, 1841 - Jun 30, 1920

CURL CEMETERY

Located on the north side of the Little Southern Railroad (abandoned) about 5 miles east of York.

Curl
  Infant ---------- Dau of Willis & Penelope Curl
                 Sep 1859

  Jefferson Davis - May 1, 1860 - Sep 28, 1861

  Sarah Ann ------- Nov 20, 1863 - Aug 5, 1864

DAVIS CEMETERY

Located on the south bank of the Sucarnoochee River, approximately 1 mile west of the intersection of the river with Interstates 20 and 59.

Danner
    Robert G. ----- Son H. G. & E. G. Danner
                     Born 1860   Died 1863

    Susan Emmer --- Dau H. G. & E. G. Danner
                     Feb 2, 1864   Died 1868

Davis
    William R. ---- Oct 8, 1831 - Dec 11, 1871

DENTON CEMETERY

Located approximately 3 1/2 miles east of Geiger on land of Sumter Farm & Stock Company.

Parker
    E. J. --------- Born 29 Feb 1814
                    Died 5 Feb 1888

DILLARD CEMETERY
(Destroyed)

Located on the south bank of Bodka Creek, about 2 miles north of County Road 24 and about 2 miles west of State Highway 17.

Dillard
    Eliza --------- Dau Dr. J. J. & N. C. Dillard
                   Oct 31, 1829 - Oct 17, 1851

    John J. ------- Born in Amherst Co. Va.
                 Mar 7, 1797 - Oct 10, 1850

    Watson W. ----- Jun 22, 1843 - Aug 14, 1856

ELIZABETH CHURCH CEMETERY

At 9 2/10 miles south of York on State Highway 17, turn southeast on Bragg Road. The church and cemetery are on the south side of this road at a distance of approximately 7/10 mile.

Alexander
Eli E. -------- Aug 1849 - Jun 1918

Hezekiah ------ B Abt 1800 Charlotte, N.C.

Ibbie E. L. --- Jun 30, 1821 - Sep 12, 1889

Samuel
Caldwell ------ 1855 - 1926

Susie H. ------ Wife of Eli
              Jul 1865 - Dec 1905

William Hiram - Nov 23, 1860 - Dec 5, 1927

William S. ---- Aug 4, 1817 - Dec 29, 1878

Allison
William O. ---- Aug 5, 1852 - Nov 18, 1865

Beggs
Frank A. ------ Son William & Martha
              1859 - 1864

Louisa V. H. -- Dau William & Martha
              1862

Bingham
Mary ---------- Jul 27, 1786 - Jan 21, 1853

Col. Samuel --- Apr 12, 1780 - Feb 21, 1853

Brown
Infant -------- Of H. & E. B.
              Died May 10, 1855

Carrigan
George
Theodore ------ Son J. W. & O. C.
              Oct 25, 1851 - Oct 25, 1852

Carrigan (contd)
  Infant -------- Of J. W. & O. C.
                  Died Jan 27, 1849

Hale
  Joseph Warren - Nov 18, 1817 - Nov 24, 1886

  Margaret
  Alexander ----- Nov 8, 1824 - Jul 5, 1901

  Mary
  Catherine ----- Oct 11, 1851 - Sep 8, 1877

  Mary E. ------- Dau J. W. & M. A.
                  Nov 14, 1859 - Aug 5, 1884

  Mary Emma ----- Wife of W. F.
                  Oct 12, 1856 - Sep 23, 1918

  William Frank - Aug 4, 1855 - Oct 27, 1930

Herd
  Eleanor ------- Died 4/27/1887   Age 80
                  (No marker)

Holley
  W. G. --------- Sep 20, 1859 - May 29, 1918

McDonald
  Daniel A. ----- May 17, 1807 - May 20, 1858

  Daniel B. ----- Apr 27, 1849 - May 20, 1885

  Louisa M. ----- Apr 29, 1856 - Jan 16, 1941

  Martha A. ----- Sep 20, 1821 - Feb 1, 1889

Nix
  Mrs. M. L. ---- Aug 17, 1843 - Aug 31, 1911

Pendergrass
  John H. ------- Apr 22, 1862 - Oct 19, 1938

Phillips
  Annie E. ------ Nov 27, 1862 - Feb 24, 1932

  Thomas A. ----- Mar 1, 1858 - Aug 9, 1917

Salmon
  William
    Thomas -------- Nov 8, 1838 - Dec 6, 1868

Shelby
  Martha N. ----- Wife of J. T.
                  Oct 18, 1845 - Jan 3, 1883

Sprott
  Robert -------- Born County Down, Ireland
                  Aug 8, 1808 Died in Sumter Co.
                  Ala. Aug 25, 1862

Williams
  Maggie W. ----- Dec 25, 1838 - Jul 31, 1910

ELLIOTT CEMETERY

From State Highway 17 at Boyd, approximately 9 miles north of York, turn west on County Road 12. At 1 1/2 miles, turn north on the Frank Dial Road. The cemetery is in the yard of a home on the east side of the road at a distance of approximately 1/10 mile.

Elliott
  Elizabeth
    Jane ---------- Born in Hanover Co. N.C.
                    Nov 16, 1826 - Feb 14, 1893

    John Knox ----- Born in Pulaski, Tenn.
                    Mar 1, 1819 - Feb 13, 1892

    John Luther --- Son of John K. & Elizabeth Jane
                    May 28, 1859 - Sep 21, 1878

    William
    Melangthon ---- Son of John Knox & Elizabeth
                    Jane Eakins Elliott
                    Feb 8, 1861 - Jun 9, 1919

ESKRIDGE CEMETERY

Located between U. S. Highway 11 and the adjoining Norfolk Southern Railroad, approximately 3 miles north of the intersecton of U. S. Highway 11 and State Highway 28 north of Livingston.

Eskridge
J. H. Pettigrew ----- Born Jun 7, 1805   Died 1877

Lemuel -------- 1807 - Mar 17, 1879

S. ------------ Dec 12, 1798 - Dec 18, 1866

Lancaster
Albert -------- May 6, 1810 - May 1870

Joseph -------- Oct 18, 1850   Died 1871

ESTES CEMETERY

From County Road 21, approximately 6/10 mile south of Epes, turn east on the Port of Epes Road. After 3/4 mile, continue straight ahead on an unnamed dirt road. The cemetery is located approximately 2/3 mile north of this road at a total of 2 3/10 miles from County Road 21.

Estes
R. A. --------- Jul 3, 1839 - May 14, 1922

Susian -------- Jul 13, 1840 - Mar 26, 1917

EVANS CEMETERY

Follow County Road 6 south of Kinterbish for approximately 1 1/10 mile to the crossing of Mundy Branch. The cemetery is about 1/4 mile southeast of the road at that point.

Evans
  Rev. A. P. ---- Born Mar 6, 1833
                  Died Jul 17, 1905

EVINGTON CEMETERY
(Choctaw County)

From State Highway 17, approximately 11 1/2 miles south of York, turn east on County Road 42. Continue for approximately 13 1/2 miles to the Choctaw County line. After another 1/10 mile, turn east on a dirt drive to the Oakchia Estate house and cemetery.

Evington
  Caroline L. --- Wife of Wm. H. Evington Jr.
                  Nov 17, 1846 - Jan 21, 1897

EZELLE CEMETERY
(Choctaw County)

From State Highway 17, approximately 17 miles south of York, turn east on Choctaw County Road 42. The cemetery is about 50 yards south of this road at a distance of approximately 4 7/10 miles, across the road from the old J. M. Young home.

Ezelle
  Delia E. ------ Dau of John & M. M. Ezelle
                  Jan 24, 1852 - May 21, 1864

  John ---------- Died Jul 6, 1853   Age 60

  Margaret T. --- Wife of W. J. Ezelle
                  Oct 15, 1835 - Jul 25, 1885

Walton
  LeVert F. ----- Son of Dr. S. & M. M. Walton
                    Oct 20, 1862 - Jun 25, 1864

Ward
  A. E. --------- Wife of E. H. Ward
                    Aug 12, 1847 - Jul 9, 1864

GAINESVILLE ODD FELLOWS CEMETERY

Located on the south side of State Highway 116 in the west side of Gainesville.

Anderson
  Hannah Wright - Died Jul 23, 1860 Age 65

Avery
  Joseph C. ----- Died Mar 22, 1862 Age 36

Beavers
  Thomas W. ----- Nov 18, 1818 - Jun 22, 1851

Bell
  Effie H. ------ Dau Turner & Sallie H. Bell
                Mar 4, 1864 - Aug 5, 1864

  Lillian L. ---- Dau Turner & Sallie H. Bell
                Mar 4, 1864 - Jul 4, 1864

Bradshaw
  Elizabeth R. -- Born Feb 16, 1811 Age 74

  James --------- Born Sep 3, 1835

  Janie --------- Wife of John W. Bradshaw
                Jul 23, 1843 - Sep 12, 1893

  R. T. --------- Born Mar 4, 1841

  Robert -------- Born Jan 1, 1798 Age 74

  Thomas W. ----- Born Feb 22, 1853

Brown
  Jere Chapman -- Son I. C. & M. A. Brown
                    Died Sep 20, 1865
                    Age 3 yr 10 mo

Childe
  Amanda M. ----- 2nd Wife William H. Childe
                    Dau G. B. Mobley
                    Oct 22, 1828 - Jan 17, 1910

  Mary H. ------- Dau W. H. & Emma Childe
                    Died Oct 11, 1877
                    Age 19 yrs 8 mo 16 days

  W. H. --------- Dec 23, 1826 - Oct 25, 1907

Cooke
  Katie G. ------ Dau C. & S. G. Cooke
                    Died Aug 5, 1859

  Susan Reavis -- 1863 - 1941

  Turner R. ----- Infant son C. & S. G. Cooke
                    Died Aug 12, 1859

Crow
  Walter Elmer -- Mar 24, 1862 - Nov 20, 1937

Derryberry
  Celestia
  Jolly --------- Died Oct 21, 1918

  Thomas Jacob -- Died Feb 27, 1917

Dillard
  Edward W. ----- Died Apr 7, 1857

Dimick
  Clara L. ------ Died Nov 15, 1868
                    Age 6 yrs 11 mo

  George
  Hamilton ------ Died Jul 19, 1865 Age 2

  Nelson T. ----- Died May 22, 1868 Age 34

Eaton
  H. F. --------- Died May 2, 1859 Age 45

Eaton (contd)
  T. ------------ Died Oct 10, 1840 Age 58

Fields
  Frank P. ------ Dec 6, 1854 - Jun 18, 1948

Flamme
  Freeda Mary --- Wife of J. P. Flamme
                  Oct 10, 1839 - Mar 6, 1916

  John P. ------- Born 1835 Died Mar 29, 1900

Gast
  Edward
  Harrison ------ Episcopalian Lay Reader
                 Confederate soldier
                 Died 1885

  Ellen Sharon -- Died 1895

  Madden -------- Son Edward & Ellen Gast
                 (No dates)

  Pierre Du Gast
  Siieur De
  Months -------- Protestant Viceroy of France
                 to New France 1603

  Thomas -------- Son Edward & Ellen Gast
                 (No dates)

  William ------- Son Edward & Ellen Gast
                 (No dates)

Gates
  Eddie ---------- Son of S. A. & M. A. Gates
                 Died Jun 15, 1860

Gibbens
  Winfield
  Scott ---------- Son H. D. & Mary E. Gibbens
                 Oct 2, 1852 - Oct 3, 1853

Gibbs
  H. T. ---------- Oct 26, 1848 - Apr 7, 1921

  Mattie Scott -- Dec 7, 1855 - Nov 15, 1938

Harris
   Augustin H. --- Nov 20, 1808 - Feb 3, 1864

   Edwin Percy --- Oct 29, 1851 - Jun 8, 1852

   M. W. --------- Wife of A. H. Harris
                      Jan 20, 1813 - Jan 16, 1852

   Mary E. ------- Feb 5, 1849 - Jul 26, 1949

   Y. W. --------- Age 54 (No dates)

Harwood
   Mary Scott
   Gray ---------- Wife of S. B. Harwood
                    Aug 28, 1835 - Nov 30, 1897

   Robert
   Ellyson, M.D. - Feb 4, 1863 - Mar 23, 1953

   Ruffin Gray --- Aug 20, 1861 - Oct 6, 1886

   Samuel B. ----- Sep 27, 1817 - Nov 22, 1901

Herndon
   John Minor ---- Son Dabney & Margaret Herndon
                    Mar 7, 1851 - Jun 18, 1852

   Lucy Chew ----- Youngest dau of Edward and
                    Malvina Ann Herndon
                    Died Aug 24, 1843 Age 7

Hill
   Emma ---------- Dau J. D. & R. F. Hill
                    Aug 4, 1855 - Apr 2, 1862

   Kate ---------- Dau J. D. & R. F. Hill
                    Aug 21, 1861 - Apr 15, 1862

   Sallie
   Roberts ------- Dau J. D. & R. F. Hill
                    Died Jul 23, 1857
                    Age 7 mos 4 days

Horn
   Elizabeth A.
   Massey -------- Wife of Iredell Horn
                    Feb 1828 - Jan 1897

Horn (contd)
  Iredell H. ---- Apr 22, 1818 - Jul 5, 1886

  Nancy A. ------ Aug 31, 1786 - Aug 14, 1874

Hutchins
  James L. ------ Died Apr 6, 1872
                  78 yrs 2 mos 9 days

  Sarah R. ------ Wife of James L. Hutchins
                  Feb 22, 1804 - Oct 27, 1887

Jackson
  Henry M., MD -- Died Jul 21, 1853

  James --------- (No dates)

Lee
  John William -- Jul 19, 1850 - Jan 9, 1932

Long
  Alice M.
  Eaton --------- Wife of H. D. Long
                  Died Oct 24, 1880
                  Age 28 yrs 2 days

  Annie Horn
  "Muddie" ------ Wife of Thomas Long
                  1846 - 1937

  Donna Julia --- Jul 8, 1851 - May 6, 1852

  Henry D. ------ Born in Russell Co. Va.
                  Oct 6, 1837 - Nov 30, 1912

  Julia Jackson - 2nd Wife of H. D. Long
                  Died Sep 21, 1893
                  55 yrs 2 mos 12 days

  Thomas M. ----- Born in Russell Co. Va.
                  Dec 13, 1840 - Jul 26, 1915

McMahon
  A. W. --------- Jan 24, 1817 - May 8, 1889

  E. R. C. ------ Wife of Col. R. G. McMahon
                  Died Oct 2, 1883
                  A 73 y 3 m 15 d

McMahon (contd)
Mattie ? ------ (No dates)

Col. R. G. ---- Died Aug 8, 1880
                A 66 y 10 m 14 d

McTurk
Isabella ------ Died Sep 17, 1862   Age 24

Meredith
Ann Eliza ----- Wife of Reuben A. Meredith
                Jan 19, 1820 - Apr 29, 1869

Reuben
Anderson ------ May 29, 1817 - Aug 29, 1878

Metcalf
Jacob R. ------ Born in Kentucky
               Aug 10, 1815 - Jan 19, 1864

Mitchell
Daniel -------- Apr 7, 1829 - Mar 11, 1890

James --------- Born in Abvil Dist. S.C.
               1787 - Dec 17, 1855

Martha
Augustus ------ Apr 19, 1844 - Mar 13, 1934

Moore
Jemima -------- Consort of A. L. D. Moore
               Dau Jemima & James Mitchell
               Nov 24, 1826 - May 22, 1852

Mooring
J. A. --------- Born in Edgecombe Co. N.C.
               Jun 21, 1821 - Jul 14, 1874

John Scott ---- 1862 - 1932

Lizzie LeRoy -- Dau J. A. & M. A. Mooring
               Sep 9, 1856 - Sep 26, 1859

Martha A. ----- Wife of J. A. Mooring
               Mar 27, 1831 - Dec 4, 1867

Nance
Averrila ------ Wife of W. T. Nance
          Mar 2, 1828 - Nov 11, 1859?

James Walter -- Aug 15, 1855 - May 10, 1858

Sarah --------- Wife of W. T. Nance
          Died Oct 4, 1855
          A 29 yrs 13 days

William ------- Pvt., Co. A, 36th Regt.,
          Alabama Infantry, CSA
          Sep 29, 1824 - Sep 15, 1864

William H. ---- Son of W. T. & Sarah Nance
          Died Jun 31, 1851
          A 2 yrs 21 days

Nelson
F. J. W. ------ A native of Carterret Co. N. C.
          Sep 29, 1799 - Feb 11, 1851

O'Neil
Addie E. ------ Wife of J. H. O'Neil
          Feb 26, 1858 - Oct 20, 1902

Paash
Sophia E. ----- Wife of Henry Paash
          Died Dec 9, 1860
          A 36 yrs 6 mo 28 days

Parker
Arthur
Theophilus ---- Son C. & A. A. Parker
          Died Jul 6, 1856

Parks
Reubin A. ----- Dec 7, 1853 - Feb 3, 1870

Post
Agmon --------- Dec 21, 1794 - Sep 1871

Azubah
Chapman ------- Mar 4, 1809 - Apr 9, 1852

Ragsdale
Hiram C. ------ Mar 1812 - Nov 19, 1891

Rambo
    Jincy --------- Jun 21, 1789 - Sep 27, 1852
    Mary J. ------- Feb 4, 1855 - Jan 1, 1857
Reavis
    Robert E. ----- May 21, 1852 - Sep 25, 1855
Rogers
    John Aduston -- Sep 1, 1861 - Sep 22, 1936
Sanders
    Edward C. ----- Jan 7, 1825 - Apr 15, 1879
    William ? ----- (No dates)
Scott
    John B. ------- Sep 13, 1828 - Aug 4, 1856
    Kate W. ------- Born in Camden, Arkansas
                    Died Nov 29, 1863 Age 17
Smith
    Albert Henry -- Son Dr. A. H. & L. A. Smith
                    Apr 7, 1850 - Jun 27, 1867
    Harriet
    Harris -------- 1838 - 1925
    Louisa Ann ---- Consort of Dr. A. H. Smith
                    Jan 6, 1823 - Nov 4, 1852
Smithline
    Charles ------- Aug 15, 1861 - Apr 3, 1944
Snow
    Hamilton Post - Apr 4, 1826 - Mar 21, 1907
    Kate Amelia --- Dau H. P. & M. E. Snow
                    Died Aug 12, 1862
                    Age 5 mo
    Leveret ------- Son H. P. & M. E. Snow
                    Died Dec 23, 1862
                    A 2 yr 1 mo
    Maria Esther -- Wife of Hamilton P. Snow
                    Apr 10, 1832 - Jun 16, 1912

Snow (contd)
  Willie
  Atwater ------- Son H. P. & M. E. Snow
                   Died Sep 21, 1859
                   A 2 yr 4 mo

Soule
  Abigail ------- Dau John M. & Virginia Soule
                   Died Jul 18, 1851
                   1 yr 9 mo 6 days

  Fannie -------- Dau John M. & Virginia Soule
                   Jun 27, 1852 - Jul 10, 1853

  John M. ------- Apr 11, 1812 - Oct 3, 1860

Stewart
  Samuel A. ----- Dec 24, 1856 - Nov 10, 1933

Stillman
  Carrie Fraser - Dau Rev. C. A. Stillman
                   Dec 27, 1852 - Jun 3, 1880

  Fannie R.
  Collins ------- Wife Rev. C. A. Stillman
                   Jul 14, 1838 - Jan 7, 1868

  Martha
  Hammond ------- Wife Rev. C. A. Stillman
                   Born in Milledgeville, Ga.
                   Oct 15, 1816 - Aug 8, 1863

  Mary ---------- Born Eutaw, Ala. Nov 2, 1847
                   Died Tuscaloosa, Ala.
                   Nov 24, 1870

  Sallie Dudley - Died Apr 29, 1864
                   14 yrs & 6 mo

Stuart
  Bettie -------- Dau Dr. R. F. & M. A. Stuart
                   Age 10 mo   (No dates)

  Martha A. ----- Wife of Dr. R. F. Stuart
                   Sep 21, 1821 - Mar 10, 1863

Tureman
    Matilda H. ---- Wife of Z. Tureman
                    Died Aug 13, 1852 Age 40

Turrentine
    Joshua Lucy --- Born in Gadsden, Alabama
                    Dec 27, 1849 - Dec 24, 1910

Williamson
    Lena Harris --- Died Jul 7, 1869

    Susan D. ------ Wife of James Williamson
                    Apr 15, 1836 - Dec 18, 1855

    Virginia B. --- Died Feb 22, 1858

GAINESVILLE OLD CEMETERY

From the intersection of State Highway 39 and County Road 21 in Gainesville, follow County Road 21 south for 6/10 mile and turn east on a dirt road. After 300 feet, turn north on a dirt drive to the cemetery.

Abrams
    Georgianna
    Lee ----------- Dau William P. & S. L. Abrams
                    Died Dec 4, 1847
                    Age 2 yr 1 mo 10 days

Alexander
    Caroline A. --- Wife William Alexander Jr.
                    Dau J. C. & A. C. Coward
                    Jun 25, 1852 - Sep 3, 1873

    James Tytler -- Son William & M. T. Alexander
                    Oct 29, 1853 Age 7 mo

    Margaret
    Tytler -------- Wife of William Alexander
                    Died Jan 21, 1856 Age 39

    Mary Jane ----- Dau William & M. T. Alexander
                    Died Jul 1, 1858
                    Age 3 mo 5 days

Alexander (contd)
Shadrack
  Minniece ------ Son William & M. T. Alexander
                   Feb 19, 1856   Age 6 wks

Barret
  Ann B. -------- Wife of Dr. John S. Barret
                  Born in Presque Isle, King
                  William Co. Va.
                  Jul 9, 1781 - Mar 2, 1857

  Caroline ------ Jul 15, 1821 - Oct 27, 1872

  Dr. John S. --- Born in Richmond, Va.
                  Jun 18, 1782 - Nov 14, 1856

  Pattie
  Virginia ------ Wife of Benjamin T. Barret
                  Born in Louisa Co. Va. 1832
                  Died in Mobile Ala. 1859

Bennett
  B. Maria ------ Wife of John Bennett
                  Died Jan 24, 1862   Age 33

  Katey --------- Dau J. & B. M. Bennett
                  Died Sep 17, 1858
                  1 yr 1 mo 6 days

  Mary ---------- Dau J. & B. M. Bennett
                  Died Sep 17, 1857
                  Age 2 yrs 5 mo 22 days

Bickley
  Margaret
  Alice --------- Born in Lebanon, Va.
                  Nov 24, 1862 - May 5, 1919

  Thomas
  Jefferson ----- Born in Castlewood, Va.
                  May 5, 1862 - Sep 4, 1914

Bliss
  James --------- Died Apr 17, 1891   Age 74

  Jonathan ------ Born Randolph, Vt. Jul 15, 1799
                  Came to Ala. 1/8/1836
                  Died Jul 27, 1879

Bliss (contd)
    Laura --------- Feb 4, 1806 - Jun 9, 1844

    Lucretia
    Leverett ------ Wife of Jonathan Bliss
                    Apr 30, 1805 - Mar 26, 1842

    Lucy M. ------- Apr 21, 1819 - Apr 22, 1843

    Mary Kidder --- Wife of Jonathan Bliss
                    Mar 6, 1809 - Apr 12, 1857

    William L. ---- May 9, 1837 - Aug 28, 1842

Blue
    Lucy ---------- Born 1855 Died Jul 14, 1910

Brackett
    Dr. Anson ----- Born in Wheelock, Vt.
                    Feb 20, 1803 - Dec 11, 1855

    Mary
    Chamberlin ---- Wife Dr. Anson Brackett
                    May 23, 1806 - Feb 25, 1851

Bryant
    J. T. --------- Oct 19, 1832 - Nov 10, 1859

Bush
    Mary E. ------- Born 1847

    William H. ---- Nov 12, 1832 - Sep 22, 1904

Byrd
    Jessie -------- Born 1844 - Died 1894

    Matilda ------- (No dates)

Carroll
    Samuel J. ----- Dec 16, 1858 - Oct 12, 1914

Christian
    Elizabeth C. -- May 30, 1831 - Nov 10, 1887

    Mary B. and her
    children, Thomas
    & Lucretia ---- Mar 14, 1806 - Mar 19, 1842

Christian (contd)
Mollie -------- Dau T. C. & E. C. Christian
Mar 22, 1858 - May 8, 1859

Turner C. ----- Died Nov 11, 1860
34 yrs 3 mo 4 days

Clark
Sylvia -------- Died Aug 12, 1912   Age 65 years

Clarke
George A. ----- Former Resident Malone, N. Y.
Died Jul 18, 1841

Colgin
Mary Ann ------ Dau John & Mary E. L. Colgin
Oct 18, 1857 - Dec 24, 1881

Mary E. L.
Neville ------- Wife of John Colgin
Mar 9, 1825 - Oct 28, 1880

Sallie Elyson - Dau John & Mary E. L. Colgin
Jan 24, 1853 - Apr 1903

Dabbs
Sarah --------- Died Oct 25, 1904   Age about 70

Dandridge
J. N. --------- Aug 7, 1856 - Apr 17, 1914

Davis
Hannah -------- Died Jan 15, 1891   Age about 80

Doss
Elizabeth
Grizzle ------- Dau John & Mary Doss   Born
Elbert Co. Ga.   May 15, 1806
Died Jul 24, 1850   Age 44

Dunning
Robert Wiley -- May 4, 1848 - Sep 26, 1916

Sallie Ann ---- Aug 7, 1845 - Jun 23, 1915

Ellis
Fannie M. ----- Jun 24, 1859 - Jan 9, 1926

Ellis (contd)
   Gray ---------- Born Dec 29, 1845
                        Died __?__

Embree
   Infant -------- Dau Sarah L. & Albert Embree
                       Born and Died Nov 8, 1857

   Mary
   Elizabeth ----- Dau Sarah L. & Albert Embree
                       May 1, 1855 - Aug 1, 1857

Fawcett
   Maj. Lyle B. -- Died Mar 25, 1838 Age 35

   Robert B. ----- Died Sep 22, 1842
                       Age 4 yrs 11 mo 13 days

Foster
   Mary Mobley --- Wife of R. H. Foster
                       Died May 5, 1860 Age 25

Frost
   Ezekial and
   M. D. (twins) - Sons J. W. & M. V. Frost
                       Died Apr 27, 1855

   N. S. --------- Jan 4, 1855 - Oct 15, 1859

Gill
   Mrs. M. M. ---- Born in Franklin Co. N. C.
                       Nov 16, 1797 - Jan 26, 1883

   William H. ---- Jun 24, 1825 - May 29, 1912

Gray
   Nancy Berton -- Born in Lebanon, Va.
                       Jan 10, 1819 - Feb 10, 1904

Greenlee
   Hugh ---------- Nov 16, 1826 - Nov 1, 1904

   Mary
   Elizabeth ----- Mar 28, 1838 - Sep 27, 1914

Griffin
   Anderson ------ Born 1847 - Died 1891

Griffin (contd)
  Rev. Dandridge
    G. ------------ Oct 1, 1860 - Oct 24, 1901

  Rev. Edward --- Dec 25, 1811 - Aug 8, 1886

  Eliza Jane ---- Wife of A. H. Griffin
                  Born Franklin Co. N. C.
                  May 4, 1817 - Jun 5, 1851

  George -------- Born 1844 - Mar 4, 1904

  J. E. --------- 1856 - 1934

  Mary ---------- Wife of Edd Griffin
                  Born 1817 - Died 1893

Guard
  A. J. --------- Died Dec 6, 1900 Age 85

  Mary A. ------- Wife of A. J. Guard
                  Died Nov 1, 1904 Age 84

Harris
  Dora O. ------- Wife of Y. W. Harris
                  Aug 20, 1842 - Mar 16, 1874

Harrison
  Harriet ------- Died Apr 28, 1903 Aged 69 yrs

Henning
  George -------- A native of Newry, Ireland
                  & a resident of Moile, Ala.
                  Born 1803 Died Jul 21, 1840

Hibbler
  Eliza Watkins - 1844 - 1917

  Robert -------- 1845 - 1920

Hill
  Robert -------- Aug 1, 1823 - Nov 25, 1898

  Capt. Robert
  & Wife
  Elizabeth ----- Died 1846

Hughes
H. H. ---------- Oct 16, 1862 - Sep 12, 1897

Hutton
Anderson ------ Jun 22, 1938 - Jan 10, 1898

Ann ----------- Died Jun 4, 1925   Age 74 yrs

Emmett
Calhoun ------- Born in Greene Co. Ala.
May 4, 1850 - Jul 2, 1880

Jackson
Lucy Barret
Reavis -------- Aug 24, 1842 - Jul 15, 1876

Thomas Klugh -- Dec 17, 1828 - Aug 5, 1902

Jeter
Sarah M. ------ Died Jul 31, 1849   Age 70

Johnston
Ella ---------- Mar 13, 1855 - Jan 28, 1874
(Same marker with Mollie McMahon)

Jones
John Wootten -- Drowned Jun 2, 1851
Age 21 yr 10 mo & 6 days

South West ---- Mar 20, 1856 - Jun 26, 1904

Kemble
Sarah J. ------ Died Mar 21, 1847

Knox
Frank M. ------ Jun 5, 1853 - Feb 14, 1864

Little Maggie - (No dates)

Kring
Bettie G. ----- Wife of E. N. Kring
1845 - 1921

E. N. --------- 1836 - 1910

Lanford
John B. ------- Dec 3, 1840 - Sep 2, 1888

Lanford (contd)
  Maria Adeline
  Rogers -------- Wife of John Bibb Lanford
                        Nov 4, 1844 - Jun 14, 1932

Lewis
  Aurelia
  Axtell -------- Wife of William M. Lewis
                        Oct 6, 1811 - Jul 15, 1865

  Eliza Webster - Dau Moses & Sallie Lewis
                        Born Bristol, N.H.
                        Died Kemper Spgs, Miss.
                        Oct 1, 1843

  Laura Aurelia - Apr 6, 1844 - Apr 6, 1845

  Mary Russell -- Sep 30, 1848 - Aug 16, 1850

  Mattie G. ----- Dau William & Aurelia Lewis
                        Died Oct 19, 1862
                        16 yrs 5 mo & 5 days

  Col. Moses ---- Died Oct 7, 1836 Age 66

  Moses
  Boardman ------ Son William M. & Aurelia Lewis
                        Apr 6, 1842 - Jan 15, 1844

  Sallie Martin - Wife of Col. Moses Lewis
                        Born in Alexandria, N. H.
                        Jul 21, 1770 - Jan 10, 1852

  William M. ---- Died Feb 13, 1881 Age 83

Long
  Henderson W. -- Nov 24, 1849 - May 30, 1879

  Precilla
  Dickinson ----- Born in Russell Co. Va.
                        Aug 17, 1817
                        Died in Gainesville, Ala.
                        Oct 31, 1912

  Richard B. ---- Born in Russell Co. Va.
                        Jan 2, 1807
                        Died in Atlanta, Ga.
                        Sep 24, 1864

Manasco
  Phoebe Hill --- Died 1847

Maniece
  Thomas Oden --- Feb 1, 1859 - Mar 14, 1942

Marshall
  Mattie H.
  Rogers -------- Wife of Dr. J. B. Marshall
                Dec 3, 1853 - Jul 18, 1932

McKinney
  John ---------- Died Oct 23, 1905 Age 69 yrs

  Julia --------- 1849 - 1926

McMahon
  Carl W. ------- 1851 - 1927

  John J. ------- Feb 1, 1846 - Apr 4, 1913

  Kate ---------- Dau R. C. & E. R. C. McMahon
                Died Nov 16, 1845
                Age 1 yr 5 mo & 26 days

  Mollie -------- Oct 16, 1847 - Nov 26, 1858
  (Same marker with Ella Johnston)

Mobley
  Green B. ------ Born Fairfield Dist. of S. C.
                Died Jan 14, 1877
                Age 70 yrs 5 mo & 19 days

  Henrietta ----- 2nd Wife of Green B. Mobley
                Born in Bradford, Vermont
                Died Apr 2, 1873
                Age 71 yrs 2 mo & 2 days

  N. B. --------- Died Mar 15, 1869 Age 34

  Savilla ------- Consort of G. B. Mobley
                Died Aug 29, 1840
                Age 33 yrs 9 mo & 13 days

Moore
  Mittie T.
  Reavis -------- Wife of John V. Moore
                Aug 25, 1846 - Apr 18, 1870

Morris
  Betty S. ------ Wife of R. W. Morris
                  Dau Capt. Robert & E. S. Hill
                  Born in King William Co. Va.
                  Feb 6, 1825 - Aug 25, 1846

Morse
  Henry --------- Died Apr 1846 Age Abt 47

  Mary Ina ------ Jan 24, 1858 - Nov 8, 1874
                  Dau A. A. & C. T. Morse

O'Neal
  E. A. B. ------ Wife of Eli O'Neal
                  Born in Wythe Co. Va.
                  Died Jan 6, 1882 Age 74

Oswalt
  Minor C. ------ Pioneer of Indian Territory
                  Confederate Soldier
                  D Aug 18, 1871

  Nancy Sanford - Died Mar 6, 1876

  Robert M. ----- Nov 16, 1853 - Nov 18, 1901

Parham
  Dr. John C. --- Nov 11, 1847 - Jul 25,1903

  Lena Winston -- Sep 2, 1852 - Nov 26, 1925

  Sallie
  Whitsett ------ 1856 - 1920

Patterson
  John William -- 1847 - 1934

  Nannie P. ----- Wife of J. W. Patterson
                  Jul 26, 1844 - Dec 18, 1909

Pearson
  Dr. Isaac F. -- Apr 8, 1836 - Mar 30, 1876

  Sarah --------- Wife of Dr. E. H. Pearson
                  Died Dec 8, 1863 Age 28

Phelps
George R. ----- A native of Hill, N. H.
Died Dec 14, 1844 Age 27

Reavis
Mary B. ------- Second Dau Turner & Mary S.
Reavis
Born in Kemper Springs, Miss.
Jun 22, 1846 - May 4, 1847

Hon. Turner --- Born in Wayne Co. N. C.
Jun 18, 1811 - Jun 13, 1872

Roberts
Baker L. ------ 1839 - 1920

Lucy C. ------- 1851 - 1931

Robertson
Ida Lee ------- Dau J. G. & F. J. Robertson
Sep 29, 1860 - Jan 13, 1865

Maria E. ------ Wife of James G. Robertson
Dau W. H. & M. E. Dandridge
Born in Richmond, Va.
Jul 15, 1824 - Feb 5, 1855

Virginia ------ Dau J. G. & M. E. Robertson
Oct 14, 1843 - Jul 16, 1844

William
Francis ------- Son J. G. & M. E. Robertson
May 4, 1845 - May 3, 1846

Russell
David Moor ---- Hus Margaret McManus Russell
Apr 19, 1836 - Aug 5, 1919

Mary Bliss ---- Wife of David Moor Russell
Oct 8, 1839 - Feb 17, 1910

Mary Flint ---- Born in Massachusetts
Resident Gainesville
1836 to 1876
Died in 1876

Walter W. ----- Born in New Hampshire
Died Jun 17, 1878 Age 72

Sanders
Elizabeth J. -- Dau J. P. & R. M. Sanders
Jan 26, 1827 - Aug 29, 1840

Rosey M. ------ Oct 18, 1805 - Jan 20, 1847

Thomas J. ----- Son J. P. & R. M. Sanders
Jan 27, 1829 - Nov 27, 1841

Scott
Eln ? --------- Died Nov __?__ Age 80 yrs

Smith
Alice --------- Dau T. W. & Ann Smith
Jun 8, 1855 - Mar 18, 1859

Ann Berlin ---- Wife T. W. Smith
Born Warren Co. Va.
Aug 2, 1832 - Jan 21, 1904

Charles C. ---- Son T. W. & Ann Smith
May 3, 1857 - Mar 20, 1859

Isaac --------- Died Jun 19, 1838 Age 47

Mary ---------- Died Oct 27, 1876 Age 82

Meliss Ann
Henderson ----- Wife of O. E. Smith
Oct 1, 1843 - Jan 4, 1903

Ottaway E. ---- Mar 9, 1832 - Jan 4, 1900

Miss P. ------- Born 1830 - Jul 27, 1893

Thomas W. ----- Born in Culpepper Co. Va.
Jan 30, 1828 - Sep 3, 1884

Stanton
Joseph H. ----- Jun 29, 1860 - Feb 5, 1898

Steele
Eliza Ann ----- Dau William J. & Mary D. Steele
Aug 4, 1849 - Jul 1850

Theophilus ---- Son William J. & Mary D. Steele
Aug 24, 1846 - Jul 13, 1850

Tolbert
  Mary Ellen ---- Died May 31, 1890 Age 59 yrs

  Rhoda --------- Died Mar 12, 1908 Age 47 yrs

Turner
  Anne
  Alexander ----- Relict of Rev. William L.
               Turner of Fayetteville, N. C.
               Born in Lexington, Va.
               Died Aug 28, 1843 Age 57

Tytler
  S. J. --------- Born Nerry Co., Armach, Ireland
               Died Apr 29, 1867 Age 85

Vandegraff
  Agnetta ------- Daughter of William J. &
               Juliette Vandegraff
               Born in Mobile, Ala. Jan 2,
               1837 Died Gainesville, Ala.
               Jun 2, 1842 Age 6

  Juliette E. --- Daughter S. and Mary C.
               Vandegraff
               Dec 2, 1857 - Jul 7, 1858

  Juliette
  Ewing --------- Wife William Jacob Vandegraff
               Died Feb 17, 1874 Age 79

  Samuel B. ----- Son W. J. & Juliette Vandegraff
               Mar 1, 1842 - Feb 13, 1843

  William J. ---- Born in Scott Co. Ky. Mar 31,
               1802. Removed to Erie, Greene
               Co. Ala. in Nov 1824 where he
               resided until 184? at which
               time moved to Gainesville where
               he died May 10, 1842

Waller
  B. ------------ Born in King & Queen Co. Va.
               Aug 1789 - Jan 14, 1844

Waller (contd)
  John W., His
    Wife Lucy ----- Children Leon P., Samuel, Lucy
                      W., Corbin B., Logan, Mary B.,
                      Cary A., Bettie B. & Arthur T.

(One marker, nine foot markers, no dates)

Washington
  Bettie -------- Dau Robert & Martha Washington
                 Feb 18, 1856 - Apr 29, 1857

  Robert, Esq. -- Nov 13, 1829 - Sep 29, 1857

Watson
  Alabama W. ---- 1860 - 1835

  Hattie E. ----- 1853 - 1933

White
  John M. ------- Son George & Mary Ann White
                Mar 26, 1832 - Jul 23, 1842

  Mary Ann ------ Wife of George W. White
                Dau John & Margaret Shawver
                Born in Monroe County, Va.
                Apr 20, 1809 - Jun 21, 1842
                Age 32

Whitney
  David S. ------ Of Northampton, Mass.
                Died Apr 1, 1840 Age 51

Whitsett
  Maj. John C. -- Died Sep 14, 1860

  John G. ------- Only son of J. C. & M. B.
               Whitsett Died Apr 18, 1845
               Age 5 mo

  Laura Bliss --- Dau John C. & Martha B.
               Whitsett Died May 20, 1841
               Age 5 yr 10 mo

  Martha B. ----- Wife of John C. Whitsett
               Dec 9, 1811 - Feb 24, 1846

Whitsett (contd)
Martha
 Lucretia ------ Dau John C. & Martha B.
        Whitsett Died May 12, 1844
        Age 1 yr 8 mo

W. J. --------- Died Apr 23, 1901

Wilson
 Boyd H. ------- Died Mar 17, 1840 Age 9

Wright
 W. A. --------- Sep 30, 1847 - Aug 31, 1849

CONFEDERATE SOLDIER SECTION
GAINESVILLE OLD CEMETERY

Droll
 J. F. --------- Jun 29, 1862 Age 21

Frittenden
 James J. ------ Born Franklin Co. Alabama
       Died Gainesville, Alabama
       Aug 24, 1862 Age 32

Lowe
 Baker M. ------ Jun 7, 1862 Age 27

Turner
 C. K. --------- Of New Orleans, La.
       Died Jul 1, 1862 Age 17

(There are 115 graves of unknown soldiers)

GARBER CEMETERY

From the intersection of U. S. Highway 11 and County Road 13 south of Livingston, proceed southeast on County Road 13 for approximately 3/10 mile to an industrial plant on the north side of the road. The cemetery is approximately 500 feet from the road, behind the plant.

Browder
- Annie Bass Garber -------- Wife James Chapron Browder May 7, 1854 - Feb 1, 1922
- James Chapron - Born Hale Co. Ala. Sep 28, 1853 Died here at Chessland Jun 7, 1909

Garber
- Alexander Menzies ------- Born Stanton, Va. Apr 1, 1815 Died here at Chessland Jan 26, 1891
- Anna Maria Rhodes -------- Born Goldsboro, N. C. Aug 10, 1826 Died here at Chessland May 17, 1911
- Eugene Rhodes - Born Mar 22, 1856 Livingston, Ala. Died Jul 12, 1898 San Francisco, Cal.
- James Rhodes -- Born at Chessland, Sumter County, Ala. Feb 14, 1847 Died Uniontown, Ala. Mar 6, 1896
- Joseph Baldwin ------- Born Mar 19, 1849 at Chessland Died Apr 14, 1915 at Demopolis
- Juliet Elizabeth ----- Mar 11, 1864 - Aug 8, 1871 Age 7 yrs 5 mo

Garber (contd)
William
Coleman ------- Sep 21, 1859 - Aug 22, 1861
                Age 1 yr 11 mo 1 day

Kornegay
Danl. --------- Oct 29, 1855 - Aug 20, 1862

Elizabeth B. -- 1825 - 1890

George -------- 1816 - 1865

Robert -------- Feb 20, 1862 - Jun 12, 1863

Pope
Geo. L. ------- Oct 31, 1834 - Feb 14, 1851

Rhodes
Capt. Charles
E. ------------ Of the Confederate Army
               Jul 5, 1838 - Dec 30, 1866

Constance L. -- Oct 20, 1834 - Aug 13, 1876

E. M.
"Mother" ------ Jun 5, 1816 - Mar 14, 1873

James --------- Nov 20, 1805 - Aug 6, 1886

Wessenburg
Maggie
Kornegay ------ 1851 - 1897

William W. ---- Husband Maggie Kornegay
               (No dates)

GASTON CEMETERY

From the intersection of State Highway 17 and County Road 10 south of York, proceed west on County Road 10 for 3 1/10 miles to a forestry station on the north side of the road. The cemetery is behind the forestry station.

Gilmore
  (Child) ------- (Marker too faint)

  (2 Children) -- (Markers too faint)

  James --------- February 1762 - May 5, 1841

  Jane ---------- Relict of James Gilmore
                  Died 10/12/1855
                  79 yrs 2 mo & 5 days

  Nathaniel G. -- 8/3/1820 - 4/17/1847

  Willie Ann
  Eskridge ------ Wife of J. N. Gilmore
                  Died 2/8/1882 at Gaston
                  43 yrs 11 mo & 28 days

Lawson
  Alex. --------- 11/20/1822 - 10/5/1863

Peteet
  Aseneth
  Clementine ---- 8/30/1830 - 6/18/1860

Shurley
  Dora ---------- Dau Thomas & America
                  5/17/1851 - 8/21/1866

  Glemma -------- Dau Thomas & America
                  5/7/1861 - 12/21/1865

  Sarah E. ------ Dau Thomas & America
                  5/25/1849 - 5/24/1851

Watson
  Alice --------- Dau J. J. & H. A. Watson
                  3/22/1851 - 10/18/1852

Watson (contd)
  Harriet A. ---- Wife of J. J. Watson
                  Died 2/18/1852
                  24 yrs, 12 days

White
  George Sydney - 7/2/1837 - 4/4/1876

  Mary E. ------- Wife of J. H. White
                  3/6/1835 - 5/11/1852

  Pleasant ------ 1/3/1797 - 9/9/1865
                  68 yrs, 8 mo, 6 days

GASTON VALLEY CHURCH CEMETERY

From State Highway 17, approximately 13 miles south of York, turn west on County Road 10. The cemetery is approximately 2 4/10 miles down this road on the east side of the road.

Babb
  Miner --------- Born 1862
                  Nov 6, 1934

Ward
  Will ---------- Died Mar 5, 1906

White
  Miner --------- 1860 - 1846

Woodward
  Priscilla ----- May 5, 1863 - Aug 18, 1919

GEIGER CEMETERY

Located approximately 100 feet west of State Highway 17, approximately 4/10 mile north of its intersection with County Road 34.

Geiger
  Carolinus ----- Son of John W. Geiger
                      Died Nov 27, 1837
                      Age 10 months

  John W. ------- Died Jul 19, 1837
                      Age 33 yrs 10 mo

GILES CEMETERY

From the intersection of U. S. Highway 11 and County Road 10 in Cuba, go north on 10 for 1 6/10 miles. At that point, the cemetery will be about 1/4 mile to the east of the road on a hill.

Giles
  John Hiram ---- Born Cumberland Co. N. C.
                     Feb 3, 1823   Died Dec 17, 1898

  Martha Sarah -- Born Anson Co. N. C.
                     Mar 25, 1845 - Oct 25, 1908

  Sarah Moore --- Born Cumberland Co. N. C.
                     Sep 4, 1820 - Mar 16, 1884

GILES - NEVILLE or GRACE EPISCOPAL CEMETERY
(Kemper County, Mississippi)

From State Highway 17, 6 8/10 miles north of Emelle, turn west on County Road 30. The cemetery is at 4 miles on the north side of the road, in Kemper County, Mississippi.

Blocker
  Betty
  Robinson ------ Aug 30, 1856 - Feb 24, 1903

Blocker (contd)
  George M. ----- Aug 21, 1852 - Aug 29, 1901

Carr
  Charlotte M. -- Oct 24, 1818 - Aug 2, 1895

Coleman
  Mary I. ------- Wife of Wiley T. Coleman
                  Mar 20, 1856 - Aug 2, 1953

  Wiley T. ------ Jul 16, 1840 - Sep 1, 1921

Dillon
  R. G., M.D. --- Born in Dublin, Ireland
                  Died Apr 2, 1897 Age 68

  William E. ---- Born in Wahalak, Mississippi
                  Nov 16, 1860 - Aug 7, 1913

Giles
  Jacob --------- Jul 27, 1799 - Apr 22, 1860

  Maria F. ------ Wife Simmons H. Giles
                  Died May 28, 1891 Age 55

  Nancy A. ------ Wife of Jacob Giles
                  Died Jan 3, 1866
                  85 yrs 1 mo & 10 d

  Simmons H. ---- Apr 6, 1827 - Sep 8, 1870

Grant
  Helen Neville - Nov 17, 1856 - Jan 14, 1922

Jones
  Addison Ward -- Oct 9, 1831 - Jun 15, 1857

  Benjamin A.,
  Dr. ----------- Jun 10, 1791 - Jan 28, 1859

  Benjamin A.
  Jr. ----------- Sep 11, 1838 - Aug 29, 1852

  Maria A. ------ Wife of B. A. Jones
                  Aug 27, 1798 - Jun 20, 1858

Kerr
  Daniel W. ----- 1832 - 1895

Kerr (contd)

Peggy M.
Jones ---------- Wife of Daniel W. Kerr
1845 - 1915

Lacy

Mart ---------- Jan 30, 1863 - Sep 2, 1896

Neville

A. L. ---------- Jun 29, 1815 - Apr 21, 1882

Amelia --------- Wife W. H. Neville Jr.
Died Mar 10, 1929

Andrew L. ----- Feb 29, 1848 - Feb 14, 1926

Maria Cross
Giles ---------- Feb 20, 1859 - Jan 20, 1929

Martha
Washington ---- Dau W. H. & Sarah Neville
1862 - 1957

Mary Russell -- Dau W. H. & Sarah Neville
1864 - 1942

Mattie E.
Massey --------- Wife Andrew L. Neville
Jul 29, 1849 - Jul 19, 1929

Nancy J. ------ Apr 25, 1833 - Jun 23, 1892

Robert S. ----- Dec 7, 1849 - May 17, 1916

Sallie
Blocker ------- Nov 1, 1848 - Apr 28, 1881

Sarah H.
Spencer ------- Oct 13, 1829 - Jun 13, 1906

Shepard
Spencer ------- Sep 16, 1858 - Jan 7, 1920

William ------- May 26, 1839 - Jun 14, 1903

William
Hervey -------- Son William & E. L. Neville
Nov 12, 1812 - Jul 25, 1887

Neville (contd)
William
Hervey Jr. ---- Apr 12, 1852 - Nov 14, 1922

Pearson
Cordelia F. --- Wife of Dr. W. E. Pearson
Jun 22, 1831 - Nov 30, 1907

W. E., Dr. ---- May 14, 1836 - May 31, 1909

Perrin
Mary Florida
Lacy Jones ---- Apr 26, 1841 - Jan 10, 1920

Capt. T. U. --- Born in Edgefield, S. C.
Sep 23, 1832 - Jul 5, 1887

William A. ---- Sgt Major, Co. C, Jeff Davis
Legion, CSA (No dates)

Robinson
James B. ------ Died Feb 8, 1905

Laura K. ------ 1854 - 1903

Stuart
J. T. --------- Sep 13, 1856 - Jan 18, 1926

John B. ------- Oct 28, 1842 - Dec 26, 1915

Mary E. ------- Feb 24, 1858 - Aug 26, 1954

GRAHAM - PETEET CEMETERY
(Destroyed)

Located behind Chestnut Grove Church on State Highway 17, 7 1/10 miles south of York.

Graham
Harriet ------- Wife of Jim Graham
Mar 15, 1821 - Sep 4, 1886
Age 43 yrs 10 mo

Wife S. M. ---- Died Sep 6, 1891
Age 44 yrs 11 mo

Peteet
  Anderson ------ 1815 - May 24, 1893

GREENLEES CEMETERY
(Destroyed)

Believed to be located on the homesite of Fred Dial, on the north side of County Road 12, approximately 4 1/2 miles west of State Highway 17.

Greenlees
  John ---------- Born in County Down, Ireland
                        May 11, 1796 or 1797
                        Died Sep 2, 1855

  Joseph -------- Died about 1880

HARRIS CEMETERY

Located on the north side of a newer cemetery, about 500 yards northeast of the intersection of County Roads 2 and 27 near the old Town of Dove.

Bourdeaux
  Laura --------- Wife of T. D. Bourdeaux
                       Jan 19, 1821 - Jul 10, 1856

  Laura Harris -- Dau T. D. & Laura Bourdeaux
                       Mar 10, 1839 - Jun 1, 1840

  Mary
  Catherine ----- Dau T. D. & Laura Bourdeaux
                     Nov 9, 1853 - Sep 28, 1855

  Thomas Devane - Born in New Hanover Co. N. C.
                     May 3, 1806 Died Lauderdale
                     Co. Miss. May 10, 1885

Grant
  Green W. ------ Born in Greenville Dist. S. C.
                     Died in Sumter County, Alabama
                     Apr 3, 1876

Harris
  Richard ------- Born in Abbeville Dist. S. C.
                  Jan 27, 1778
                  Died in Sumter County, Alabama
                  Jul 29, 1851

HATCH CEMETERY

Located approximately 1 mile south of Geiger, about 150 yards west of State Highway 17.

Curry
  Martha -------- Born in Virginia
                  Died Jul 8, 1884   Age 81
                  (No marker)

Hatch
  Ann ----------- Wife of C. A. Hatch
                  Died Jun 22, 1841

  Catherine E. -- Wife of C. A. Hatch
                  Died Sep 16, 1844   Age 34

  Lemuel B. ----- Son C. A. & Ann Hatch
                  Died Jan 22, 1841   Age 4 mo

  Noble --------- 1812 - 1842

  William A. ---- Son C. A. & Ann Hatch
                  Died Oct 15, 1847   Age 14

Kennedy
  Margaret ------ Died Jul 19, 1843

Williamses
  Col. Edward --- A native of Onslow Co. N. C.
                  Died Mar 31, 1844   Age 77

HAUPT CEMETERY

From Belmont, proceed east on County Road 23 for approximately 3 3/10 miles. The cemetery is approximately 50 yards south of the road in heavy overgrowth.

Duncan
  Matilda
  Elizabeth ----- Jan 25, 1854 - Jul 30, 1858

Haupt
  Infant -------- May 8, 1835 - Aug 3, 1835

  Lewis --------- May 3, 1820 - Jan 19, 1873

  Matilda ------- Wife of Sebastin Haupt
                     B 1794 in Ga.
                     D May 19, 1880 in Ala.

  Matilda Dale -- Wife of Lewis Haupt
                     Jan 15, 1833 - Jan 25, 1921

  Sebastin ------ Born 1784   Died Oct 3, 1835

  Sebastin ------ Jan 21, 1836 - Dec 25, 1843

Hodgins
  Merrit -------- Born in Bucks Co. Pa. 1796
                     Died Nov 22, 1868

McDowell
  Ann Marshall -- Dau Alexander & Anna McDowell
                     Feb 9, 1849 - Jan 2, 1873

  Anna ---------- Sep 24, 1821 - Dec 28, 1866

  Baby Brother -- May 12, 1852 - Sep 17, 1852

  Joseph
  Sebastin ------ Son Alexander & Anna McDowell
                     Sep 4, 1847 - Dec 7, 1851

  Marshall ------ Son Alexander & Anna McDowell
                     May 4, 1845 - Sep 21, 1846

  William H. ---- Son Alexander & Anna McDowell
                     Jun 17, 1843 - Oct 25, 1853

Smith
  Lela Haupt ---- Oct 22, 1864 - Jul 1, 1894

Weller
  Erin H. ------- Jan 29, 1859 - Jul 28, 1942
  William H. ---- Jul 7, 1838 - Dec 25, 1916

HAWKINS CEMETERY

Located approximately 1/2 mile north of the old Hawkins home on the west side of County Road 21, approximately 3 1/2 miles south of Epes.

Hawkins
  Ann Caroline -- Dec 12, 1844 - Apr 6, 1912

  Elizabeth W. -- Mar 8, 1832 - Mar 6, 1862

  John T. ------- Nov 20, 1834 - Oct 23, 1915

  Martha A. ----- Born in North Carolina
                  Nov 6, 1811 - Mar 25, 1869

  Martha A. ----- Who departed this life
                  January 29, 1856
                  7 yrs 2 mo & 12 days

  Susan M. ------ Born Albemarle Co. Va.
                  Wife of T. H. Hawkins
                  Nov 22, 1826 - Oct 4, 1891

  Thomas Hewitt - Nov 2, 1802 - Feb 24, 1879

  W. H. --------- Jun 12, 1838 - Nov 18, 1900

Read
  Rhoda --------- Feb 9, 1790 - Jan 1, 1841

Tillman
  Sallie -------- Died Oct 24, 1912 Age 66 years

HENAGAN CEMETERY

From U. S. Highway 11, 1 1/2 miles south of Epes, turn east on a dirt road. The cemetery is at the end of this road, at a distance of 1/2 mile.

Abbott
Alice Kennedy - Wife C. H. Abbott
Jun 27, 1858 - Sep 22, 1889

Anderson
Josephus M. --- Sep 25, 1861 - Jul 15, 1927

Arnold
Hettie H. ----- 1856 - 1932

J. W. --------- Apr 10, 1830 - Jul 16, 1902

Arrington
Andrew J. ----- Jul 19, 1827 - Nov 6, 1909

Helen Amelia -- Wife of Andrew J. Arrington
Oct 20, 1837 - Dec 25, 1865

Helen Ora ----- Dau A. J. & Helen A. Arrington
Dec 29, 1857 - Nov 7, 1878

Infant -------- Dau Andrew J. & Helen A.
Born & Died Feb 13, 1856

Joseph J. ----- Son Joseph & M. G. Arrington
Mar 13, 1849 - Sep 11, 1850

Margaret G. --- Wife of Joseph Arrington
May 27, 1820 - Sep 20, 1855

Autrey
Rev. H. R. ---- Oct 12, 1814 - Aug 14, 1888

Brenneman
Nannie R. ----- 1865 - 1924

Cathey
Martin A. ----- Feb 1, 1845 - Jan 21, 1901

Susie Dial ---- Nov 13, 1855 - Mar 4, 1921

Collier
    Permelia ------ Died Apr 29, 1842 (1812?)
                   Age 13 yrs 2 mo & 2 days

David
    Bettie -------- Dau J. E. & C. J. David
                   Born in Bennettsville, S. C.
                   Oct 18, 1857 - Oct 4, 1907

    E. C. --------- Born in Bennettsville, S. C.
                   Mar 26, 1844 - Feb 6, 1909

    John J. ------- Sep 1852 - Mar 18, 1905

Dial
    Mattie A. ----- Jan 3, 1863 - Oct 10, 1890

    Willie A. ----- Sep 16, 1860 - Apr 15, 1898

Ellis
    Octavia
    Josephine ----- Jun 11, 1849 - May 18, 1851

Fitzpatrick
    Isabella A. --- Aug 10, 1853 - May 24, 1902

    Thomas F. ----- Mar 30, 1842 - May 30, 1895

Godfrey
    Dozier -------- Died Aug 24, 1843 Age 32

    Dozier
    Elizabeth ----- Dec 28, 1843 - Sep 5, 1845

    Harriet P. ---- Consort of William Godfrey
                   Died Sep 30, 1845
                   Age 54 yrs 1 mo & 22 days

    John D. ------- Died Apr 27, 1843 Age 24

    Mary E. ------- Dau J. M. & L. A. Godfrey
                   Sep 3, 1862 - May 27, 1864

    William ------- Died Jan 22, 1854
                   Age 69 yrs 6 mo & 4 days

Greenlee
  Hugh
  Washington ---- Oct 28, 1851 - Nov 17, 1929

  Katie
  Coblentz ------ Apr 20, 1854 - Jul 9, 1928

  Lilly May ----- Wife of John Greenlee
                   1889 - 1907

Jones
  Isaac Hull ---- Mar 7, 1847 - Mar 10, 1917

Kennedy
  Catharine
  Lowery -------- Wife of J. T. Kennedy
                 Feb 15, 1837 - Dec 16, 1915

  George
  Earnest ------- Son T. H. & S. J. Kennedy
                 Died Feb 22, 1859
                 Age 6 mo 22 days

  Sallie J. ----- Wife of T. H. Kennedy
                 Jul 24, 1830 - Apr 6, 1860

  Vernal Hardy -- Aug 16, 1855 - Jan 8, 1896

  Willie B. ----- Son T. H. & S. J. Kennedy
                 Died Dec 9, 1859
                 Age 3 yrs 7 mo & 25 days

Lawler
  M. E. --------- Wife of T. B. Lawler
                 Apr 23, 1848 - Jul 26, 1899

Lee
  Bettie J. ----- Wife of James B. Lee
                 Jul 5, 1847 - Jan 17, 1918

  J. B. --------- May 27, 1823 - Dec 23, 1902

  J. W. W. ------ Nov 21, 1854 - Jan 29, 1901

  Jennie Lee ---- Wife of Tom Lee
                 1864 - 1929

  Thomas J. ----- Oct 4, 1855 - Sep 3, 1906

Lewis
   William
      Garrett ------- Jul 2, 1848 - Dec 19, 1914

Lipscomb
   G. W. --------- Son A. & M. Lipscomb
                   Aug 16, 1850 - May 7, 1851

   J. E. --------- Son A. & M. Lipscomb
                   Oct 31, 1857 - Sep 24, 1859

   M. G. --------- Son A. & M. Lipscomb
                   Jul 9, 1852 - Jun 31, 1852

   Mary M. R. ---- Wife of A. Lipscomb
                   Died Jun 2, 1858 Age 37

   Willie A.
   Ogletree ------ Wife of __?__ Lipscomb
                   Dec 6, 1848 - Mar 15, 1877

Love
   Ida K. -------- Mar 18, 1860 - Apr 19, 1946

Lowry
   Florence G. --- Feb 15, 1847 - Jun 3, 1847

   George W. ----- Oct 29, 1840 - Jul 22, 1853

   Joseph J. ----- Aug 29, 1827 - Aug 16, 1853

   Margaret A. --- Jun 17, 1832 - Dec 24, 1837

   Prudence H. --- Dec 22, 1809 - Jul 10, 1873

   Robert H. ----- May 20, 1839 - Aug 24, 1840

   Vernal -------- Apr 29, 1807 - Sep 29, 1851

   Vernal L. ----- Jan 29, 1843 - Oct 6, 1853

May
   Florence P. --- 1857 - 1902

   James --------- 1841 - 1910

Mitchell
  Benjamin
  George -------- Nov 18, 1856 - Oct 21, 1936

  Elizabeth
  Lowry --------- Wf of J. M. Mitchell
                  Jun 17, 1835 - Jun 5, 1907

  Franklin
  Lowry ---------- Youngest son of J.M. &
                   Elizabeth Lowry Mitchell
                   Jul 4, 1865 - Mar 28, 1924

  John
  Montgomery ---- Dec 13, 1832 - Dec 12, 1928

Myers
  Asbury -------- Mar 4, 1816 - Mar 29, 1843

  James Asbury -- Died Aug 17, 1849   Age 6

  James G. ------ Dec 12, 1811 - Oct 21, 1840

  Martha -------- Oct 10, 1780 - Feb 27, 1845

Ogletree
  Amelia J. ----- Wife of B. H. Ogletree
                  Feb 25, 1842 - Oct 11, 1908

Patterson
  James D. ------ Sep 3, 1862 - Aug 11, 1898

Pettigrew
  Louise
  Eskridge ------ 1827 - 1912

  William
  Beauregard ---- 1860 - 1912

Phillips
  Florence M. --- Dau John & Martha G. Phillips
                  Jul 19, 1845 - Oct 9, 1846

  Maj. John ----- Died Mar 18, 1846   Age 60

Phillips (contd)
  Margaret
   Lawrence ------ Dau Lawrence D. & H. M. M.
                    Phillips
                    Jul 6, 1845 - Sep 8, 1845

  Martha G. ----- Died May 7, 1853 Abt 44

Pruitt
  Leanora ------- 1851 - 1911

Richie
  Jabes C. ------ May 20, 1862 - Mar 28, 1938

Saunders
  Ellen J.
   Wedgeworth ---- Wife of J. L. Saunders
                    ? 14, 1861 - Dec 16, ?

Sawls
  Ella J. ------- Wife of W. B. Sawls
                    Nov 7, 1853 - Nov 17, 1911

Smith
  Maggie J. ----- Aug 19, 1851 - Nov 11, 1929

  W. W. --------- Sep 21, 1854 - Apr 19, 1936

Underwood
  Infant -------- Son William D. & Olivia E.
                    Born & Died Jan 9, 1854

  Infant -------- Dau William D. & Olivia E.
                    Aug 12, 1855 - Aug 18, 1855

Williams
  Albert A. ----- Sep 29, 1865 - Jan 3, 1958

Willis
  J. P. --------- Jan 14, 1846 - Jun 28, 1904

  Sallie
   Elizabeth ----- Sep 9, 1848 - Sep 29, 1902

HIBBLER CEMETERY

Located a few hundred feet south of County Road 34, approximately 1/4 mile east of the intersection of County Road 34 and State Highway 17.

Hibbler
- Charlie ------- Son W. H. & F. A. Hibbler
  Mar 24, 1853 - Nov 16, 1855

- Frances A. ---- Consort of W. H. Hibbler
  Born in Greene Co. Ga.
  Apr 13, 1824 - Mar 25, 1861

- Infant -------- Son W. H. & F. A. Hibbler
  (No dates)

- Infant -------- Of W. H. & M. N. Hibbler
  (No dates)

- Martha N. ----- Died Sep 24, 1842
  34 yrs 3 mo 8 days

- Martha S. ----- Dau W. H. & M. N. Hibbler
  Sep 1842 - Sep 1843

- Sarah Jane ---- Died Jun 28, 1840
  Age 11 yrs 11 mo & 10 days

- William ------- Son W. H. & M. N. Hibbler
  Jun 10, 1839 - Aug 30, 1849

- William H. ---- Born in Edgefield Dist. S. C.
  Jan 11, 1804 - Nov 17, 1862

HICKS CEMETERY

From U. S. Highway 80, approximately 2 3/10 miles east of its intersection with State Highway 17, turn north on the Lynn Bennett Road. The cemetery is approximately 1 7/10 miles down this road on the north side of the road.

Hicks
- William ------- Died Apr 3, 1909 Age Abt 70

HORN CEMETERY

Located on the north side of the Sucarnoochee River in Section 14, Township 19 North, Range 3 West, approximately 1 mile south of State Highway 28.

Killen
    Aramenta ------ Dau Harris W. & Mary Killen
                           Oct 1, 1843 - Oct 17, 1844

    Infant -------- Son Harris W. & Mary Killen
                           Jul 22, 1840 - Jul 24, 1840

    Mary ---------- Consort of Harris W. Killen
                           Dau John & Asenath Horn
                           Sep 15, 1811 - Nov 4, 1843
                           Age 32 yrs 1 mo & 19 days

HOUSTON CEMETERY
(Mostly Destroyed)

Located approximately 3/4 mile north of Livingston North Industrial Park Road and 75 yards east of the Norfolk Southern Railroad.

Houston
    Davis
    Caldwell ------ Born Mar 31, 1827
                           Died Sep 6, 1836
                           Age 9 yrs 5 mo 6 days
                           (Only marker remaining)

INGE CEMETERY

Located in Section 24, Township 21 North, Range 3 West.

Inge
    John ---------- Dec 4, 1842 - May 1935

JAMESTOWN CEMETERY
(Mostly Destroyed)

From the intersection of County Roads 34 and 35 east of Panola, proceed west on County Road 34 a distance of approximately 1/2 mile to the cemetery on the north side of the road.

Cattle have almost destroyed this cemetery.

Allgood
  Altazana ------ Oct 2, 1846 - Jul 8, 1848

  Blake Baker --- Jul 14, 1842 - Jan 1, 1843

  Darthula D. --- Jan 30, 1826 - Jul 31, 1826 ?

  James William - Jun 9, 1845 - Sep 11, 1846

  Sterling H. --- Apr 7, 1848 - Jul 28, 1849

  Sterling
  Henry --------- Apr 7, 1848 - Jul 28, 1849

Beavers
  Thomas Walter - Aug 12, 1851 - Feb 22, 1880

Gattis
  Susan E. S. --- Apr 27, 1834 - Jan 22, 1841

Houston
  Hamilton ------ Dec 12, 1833 - Feb 18, 1860

  John ---------- Born in Jones Co. N. C.
                     Jan 10, 1800 - Dec 6, 1849

Johnson
  Elizabeth ----- Consort of Henry Johnson
                     Oct 24, 1790 - Aug 1, 1842

  Rev. Henry ---- May 9, 1791 - Jul 16, 1844

Jones
  James W. ------ Apr 12, 1832 - Nov 6, 1860

Stone
  George W. ----- Son George W. & Nannie A.
                     Dec 17, 1860 - Nov 11, 1861

Stone (contd)
Lizzie -------- Dau George W. & Nannie A.
May 14, 1862 - Jul 6, 1863

Tartt
Cadmus E. ----- Dec 23, 1865 - Sep 20, 1866

Martha M. ----- Jul 27, 1863 - Mar 14, 1880
Typhoid fever

Nannie A. ----- Jul 28, 1864 - Mar 4, 1880
Typhoid fever

JARMAN CEMETERY

From County Road 10, approximately 3 3/10 miles south of Cuba, turn south on County Road 5. After 1 2/10 miles, turn west on Campbell Road. Turn further right onto Jarman Road. The cemetery is approximately 1 mile down this road, several hundred yards northwest of the road.

Jarman
Mary ---------- Wife of Thomas Jarman Sr.
Feb 12, 1799 - Sep 7, 1871

Thomas Sr. ---- Mar 30, 1797 - Dec 16, 1869

JEMISON CEMETERY

Located a few hundred yards northeast of the intersection of County Road 2 with Interstate Highways 20 and 59, west of York.

Green
Rolly --------- A native of Virginia who died in 1857 in the 48th year of his age

Jemison
Harriet P. ---- Feb 19, 1819 - Dec 16, 1855

Jemison (contd)
J. S. --------- Jun 28, 1854 - Jul 20, 1856

Jane E. ------- Nov 30, 1815 - Sep 13, 1840

Joseph -------- Nov 3, 1836 - Jul 1, 1844

Robert -------- Dec 1, 1855 - Dec 3, 1855

William H. ---- Feb 22, 1805 - May 12, 1866

JENKINS CEMETERY

Located on the north side of U. S. Highway 11, approximately 4 3/4 miles north of York.

Jenkins
Jennett L. ---- Born Jan 27, 1852
              Died Oct 8, 1853

JONES CEMETERY

Located near the common corner of Sections 7, 8, 17 and 18, Township 23 North, Range 3 West.

Jones
Alexander P. -- Dec 25, 1829 - Dec 27, 1851

Gabriel ------- Jun 1770 - Sep 1842 Age 72

Little Rollie - Feb 14, 1866 - Nov 19, 1868

Victoria ------ Aug 25, 1829 - Dec 27, 1851

Zechariah ----- Jan 27, 1805 - Mar 23, 1843

Richardson
Freeman ------- Born Aug 1812
              Died Apr 27, _?_

JONES CEMETERY
(Kemper County, Mississippi)

From State Highway 17, approximately 2 1/2 miles south of Geiger, turn west on County Road 30. At approximately 3 1/10 miles, turn south into the driveway of a home. The cemetery is located approximately 2/10 mile behind this home.

Jones
    Martha Ann ---- Wife of Henry Jones
                    Dau Thomas & Susanna Jones
                    Oct 22, 1817 - Mar 11, 1853

Vaughn
    Mary S. ------- Born Jan 29, 1842
                   Died Aug 14, 1868

KING CEMETERY

Located in the southwest one-quarter of the northwest one-quarter of Section 20, Township 18 North, Range 1 East.

King
    Mrs. Sallie
    T. ------------ Born Washington Co. Ala.
                   Mar 26, 1841 - Aug 18, 1878

KNOX CEMETERY

Located on the south side of U. S. Highway 80, approximately 1 1/4 miles east of the intersection of U. S. Highway 80 and State Highway 17.

Fincher
    J. ------------ 1815 - Apr 15, 1869

Knox
    John ---------- Dec 6, 1782 - Apr 3, 1840

Knox (contd)
John
Clementine ---- Nov 15, 1840 - Mar 6, 1851

Mary Jane ----- 4/4/1839 - 10/17/1840

LACY CEMETERY
(Destroyed)

From State Highway 17, approximately 4 1/10 miles south of Emelle, turn east on the Looksookold Road. At approximately 8/10 mile, go through a pasture gate on the south side of the road. The cemetery is approximately 3/4 mile from the gate.

Lacy
Mary ---------- Born 1793 Died 1843

Nicholas ------ Oct 4, 1790 - Jul 20, 1858

LEE CEMETERY

From State Highway 28, approximately 6 4/10 miles southeast of Livingston, turn east on County Road 22. The cemetery is approximately 1 6/10 miles down this road, behind the Zion Hill Church and cemetery, in heavy overgrowth.

Lee
Adeline ------- Dec 9, 1818 - Nov 30, 1901

An older resident stated that, years ago, there were several tall markers in this cemetery.

LEE HAVEN CEMETERY

Located at "Lee Haven", several hundred feet east of County Road 21, approximately 2 1/2 miles south of the intersection of County Road 21 and State Highway 28, southeast of Livingston.

Patton
    Nancy --------- Consort of Joseph Patton
                           11/20/1796 - 6/7/1841

LIBERTY BAPTIST CHURCH CEMETERY

From County Road 10, 3 3/10 miles south of Cuba, turn south on County Road 5. At 5 miles, turn northwest on County Road 6. At 1 3/10 miles, turn west on the Liberty Church Road. The church and cemetery are located on the north side of this road at a distance of 9/10 mile.

Blann
    Antoinette ---- Jan 19, 1848 - Sep 10, 1930

Boswell
    Bellzora ------ Wife of K. W. Boswell
                     Died Jul 13, 1884 Age 54

    Bill ---------- (No dates)

    Jerusha ------- Aug 25, 1864 - Jun 19, 1935

    Kommie C. ----- Oct 31, 1857 - Jan 8, 1901

    Nancy C. ------ Wife of Kommie Boswell
                     Jan 4, 1851 - Oct 7, 1912

Brewster
    Dora Ann ------ 1st Wife George J. Brewster
                     Jun 7, 1852 - May 5, 1887

    Emily Smith --- Jul 10, 1841 - Nov 21, 1913

Culpepper
    Alfred
    Mickens ------- Mar 8, 1863 - Aug 14, 1925

Culpepper (contd)
  Ambrose ------- Dec 8, 1829 - May 21, 1892
  Caroline C. --- Wife of John J. Culpepper
                  Jan 15, 1865 - Feb 3, 1931
  Emma G. ------- May 23, 1850 - Jul 3, 1924
  Hardin -------- Feb 1, 1840 - Oct 22, 1882
  James --------- Sep 24, 1824 - Jun 10, 1890
  John J. ------- Jan 10, 1862 - Aug 5, 1934
  John L. ------- May 3, 1858 - Jul 4, 1924
  Julia Ellis --- Apr 3, 1856 - Aug 29, 1893
  Karon J. ------ Wife of Rev. W. S. Culpepper
                  May 14, 1855 - Jul 23, 1932
  M. A. --------- Wife Ambrose Culpepper
                  Jan 28, 1830 - Jun 11, 1880
  Mary ---------- Wife of Hardin Culpepper
                  Dec 19, 1841 - May 20, 1913
  Mary A. ------- Wife of James Culpepper
                  Apr 25, 1839 - Dec 7, 1923
  Mary Ann ------ Wife of Rubin Culpepper
                  Aug 21, 1849 - Jun 21, 1924
  Matthew ------- Co. C, 40th Ala. Inf., CSA
                  (No dates)
  Nancy J. ------ Wife of M. J. Culpepper
                  Jan 12, 1843 - Mar 16, 1892
  Rubin --------- Dec 22, 1847 - Jan 24, 1927
  Thomasetta ---- Wife of H. M. Culpepper
                  1861 - 1884
  Willie Ann ---- Feb 1862 - Nov 1922

Goodwyn
  Eliza W. ------ (No dates)

Goodwyn (contd)
James W. ------ Jan 31, 1840 - Jul 11, 1880

Thomas H. ----- (No dates)

Hall
Caloway ------- Born 1838 - Oct 14, 1860

Hardin
Elmie --------- Wife of J. M. Hardin Sr.
Mar 22, 1855 - Jun 6, 1940

J. M. Sr. ----- Jan 15, 1844 - Jul 4, 1924

Jessie
Columbus ------ 1851 - 1925

Joseph Y. ----- Aug 3, 1835 - Jul 28, 1906

Julia E. ------ Wife of J. M. Hardin
Aug 1, 1852 - May 26, 1869

Lauizer ------- 1863 - 1931

Martha A. ----- Wife of Simeon C. Hardin
Apr 18, 1848 - Mar 6, 1931

Mary
Culpepper ----- Wife of Spinks Hardin
Sep 13, 1856 - Aug 25, 1899

Simeon C. ----- Apr 9, 1839 - Oct 28, 1921

Spinks -------- Oct 11, 1858 - Apr 23, 1917

Tiny ---------- Aug 21, 1840 - Feb 23, 1928

Harris
Jacob P. ------ Son A. M. & Nancy Harris
Aug 10, 1854 - Nov 15, 1857

Lacy
Martha Lela --- Wife W. A. Lacy
Sep 5, 1860 - Sep 23, 1891

William ------- Jul 22, 1859 - May 24, 1923

McCann
  Amanda L. ----- Dec 1, 1850 - Sep 6, 1938

  Hugh ---------- Sep 20, 1838 - Feb 8, 1919

McMurry
  Millie
  Culpepper ----- Wife J. R. McMurry
                 Aug 13, 1855 - Jun 16, 1911

Rainer
  Charles F. ---- Husband Sarah E. Rainer
               Mar 7, 1829 - Jan 26, 1901

  W. J. --------- Apr 5, 1858 - Apr 8, 1885

Robinson
  B. R. --------- Mar 28, 1851 - Mar 14, 1925

  Sarah C. ------ May 21, 1852 - Sep 17, 1929

Smith
  William Wiley - Co. A, 37th Regt., Miss. Inf.,
               CSA Mar 15, 1840 - Jun 20, 1870

Tims
  W. R. --------- Aug 8, 1863 - Feb 18, 1925

Watts
  Martha
  Elizabeth ----- Mar 23, 1857 - Feb 18, 1931

Willis
  Martha
  Culpepper ----- Wife of Abner Willis
                 Sep 13, 1856 - Nov 11, 1890

Yarbrough
  Rev. Ambrose -- Feb 19, 1772 - Jul 20, 1861
               Founded Liberty Baptist Church
               May 31, 1845

  Joseph -------- Co. K, 12th Miss. Cav., CSA
               Oct 3, 1842 - May 16, 1891

LITTLE CEMETERY

From State Highway 17, approximately 6 miles north of Geiger, turn east on County Road 34. At 2 1/10 miles, turn north on County Road 83. The cemetery is at approximately 9/10 mile, a few hundred feet behind a home west side of the road.

Little
   Margaret L. --- Dau of Will & Tempe Little
                     3/1/1838 - 4/26/1838

   Mary E. ------- Dau of Will & Tempe Little
                     Born in Edgecombe Co. N.C.
                     12/3/1833 - 2/14/1836

LOCKARD CEMETERY
(Choctaw County)

From State Highway 17, 50 yards south of the Choctaw County line, turn east through a gate and follow a road for 3/10 mile to the cemetery.

Lockard
   Caroline ------ Family Slave
                     Age 110 years

   John ---------- Born in South Carolina
                     Aug 19, 1805 - Aug 7, 1866

   Nancy L. ------ Dau John & Nancy Lockard
                     Jul 12, 1851 - Sep 15, 1851

   Nancy Stewart - Wife of John Lockard
                     Born in Tennessee
                     Jul 27, 1810 - Mar 11, 1872

   Robert F. ----- Son John & Nancy Lockard
                     Jun 8, 1844 - Dec 15, 1872

   Sarah A. ------ Dau John & Nancy Lockard
                     Sep 11, 1842 - Sep 8, 1843

   William J. ---- Son John & Nancy Lockard
                     Mar 6, 1834 - Jun 21, 1862

MAY CEMETERY

From State Highway 28, approximately 10 miles southeast of Livingston, turn east on County Road 23. The cemetery is on the right side of the road, approximately 6 4/10 miles from the intersection, behind a newer cemetery.

Butler
  Sarah S. ------ A native of Middletown, Conn.
                   Died Sep 15, 1864 Age 74

May
  Ann ----------- Dau of P. & C. L. May
                   Died Oct 20, 1856 Age 10

  Catharen
  Louisa -------- Consort of Phillip May Sr.
                   Died Oct 26, 1862 Age 36 yrs

  Frank --------- Son of P. & C. L. May
                   Died Oct 21, 1855 Age 13

  Mary ---------- Died Sep 8, 1849
                   In her 79th year

Parker
  Ellen --------- Wife of P. W. Parker
                   Jan 25, 1850 - Nov 8, 1870

Rothrock
  Geo. T. ------- Of Ray Co. Me.
                   Son H. & M. Rothrock
                   Born Dec 23, 1844
                   Died Jul 2, 1865

MAYS CEMETERY

From Epes, go south on County Road 21. The cemetery is at 4 6/10 miles, approximately 50 yards west of the road.

Clark
  Jesse --------- Born Feb 2, 1848
                   Died Feb 10, 1933

Clark (contd)
    Laura --------- Born Dec 25, 1840
                    Died May 18, 1940
Freeman
    Thomas W. ----- Who departed this life
                    24th July 1840
                    Age 25 years & 7 months
May
    Green --------- Born Jan 1820
                    Died Feb 21, 1897
Megerson
    Frank --------- Born 1849
                    Died Aug 11, 1896
Williamson
    Eliza --------- Born Sep 16, 1958 (1858?)
                    Died Aug 12, 1940

    Squire -------- Born Sep 1, 1857
                    Died Sep 21, 1914

McCAIN CEMETERY

From State Highway 28, approximately 5 miles east
of State Highway 17, turn north on a dirt road.
The cemetery is about 1/4 miles west of the road,
at a distance of approximately 1 1/2 miles.

Lavender
    Margaret ------ Wife of Robert Lavender
                    May 22, 1815 - Jun 28, 1871
McCain
    Adam ---------- Died Apr 24, 1841   Age 61

    Adam S. ------- Jul 23, 1835 - Jun 3, 1870

    Elizabeth ----- Consort of Adam McCain
                    Mar 13, 1798 - Mar 11, 1867

    Lelia Marion -- Dau A. S. & F. L. McCain
                    May 5, 1863 - Sep 4, 1868

McELROY OR TABERNACLE CEMETERY

From County Road 10, approximately 2 8/10 miles south of Cuba, turn east on Wilson Road. The cemetery is at approximately 9/10 mile on the north side of the road.

Beavers
Eld. A. E. ---- 1844 - 1902

    Elizabeth ----- Wife James Beavers
                         Jan 31, 1811 - Dec 16, 1883

S. M. --------- 1842 - 1915

Garden
Phila S. ------ Jan 4, 1862 - Aug 4, 1917

McElroy
A. P. --------- Jan 10, 1845 - Oct 21, 1900

Andrew J. ----- Jul 3, 1849 - Nov 22, 1922

Anna E. ------- Feb 11, 1853 - Feb 24, 1928

Aseneth E. ---- Nov 8, 1859 - Mar 11, 1942

E. M. --------- Aug 30, 1845 - Jul 16, 1925

G. W. --------- Apr 5, 1817 - Jan 14, 1879

G. W. --------- Jan 25, 1849 - Aug 13, 1929

I. R. --------- Apr 4, 1840 - Jan 20, 1914

Col. Isaac R. - May 1, 1805 - Jul 22, 1885

J. J. --------- Age 72 yrs

Jasper Newton - Apr 1, 1859 - Nov 7, 1927

Jesse W. ------ Son A. P. & Esther McElroy
                  Age 1 yr

M. E. --------- Wife I. R. McElroy
                  Jul 4, 1842 - Jul 6, 1896

Mariah -------- Wife J. J. McElroy   Age 83

McElroy (contd)
Matilda T. ---- Wife G. W. McElroy
                1822 - Sep 6, 1885

Nancy --------- Wife Col. J. R. McElroy
                Feb 27, 1839 - May 24, 1899

Sallie -------- May 11, 1843 - Mar 14, 1920

Sarah
Elizabeth ----- Wife G. W. McElroy
                Oct 14, 1846 - Apr 16, 1926

Son ----------- of J. J. & Mariah McElroy
                Age 7 yr

Phelps
Walter Helen -- Oct 19, 1855 - Nov 1891
                Age 36

William F. ---- Son Wm. & Nicia H. Phelps
                Oct 19, 1854 - Feb 8, 1885

Shaw
E. M. --------- Mar 27, 1838 - Dec 2, 1922

Eastern ------- Wife Orson Shaw
               Mar 22, 1816 - Oct 7, 1890

Emeline R. ---- Wife R. W. Shaw
               Jun 10, 1841 - Feb 3, 1916

Frances
Elizabeth ----- Wife E. M. Shaw
               Apr 10, 1835 - Aug 17, 1869

Marthie A. ---- Feb 22, 1848 - Jul 14, 1893

Orson --------- Jul 28, 1802 - Jun 10, 1868

R. W. --------- 1835 - 1900

Sarah
Cornelia ------ Wife E. M. Shaw
               May 19, 1849 - Aug 11, 1901

W. O. --------- Feb 22, 1848 - Mar 10, 1922

Watson
  Elizabeth ----- Born in Anson Co. N. Carolina
                  Oct 24, 1818
                  Died Cuba Station, Ala. Sumter
                  Co. Oct 1, 1902

Webb
  Archibald C. -- 40th Ala. Inf., CSA
                  Dec 21, 1828 - Nov 28, 1915

  C. H. --------- Husband of Amelia Webb
                  Jun 19, 1858 - Feb 16, 1889

  S. A. --------- Mar 27, 1829 - May 14, 1896

  V. P. --------- Nov 8, 1844 - Nov 30, 1893

  William B. ---- 1859 - 1926

McGREW - HART CEMETERY

From U. S. Highway 80, approximately 3 miles west of the Tombigbee River Bridge, turn south on County Road 25. The cemetery is on the north side of the road, a few hundred yards from the end of the road at the river.

Fluker
  Isabella ------ Consort of Dr. William Fluker
                  Dau Nathaniel & Isabella Abney
                  of the Edgefield District of
                  S. Carolina. Born Jan 14, 1788
                  Died May 22, 1847
                  Age 59 yrs 4 mo 8 days

Gregory
  J. J. --------- Who departed this life
                  Oct 1, 1853 Age 38 yrs

Hart
  J. N. --------- Jul 16, 1851 - Dec 25, 1942

  Mary ---------- Feb 19, 1859 - Feb 20, 1944

McGrew

Clark ---------- Oct 26, 1804 - Nov 14, 1855

Infant --------- Son of J. C. & Cebell McGrew
Died Sep 2, 1834 Age 5 hrs

Infant --------- Dau of J. C. & Cebell McGrew
Died Aug 7, 1835 Age 12 hrs

Infant --------- Dau of J. C. & Cebell McGrew
Feb 22, 1839 Age 1 hr

William
Patterson ----- Died Feb 4, 1838
Age 26 yrs 3 mo 6 days

McINNIS OR JONES CREEK CEMETERY

From U. S. Highway 11, approximately 1 1/2 miles south of Epes, turn west on a dirt road. At approximately 2/10 mile, go through a gate on the north side of the road. Follow a pasture road for approximately 1 3/10 miles to the cemetery.

Bronaugh
Andrew -------- Born in Louisa Co. Virginia
Feb 7, 1824 - Sep 3, 1851

Epes
James Vernon -- Aug 5, 1861 - Dec 23, 1913

Gibson
William A. ---- Jul 1, 1813 - Apr 9, 1853

Greer
Martha A. ----- Who departed this life
Aug 6, 1854 in the 24th
year of her age

Henagan
Ann ----------- Born in South Carolina
Mar 22, 1801 - Jan 10, 1884

Effie M. ------ Born in South Carolina
Jan 17, 1838 - Died 1886

Henagan (contd)
Julia A. ------ Dau E. L. & Ann Henagan
                 Born in Marlboro Dist. of S. C.
                 Died Jul 5, 1900

Hilman
Emma R. ------- Apr 17, 1852 - Dec 26, 1920
                 (Shared marker with Joseph J.)

Jezreel P. ---- Mar 22, 1819 - Oct 25, 1904

Joseph J. ----- Oct 12, 1846 - Apr 19, 1910

Joshua W. ----- A native of Orange Co. Va.
                 Aug 4, 1809 - May 31, 1853

Mary Jane ----- Wife Jezreel P. Hilman
                 Aug 15, 1825 - Mar 23, 1890
                 (Shared marker with Jezreel P.)

Nimrod -------- A native of Orange Co. Va.
                 Dec 9, 1807 - Dec 17, 1853

Hudson
Sarah B. ------ Consort of William Hudson
                 Died May 23, 1847
                 Age 28 yrs 3 mo 1 day

Kennedy
Franklin ------ Son of B. F. & S. A. Kennedy
                 Who departed this life
                 Jun 14, 1853
                 Age 6 months & 12 days

Sallie A. ----- Consort B. F. Kennedy
                 Who departed this life
                 May 27, 1853
                 Age 20 yrs 9 mo 14 days

McInnis
Julia Ann ----- Died Sep 7, 1851
                 In the 11th year of her life

Malcolm ------- Died Nov 2, 1854   Age 34

Malcolm E. ---- Died Sep 13, 1849
                 Age 14 yrs 10 mo

McInnis (contd)
  Robert H. ----- Died Dec 3, 1854
                    In the 21st year of his age

Pate
  Martha -------- Consort of S. R. Pate
                    Died May 12, 1848

  Sam'l R. ------ Died Nov 8, 1854   Age 52

Phillips
  Elizabeth D. -- Dau John & Martha G. Phillips
                    Apr 26, 1833 - May 1, 1835

  Infant Son ---- John & Martha Phillips
                    (No dates)

Prince
  Richard ------- A native of South Carolina
                    Who died at Jones Bluff, Ala.
                    Nov 27, 1849
                    In the 45th year of his age

Whitely
  C. H. --------- Mar 22, 1861 - Oct 31, 1918

MILLER CEMETERY

From the intersection of County Roads 20 and 21 in Epes, follow County Road 21 north for approximately 2 1/2 miles to a paved drive to the east. A church and the cemetery are at the end of this 3/10 mile drive.

Dickinson
  Caroline ------ Departed this life Apr 7, 1843
                    Age 36 yrs 23 days

  Martha P. ----- Departed this life Jul 3, 1842
                    Age 21 yrs 1 mo 14 days

Forman
  Catherine ----- Departed this life Feb 12, 1845
                    Age 26 yrs 10 mo 10 days

Miller
  Dr. John
  Francis ------- Departed this life Jul 12, 1844
                     Age 21 yr 4 mo 13 days

  William E. ---- Who died Aug 13, 1848
                   66 yr 8 mo 28 days

MIMS CEMETERY

Located a few hundred yards northeast of the intersection of County Road 12 with Interstate Highways 20 and 59, in the corner of a newer cemetery.

Mims
  Elizabeth
  Hubbard ------- Died Oct 14, 1842
                    Age 50 yrs 6 mo & 23 days

  Seabourn ------ Died Dec 17, 1842
                   Age 55 yrs 8 mo & 4 days

MT GILEAD BAPTIST CHURCH CEMETERY

From County Road 10, approximately 1 1/4 miles southeast of Cuba, turn east on a dirt road, keeping to the right, for approximately 3 miles to the cemetery on the north side of the road.

Bartlett
  Penelopie ----- Wife T. J. Bartlett
                   Sep 12, 1843 - Jun 11, 1896

  T. J. --------- Jun 15, 1840 - Dec 7, 1900

Brown
  M. J. --------- Wife J. D. Brown
                   Jan 9, 1833 - Jan 28, 1897

Bunyard
  I. B. --------- Dec 21, 1825 - Jul 1, 1890

Dearman
  Anjelico ------ Dec 24, 1833 - Mar 17, 1895
  Mally --------- Feb 1, 1827 - Aug 17, 1906
  Sarah C. ------ Apr 28, 1838 - Nov 28, 1877
  T. L. --------- Jun 9, 1833 - Feb 28, 1907
Hitt
  Martha Jane --- Jan 27, 1845 - Oct 8, 1904
  Robert Clark -- Sep 12, 1843 - Oct 2, 1924
Knight
  B. F. --------- Jan 19, 1851 - Jul 23, 1929
  Mary A. ------- Wife B. F. Knight
                  Jun 5, 1856 - Oct 5, 1925
Steavens
  H. H. --------- Aug 8, 1822 - Oct 30, 1879
Stephens
  Elizabeth ----- Wife of H. H.
                  Apr 29, 1838 - May 20, 1917
Thorne
  T. L. --------- Aug 22, 1863 - Feb 21, 1908
Williams
  Z. R. --------- Sep 1, 1857 - Jul 1, 1881

MT HERMAN NEW CHURCH CEMETERY

Located on the south side of County Road 19, approximately 2 1/2 miles west of York.

Bryant
  Atline -------- Died Sep 22, 1923 Age 71
Clark
  Jesse --------- Nov 14, 1861 - Nov 15, 1949

Cospey
  Rev. J. M. ---- Mar 4, 1861 - Jan 24, 1928

Grant
  Frank T. ------ Jul 4, 1865 - Mar 1, 1918

  Susan --------- Jan 20, 1836 - Nov 10, 1913

  Rev. Thomas --- Died Oct 4, 1900 Age 63 yrs

Harris
  Susan --------- 1853 - Dec 20, 1917

Henderson
  Nathan -------- Died Sep 14, 1911 Age 65

Henry
  James --------- Died Jan 3, 1906 Age 64

Houston
  Caroline ------ Died Aug 16, 1904 Age 54 yrs

Moore
  Wesley -------- May 12, 1849 - Jan 30, 1923

Nicholson
  Cherry -------- Died Dec 22, 1900 Age 69 yrs

  Henry --------- Died Feb 17, 1889 Age 62 yrs

Peterson
  Bill ---------- 1861 - 1953

Ward
  Will ---------- Sep 17, 1863 - Sep 14, 1926

Woodward
  L. A. --------- Jul 10, 1860 - Jun 6, 1912

MT HERMAN CHURCH OLD CEMETERY

Located on the north side of County Road 19, approximately 5 miles northwest of York.

Bell
L. C. --------- Born in Marlboro District of
S. Carolina Jan 29, 1836
Nov 20, 1868 32 yrs 9 mo 22 da

Burton
Amanda C. ----- May 28, 1845 - Dec 14, 1901

Jefferson C. -- Apr 27, 1839 - Jan 10, 1902

Cameron
Nancy --------- Dec 3, 1858 - Oct 28, 1937

Nathaniel ----- Oct 22, 1852 - Nov 6, 1911

Cobb
Martha A. ----- Wife of I. M. Cobb
Born Sumter Co. Ala.
Apr 27, 1855 - Nov 15, 1884

Mary ---------- Jun 11, 1808 - Oct 29, 1889

Tresa C. ------ Wife I. M. Cobb
Aug 20, 1863 - Nov 15, 1885

Dewitt
Mary A. ------- Wife of J. L. Dewitt
Mar 23, 1848 - Jul 17, 1889

Dial
John ---------- Nov 27, 1843 - Dec 28, 1925

Mary F. ------- Mar 14, 1848 - Dec 17, 1920

Gregory
Sarah A. ------ Born in Orange County, Virginia
Jan 10, 1804 - Jul 1, 1879

Harry
Francis
Marion -------- Mar 26, 1833 - Oct 3, 1875

Kay
  Dora ---------- 1818 - 1878

Kent
  Nancy Ann ----- Apr 9, 1812 - Apr 20, 1896

  Sarah Winn ---- May 16, 1854 - Jul 24, 1934

Lancaster
  James Edwin --- Dec 29, 1840 - Mar 17, 1925

Leard
  James O. ------ Born in 1817
                  May 10, 1905   88 yrs

  Louvenia ------ Wife J. O. Leard
                  Sep 16, 1820 - Sep 28, 1895
                  Age 75 yrs

Lynn
  Ella ---------- Sep 1, 1854 - Nov 3, 1873

  James --------- Feb 2, 1861 - Aug 16, 1865

  M. W. --------- Nov 19, 1819 - Mar 2, 1867

McGowen
  J. C. --------- Husband of Nancy McGowen
                  Jan 13, 1813 - Feb 9, 1900

  Nancy --------- Wife J. C. McGowen
                  Oct 22, 1818 - Jul 29, 1899

  R. J. --------- Husband of S. A. McGowen
                  Jul 1, 1839 - Oct 22, 1886

  William F. ---- Pvt., Co. K, 16th Regt., Ala.
                  Cav., CSA
                  Oct 26, 1846 - Apr 11, 1931

Sanders
  A. J. --------- Jan 6, 1828 - Dec 27, 1864

Known to be buried here:

      Lancaster, Agnes C.
      Lancaster, Lucy A.

Probably buried here:

    Lancaster, Sarah M.
    Lancaster, Talitha Ann Elizabeth

MT MORIAH CHURCH CEMETERY
(Destroyed)

From County Road 10, approximately 2 8/10 miles south of Cuba, turn east on Wilson Road. The cemetery is at approximately 3/10 mile, several hundred feet north of the road.

This cemetery has been destroyed. According to the Sumter County Register of Deaths, 1881 - 1892, the following persons are buried there.

Beavers
    Ida ------------ Sister of Henry Brewer

    Miss ----------- Born in N. Carolina
                        Died Dec 20, 1883   Age 40

Math(?)
    Fannie --------- Died Mar 7, 1884   Age 29

McElroy
    Miss ----------- Died Feb 27, 1884   Age 28

Reed
    Miss ----------- Died Sep 11, 1884   Age 36

MT TABOR BAPTIST CHURCH CEMETERY

From U. S. Highway 80, approximately 2 1/10 miles west of its intersection with State Highway 28, turn north on a dirt road. The church and cemetery are at approximately 1/2 mile, on the east side of road.

Brown
    Rolley --------- 1828 - Oct 12, 1901

Hardge
  Simon ---------- Nov 2, 1865 - Feb 8, 1948

Johnson
  S. A. ---------- 1859 - 1933

Kelly
  Julis ---------- Mar 3, 1856 - Feb 5, 1940

May
  Sam ------------ 1851 - 1924

  Susan ---------- 1854 - 1939

McCall
  Fannie --------- 1844 - Dec 17, 1917

Shackelford
  R. D. ---------- Jul 31, 1865 - Mar 15, 1948

Simpson
  Mat ------------ Wife of Zack Simpson
                   1852 - ?
                   Marker broken

Smith
  M. S. ---------- 1857 - Jan 2, 1929

Wabbington
  Ed ------------- Died Jun 24, 1914 Age 75 yrs

Wyatt
  John ----------- Jan 12, 1863 - Nov 10, 1939

MYRTLEWOOD CEMETERY

Located on East South Street in Livingston.

Abrahams
  James ---------- Son J. A. & S. T. Abrahams
                   Died Jul 31, 1839 1 yr & 4 mo

  James A. ------ Born Buckingham Co. Va.
                   Nov 12, 1804 - Jan 6, 1881

Abrahams (contd)
  James
    Randolph ------ Son J. A. & S. T. Abrahams
                    Died Jul 27, 1837
                    10 mo & 10 days

  Sarah T. Ward - Wife of J. A. Abrahams
                    Aug 15, 1812 - Aug 16, 1901

Adams
  Elvira L.
    Ustick -------- Relict of John W. Adams
                    A native of Abingdon, Virginia
                    Died Dec 11, 1887 Age 75

  John W. ------- Died Jun 6, 1843 Age 35

  John William -- (No dates) Age 11 months

  Lockey H. ----- Mar 28, 1824 - May 3, 1883

  Susan Ustick -- Died Dec 16, 1846 Age 6

  William F. L. - Born Montgomery Co. Tenn.
                    Jun 20, 1809 - Oct 24, 1855

  William F. L.
    Jr. ----------- Jul 24, 1853 - Mar 15, 1871

Allen
  Belle S. ------ Feb 16, 1859 - May 7, 1930

  Charles H. ---- Jul 15, 1857 - Jul 19, 1912

Amason
  Lydia C. ------ Wife of Asa Amason
                    Feb 1, 1929 - Apr 9, 1906

  S. C. M. ------ Aug 16, 1863 - May 28, 1927

Arrington
  Charles O. ---- Son Joseph & E. C. Arrington
                    Dec 20, 1858 - Oct 12, 1859

  Edward -------- Son Gen. Joseph & Mary J.
                    Arrington
                    Aug 27, 1826 - Jun 13, 1885

Arrington (contd)
Eugenia C. ---- 2nd Wife of Joseph Arrington
Nov 21, 1831 - Oct 17, 1871

Henry --------- Jan 22, 1864 - Aug 5, 1899

James C. ------ Dec 17, 1841 - Nov 6, 1904

Joeanner ------ Jan 16, 1862 - Dec 13, 1934

Joseph -------- Son Gen. Joseph & Mary J.
Arrington
Mar 26, 1817 - Sep 24, 1887

Joseph J. ----- Mar 13, 1827 - Nov 14, 1867

Lucy B. ------- Wife W. R. Arrington
Feb 21, 1851 - Nov 2, 1900

Mary ---------- Wife of William Arrington
Born in Brunswick Co. Va.
Died May 21, 1869

Mary Eliza ---- 3rd Wife of Joseph Arrington
Jan 28, 1841 - Dec 1, 1920

Mary F.
America ------- Apr 22, 1840 - Sep 6, 1935

Mary M. ------- Wife Dr. H. F. Arrington
Dau William & Sarah Jemison
Sep 1, 1817 - Nov 24, 1863

Patience Ann -- Born Nash Co. N. C. (No dates)

Robert -------- Born in Nash Co. N. C.
Mar 8, 1801 - Sep 16, 1867

Dr. Robert H. - Born in Halifax Co. N. C.
Apr 26, 1825 - Sep 27, 1892

W. R. --------- Jan 5, 1840 - Sep 8, 1894

Willie Ann ---- Sep 17, 1856 - Jul 19, 1936

Ayers
Daniel -------- Died Jan 3, 1871
60 yr 9 mo & 16 days

Baldwin
  Helen
  Vandegraff ---- Nov 18, 1860 - Feb 4, 1883

Bancroft
  Rev. J. ------- Apr 8, 1833 - Dec 15, 1901

Bardwell
  Hiram Francis - Son Hiram & Frances J. Bardwell
                  Apr 22, 1846 - Sep 24, 1849

Barker
  Benjamin ------ Mar 26, 1833 - Dec 21, 1874

  Cordine H. ---- Jun 14, 1865 - Mar 4, 1880

Barnes
  Robert A. ----- Nov 9, 1858 - Aug 11, 1895

Barnett
  Samuel A. ----- Born Abbeville Co. S. C.
                  Dec 24, 1832 - May 25, 1904

Battle
  D. T. --------- Feb 21, 1852 - May 3, 1931

  Ludie S. ------ Wife of W. D. Battle Jr.
                  Apr 9, 1846 - Mar 23, 1913

  Mollie
  Kornegay ------ Apr 28, 1853 - Jan 21, 1919

  Mrs. S. E. S. - Born in Nash Co. N. C.
                  Jan 12, 1824 - Aug 26, 1878

  W. D. Jr. ----- Apr 23, 1845 - Mar 12, 1917

  William D. ---- Born in Franklin N. C.
                  Aug 24, 1822 - Dec 27, 1896

  Willie D. ----- Son W. D. & Ludie Battle
                  (No dates)

Beach
  Erasmus
  Darwin -------- Son E. D. & Jane C. Beach
                  Died May 4, 1856 Age 8

Bedwell
  Albert M. ----- Jun 15, 1856 - Apr 8, 1882, CSA

Beggs
  Martha
  Alexander ----- Wife of William Beggs
                  1826 - 1883

  William ------- Born in Ireland
                  Aug 1, 1825 - Dec 19, 1893

Bell
  Mattie D.
  Powell -------- Wife of W. W. Bell
                  Born Corinth, Miss.
                  Sep 6, 1865 - May 21, 1899

Binns
  Henrietta
  Caroline ------ Dau Charles H. & Adeline Binns
                  Oct 17, 1839 - Mar 17, 1841

  Martha
  Eleanor ------- Born in New Kent Co. Va.
                  Sep 24, 1814 - Jun 2, 1836

Blackwell
  Thomas J. ----- Born in Trenton, N. J.
                  May 19, 1801 - Oct 9, 1847

Boggs
  Louisa Ann ---- Wife Rev. G. W. Boggs
                  Born Anderson Dist. S. C.
                  Jan 20, 1821 - May 28, 1854

Boyd
  Isarella
  Stephenson ---- Eldest Dau Sam B. & Susan H.
                  Boyd Apr 6, 1831 - Jun 29, 1836

Boynton --------- Four-grave lot. No markers.

Bradford
  James Thomas -- Born Plainfield, Conn.
                  Oct 13, 1806 - Feb 17, 1863

259

Bradford (contd)
  Jerusha L. ---- Wife of James T. Bradford
                   Born Willingford, Conn.
                   Nov 3, 1806 - Jul 4, 1852

Bradshaw
  John W. ------- Sep 18, 1837 - Mar 8, 1899
                 CSA

  Lizzie -------- Jan 1, 1834 - Apr 26, 1902

Branch
  Sarah Rebecca - Wife of James Branch
                 Aug 6, 1829 - Jun 10, 1886

Breitling
  Otto G. ------- Jul 9, 1860 - Sep 11, 1930

Brock
  George
  William ------- Feb 18, 1864 - May 20, 1941

Brockway
  Carrie L. ----- Jul 5, 1855 - Jan 13, 1921

  Charles J. ---- Sep 13, 1851 - Oct 7, 1916

  Martha E. ----- Wife Dr. A. E. Brockway
                 Jun 11, 1830 - Apr 1, 1908

Brown
  George A. ----- Apr 12, 1815 - Apr 5, 1896

  John C. ------- Jul 16, 1817 - Oct 17, 1871

  John Louis ---- Son Louis L. & Amaranth Parker
                 Brown. Born in Sumterville,
                 Ala. 1841. Died in Livingston,
                 Ala. May 22, 1917. Lieut.
                 Hamptons Brigade in Va., CSA

  Laura --------- Dau J. C. & M. B. Brown
                 (No dates)

  Lula Godfrey -- Nov 14, 1860 - Dec 8, 1900

  Rosa Knox ----- Wife J. L. Brown
                 Jul 13, 1845 - Feb 18, 1928

Brown (contd)
  Sarah Godfrey - Wife George A. Brown
                    Feb 6, 1822 - Jul 16, 1896

Bullock
  Charlie H. ---- Aug 10, 1842 - Feb 14, 1899

  Susan F. ------ Dec 8, 1854 - Sep 25, 1899

Butler
  Leonidas W. --- A native of N. Carolina
                  D Aug 30, 1847

Callaway
  Maggie Bryan -- Dau R. B. & M. E. Callaway
                  (No dates)

  Margaret
  Edmundson ----- (No dates)

  Robert Baker -- (No dates)

Chapman
  Alta ---------- Apr 9, 1863 - May 28, 1947

  Mary
  Catherine ----- Wife of Reuben Chapman
                  Dau J. L. & T. M. Scruggs
                  Jul 22, 1842 - Jun 29, 1912

  Mary Lucinda
  Newell -------- Wife Judge Samuel Chapman
                  Feb 24, 1799 - Aug 29, 1836

  Rebecca S. ---- Wife of Reuben Chapman
                  Dau Robert & Patience Arrington
                  Jan 16, 1835 - Mar 1, 1866

  Capt. Reuben -- May 25, 1833 - Apr 30, 1902

Chilcoat
  Martha Betty -- Jun 28, 1833 - Nov 29, 1836

Chiles
  Jane Harper --- 1865 - 1949

  Samuel H. ----- (No dates)

Chiles (contd)
William
Sidney -------- 1853 - 1928

Clark
Jack ---------- (No dates) CSA

Cleveland
Lucy Adela ---- Wife of A. A. Cleveland
May 28, 1854 - Feb 19, 1901

Cobbs
Bettie Gaines - Jul 10, 1858 - Jan 9, 1869

James --------- Born in Raleigh, N. C.
Oct 22, 1830 - Jun 3, 1889

Julia Boon ---- Oct 7, 1862 - Sep 16, 1863

Lucy Thom ----- 1832 - 1911

Maggie A. ----- Jun 1, 1860 - Nov 3, 1875

Margaret Lake - Wife of James Cobbs
Apr 22, 1836 - Jul 22, 1914

Thomas -------- Aug 5, 1826 - Jun 19, 1902

Cockrell
Eleanor ------- Wife of L. A. Cockrell
Nov 3, 1858 - Apr 16, 1890

Eva Nash ------ 1850 - 1872

Hester
Elizabeth
Gulley -------- Sep 29, 1860 - Jun 20, 1939

Two Infants --- (No dates)

__?__ Jamie --- (No dates)

L. A. --------- Nov 17, 1839 - Nov 27, 1922

__?__ Lily
Belle --------- (No dates)

Cockrell (contd)
  Minna --------- Wife of L. A. Cockrell
                    Mar 23, 1842 - Jun 11, 1883

  Susan Spratt -- Wife A. W. Cockrell
                 Mar 9, 1842 - Apr 10, 1871

Coleman
  Emma S. ------- Wife Dr. William Harris Coleman
                  Died May 5, 1854 Age 26

  Jesse Bell ---- Jun 7, 1839 - Jul 10, 1892

  Sarah Kynerd -- Mar 5, 1843 - Oct 8, 1911

Cook
  Chauncy ------- Born in Utica, N. Y.
               Nov 10, 1800 - Oct 15, 1853

  J. M. --------- (No dates) CSA

Cooper
  William Frank - May 14, 1863 - Aug 27, 1931

Copeland
  Nathan -------- (No dates) CSA

Cornick
  Mary ---------- Dau T. R. & S. H. Cornick
              Oct 6, 1843 - Oct 9, 1843

Cowin
  Cornelia C. --- Sep 18, 1847 - Jul 5, 1921

Cravens
  Margaret E. --- Born Marengo Co. Alabama
              Jan 2, 1821 - Oct 18, 1853

Crenshaw
  Frances ------- Died Jul 20, 1840 Age 44

  Mary H. ------- Dau Gen. Davie Crockett
              Born Halifax Co. N.C.
              Jun 25, 1790.
              Married Feb 17, 1825
              Died Nov 24, 1849

Crenshaw (contd)
Thomas A. ----- Son Willis & Amanda Crenshaw
                 Died Apr 15, 1845 Age 2

__?__ --------- Son Willis & Amanda Crenshaw
                 Died 1844 Age 10

Cunningham
Evelyn -------- (No dates)

Tully R. ------ (No dates)

William ------- (No dates)

Daily
Etta ---------- Mar 30, 1865 - Apr 3, 1932

Dainwood
George W. ----- Jan 23, 1829 - May 22, 1905

George
William ------- (No dates)

Lilburn ------- Son G. W. & M. U. Dainwood
                 (No dates)

Lydia Weir ---- Dau G. W. & M. U. Dainwood
                 May 14, 1860 - Jul 22, 1896

Matilda Baldwin
Ustick -------- Jul 11, 1836 - Jan 12, 1911

Daly
Maria --------- Dau Peter & Mary E. Daly
                 Born & Died Jan 1, 1850

Martha C. ----- Dau Peter & Mary E. Daly
                 Died May 1836 Age 6

Davidson
Augustus
Cleveland ----- Dec 3, 1846 - Mar 31, 1840

Elizabeth
Keene --------- Wife of A. C. Davidson
                 Aug 6, 1851 - Feb 16, 1922

Davis
   Hugh ---------- (No dates) CSA

DeLoach
   Alfred B. ------ 1811 - 1854

   Etheldra C. --- 1818 - 1857

   Susan
   Thornton ------ Wife Judge W. R. DeLoach
                   Dec 16, 1842 - Jan 15, ?

   Capt. W. R. --- Jun 4, 1842 - Aug 5, 1910

Desha
   Eleanor ------- Dau of Robert Desha
                   Aug 31, 1926 - Sep 30, 1840

   Euphemia ------ Consort of Robert Desha
                   Jul 16, 1812 - Dec 13, 1840

Dodson
   Elizabeth ----- May 5, 1838 - Aug 23, 1861

   Ernest Clark -- Mar 16, 1862 - Jun 27, 1862

   Juliett T. ---- Aug 24, 1832 - Oct 9, 1872

   Robert Wesley - Dec 2, 1857 - Aug 24, 1859

Dotti
   Maria
   Soberling ----- Jan 10, 1837 - Jun 9, 1905

Eason
   John Mitchell - Nov 10, 1858 - Jun 3, 1892

   Joseph
   Addison ------- Died Sep 20, 1880 Age 21

   M. L. G. ------ Nov 19, 1816 - Apr 27, 1900

Edwards
   Alonzo Jones -- Mar 25, 1824 - Jan 15, 1841

   Narcissa
   Hansford ------ Jul 24, 1829 - Jul 15, 1847

Ennis
   Annie E. ------ Dec 18, 1845 - Dec 4, 1913

   Robert
   Washington ---- Mar 6, 1842 - Oct 29, 1918

Evans
   A. P. --------- Dec 8, 1849 - Jul 2, 1903

   Frederick P. -- Born Edgecomb Co. N. C.
                  Dec 29, 1809 - _?_

   Joe Helen ----- Aug 9, 1853 - Aug 3, 1922

   Paul Emmet ---- Son of F. P. & Arabella Evans
                  Died Jan 19, 1869   27 yr 9 mo

Everett
   W. G. J. ------ 1862 - 1908

Faust
   Rev. John E. -- Died Jun 7, 1882   Age 46

Fellows
   Delphine ------ Wife of H. D. Fellows
                  Nov 6, 1841 - Sep 24, 1886

   G. B. --------- Jul 25, 1859 - May 19, 1907

   H. D ---------- Sep 29, 1833 - Jul 23, 1884 CSA

   Hortense
   Parrent ------- Wife George B. Fellows
                  Jan 24, 1861 - Sep 30, 1918

Fluker
   Emmie K. ------ 1851 - 1894

   George M. ----- 1850 - 1907

Foard
   Francis ------- Died Jun 18, 1850   Age 62

Forster
   Laura Brown --- Mar 15, 1836 - Mar 5, 1893

Fortner
   A. D. --------- (No dates) CSA

Fortner (contd)
  Mrs. L. A. ---- Died May 29, 1897

Gage
  Olive Winston - Jun 11, 1864 - Mar 4, 1942

Gaines
  Fannie -------- (No dates)

  Susan Frances - (No dates)

Gardner
  Melvina
  Sledge -------- Dec 7, 1862 - Dec 5, 1921

Gee
  Betty Isaacs -- Wife of Paul J. Gee
               Dec 7, 1856 - Sep 12, 1906

  Paul J. ------- Dec 23, 1853 - Jan 8, 1917

Gibbs
  Anne Frances -- Consort of R. T. Gibbs
               Dau George S. & Mary Thom
               Born in Culpepper Co. Va.
               Mar 1, 1818 - Aug 21, 1848

Gould
  Bettie Beebe -- Apr 27, 1861 - Dec 14, 1939

Gowdey
  George
  Clarence ------ Aug 19, 1850 - Feb 2, 1927

Hainsworth
  J. L. --------- Born in Linden, Alabama
              Feb 28, 1825 - Oct 19, 1857

Hair
  Elizabeth W. -- Consort of James Hair, Esq.
              Jun 20, 1800 - Mar 5, 1837

  James --------- Jun 1790 - Jan 9, 1863

  Martha A. A. -- Mar 5, 1835 - Aug 28, 1836

  Martha W. ----- Apr 3, 1799 - Oct 13, 1874

Hair (contd)
      Robert A. ----- Apr 1, 1836 - Jan 20, 1837

      William A. ---- Nov 15, 1833 - Aug 19, 1850

Hale
   Harvey
   Stewart ------- Only Child S. A. & M. A. Hale
                   Mar 30, 1859 - Mar 28, 1863

   Mary Ann ------ Wife of Samuel A. Hale
                   Died Oct 18, 1860 Age 24

Harris
   Eva ----------- (No dates)

   Gertrude ------ Dau of H. H. & M. S. Harris
                   Aug 9, 1847 - Jul 9, 1850

   H. H. --------- Feb 15, 1815 - Sep 1, 1862

   Henry C. ------ (No dates) CSA

   Irene --------- Dau of H. H. & M. S. Harris
                   (No dates)

   Lizzie -------- Jul 14, 1838 - Feb 13, 1894

   Mary S. ------- Born in Knoxville, Tenn.
                   Feb 20, 1826 - Aug 4, 1896

   Norlet T. ----- Feb 18, 1859 - Apr 11, 1916

   Park
   McClelland ---- Feb 20, 1846 - Mar 1, 1882

   R. M. --------- Jun 30, 1831 - Mar 3, 1904

   Robert -------- Jul 20, 1853 - Oct 2, 1888

   Sam B. -------- (No dates)

   Willie -------- Child of H. H. & M. S. Harris
                   (No dates)

Hawkins
   D. B. --------- (No dates) CSA

Henagan
  James M. ------ Died May 22, 1903

  Kate Brown ---- Aug 8, 1850 - Dec 26, 1910

Henderson
  Mary E. ------- Born in Onslow Co. N. C.
                  Nov 26, 1837 - Oct 5, 1850

  Thomas -------- Born in Onslow Co. N. C.
                  Mar 18, 1815 - Sep 27, 1850

Herr
  Ben F. -------- May 16, 1830 - Nov 14, 1898
                  CSA

  Ernest -------- Son B. F. & Mary A. Herr
                  Nov 10, 1865 - May 10, 1876

Hill
  James Twyman -- Son Ambrose & Frances Hill
                  Born in Culpepper Co. Va.
                  Jan 20, 1809 - Feb 4, 1851

Hoit
  Elizabeth
  Hair ---------- Jul 18, 1820 - Jan 6, 1890

  Hamilton Hair - Son I. D. & Elizabeth Hair Hoit
                  Feb 2, 1854 - Oct 6, 1854

  Isiah D. ------ Feb 9, 1818 - 1895

  Zane M. ------- Jul 18, 1846 - Sep 19, 1882

Hooks
  Coster -------- May 20, 1855 - Dec 17, 1907

  E. W. --------- (No dates) CSA

  Margaret
  Adeline ------- Wife David William Hooks
                  Jul 13, 1824 - May 17, 1906

Hopkins
  Elizabeth W. -- Wife of D. Hopkins
                  Born in Greensboro
                  Dec 13, 1821 - Mar 2, 1881

Hopkins (contd)
  Julia B. ------ Dec 6, 1856 - Nov 27, 1933

  Kate E. ------- Dau Devereaux & Elizabeth W.
                  Hopkins
                  Jul 6, 1846 - Dec 24, 1928

  William W. ---- Jun 21, 1841 - May 31, 1914

Houston
  Florence May -- Dau M. C. & M. L. Houston
                  Sep 22, 1843 - Sep 17, 1862

  J. Sanford ---- Apr 24, 1861 - Feb 19, 1898

  Joe Clint ----- Feb 17, 1864 - Nov 8, 1883

  John Clinton -- Jul 11, 1831 - Dec 17, 1910

  Lizzie -------- Dau of M. C. & E. H. Houston
                  Nov 14, 1825 - Mar 6, 1873

  M. C. --------- Born in Blount Co. Tenn.
                  Oct 21, 1799 - Feb 22, 1872

  Martha L. ----- Wife of M. C. Houston
                  Born in Blount Co. Tenn.
                  Dec 22, 1806 - Jun 11, 1884

  Mollie G. ----- Dau J. C. & Ginnie Houston
                  Oct 4, 1856 - May 13, 1873

  S. A. --------- Sep 18, 1838 - Sep 9, 1843

  Sallie M. ----- Dec 1, 1842 - Dec 23, 1928

  Virginia ------ Wife of J. C. Houston
                  Dec 18, 1829 - Oct 20, 1898

  W. A. --------- Died Sep 24, 1851
                  4 yrs & 7 mo

Hull
  Adah W. ------- Wife of Frank Hull
                  Aug 8, 1847 - Jul 31, 1888

Hunter
  Anna J. ------- May 30, 1849 - Nov 17, 1889

Hunter (contd)
  Boanerges
    Clay ---------- Born in Logan Co. Ky.
                        Feb 22, 1842 - Oct 22, 1922
                        CSA

  Ella Lake ----- Feb 12, 1863 - May 10, 1934

  James Howlett - Mar 1, 1858 - Jan 11, 1930

  Mary
    Elizabeth ----- Sep 24, 1864 - Nov 14, 1946

  Dr. Robert L. - Died Aug 7, 1856 Age 46

Hutchinson
  Virginia
    Richardson ---- Wife Alfred H. Hutchinson
                      Mar 19, 1841 - Nov 2, 1925

Hyatt
  Devereaux M. -- 1856 - 1937

Ivy
  Ben ----------- Apr 11, 1806 - Sep 25, 1858

Jackson
  Eliza M. ------ Wife of John Jackson
                Oct 12, 1843 - Dec 13, 1912

  James B. ------ Sep 6, 1857 - Mar 21, 1937

  John ---------- Sep 26, 1823 - Sep 26, 1893

  John ---------- Apr 19, 1836 - Jan 18, 1915

  Mollie B. ----- Oct 25, 1861 - Jan 26, 1952

Jarman
  Hunter Gordon - Wife of P. B. Jarman
                  1860 - 1932

  Peter Bryant -- 1857 - 1934

Jemison
  Jane ---------- Jan 15, 1785 - Oct 5, 1860

  John Steel ---- Died Aug 10, 1843 Age 30

Jemison (contd)
  ? --------- (No dates) CSA

Jenkins
  Jane L. ------- Mar 9, 1830 - Nov 16, 1895
  Joseph W. ----- May 8, 1820 - Mar 24, 1894
  Leroy --------- Jul 11, 1805 - Feb 2, 1888

Johnston
  Emily H. ------ Wife Thomas A. Johnston
                Born Wayne Co. N. C.
                Jan 20, 1824 - Dec 5, 1893

  John S. ------- 1853 - 1917

  Margaret V. --- 1856 - 1932

  Mattie M. ----- Dec 31, 1847 - Jul 5, 1864

  Thomas A. ----- Born in Herkimer Co. N. Y.
                Jun 4, 1813 - Nov 16, 1872

Jones
  D. Bestor ----- Feb 10, 1799 - Feb 19, 1887

  Frederick
  Houston ------- Oct 3, 1858 - Jul 16, 1921

  Harden L. ----- Jun 19, 1864 - Apr 19, 1908

  Mary Esther --- Wife of W. A. C. Jones
                Aug 26, 1830 - Jan 11, 1909

  Mary
  Hutchinson ---- Wife of F. H. Jones
                Sep 18, 1862 - Jan 9, 1930

  W. A. C. ------ Jun 17, 1829 - Aug 17, 1911

  William H. ---- Son W. A. C. & M. E. Jones
                Apr 16, 1862 - Aug 21, 1862

Kenard
  John M. ------- Died Apr 17, 1843
                36 yrs & 14 days

Kennard
  Amanda -------- Wife of James Kennard
                  Feb 17, 1812 - Aug 24, 1870

  Bettie -------- Dau J. P. & Amanda Kennard
                  Jun 25, 1852 - Nov 8, 1856

  James P. ------ Son J. P. & M. A. Kennard
                  Aug 8, 1836 - Apr 12, 1843

  Minerva Ann --- Wife of James P. Kennard
                  Died Apr 6, 1843
                  28, 11, & 19

  Missouri
  Phillips ------ Dec 15, 1864 - Jul 25, 1955

  Nancy D. ------ Dau J. P. & N. D. Kennard
                  Jul 7, 1830 - Apr 22, 1843

  Sally J. ------ Wife of John Kennard
                  Apr 2, 1845 - Oct 11, 1872

  Smith O. ------ Son J. P. & N. D. Kennard
                  Sep 23, 1828 - Oct 9, 1854

Kinnard
  Calvin -------- Died Mar 8, 1905   Age 79 yrs

  Michael
  Claiborne
  M.D. ---------- Born Williamson Co. Tenn.
                  Nov 30, 1831 - Sep 12, 1878

Lake
  Ella ---------- Dau Joseph & Margaret Lake
                  Jan 25, 1839 - Jun 27, 1858

  Joseph Henry -- Son Joseph & Margaret Lake
                  Aug 17, 1842 - Jul 15, 1843

  Joseph J. ----- Son T. H. & Sarah Lake
                  Died Oct 27, 1855 Age 6 mo

  Margaret
  Gains --------- Consort of Joseph Lake
                  Born in Tennessee
                  Feb 5, 1802 - May 21, 1843

Lake (contd)
N. Scales ----- May 8, 1825 - Jul 5, 1847

Sarah Lane ---- Wife of T. H. Lake
Dau M. C. & M. L. Houston
Jun 10, 1836 - Dec 11, 1870

Lamberson
J. L. --------- Jul 9, 1849 - Jan 18, 1851

Lancaster
Albert Jr. ---- Jun 15, 1855 - 1883

Ben ----------- Oct 6, 1847 - Oct 2, 1902

Elizabeth ----- Died Oct 30, 1900

Martha Jane --- Jun 18, 1846 - Apr 21, 1932

Sally --------- Apr 23, 1849 - 1881

Lawhon
Annie H. ------ Wife of John Lawhon
Dau of E. & A. Porter
Apr 22, 1849 - Jun 6, 1880

Infant -------- Died Aug 2, 1869

John ---------- Died Apr 17, 1920
Lt., Co. F, 3rd Ala. Cav., CSA

Lawrence
William
Haywood ------- Mar 18, 1860 - Jun 1, 1938

Lee
Frank --------- (No dates) CSA

Leverett
H. B. --------- Died Jul 6, 1867

Lide
Hugh S. ------- Mar 25, 1831 - Jan 21, 1879

Little
    Capt. Ben B. -- Born Edgecomb Co. N. C.
                    Jan 25, 1831
                    Killed in battle Jonesboro, Ga.
                    Aug 31, 1864 CSA

    Dr. Blake ----- Died Mar 8, 1873

    H. Emmett ----- Died May 6, 1898

    James Hibbler - Feb 27, 1862 - Nov 8, 1897

    Manie --------- Died May 11, 1913

    Mrs. S. B. ---- Died Mar 13, 1924

    Mrs. Susan ---- Born in Georgia in 1835
                    Died Aug 21, 1863

    Willie Gray --- Son Ben B. & Susan Little
                    Feb 24, 1857 - Apr 25, 1857

Lockard
    Amanda F. ----- Jun 28, 1815 - Jul 1, 1882

    Gertrude
    Alice --------- Sep 1, 1848 - Jun 12, 1912

    Lucinda
    Adeline ------- Jul 14, 1838 - Feb 13, 1910

    T. E. --------- 1845 - 1929
                    Phelans Battery, CSA

    William ------- Apr 16, 1807 - May 22, 1872

Lott
    Henrietta T. -- 1865 - 1936

Lowe
    Catherine ----- 1863 - 1951

Luke
    Marion -------- May 4, 1857 - Mar 26, 1914

    Mary E. ------- Jun 22, 1861 - Mar 21, 1926

Maggard
  Joseph A. J. -- Son David & Pernelia Maggard
                   Died Oct 18, 1843 Age 7 mo

Makin
  Mary Alice ---- Wife Thomas G. Makin
               Jun 27, 1864 - Dec 28, 1915

Mason
  Ann ----------- Consort Robert S. Mason
               Apr 16, 1839 - Mar 11, 1881

  George -------- (No dates) CSA

  Robert -------- Sep 9, 1815 - Dec 23, 1899

  Robert
  Saunders ------ Aug 23, 1840 - Jun 6, 1923
               1st Lt., Co. D, Stuart's Cav.,
               CSA

  Sarah A. ------ Sep 6, 1817 - Dec 1, 1904

  Sophia
  Slaughter ----- Wife of John Mason
               Aug 21, 1792 - Mar 21, 1850

Maury
  Alexander C. -- Lieutenant, U.S. Navy
               Jun 5, 1805 - Jun 23, 1840

McCain
  Clarence M. --- Oct 18, 1860 - Nov 28, 1905

  Frances Lou
  Hodges -------- Wife of Adam S. McCain Mother
               of A. C., C. M., Leila, W. J. &
               Lula McCain 1838 - 1908

  Isabella M. --- Apr 10, 1857 - Oct 31, 1931

  Dr. W. J. ----- 1864 - 1952

McConico
  Eliza --------- Died Jan 27, 1924 Age 93

McConnico
Bettie Ann ---- Dau C. S. & J. S. McConnico
Died May 10, 1851

C. S. --------- Aug 13, 1820 - Aug 5, 1868

Garner M. ----- Son C. S. & Ann McConnico
D Dec 1, 1860 8 mo & 18 days

Jacqueline S. - Wife of C. S. McConnico
Died Jun 12, 1853

Jacqueline S. - Dau C. S. & J. S. McConnico
Died Aug 4, 1854

Maggie Jane --- Dau C. S. & J. S. McConnico
Died Oct 4, 1852

Zora Jane ----- Dau C. S. & J. S. McConnico
Died Sep 17, 1849

McDonald
James --------- Apr 4, 1848 - Aug 27, 1910

Malcolm Boyd -- Apr 23, 1845 - Nov 5, 1890

Martha A. ----- Apr 6, 1845 - Feb 2, 1882

_?_ --------- Feb 11, 1847 - Dec 24, 1924

McHelm
R. Melville --- Died May 10, 1893 Age 45

McKnight
F. H. --------- Jul 22, 1814 - Nov 5, 1880

Margaret
Sprott -------- May 2, 1848 - Jun 22, 1919

Susan A. ------ Jul 1, 1822 - Jul 1, 1889

William
Thomas -------- Jun 19, 1846 - Sep 28, 1922
CSA

McRae
Martha H. ----- Nov 3, 1852 - Jul 29, 1853

McRae (contd)
W. B. --------- (No dates) CSA

William P.
M.D. ---------- Dec 2, 1821 - Mar 3, 1853

Willie -------- Apr 15, 1850 - Oct 30, 1938

Mellen
George
Frederick ----- 1859 - 1927

Henry Levi ---- Dec 18, 1865 - Aug 25, 1941

Mary Briscoe
Baldwin ------- Wife Dr. G. F. Mellen
                     Born Houston, Miss. 1862
                     Died Knoxville, Tenn. 1946

Prof. S. S.,
L.L.D. -------- Born Pelham, Mass.
                     Feb 7, 1821 - May 30, 1893

Susan H. ------ Born in Whateley, Mass.
                     Nov 18, 1830 - Mar 17, 1898

Miller
Charles
Brooks -------- Son T. K. & C. B. Miller
                     Mar 14, 1858 - Dec 7, 1858

Mitchell
Annie P. ------ Wife of D. W. Mitchell
                     Dec 7, 1844 - Feb 15, 1884

D. W. --------- May 30, 1842 - Jan 20, 1888

Edwin L. ------ Apr 28, 1858 - May 5, 1941

James A. ------ Mar 28, 1865 - Aug 20, 1941

Jessie
Nichols ------- Dec 6, 1861 - Feb 20, 1888

Preston
Augustus ------ Oct 8, 1859 - Apr 15, 1944

Monett
  Samuel -------- Died Jul 14, 1854 Age 52

Moore
  Dr. A. E. ----- Sep 21, 1834 - Apr 23, 1911

  Aaron --------- Dec 3, 1804 - Aug 20, 1841

  Amanda E. ----- Jul 1, 1825 - Nov 10, 1912

  Josiah -------- Jun 12, 1813 - Mar 7, 1859

  W. H. --------- Dec 13, 1852 - Mar 7, 1860

  William F. ---- Jun 28, 1806 - Apr 29, 1845

Mooring
  Theodocia
  Hainsworth ---- May 22, 1831 - May 14, 1912

Murley
  Anne ---------- Consort of Stephen W. Murley
                  Dau Asa Beebe of Fayetteville,
                  N. C. Died Apr 24, 1852 Age 38

  D. S. M. ------ Died Sep 12, 1847 Age 20 days

  J. S. M. ------ Died Jan 3, 1844 Age 18 days

  Mary Alice ---- Dau S. W. & H. D. Murley
                  Died Nov 24, 1861 Age 7

  S. W. M. ------ Died Jun 6, 1844 Age 21 days

  W. A. --------- (No dates) CSA

Murray
  Belle Trott --- Wife of Lewis Murray
                  May 4, 1820 - Jan 28, 1893

  Robert Lewis -- Sep 7, 1851 - Sep 3, 1928

Myers
  Ann ----------- 1849 - 1924

  Tom ----------- 1847 - 1914
  (Above inscriptions are on a single marker.)

Nash
Cora (?) ------ (No dates)

Dr. Joe T. ---- Mar 13, 1857 - Nov 26, 1909

Lampedo ------- 1822 - 1885

P. G. --------- Born Lovingston, Va.
Jul 3, 1820 - Feb 20, 1883

Paulina (?) --- (No dates)

Neilson
Eugenie
Amason -------- Wife Robert C. Neilson
Aug 20, 1857 - Oct 19, 1883

Nelson
Phillip Meade - Jan 20, 1844 - Jul 16, 1929
CSA

Newman
Frank --------- Died May 12, 1853 Age 10 mo

Nichols
Annie M. ------ Jun 18, 1839 - Nov 21, 1896

W. J. --------- Died Dec 10, 1868 Age 35

William
Sanders ------- Jun 25, 1863 - Jul 26, 1931

Norville
Hardy W. ------ Born Edgecomb Co. N. C.
Jun 3, 1813 - Apr 10, 1878

Hardynia Kate - Oct 1, 1863 - Feb 3, 1941
Missionary to Mexico 1891 -
1911 Missionary to S. America
W.C.T.U. 1913 - 1931

John H. ------- Aug 28, 1854 - Sep 30, 1918

Jordon Short -- Aug 30, 1861 - Sep 7, 1887

Mary Ann
Hodges -------- Born in Greene Co. Ala.
Oct 11, 1830 - Jul 11, 1890

Norwood
  Lt. Col. James
   K. ------------ Son Daniel H. & Milly Norwood
                   Jan 7, 1831 - Aug 22, 1866, CSA

Nowles
  Sarah A. M. --- Died 1847

Park
  Irene H. ------ Consort of Robert N. Park
                  Dau of M. C. & M. L. Houston
                  Jan 20, 1841 - Oct 19, 1858

Parker
  Elizabeth P. -- Feb 3, 1828 - Dec 26, 1900

  James Lake ---- 1859 - 1946

  Mary M. ------- Dau Socrates & Elizabeth Parker
                  Mar 11, 1853 - Nov 6, 1853

  Socrates ------ Jul 22, 1820 - May 6, 1881

  Tennie
  Letcher ------- Jan 27, 1864 - Jan 22, 1875

Parrent
  Cornelia Ann -- Jan 28, 1834 - Apr 19, 1913

  Ellen M. ------ Died Dec 17, 1856 Age 30

  James L. ------ Jul 3, 1842 - May 28, 1861

  Mary Caroline - Wife of L. Parrent
                  Died May 2, 1848 Age 24

  Preston Nash -- Aug 11, 1846 - Feb 27, 1860

Perkins
  John ---------- A native of Lincoln Co. N. C.
                  Died Sep 27, 1834 Age 30

Petty
  L. B. --------- May 18, 1851 - Mar 30, 1915

Phillips
  Adam E. ------- 1853 - 1881

Phillips (contd)
Ellen Cobbs --- Wife of J. H. Phillips
　　　　　　　　Jul 29, 1854 - May 27, 1893

John T.,
D.D.S. -------- May 20, 1860 - Nov 8, 1948

Pickens
Fannie West --- 1849 - 1931

William King -- 1847 - 1923

Posey
Eleanor ------- Consort of Capt. Jesse H. Posey
　　　　　　　　Died Jan 7, 1837 Age 55

Powell
E. A. Jr. ----- Jan 31, 1855 - Aug 17, 1883

Pratt
Maude Callaway - Wife of Charles P. Pratt
　　　　　　　　 Dau Robert & Margaret Callaway
　　　　　　　　 (No dates)

Praytor
Middleton A. -- Feb 20, 1852 - Aug 11, 1894

Price
Rev. E. G. ---- Jan 10, 1849 - Aug 4, 1906

Pruitt
Dewitt A. ----- Feb 13, 1855 - Aug 10, 1889

Quarles
Garrett Minor - Dec 16, 1848 - Oct 26, 1897

Randall
Clara B. ------ Dec 26, 1853 - Apr 30, 1918

Dr. Newton ---- Sep 28, 1851 - Aug 23, 1904
　　　　　　　　CSA

Rast
David Irvin --- Born in Orangeburg Dist. S. C.
　　　　　　　　Jan 17, 1830 - Sep 29, 1870

Ellen Ustick -- Wife of D. I. Rast
　　　　　　　　May 12, 1834 - Jul 5, 1901

Ratican
    Michael ------- A native of Ireland
                    Died 1834   Age 38

Reynolds
    Col. Alfred
    C. ------------ Born in Georgetown, Va.
                    Nov 2, 1843 - Apr 28, 1915

    Ella B. ------- Feb 19, 1846 - Feb 17, 1914

Roan
    G. T. --------- Died Oct 9, 1907   Age 67

Robinson
    Eliza M. ------ Consort of Leroy Robinson
                    Died Dec 18, 1852   Age 33

Sanders
    Maggie B. ----- Dau B. B. & Beatrice Sanders
                    Jun 24, 1864 - Dec ?, 1867

Saunders
    Sophia -------- Wife George B. Saunders
                    Feb 8, 1829 - Aug 20, 1847

Savage
    James Esq. ---- Born in Ireland
                    1780 - Dec 19, 1837

Scales
    Martha
    Elizabeth ----- Dau Peter Perkins & Caroline
                    Hancock Scales.
                    Born in Tennessee
                    Feb 5, 1829 - Feb 7, 1842

Scarbrough
    William H. ---- Oct 30, 1854 - Dec 18, 1933

Scruggs
    Etta Elizabeth
    Houston ------- Wife of J. O. Scruggs
                    Feb 21, 1854 - Feb 5, 1937

    Fannie Lowe --- Wife of J. L. Scruggs
                    Jun 28, 1822 - Feb 2, 1896

Scruggs (contd)
  Infant -------- J. L. & M. T. Scruggs
                  (No dates)

  J. L. --------- Born Buckingham Co. Va.
                  May 2, 1816 - Mar 18, 1891

  James
  Whitehead ----- Son J. L. & M. T. Scruggs
                  Sep 24, 1857 - Oct 8, 1858

  Joseph
  Oglesby ------- Mar 19, 1859 - Dec 5, 1923

  Malvina T. ---- Dau J. L. & M. T. Scruggs
                  Feb 26, 1852 - May 18, 1853

  Tempie M. ----- Born Nash Co. N. C.
                  Sep 29, 1817 - Mar 31, 1873

Seely
  Caroline M. --- 1845 - 1856

  James D. ------ 1847 - 1856

Shearer
  Ellen --------- Consort W. Waldo Shearer
                  Died Oct 17, 1844 Age 18

  William Kirby - Son W. W. & E. A. Shearer
                  Aug 24, 1844 - Jun 3, 1848

Shelton
  R. J. --------- Jun 10, 1860 - Jan 16, 1927

Sherard
  Alfred D. ----- Son J. H. & M. M Sherard
                  Jul 26, 1847 - Sep 7, 1848

  John H. ------- Feb 8, 1798 - Jun 26, 1855

  Solon L. (?) -- Jan 1840 - Mar 1871

Sims
  Aline J. ------ 1860 - 1927

  W. A. --------- 1858 - 1924

Sledge
  Annie H. ------ Sep 15, 1865 - Mar 20, 1905

  Edward
  Simmons ------- Jan 8, 1852 - Nov 21, 1933

Smith
  Addison
  Gillespie ----- Oct 1, 1851 - May 16, 1933

  Cornelia E.
  Houston ------- Wife of John T. Smith
                  Dec 5, 1833 - Sep 14, 1920

  E. W. --------- Born Wayne Co. N. C. 1825
                  Died Livingston, Ala.
                  Feb 25, 1874

  Florence D. --- Wife of A. G. Smith
                  Dau Devereus & Elizabeth W.
                  Hopkins Died Jan 24, 1928

  Helen E.
  Cusack -------- 1862 - 1944

  John D. ------- A native of Goram, Maine
                  Died May 29, 1836

  John T. ------- Son Stephen & Sally Smith
                  Born in Wayne Co. N. C.
                  Jan 15, 1823 - Apr 6, 1891

  Joseph A.,
  MD ------------ Son Stephen & Sally Smith
                  Born in Wayne Co. N. C.
                  Sep 19, 1812 - Dec 7, 1873

  Lena Hadden --- Wife of Thomas B. Smith
                  Nov 27, 1852 - Sep 28, 1918

  Martha E. ----- Wife of E. W. Smith
                  Dau M. C. & M. L. Houston
                  Born in Morgan Co. Ala.
                  Nov 21, 1831 - Apr 12, 1858

  Mary Phifer --- Dec 25, 1856 - Feb 4, 1936

Smith (contd)
S. A. E. ------ Dau Stephen & Sally A. Smith
              Dec 25, 1828 - Aug 6, 1908

Sally Ann ----- Wife of Stephen Smith Born
              Wayne Co. N. C. Jan 10, 1794
              Died Livingston Ala. Aug 9,
              1854 Married Aug 8, 1811
              Dau Gen. James & Anna Rhodes

Samuel -------- Dec 14, 1856 - Apr 23, 1881

Sarah Ramsay -- Jul 13, 1862 - May 8, 1944

Stephen N. ---- Aug 9, 1853 - Jun 23, 1905

Rev. Stephen
Uriah --------- Son Stephen & Sally Smith
              Jan 2, 1817 - May 18, 1888

Susan T. ------ Wife of Walter K. Smith
              Feb 12, 1860 - Feb 21, 1946

Thomas B. ----- Dec 31, 1852 - Jul 28, 1938

Walter K. ----- Oct 31, 1855 - Apr 23, 1908

Spratt
James P. ------ Feb 10, 1844 - Mar 25, 1920

Lillis
Barnett ------- Wife of Robert D. Spratt
              1818 - 1864

Mattie A.
Beggs --------- Wife James P. Spratt
              Sep 10, 1853 - Nov 2, 1913

Robert
Barnett ------- 1847 - 1864, CSA

Robert D. ----- Born York District, S. C.
              Jul 21, 1806 - Nov 16, 1879

Sprott
John ---------- Jul 17, 1837 - Oct 7, 1874

Sprott (contd)
  Leonora
    Brockway ------ Wife of S. H. Sprott
                    Nov 25, 1848 - Aug 3, 1926

    Mary ---------- Born in County Down, Ireland
                    1808 - Nov 21, 1882

    Mary A. V. ---- Wife of John Sprott
                    Feb 20, 1853 - May 18, 1873

    Samuel Henry -- Jun 24, 1840 - Apr 12, 1916

Staples
  Elizabeth A. -- Consort of W. N. Staples
                  Dau John & Rebecca Lang
                  Died Jun 14, 1847 18 yrs 9 mo

Stephens
  John H. ------- Born in Alexandria, D. C.
                  Aug 1, 1805 - Dec 13, 1855

  Penelope R. --- Consort of John H. Stephens
                  Born in Beaufort, N. C.
                  May 13, 1808 - Jul 9, 1856

Stillings
  James N. ------ Born at Covington, Virginia
                  Nov 28, 1821 - Oct 23, 1848

Sturdivant
  Martha Troup -- Dau Edward & Louisiana Troup
                  May 6, 1852 - Feb 19, 1853

Swan
  Mrs. Tency ---- Dec 23, 1815 - Aug 1851

Tankersley
  Eva Luvenia --- Jun 18, 1838 - Mar 11, 1906

  Robert -------- Jan 21, 1832 - Oct 20, 1894

  Sarah F. H. --- Consort G. C. Tankersley
                  Born in Columbia, Ga.
                  Oct 29, 1808 - Oct 18, 1892

Tartt
  Annie M. ------ Jan 8, 1841 - Jan 15, 1928

Tartt (contd)
Thomas
  Morrison ------ Born in Edgecombe Co. N. C.
                     Apr 1, 1821 - Aug 9, 1885

Thom
  Mrs. Margaret - Jan 11, 1800 - Sep 14, 1854

Thompson
  Angelina S. --- Wife James Harvey Thompson
               Died Mar 14, 1850   24 yrs

  Felix Gibson -- Son J. H. & A. S. Thompson
               Died Mar 14, 1847   Age 18 mo

  James Harvey -- A native of Mt Sterling, Ky.
               Died Mar 7, 1855   Age 37

  Rufus K. ------ 1842 - 1910

Thornton
  Ellen Thom ---- Wife Henry R. Thornton
               Died Mar 30, 1903

  Henry
  Randolph ------ Died Nov 21, 1862

  Hortense
  Randolph ------ Jul 15, 1851 - Jul 1, 1927

  Lucy Cobbs ---- Oct 1, 1858 - May 4, 1917

  Mrs. Maria A. - Consort Henry R. Thornton
               Born in Culpepper Co. Va.
               Died Jul 5, 1847   Age 37

  Reuben Thom --- Jun 27, 1849 - Mar 4, 1910

  Seth B. ------- Capt, 2nd Dragoons, USA
               Born Orange Co. Va.
               May 28, 1815
               Killed in service - Mexico
               Aug 18, 1847

  Seth Brett ---- Son H. R. & E. T. Thornton
               Jul 29, 1862 - Aug 21, 1866

Tisdale
  J. W. --------- Mar 8, 1851 - Apr 18, 1910

    Malcolm
    Henagan ------- Aug 27, 1862 - Mar 21, 1938

Travis
  Jesse Cobb ---- Jul 21, 1862 - Jan 21, 1929

    Rosa S. ------- Wife of Anderson Moore
                   Died Aug 10, 1929 Age 77 yrs

Trigg
  William S. ---- 1828 - 1868, CSA

Trott
  David H. ------ Born in Salisbury, N. C.
                Oct 11, 1811 - Jun 21, 1886

    David H. Jr. -- Sep 2, 1851 - Nov 2, 1885

    John J. ------- May 7, 1845 - Jan 30, 1897

    Margaret Ann -- Wife of David H. Trott   Age 45
                    (No dates)

Tureman
  F. S. --------- May 30, 1837 - Jun 26, 1866

    Sallie McGrew - Dau W. S. & S. E. Tureman
                    Died Jul 9, 1860   7 mo & 2 days

    Zack ---------- (No dates) CSA

Turk
  Etta ---------- 1844 - 1933

    S. B. --------- Aug 19, 1841 - May 18, 1922

Underwood
  Mallie -------- Dau T. R. & E. J. Underwood
                 Jun 13, 1858 - Jul 30, 1876

Ustick
  John G. ------- Died Sep 4, 1844

    Lydia Farand -- Born in Albany N. Y.
                   Jun 12, 1808 - Nov 16, 1880

Ustick (contd)
    William King -- Born in Abingdon, Va.
                    Dec 27, 1806 - Sep 1, 1872

Vary
    Elbert M. ----- Born Rensselaer Co. N. Y.
                    Mar 18, 1819 - Aug 11, 1850

    John F. Jr. --- Son J. F. & A. A. Vary
                    Apr 23, 1851 - May 17, 1851

Vaughan
    Edward C. ----- Aug 28, 1862 - Dec 29, 1928

Verell
    Mrs. Mary ----- Died Nov 18, 1844

Voss
    H. Otto ------- (No dates) CSA

    W. H. A. ------ (No dates) CSA

Wallace
    James --------- Jun 25, 1908 - Nov 8, 1910

Walton
    James F. ------ Born in Oglethorpe Co. Ga.
                    Oct 27, 1815 - Nov 26, 1843

Ward
    Ann ----------- Wife of Capt. Leonard Ward
                    Oct 21, 1778 - Mar 11, 1857

    Jane Margaret - Wife Thomas Ward
                    (No dates, marker unreadable)

Wetmore
    Laura Ledelle - Wife of R. P. Wetmore
                    Died Dec 13, 1931

    Richmond
    Pearson ------- Aug 17, 1861 - Jan 31, 1912

White
    Daniel O. ----- Born in Dallas Co. Ala.
                    Jul 16, 1826 - Aug 23, 1882
                    CSA

Whitehead
  Lemuel F. ----- May 19, 1809 - Jun 9, 1894

  Mary E. ------- Wife of Lemuel F. Whitehead
                  Dau Gen. Joseph & Mary J.
                  Arrington Died 1909

  Redding ------- Born in Nash Co. N. C.
                  D Feb 22, 1864 Age 69

Williams
  George W. ----- Sep 29, 1844 - Oct 22, 1921

  Johnson C. ---- Son William O. & Wineford
                  Williams Died Jun 13, 1849
                  Age 28

  Sarah H. ------ Wife of J. C. Williams
                  Dau Seaborn & Elizabeth Mims
                  Died May 21, 1848 Age 22

Wilson
  Alex ---------- (No dates) CSA

  George W. ----- Born in Sweden
                  Mar 1, 1818 - Feb 12, 1895

  George
  Westley ------- Son George & Mary A. Wilson
                  May 28, 1847 - Sep 2, 1848

  Infant -------- Son George & Mary A. Wilson
                  Apr 19, 1847

  James Cobbs --- Son George & Mary A. Wilson
                  Oct 12, 1855 - May 3, 1856

  Jane Olivia --- 1857 - 1929

  Mary Rebecca -- Dau George & Mary A. Wilson
                  Died Mar 20, 1854 Age 2

  R. D. --------- May 11, 1848 - Aug 11, 1912

Wimbish
  L. J. --------- Feb 8, 1843 - Apr 26, 1917

Witt
  Monan --------- Born Jul 1854
                  Died Mar 16, 1940

Wooten
  Joseph
  Richard ------- Son Richard & Malvina Wooten
                  Mar 22, 1862 - Jun 7, 1915

  Mary Martha
  Malvina ------- Dau Gen. Joseph & Mary J.
                  Arrington
                  Aug 3, 1820 - Mar 30, 1862

Wright
  Ida Coleman --- Dau A. D. & S. A. M. Wright
                  Died Aug 27, 1846

  Samuel Inge --- Son A. D. & S. A. M. Wright
                  Died Nov 23, 1855

  Sarah DeV. ---- May 22, 1818 - Nov 12, 1875

(Three unknown soldiers are buried here)

NEW PROSPECT CHURCH CEMETERY

From State Highway 28, approximately 3 miles east of Livingston, turn north on County Road 21. The church and cemetery are 2 9/10 miles down this road on the east side of the road.

Beazley
  Nancy --------- Dau W. H. & Elizabeth Beazley
                  Born & Died Oct 11, 1861

Blakeny
  Louisa -------- Aug 28, 1848 - Aug 15, 1858

Brewer
  Eliza J. ------ Wife of W. P. Brewer
                  Dau W. H. & G. Talbot
                  Born Boligee Jan 16, 1832
                  Died Sep 29, 1904

Brewer (contd)
Mary ---------- A native of Virginia
Feb 12, 1774 - Jan 11, 1859

W. P. --------- May 6, 1822 - Nov 23, 1907

William ------- A native of North Carolina
Sep 14, 1770 - Mar 26, 1852

Casey
J. T. --------- Dec 25, 1848 - Jan 21, 1892

Cates
B. R. --------- Mar 1, 1840 - May 24, 1862

J. W. --------- May 11, 1847 - May 2, 1914

Sallie A. ----- Wife of J. W. Cates
Jan 18, 1840 - May 29, 1908

William ------- Oct 26, 1792 - Dec 9, 1867

Chapman
Adline -------- Jul 4, 1863 - Jan 9, 1964

Cholmon
Pink ---------- Born Oct 15, 1861
Died Mar 10, 1952

Etheridge
J. T. --------- Dec 20, 1817 - Jan 5, 1874

Martha J. ----- Dec 14, 1822 - Jan 21, 1886

Gibbins
M. A. --------- Died Oct 15, 1917
Age 86 yrs 6 mo

Hawkins
Alice G.
Scarborough --- Wife of W. H. Hawkins
Nov 20, 1852 - Jun 19, 1931

Henagan
Dr. Darby ----- Apr 21, 1831 - Dec 7, 1899

Kate L. ------- Jan 25, 1839 - Sep 5, 1900

Hoit
    Mary E.
        Scarborough --- Wife of Zane Hoit
                        Dec 1, 1848 - Jul 14, 1925

Hunter
    Thomas -------- Dec 13, 1862 - Feb 7, 1931

Jackson
    Charlotte ----- Wife of James Jackson
                    1820 - 1897

    Louisa -------- 1853 - 1899

Lammers
    Betty G. ------ Dau F. D. & Delia Lammers
                    Nov 29, 1882 - Sep 18, 1899

    Delia --------- Wife of F. D. Lammers
                    Jan 1, 1860 - Feb 17, 1909

Leitch
    H. B. --------- Jan 29, 1833 - Apr 14, 1903

    Sarah
    Catherine ----- Wife of H. B. Leitch
                    Feb 14, 1842 - Aug 22, 1931

May
    Jefferson ----- Born & Died Dec 14, 1845

    Marsaline ----- Born & Died Jul 14, 1854

    Sally --------- Born May 3, 1853
                    Died Mar 19, 1975
                    Age 122

Maye
    Andrew W. ----- Born Aug 13, 1865
                    Died Apr 28, 1957

McGehee
    Cora
    Etheridge ----- 1849 - 1932

McLean
    Eliza H. ------ Sep 20, 1811 - Mar 26, 1871

McLean (contd)
Emma ---------- Wife of Lewis A. McLean
                Feb 3, 1855 - Feb 20, 1913

Lewis A. ------ Aug 15, 1850 - May 5, 1914

Mary O. ------- 1845 - 1927

Peter --------- Jun 16, 1808 - Feb 17, 1885

Porter
Frederick ----- Who was born Nov 13, 1803
               Died Oct 12, 1857
               Aged 53 yrs 10 mos 29 days

Reynolds
Jefferson
Lavernia ------ Aug 6, 1853 - Mar 26, 1854

Sanford
Joseph L. ----- Jan 22, 1848 - Dec 16, 1879

Scarborough
Rev. A. R. ---- Born in Edgecombe Co. N. C.
               Jan 31, 1815 - Jul 10, 1888

Andrew Greer -- Apr 5, 1858 - Sep 27, 1907

Annie --------- Wife of W. H. Scarborough
               Oct 15, 1861 - Jul 17, 1909

James T. ------ Dec 18, 1849 - Jul 7, 1927

Lama A.-------- Died 1852 Age 9 mo

Nancy --------- Died 1817 Age 56

Ruth Greer ---- Wife of A. R. Scarborough
               Dau W. H. & G. Talbot
               Born in Nashville, Tenn.
               Sep 4, 1821 - May 28, 1880

William T. ---- 18_? Age 4 yrs

Sullivan
Cornelia ------ Mar 28, 1843 - Nov 14, 1908

Sullivan (contd)
Helen Terrell - Wife of J. M. Terrell
Dec 6, 1847 - May 27, 1911

James M. ------ Feb 17, 1839 - Dec 21, 1915

Talbot
Edmund -------- Died 1854   Age 26

Rhoda --------- May 1793 - Mar 1865

Sophia C. ----- Died 1844   Age 18

W. H. --------- Sep 5, 1790 - Jan 3, 1863

OLD PROVIDENCE BAPTIST CHURCH CEMETERY

From Panola, proceed south on Ginhouse Road for approximately 1 4/10 miles to a dirt road to the west that leads to the Galilee Church. Follow this road for approximately 7/10 mile to a gate on the north side of the road. The cemetery is approximately 300 yards north of this gate.

Adams
Mary E. Jones - Wife of Talbot Adams Jr.
Jun 24, 1844 - Aug 12, 1903

Talbot -------- Jul 26, 1837 - Jun 24, 1893

Brown
William A. O. - Son William & Mary Ann Jones
Hudson (?)
Feb 11, 1843 - Jul 4, 1846

Jones
William Henry - Eldest Son Jabez & Mary Ann
Jones   Died Aug 3, 1844
Age 3 yr 9 mo 7 days

Nairne
John Wiley ---- Son John W. & Nancy G. Nairne
Aug 18, 1844 - Oct 12, 1846

Nairne (contd)
Mary G. ------- Wife of John W. Nairne
Dau Wiley & Nancy Spencer
Oct 19, 1819 - Apr 22, 1858

Oliver
Eliza Perrin -- Consort of Lewellyn Oliver
Born in Edgefield Dist. N. C.
Feb 16, 1808 - Jun 11, 1851

Francis Howe -- Son Lewellyn & Eliza
Aug 19, 18_? - Jul 8, 1851
1 month after his mother

Freeman Goode - Jan 9, 1816 - Apr 1817 ?

Lewellyn ------ Born in Edgefield Dist. N. C.
Sep 24, 1805 - Jan 18, 1886

Lewellyn Jr. -- May 9, 1841 - Jan 21, 1882

Sallie G. ----- Aug 8, 1854 - Sep 5, 1881

_?_ --------- Wife of L. Oliver
Born in Charleston, S. C.
Dec 12, 1814 - Jan 7, 1898

Perrin
Elizabeth S. -- B Sep 4, 1827
D _?_
(Marker broken, part missing)

Sarah C. ------ Mar 4, 1850 - Apr 27, 1850

Russell
E. E. R. ------ (No dates)

Elizabeth
Reed ---------- Dau John B. & Nancy
Jun 16, 1824 - Jun 10, 1846

Spencer
Elizabeth B. -- Wife of Shepherd Spencer
Jan 27, 1804 - May 5, 1844

Hannah P. ----- Dec 15, 1843 - Nov 23, 1844

Spencer (contd)
Shepherd ------ Born in Edgefield Dist. S. C.
               1770 Died Oct 29, 1853

Shepherd Jr. -- Nov 8, 1804 - Sep 11, 1843

Susan E. ------ Feb 19, 1837 - Feb 16, 1880

Washington
Benjamin L. --- Son R. W. & H. P. Washington
               Age 22 mo 5 days

Bettie A. ----- Sep 20, 1832 - Mar 15, 1854

Dr. Robert W. - Born in Brunswick Co. Virginia
               Oct 15, 1795 - Aug 26, 1851

OLD SIDE BAPTIST CHURCH CEMETERY

From State Highway 17, 2 miles south of Emelle,
turn east on County Road 20. At approximately 2
1/2 miles, turn south on County Road 74. At
approximately 8/10 mile, turn east on a dirt
drive of approximately 8/10 mile to the cemetery.

Aiken
Samuel J. ----- Nov 21, 1857 - Feb 2, 1930

Amason
Asa ----------- Born in Edgecomb Co. N. C.
               Dec 3, 1804 - Aug 8, 1876

Elbert -------- Born in Edgecomb Co. N. C.
               Jun 8, 1802 - 1872

Elizabeth ----- Consort of Elbert Amason
               Born Edgefield Dist. of S. C.
               Jan 28, 1813 - Feb 1886

Emalina ------- Wife of Nathan Amason Born in
               Edgecomb Co. N. C. Oct 10, 1808
               Removed to Ala. in Oct 1836.
               Became a member of Baptist
               Church in July 1843 Died
               May 28, 185?

Amason (contd)
  Infant -------- Dau Asa & Sara Amason
                       Born & Died 1840

  Margaret L. --- Wife of E. A. Amason
                       Dec 15, 1855 - May 9, 1913

  Nathan -------- Born in Edgecommb Co. N. C.
                       Jun 6, 1800 - Feb 24, 1877

  Sara ---------- Consort of Asa Amason
                       Born in Edgecomb Co. N. C.
                       1804 - Feb 11, 1855

  Susan --------- Dau Asa & Sara Amason
                       B 1842 D 1848

  Van Buren ----- Son Asa & Sarah Amason
                       Feb 3, 1840 - Sep 26, 1840

  William ------- Born in Edgecomb Co. N. C.
                       Aug 13, 1798 - Jan 6, 1858

Bayless
  Charles
  Sidney -------- Apr 7, 1859 - Mar 4, 1911

Bell
  Elizabeth
  Goldsmith ----- Born in Tarboro N. C.
                       Mar 17, 1830

  William R. ---- Died Apr 1, 1871 Age 44

Boyette
  Ellen A. ------ Dau Locke Boyette
                       Born 1828 - __?__

  Locke --------- Born 1784 - Oct 9, 1840

  Nancy --------- Born 1793 - Oct 13, 1840

  Sarah I. ------ Sep 16, 1824 - Sep 5, 1840

Bryant
  Cherry Lane --- Wife of Evan N. Bryant
                       Dau Bryant & Uny Richardson
                       Sep 1, 1818 - Mar 18, 1881

Bryant (contd)
E. N. --------- Jun 24, 1812 - Jan 3, 1876

Mary L. ------- Dau E. N. & C. L. Bryant
Oct 16, 1842 - Sep 1, 1844

Thomas -------- Son E. N. & C. L. Bryant
Aug 13, 1839 - Nov 5, 1843

William T. ---- Son E. N.& C. L. Bryant
Born 1836 Died 1842

Buntin
Martha
A. A. P. ------ Jun 21, 1836 - Nov 24, 1853

Burton
Rev. John
Wesley -------- Sep 18, 1851 - Nov 8, 1926

Nannie Amason
Gregory ------- Oct 1, 1844 - Jul 4, 1904

Cockrell
Catherine ----- Jun 1, 1847 - Sep 4, 1893

Infant -------- Son William & Millicent
Cockrell Born Jan 28, 1846

Infant -------- Of William & Louisa Cockrell
Born & Died 1855

James A. ------ Nov 1, 1847 - Feb 2, 1884

Louisa L. ----- Wife of William Cockrell
May 21, 1826 - Apr 22, 1857

Mary S. ------- Dau W. J. & Millicent Cockrell
Jun 1, 1847 - May 6, 1865

Millicent ----- Wife of William J. Cockrell
Aug 15, 1827 - May 20, 1849

Nathan -------- Co-Founder, SAE, Univ. of Ala.

William
Joseph -------- Jan 24, 1819 - May 25, 1892

Dixon
  James J. ------ Mar 8, 1848 - Nov 22, 1923
  Mattie A. ----- Jun 13, 1856 - Feb 6, 1931
Eason
  Ann W. -------- Dau John T. & Winifred Eason
                  Oct 6, 1842 - Dec 3, 1855
  Elizabeth M. -- Dau John T. & Winifred Eason
                  Jul 15, 1833 - Jul 7, 1853
  Henry --------- Son E. C. & E. K. Eason
                  Jul 12, 1865 - Jul 31, 1865
  John Thomas --- Born in Pitt Co. N. Carolina
                  Nov 20, 1796 - Apr 6, 1864
  John Thomas --- Born in Pitt Co. N. Carolina
                  Apr 6, 1829 - May 25, 1853
  William H. ---- Son John T. & Winifred Eason
                  Born in Pitt Co. N. Carolina
                  Mar 13, 1825 - Jul 21, 1842
  Winifred W. --- Wife of John T. Eason
                  Born in Pitt Co. N. Carolina
                  Aug 14, 1800 - May 10, 1855
Epes
  Dr. John W. --- Born in Lunenburg Co. Virginia
                  May 5, 1836
  Mamie --------- Dau J. W. & M. J. Epes
                  Oct 4, 1863 - Sep 26, 1876
  Martha J. ----- Wife of Dr. J. W. Epes
                  Oct 15, 1839 - Jul 8, 1906
  Richard J. ---- Born in Lunenburg Co. Virginia
                  Sep 25, 1813 - Dec 24, 1865
Faulkner
  James Davis --- Dec 11, 1843 - Sep 7, 1910
Foy
  Davis --------- Born 1811 - Oct 17, 1877

Foy (contd)
Eliza T. ------ Wife of Davis Foy
　　　　　　　　Born in Edgecomb Co. N. C.
　　　　　　　　May 16, 1829 - Apr 7, 1893

Lemuel -------- Son William & Ellen Foy
　　　　　　　　Jun 15, 1852 - Jun 11, 1853

Mary ----------- Jul 19, 1858 - Feb 10, 1940

Nancie -------- Consort of Terrance Foy
　　　　　　　　Born in Chester Dist. S. C.
　　　　　　　　Aug 1777 - Jun 5, 1854

Patrick ------- Son Davis & Ella Foy
　　　　　　　　Aug 21, 1860 - Feb 10, 1873

Robert Emmet -- Son Davis & Eliza Foy
　　　　　　　　Aug 17, 1853 - Apr 7, 1869

Sarah K. ------ Dau William & Ellen Foy
　　　　　　　　Mar 24, 1854 - Jun 14, 1855

T. T. --------- Feb 21, 1850 - May 3, 1878

Terrance ------ Born in Co. of Meud, Ireland
　　　　　　　　Dec 25, 1775 - Oct 24, 1842

Freeman
Martha -------- Died Jan 16, 1854 Age 8

Gordon
Ella Wrenn ---- Aug 24, 1861 - Aug 18, 1923

Georgia ------- Wife of T. J. Gordon
　　　　　　　　Jul 28, 1839 - Nov 1, 1922

T. P. --------- Nov 30, 1858 - Jun 27, 1918

Gregory
William J. ---- Born Montgomery Co. Missouri
　　　　　　　　Oct 25, 1840 - Sep 26, 1870

Grice
John ---------- Born in Nash Co. N. C.
　　　　　　　　Apr 5, 1803 - Sep 1864

Grice (contd)
  Mary Simms ---- Born in Edgecombe Co. N. C.
                  Apr 27, 1809 - Aug 17, 1847

Hagood
  R. J. --------- Son R. Z. & Ida Hagood
                  Born 1847   Died 1876

Hale
  Amanda Jane --- Dau R.(or H.) & Malinda Rogers
                  Wife of J. M. Hale
                  May 21, 1830 - Oct 27, 1857

  Elizabeth ----- Dau __?__ & D. D. Hale
                  Aug 19, 1841 - Jan 12, 1843

  Malinda
  Frances ------- Dau J. M. & Amanda Hale
                  Dec 6, 1854 - Aug 21, 1856

Hendricks
  Clarra -------- Dau J. H. & V. A. Hendricks
                  May 13, 1859 - _?_ 27, 1860

High
  J. W. --------- Mar 31, 1848 - Dec 31, 1869

  Mrs. T. A. ---- Wife of William R. High
                  Born in Wayne Co. N. C.
                  (Dates unreadable)

  William R. ---- Born in Wake Co. N. C.
                  Mar 18, 1825 - Dec 25, 1866

Holcomb
  A. H. --------- Jul 21, 1813 - Jul 19, 1853

Hollis
  Emily A. ------ Mar 20, 1865 - Apr 15, 1933

Holloway
  Infant -------- Son S. M. & S. F. Holloway
                  Apr 29, 1858 - May 4, 1858

  Melvin W. ----- Son A. M. & A. B. Holloway
                  Nov 21, 1849 - Feb 9, 1862

Jackson

Isephena A.
E. ------------ 1st Wife of John R. Jackson
Nov 8, 1835 - Jan 7, 1862

John R. ------- Born 1831 Died 1924

Mary A. ------- Wife of C. M. Jackson
Dau Mrs. R. P. Bobbitt
Born in Franklin Co. Ala.
Dec 7, 1854 - Mar 27, 1877

Mary
Jacqualine ---- Wife of Will D. Jackson
Oct 26, 1864 - Dec 24, 1932

Rebecca Wrenn - 2nd Wife of John R. Jackson
Born 1840 Died 1912

Will D. ------- Son John R. & I. Holliday
Jackson
Mar 16, 1856 - Oct 22, 1924

Kennedy

Harriett A. --- Born in Jones Co. N. C.
Nov 8, 1805 - Dec 28, 1866

John ---------- Born in Lenoir Co. N. C.
Died Lauderdale Co. Miss.
Oct 27, 1796 - Jan 18, 1874

Knight

Joseph -------- Born 1806 - Mar 1849

Lacy

Mary Ann ------ Consort of H. B. Lacy
Jul 23, 1823 - Jun 27, 1856

Lewis

Lewellyn Sr. -- Oct 12, 1813 - Jul 5, __?__

Rachel -------- Wife of Lewellyn Lewis
Aug 21, 1819 - Jun 1, 1909

May

Ben ----------- Mar 5, 1852 - Dec 12, 1926

May (contd)

Nannie Foy ---- Wife of Ben May
Oct 22, 1851 - Mar 14, 1933

McClendon

Ezekiel ------- Died Apr 25, 1856   Age 30

Myers

Infant -------- Son Richard W. Myers
Died Jan 21, 1858   Age 2 mo

James W. ------ Son Wilson G. Myers
Dec 8, 1830 - May 1, 1843

Samuel W. ----- Son Wilson G. & Margaret C. Myers
Dec 8, 1850 - Oct 14, 1855

Wilson G. Jr. - Son W. G. & Margaret C. Myers
Apr 16, 1840 - Apr 13, 1855

Ormond

Cherry Ella --- Oct 19, 1851 - Jul 24, 1897

John Fletcher - Born in Green Co. N. C.
Oct 6, 1843 - May 24, 1924

Parham

Matilda ------- Wife of J. M. Parham
Apr 22, 1853 - Mar 23, 1871

Matthew ------- Born 1792 - Jan 10, 1859

Nancy --------- Born in Sampson Co. N. C.
Jul 10, 1810 - Jan 18, 1859

Renfroe

Mary M. ------- 2nd Wife of S. S. Renfroe
Nov 17, 1849 - Jul 11, 1871

Molly E. ------ 1st Wife of Steve S. Renfroe
Mar 7, 1846 - Aug 21, 1868

Richardson

A. W. --------- Died Oct 29, 1863   Age 34

Richardson (contd)
Almeta E. ----- Dau William R. & Ester
　　　　　　　　Richardson
　　　　　　　　Aug 24, 1838 - Jul 18, 1842

Arch T. ------- 1857 - 1935

John H. ------- Born in Wake Co. N. C.
　　　　　　　　Dec 5, 1809 - Nov 24, 1878

Mary Emma ----- Dau of A. W. & Martha A.
　　　　　　　　Richardson Died 1863
　　　　　　　　11 yrs 5 mo & 22 da

Sallie T. ----- 1864 - 1934

Robertson
John H. ------- Born in Wake Co. N. C.
　　　　　　　　Dec 5, 1809 - Nov 24, 1878

Sewell
Mrs. Sue ------ Died 12/11/1889   Age 82
　　　　　　　　(No marker)

Simms
Ben F. -------- Mar 29, 1869 - Jan 12, 1871

Harriett ------ Wife of William T. Simms
　　　　　　　　Dec 2, 1829 - Mar 4, 1873

Henry H. ------ Apr 6, 1865 - Jan 12, 1871

John T. ------- Apr 2, 1865 - Dec 13, 1935

Leroy --------- Jul 15, 1811 - Oct 11, 1849

Leroy L. ------ Mar 1, 1863 - Jan 12, 1871

Mary Leslie --- Dau W. T. & Harriett Simms
　　　　　　　　(No dates)

William T. ---- (No marker)

(Ben F., Henry H. and Leroy L. all died the same night of spinal meningitis.)

Tartt
    A. B.   --------- Native of Edgecombe Co. N. C.
                            Apr 26, 1827 - May 23, 1856

    Emily L.   ------   Consort of Enos Tartt
                            Dau John T. & Winifred Eason
                            Married Apr 24, 1845
                            Feb 20, 1827 - Feb 20, 1852

    James   ---------- Born in Edgecombe Co. N. C.
                            Born 1792 - Apr 11, 1857

    Mary C.   -------   Wife of Elnathan Tartt
                            Dau John T. & Winifred Eason
                            Aug 1, 1823 - Sep 20, 1866

Wilson
    Fannie   -------- Dau E. R. & Martha Wilson
                            Died Dec 27, 1871

    Henderson
    Matilda
    Malinda   -------   Dau Wm. H. & M. A. Wilson
                            Jan 30, 1857 - Jun 8, _?__

    Isaac R.   ------   Jan 6, 1838 - Dec 24, 1918

    Martha O.   -----   Consort of E. R. Wilson
                            Born at Bluffport, Ala.
                            Apr 5, 1838 - Apr 5, 1869

    Matilda Ann   ---   Wife of William H. Wilson
                            Dau R. H. & Malinda Rogers
                            Dec 10, 1833 - Feb 14, 1857

    Mollie U.   -----   Dau of Henry Wrenn
                            Sep 18, 1846 - Oct 18, 1939

    Penninah   ------   Born in Edgecombe Co. N. C.
                            Apr 1, 1821 - Nov 23, 1852

Wrenn
    Catherine W.
    Cockrell   ------   Wife of James T. Wrenn
                            Jun 1, 1849 - Sep 4, 1898

    Elias H.   ------   Apr 14, 1810 - Dec 21, 1889

Wrenn (contd)
Infant -------- Son E. H. & R. R. Wrenn
                Died Apr 13, 1863   Age 5

James T. ------ Jun 7, 1844 - Dec 18, 1899

Josiah H. ----- Apr 17, 1852 - Jan 16, 1922

Nannie E.
Cockrell ------ Wife of Josiah Wrenn
                Dau of William Cockrell
                1856 - 1932

Rixie
Richardson ---- Wife of Elias Wrenn
                Dau Bryant & Uney R. Richardson
                Born Jones Co. N. Carolina
                Jan 24, 1821 - Dec 10, 1899

O'NEAL CEMETERY

From State Highway 39, approximately 3 miles south of Gainesville, turn east on Williams Road to the Wendy Hills Subdivision. The cemetery is to the east and adjacent to apartments in the subdivision.

O'Neal
  Emily
  McCallister --- Feb 17, 1800 - Jun 29, 1846

There are signs of one or two additional graves and the remains of a Masonic marker.

OXFORD PRESBYTERIAN CHURCH CEMETERY

Located on the west side of County Road 27, approximately 3 miles south of its intersection with County Road 19.

Bond
  Ivie J. ------- Nov 8, 1861 - Mar 10, 1948

Bond (contd)
  Jacob J. ------ Co. E, 15th Miss. Inf., CSA
                (No dates)

  James --------- Died Jun 18, 1871
                Age 72 yr 3 mo 17 days

  John W. ------- Son J. W. & M. E. Bond
                Jan 11, 1862 - Feb 3, 1863
                1 yr 22 days

  Mary C. ------- Feb 22, 1861 - May 25, 1943

  Mary E. ------- Feb 29, 1808 - May 17, 1886

  Robert J. ----- Sep 9, 1840 - Nov 2, 1922

  Susan F. ------ Wife R. J. Bond
                Aug 15, 1841 - Jul 29, 1920

Campbell
  Hugh ---------- Hus Cathrian Campbell
                Aug 3, 1824 - Aug 15, 1898

  John A. ------- Feb 3, 1861 - Feb 24, 1888

  Katherine ----- Jul 1, 1834 - Nov 29, 1911

  Neal ---------- Aug 20, 1864 - Mar 7, 1948

Campbelle
  Georgia
  Garrette ------ Wife of Neal Campbelle
                Aug 8, 1859 - Jul 4, 1929

Clay
  Sgt. J. T. ---- Co. C, 37th Miss. Inf., CSA
                Sep 19, 1832 - Jan 18, 1912

  Mary ---------- Wife J. T. Clay
                Mar 16, 1837 - Mar 8, 1896

Davis
  Bessie Bell --- (No dates)

  Lela Ada ------ Jan 26, 1862 - May 16, 1922

  Thomas C. ----- Feb 14, 1860 - Jan 9, 1940

Dove
Catharine C. -- Dau M. J. & L. J. Dove
May 20, 1864 - Aug 20, 1868

John ---------- May 1805 - Sep 1893
88 yrs 4 mo

L. J. --------- Wife M. J. Dove
Apr 18, 1839 - Jan 16, 1894
54 yrs 8 mo 28 days

M. J. ---------- Jan 6, 1835 - Jul 23, 1911
78 yrs

Gillis
Anna R. ------- Wife John M. Gillis
Mar 13, 1857 - Oct 30, 1922

John M. ------- Jul 24, 1853 - Nov 23, 1921

Haguewood
Callie I. ----- Wife B. L. Haguewood
Aug 26, 1862 - Sep 3, 1900

Harper
Julia Wilder -- 1838 - 1900

Harrell
John S. ------- Aug 3, 1793 - Oct 27, 1868

L. R. --------- Jun 29, 1801 - Dec 8, 1876

Knox
J. M. --------- Apr 11, 1849 - May 30, 1878

Lancaster
Ben F. -------- 1851 - 1917

J. A. --------- Husband of Maggie Lancaster
Apr 28, 1859 - Nov 6, 1894

Laura J. ------ 1854 - 1955

McElroy
Lula Wilder --- Dec 1, 1865 - Aug 1, 1952

Mary Sybil ---- Apr 15, 1861 - Nov 5, 1938

McElroy (contd)
Thad C. ------- Dec 3, 1855 - Oct 18, 1935

McNeil
D. L. --------- Husband of Lou McNeil
Mar 18, 1812 - Jul 31, 1886

Miller
Charlie G. ---- Nov 4, 1856 - May 17, 1932

Maria F. ------ Wife Thomas J. Miller
Aug 14, 1835 - May 29, 1898

Owen Pigford -- Dec 27, 1859 - Nov 12, 1955

Thomas J. ----- Sep 25, 1831 - May 2, 1913

Willie A. ----- Apr 7, 1853 - Jan 14, 1945

Moore
Lula ---------- Feb 7, 1863 - Jul 16, 1946

Morgan
Phalby T. ----- Jan 19, 1861 - Sep 2, 1950

Thomas J. ----- Feb 19, 1855 - Nov 23, 1921

Pankey
Elizabeth ----- Wife J. B. Pankey
Sep 7, 1853 - May 26, 1908

J. B. --------- Jan 27, 1854 - Apr 17, 1920

Sara Miller --- Sep 11, 1857 - Apr 27, 1939

Pigford
Emma S. ------- Dau W. H. & L. C. Pigford
Aug 31, 1859 - Sep 23, 1859

Owen ---------- Oct 25, 1806 - Dec 31, 1881

S. M. --------- Wife Owen Pigford
Sep 25, 1806 - Aug 15, 1867

W. H. --------- Jan 31, 1834 - Dec 28, 1862

Rhaly
Bryant J. ----- Died Feb 1, 1916 Age 83

Rhaly (contd)
Margaret ------ Jan 25, 1836 - Mar 3, 1924

Shelby
Mattie E. ----- Wife S. N. Shelby
Sep 9, 1865 - Jan 19, 1902

S. N. --------- Mar 31, 1857 - Mar 1, 1939

Silliman
Alice Gibbs --- Wife Dr. W. C. Silliman
Dec 31, 1845 - Sep 1, 1923

Lizzie T. ----- Jul 7, 1842 - Dec 25, 1911

Mary A. ------- Jul 2, 1841 - Feb 25, 1898

S. M. --------- Aug 16, 1830 - Feb 1, 1902

William A. ---- Oct 22, 1825 - Apr 5, 1898

William C.,
M.D. ---------- Born in York District of S. C.
Dec 17, 1823
D Lauderdale Co. Miss
Oct 26, 1891

Smith
James M. ------ Oct 1, 1822 - Jul 14, 1890

Robert H. ----- Sep 28, 1851 - Jun 5, 1881

Stewart
Calvin L. ----- Died May 21, 1901   Age 62 yrs

Christina ----- Born 1806 Died 1883 Age 77 yr

Norman -------- Born 1772 Died 1866 Age 94 yr

Swain
Anna E. ------- Apr 15, 1814 - Dec 15, 1903

J. H. --------- Co. F, 19th Miss. Inf., CSA
(No dates)

J. N. --------- Apr 17, 1817 - Jan 25, 1891

Swain (contd)
  L. A. --------- Dau J. N. & A. E. Swain
                  Jul 15, 1852 - Feb 23, 1896

  Mary A. ------- Wife Robt. D. Swain
                  Mar 5, 1854 - Nov 11, 1922

  Mary V. ------- 1855 - 1917

  Robert D. ----- Aug 27, 1843 - Feb 24, 1922

  William S. ---- 1848 - 1922

Thomas
  Edward -------- Aug 9, 1854 - Jun 17, 1918

  Mary E. ------- Wife Ed Thomas
                  Nov 19, 1856 - Aug 27, 1879

Tucker
  Howard -------- 1856 - 1934

  Infant -------- Son H. & J. G. Tucker
                  Born Mar 22, 1861 (1881?)

  Janie Gillis -- Wife Howard Tucker
                  1852 - 1934

Twilley
  W. R. --------- Sep 27, 1864 - Mar 25, 1917

Walker
  Maggie
  Stewart ------- Wife of W. J. Walker
                  Aug 6, 1839 - Oct 7, 1917

Wilder
  R. B. --------- Husband S. O. Walker
                  Sep 10, 1829 - Oct 8, 1884

  Robert N. ----- Feb 14, 1862 - Nov 26, 1943

  Sarah O. ------ Feb 1, 1839 - Dec 29, 1910

  W. H. --------- Son R. B. & S. O. Wilder
                  Jan 8, 1864 - Apr 9, 1868

PARKER CEMETERY

Located in a pasture in Section 7, Township 19 North, Range 2 West, approximately 1/2 mile south of State Highway 28.

Brown
    James P. ------ Son Robert & Amazon Brown
                           Died Jun 7, 1852
                           Age 16 mo & 2 days
                           (Marker now missing)

Greene
    Daniel -------- A native of Greenville Dist.
                           of S. Carolina
                           Died Aug 21, 1842
                           Age 49 yrs 7 mo 20 days

    Mattie Floyd -- Inf Dau of McDuffie & Mattie
                           Greene (No dates)

    Pamelia Ann --- Dau Daniel & Stacy Greene
                           Died Apr 11, 1843
                           Age 16 yrs 6 mo 8 days

    Sue ----------- Youngest daughter of Daniel
                           & Stacy Greene
                           Died May 2, 1853
                           Age 17 yrs & 7 mo

Killen
    Amaranth M. --- Wife of H. W. Killen
                           Dau James & Mary W. Parker
                           Died Oct 10, 1851
                           Age 29 yrs 4 mo 8 days

McCown
    Charlotte ----- Died Jul 16, 1840 ?
                           (Marker is very worn)

Mitchell
    Nancy --------- Relict of Daniel Mitchell
                           Died Oct 29, 1847   Age 71

Parker
    Adamant ------- Dau James & Mary W. Parker
                           Sep 20, 1838 - Sep 30, 1847

Parker (contd)
  Infant -------- Dau Marcus & Sarah Hines
                  Parker Died Jul 15, 1853

  James --------- Jan 30, 1788 - Nov 28, 1855

  Mary ---------- Wife of James Parker Sr.
                  Died Dec 25, 1841 Age 86

  Mary W. ------- Wife of James Parker Jr.
                  Jun 28, 1804 - Sep 17, 1848

  Osceola ------- Son James & Mary Parker
                  Died Jun 21, 1842
                  Age 1 yr 3 mo

Perry
  Ann ----------- Wife of Josiah Perry
                  May 22, 1784 - Jun 28, 1840

PARKER CEMETERY

Located about 75 yards behind the old R. S. Parker home site at Coatopa, on the south side of State Highway 28, approximately 8/10 mile north of its intersection with County Road 23.

This cemetery partially destroyed by a tornado.

Nicholson
  Joseph -------- Son Stith & Ann Nicholson
                  Born in Southampton County, Va.
                  May 31, 1825
                  Died in Sumter County, Ala.
                  Oct 20, 1845
                  Age 20 yrs 4 mo 20 days

Parker
  Agnes Stewart - Died May 4, 1886
                  (Marker now missing)

  Lucy Hopper --- About 18 yrs of age
                  (Marker now missing)

Parker (contd)
  Robert
  Murphree ------ Born Drurysville, Va.
                  Died Dec 25, 1904

  Virginia
  Stewart ------- Died 1884 Age 49 years

The above two inscriptions are on a single marker

Stewart
  Emma L. ------- Died 1913
                  (Marker now missing)

  John Monroe --- (Marker now missing)

PEARCE CEMETERY

From State Highway 17, approximately 11 1/2 miles south of York, turn east on County Road 42. The cemetery is approximately 6 miles down this road, approximately 200 yards north of the road behind the Pearce home.

Flowers
  Goodman ------- Apr 5, 1836 - Dec 15, 1891

  Margaret Lee -- Jun 6, 1845 - Nov 28, 1912

Lee
  Mrs. M. P. ---- Sep 30, 1865 - Nov 22, 1894

Maggard
  Con ----------- Aug 1858 - Jan 8, 1913

Pearce
  W. E. Sr. ----- 1863 - 1936

PEAVY CEMETERY

Located on the north side of County Road 76, approximately 1 1/4 miles west of its intersection with U. S. Highway 11 in Cuba.

Peavy
L. D. --------- Dec 11, 1794 - May 12, 1838

PHARES CEMETERY

Located in the northeast one-quarter of Section 30, Township 19 North, Range 1 East.

Phares
Bolivar ------- Mar 10, 1828 - Apr 16, 1849

Cornelia E. --- Feb 28, 1838 - Feb 27, 1853

Diana --------- Sep 9, 1836 - Mar 23, 1837

Elizabeth ----- Died Sep 8, 1876
Age 72 yrs 6 mo 21 days

John G. ------- Died Mar 1, 1868
Age 69 yrs 9 mo 16 days

POTTS CEMETERY
(Destroyed)

Located approximately 1/4 mile southwest of County Road 12, approximately 1 1/4 miles northwest of its intersection with U. S. Highway 11.

Potts
Anna McCarta -- Dau Stephen and Susan T. Potts
Died Sep 4, 1861 in Warrenton, Va. Age 8 yrs 5 mo 28 days

__?__ry ------- Age 13
(No dates, marker broken. Foot marker is inscribed with H.P.)

REA CEMETERY

From State Highway 17, approximately 2 1/2 miles south of Geiger, turn west on County Road 30. At 1 3/10 miles, turn south on the Jerusalem Church Road. At approximately 2 7/10 miles, turn south into the driveway of the Nat Jones home. The cemetery is approximately 150 yards behind the home.

Rea
Hilliard W. --- Nov 12, 1813 - Jun 13, 1859

Mary ---------- Jul 26, 1823 - Oct 26, 1900

REEDS CHAPEL CEMETERY

From County Road 10, 3 3/10 miles south of Cuba, turn south on County Road 5. At approximately 5 miles, turn west on County Road 6. The chapel and cemetery are 1 2/10 miles down this road on the north side of the road.

Brown
Rev. G. W. ---- Feb 10, 1830 - Mar 16, 1891

Hunter M.
Larkins ------- Wife of Rev. G. W. Brown
Aug 22, 1842 - Jul 14, 1922

Carney
James R. ------ Sep 1, 1865 - Apr 4, 1937

Sara E. ------- Apr 30, 1843 - Apr 11, 1906

W. R. D. ------ Feb 26, 1816 - Jul 29, 1894

Dorough
Emma Ann ------ Apr 23, 1847 - Feb 2, 1937

James W. ------ Oct 26, 1845 - Aug 7, 1901

Gordon
  Ira Pearsall -- Son James Ira & Mary Catharine Gordon
  Jun 28, 1856 - May 26, 1858

  James I. ------ Son Dr. James & Mary M. Gordon
  Born in Suggsville, Ala.
  May 1, 1830 Died Jun 9, 1906

  Mary ---------- Born Randolph Co. N. C.
  Dec 23, 1795 Departed this life Lauderdale Co. Miss.
  Aug 8, 1840

  Mary C.
  Larkins ------- Wife of James Gordon
  1833 - 1917

  Mary S. ------- Dau J. I. & M. C. Gordon
  Feb 5, 1854 - Jun 29, 1900

Hinson
  Elizabeth D.
  Dorough ------- Apr 7, 1848 - Apr 7, 1911

James
  Edward Payton - (No dates)

Knott
  Virgie Portis - Dau B. T. & S. J. Portis
  Dec 18, 1865 - Jun 28, 1892

Larkins
  Elizabeth
  Pearsall ------ 1845 - 1926

Lummus
  Elizabeth Ann - Mar 22, 1856 - Mar 18, 1924

  Loueasa ------- Wife of J. W. Lummus
  Sep 3, 1848 - Apr 30, 1891

  William A. ---- Hus Willie A.
  Aug 20, 1856 - Mar 18, 1924

Marsh
  Darius -------- Jan 1772 - Sep 12, 1841

Nicholson
  Mrs. S. E.
  Gordon -------- Wife of Eld. J. M. Nicholson
                    Oct 10, 1832 - Aug 8, 1880

Portis
  Benjamin
  Person -------- Oct 30, 1822 - Dec 17, 1878

  Howard W. ----- (No dates)

  Susan Jane ---- Oct 1, 1826 - Dec 15, 1876

Shamburger
  James Andrews - Apr 12, 1849 - Jan 25, 1910

  Sarah Portis -- Jan 2, 1848 -

Stabler
  Mary M.
  Portis -------- Dau B. P. & Susie Portis
                  Wife of M. L. Stabler
                  Sep 7, 1847 - Oct 18, 1897

RHYNE CEMETERY
(Destroyed)

Located in Section 15, Township 19 North, Range 4 West, on the north bank of the Sucarnochee River, approximately 1/4 mile west of the Fred Dial Road at approximately 1/2 mile south of its intersection with County Road 12.

Griffin
  James --------- Dec 22, 1820 - Dec 11, 1851

Rhyne
  Jabez A. ------ Mar 3, 1848 - Jul 21, 1870

  John E. ------- May 27, 1858 - Sep 20, 1862

  Mary H. ------- Aug 23, 1845 - Jan 20, 1863

  Sarah A. ------ Aug 23, 1845 - Jan 20, 1863

Thetford
   J. W. --------- Jul 2, 1825 - Apr 7, 1885

RICHARDSON CEMETERY

From State Highway 39, approximately 2 1/2 miles south of Gainesville, turn east on Williams Road. At approximately 3/4 mile, turn south on Hodges Place Road. The cemetery is approximately 1/4 mile down this road, several hundred feet west of the road.

Richardson
   Bryant -------- Feb 28, 1782 - Mar 19, 1836

   F. W. --------- Born in Johnson Co. N. C.
                   May 5, 1816 - Dec 4, 1859

   George A. ----- Son Bryant & Una Ray Richardson
                   Aug 29, 1831 - Dec 16, 1841

   Infant -------- Son Curney & Matilda Richardson
                   Born & Died 1845

   Una Ray ------- Dau Furney & Margaret
                   Richardson
                   Aug 16, 1851 - Sep 23, 1852

   Uny ----------- Wife of Bryant Richardson
                   Dec 24, 1789 - Nov 12, 1843

   __?__ ---------- Born 1822 Died Sumter Co. Ala.
                   Mar 19, 1836 (Marker broken)

ROCKY MOUNT CEMETERY

From State Highway 17, approximately 13 1/2 miles south of York, turn east on County Road 15. At approximately 2 1/2 miles, turn northeast on the Rogers-Ward Road. After approximately 2/10 mile, turn north on unnamed dirt road. The cemetery is approximately 1 1/10 miles up this road, approximately 65 yards to the west of the road.

Sample
David E. ------ Nov 4, 1850 - Jun 25, 1913

Elizabeth ----- Died May 26, 1882   Age 58
No marker

R. T. --------- Died Mar 15, 1857
Age 37 yrs 3 days

Mrs. Sarah ---- Died Mar 20, 1857
In her 68th year

W. N. --------- Feb 9, 1848 - Mar 29, 1909

Woodward
Carolina ------ Sep 7, 1836 - May 31, 1881

Cora ---------- Oct 28, 1856 - Sep 12, 1859

Joseph G. ----- Jan 5, 1830 - Aug 22, 1900

Julius E. ----- Mar 31, 1858 - May 15, 1858

Sarah E. ------ Oct 3, 1853 - Sep 12, 1925

ROGERS - MANDERSON - VAUGHAN

From U. S. Highway 80, 2 3/10 miles east of its intersection with State Highway 17, turn north on the Lynn Bennett Road. At 1 1/2 miles, continue north on a logging road. The cemetery is at about 1 1/2 miles on the east side of the road.

Rogers
Eugenia A. ---- Dec 6, 1844 - May 19, 1907

Rogers (contd)

   R. T. --------- Jul 22, 1833 - Jan 2, 1895

SEALE CEMETERY

At approximately 12 6/10 miles south of York on State Highway 17, turn northeast on the B. B. Bragg Road. The cemetery on the east side of the road, a few hundred feet from the intersection.

McSween
  Benjamin
  Franklin ------ (Inscription unreadable)

  Daniel -------- Born Jan ?, 181?
                    Died in Texas 1/27/1855
                    Murdered by his slave

Seale
  Bluford ------- Born in South Carolina
                    1/28/1791   Died 10/18/1871

  Carter H. ----- Born Greene Co. Ala. 6/25/1829
                    Died Sumter Co. Ala. 6/12/1853

  Elizabeth ----- Wife of Bluford Seale
                    Born in South Carolina
                    3/8/1797   Died in Alabama
                    7/29/1857

  Frances M. ---- Dau Bluford & Florabell Seale
                    Born Greene Co. Ala. 11/5/1831
                    Died Sumter Co. Ala. 11/3/1858

  Mrs. Mary
  Culpepper ----- Born Nash Co. N. C. 1808
                    Died 10/14/1864

  Mary E.
  Lockard ------- Wife of T. F. Seale
                    Born Greene Co. Ala. 3/14/1836
                    Died Johnson Co. Texas
                    6/26/1882

Seale (contd)
    R. L., MD --- 7/9/1825 - 5/25/1897
    Thomas F. ----- Born near Greensboro Ala.
                    7/9/1825 Died near Gaston Ala.
                    6/5/1893
    William C. ---- 6/22/1860 - 12/13/1889

Strutton
    Nancy Seale --- Oct 1833 - Aug 1865

Ward
    Susan L. ------ Wife of C. S. Ward
                    Died Nov 9, 1870
                    18 yrs 4 mo

SHACKELFORD CEMETERY

Located a few hundred feet north of U. S. Highway 80 in Section 9, Township 17 North, Range 1 West, approximately 1 mile east of the intersection of U. S. Highway 80 and County Road 21.

Coleman
    Susan R. ------ Consort of Dr. W. H. Coleman
                    Dau of R. D. Shackelford
                    Who departed this life
                    Feb 11, 1844
                    Age 20 yrs 1 mo 21 days
    William H.
    Jr. ----------- Jan 8, 1846 - Sep 2, 1846

Shackelford
    Infant -------- Dau of R. D. & Jane Shackelford
                    (No dates)

    James T. ------ Son R. D. Shackelford
                    He departed this life
                    Oct 31, 1852 Age 26 years

    Jane ---------- Wife of R. D. Shackelford
                    Who departed this life in the
                    59th year of her age

Shackelford (contd)
 Kerran Ann ---- Second Dau R. D. & Susan H.
       Shackelford who departed this
       life Jul 11, 1842
       Age 24 yr 4 mo 1 day

 R. D. Jr. ----- Who departed this life
       Jan 27, 1848   Age 26 years

 Richard D. ---- Born Pittsylvania County, Va.
       Nov 11, 1793 - Nov 6, 1866
       Age 73 years

 Thomas G. ----- Who departed this life
       Mar 25, 1845   Age 20

Whitfield
 Jane ---------- Dau Nathan B. Whitfield and
       Medora Shackelford his wife
       Dec 31, 1865 - Jan 26, 1868

SHADY GROVE METHODIST CHURCH CEMETERY

Located on the west side of County Road 35, approximately 1/4 mile south of its intersection with County Road 34, southeast of Panola.

Abrams
 George Thomas - Sep 9, 1850 - Jan 17, 1918

 M. C. --------- Wife of G. T. Abrams
       Mar 22, 1854 - Jan 15, 1915

Allford
 Margaret ------ (No dates)

 Mary E. ------- (No dates)

Amason
 T. E. --------- Son G. & M. E. Amason
       Sep 23, 1849 - Oct 18, 1869

Baker
 Tempe --------- Wife of F. S. Baker
       May 27, 1858 - Dec 30, 1885

Barnes
   Bennett B. ---- (No dates)

   Harriett Ann -- Feb 9, 1842 - Apr 21, 1879

   J. W. --------- (No dates)   Age 37

   James C. ------ (No dates)

   John R. ------- Died Jan 12, 1881   Age 71

   Nancy A. ------ Wife of J. R. Barnes
                   Died Oct 5, 1875   Age 55

   Rebecca ------- (No dates)

   Rebecca Ann --- (No dates)

   Sallie W. ----- (No dates)

   Samuel Taylor - Son S. W. & H. A. Barnes
                   Dec 14, 1860 - Oct 1, 1872

   Samuel W. ----- Mar 3, 1832 - Sep 10, 1882

   __?__ T. ------ May 10, 1844 - Oct 8, 1868

Bell
   Caroline
   Amanda -------- Wife of Bennet B. Bell
                   Jun 7, 1823 - Jun 23, 1877

   James H. ------ Born in Edgecomb Co. N. C.
                   Dec 3, 1817 - Oct 17, 1887

   Patience
   Amanda -------- Wife of James H. Bell
                   Born in Wayne Co. N. C.
                   May 29, 1820 - Oct 30, __?__

   Sarah --------- Wife of Washington L. Bell
                   Born in North Carolina
                   Feb 29, 1808 - Jun 8, 1844

   Susan Rebecca - Dau W. L. & Sarah Bell
                   Dec 5, 1840 - Apr 9, 1842

Bostic
 E. A. --------- Wife of Garland Bostic
                 Died Apr 16, 1887 Age 75

 Garland ------- Died Mar 29, 1862 Age 63

Boykin
 Dr. Benjamin -- Born in North Carolina
                 1797 - Aug 14, 1857

 Benjamin B.
  B. ------------ Son Dr. W. D. & M. G. Boykin
                  Sep 17, 1858 - ___?___

 Dr. Edwin D. -- Jan 18, 1834 - Feb 18, 1875
                 Married Mary G. Cromwell
                 Sep 29, 1856

 Mrs. Martha --- Born in North Carolina
                 Jan 1, 1804 - Jan 8, 1865

 Mary Gray ----- Wife of Dr. Edwin D. Boykin
                 Mar 19, 1837 - Dec 14, 1872

 Mrs. Mary L. -- Born in North Carolina
                 Jan 26, 1823 - Dec 24, 1842

 Dr. W. D. ----- Born in Edgecomb Co. N. C.
                 Aug 18, 1829 - Jul 27, 1867

Cameron
 Alice B. ------ 1862 - 1934

 Kelly H. ------ Dec 19, 1829 - Aug 23, 1862

 Major J. ------ 1858 - 1941

Carpenter
 Annie Belle --- (No dates)

 Joel Pearson -- May 4, 1852 - Aug 16, 1878

 Mamie K. ------ Jan 5, 1862 - Sep 7, 1866

 Minnie H. ----- Dau Kelly H. & Mary G.
                 Carpenter
                 Jun 12, 1855 - Jul 30, 1857

Carpenter (contd)
Phillip N. ---- (No dates)

Carroll
Katie --------- Wife of W. G. Carroll
                Mar 23, 1838 - Aug 12, 1867

Clanton
Lucinda ------- Dau Robert & Sylvia Clanton
                Oct 23, 1845 - Aug 29, 1846

Martha Louise - Dau Robert & Sylvia Clanton
                May 28, 1842 - Sep 2, 1843

Mary
Elizabeth ----- Dau Robert & Sylvia Clanton
                Jan 3, 1844 - Jul 24, 1844

Sylvia Jane --- Wife of Robert Clanton
                Dau Blake & Mary Little
                Nov 28, 1820 - Aug 22, 1846

Temperance ---- Dau Robert & Sylvia Clanton
                Jan 14, 1841 - Jul 21, 1842

Criswell
Elijah -------- Died Nov 10, 1850   Age 41

Dancy
Edwin C. ------ Jul 14, 1811 - Jul 18, 1891

Daniel
Arthur -------- Dec 1, 1850 - Dec 7, 1873

George H. ----- Son John & Peninah Daniel
                Aug 4, ? - Dec 29, ?

Marcus C. ----- Son J. & P. Daniel
                Feb 8, 1860 - Mar 12, 1880

Peninah ------- Aug 14, 1852 - May 23, 1871

Thomas -------- Died Sep 22, 1865   Age 60

William ------- Died Mar 10, 1863   Age 22

Darden
  Clemmons ------ Born in North Carolina
                  Died Dec 24, 1842

Dyer
  P. S. --------- Dau Blake & Mary Little
                  Died Feb 1857 Age 22

Edmundson
  James --------- A native of Greene Co. N. C.
                  Soldier in War of 1812
                  Died May 18, 1854 Age 76

Ellis
  E. ------------ Oct 13, 1804 - Jul 28, 1875

Evans
  Myrtle -------- Died Jul 10, 1866

Ferrell
  Henry I. ------ (No dates) Age Abt 60 yrs

Few
  Alma A. ------- Eldest Dau A. S. N. & V. C. Few
                  Dec 9, 1856 - Aug 16, 1868

Fulton
  Mary Bell ----- Wife of Paul Fulton
                  (No dates)

  Paul ---------- (No dates)

Gay
  Benjamin ------ Apr 29, 1816 - Mar 13, 1889

  Delphia ------- Jul 27, 1819 - Jan 27, 1891

  Mittie L. ----- Dec 31, 1863 - Nov 16, 1879

  Wallace ------- Mar 12, 1858 - Mar 29, 1898

  Willie J. ----- Aug 8, 1860 - Aug 8, 1893

Geiger
  Capt. A. ------ Died Nov 16, 1871 Age 54

  William Henry - Son J. C. & E. B. Geiger
                  Aug 21, 1841 - Jul 13, 1867

Gentry
J. W. --------- Dec 18, 1853 - Sep 22, 1906

Godfrey
Julia Augusta - (No dates)
Age 19 yrs 8 mo & 21 days

Graham
Onita --------- Dau John & Ophelia Geiger
Oct 14, 1860 - Jul 17, 1871

Grove
Augustus
George -------- Mar 31, 1814 - Oct 31, 1886

Augustus J. --- Jul 16, 1846 - Nov 10, 1920

Clarence ------ Jun 27, 1849 - Nov 25, 1920

Frank M. ------ Jul 26, 1857 - Jul 8, 1909

Julian -------- Son Dr. A. G. Grove
Dec 21, 1851 - Jul 2, 1869

Lu Hill ------- Wife of A. J. Grove
Apr 15, 1849 - Apr 1, 1917

Mary E. ------- Wife of Dr. A. G. Grove
Oct 10, 1831 - Nov 2, 1869

Peninnah F. --- Apr 1, 1853 - Dec 14, 1920

Zoubie Rogers - Wife of F. M. Grove
Nov 14, 1862 - Jan 23, 1889

Halsell
Mrs. Eliza ---- Wife of William Halsell Sr.
Jul 31, 1810 - Apr 20, 1868

Ella A. ------- Dau W. M. & M. A. Halsell
Oct 10, 1861 - May 11, 1880

J. A. --------- Aug 1, 1857 - Aug 29, 1909

J. R. --------- Son W. M. & M. A. Halsell
Jan 4, 1859 - Mar 15, 1871

Halsell (contd)
Mrs. M. A. ---- Wife of W. M. Halsell
Feb 1, 1837 - Jan 29, 1885

Sallie Bess --- Dec 15, 1903 - Oct 21, 1919

Sparta L. ----- Wife of W. M. Halsell
Jul 7, 1844 - Dec 24, 1890

W. M. Sr. ----- May 18, 1832 - Jul 3, 1913

William Sr. --- Born in Chester, S. Carolina
Aug 10, 1807 - Nov 9, 1884

Hare
John ---------- (No dates)

Martha H. ----- (No dates)

Hibbler
Martha Blount - Wife of Robert Hibbler
Dau Edwin & Martha E. Speight
Jun 21, 1846 - Oct 18, 1867

Houston
Almira S. ----- Wife of J. J. Houston
Oct 29, 1841 - Jan 1, 1927

John J. ------- Died Jan 27, 1879
Age 41 yr 1 mo 27 das

Hunnicutt
Fannie
Elizabeth
Halsell ------- Wife of J. A. Hunnicutt
Born Jul 7, 1860 Houlka, Miss.
Marr Dec 22, 1887 Panola, Ala.
Died Nov 24, 1933 Meridian, Ms.

John A. ------- Apr 25, 1856 - Aug 3, 1922

Jenkins
Infants (2) --- Of J. T. & Mary L. Jenkins

J. T. --------- 5th Alabama Regiment
Born Jan 7, 1834
Died Union Hills, Va.
Oct 28, 1861

Jenkins (contd)
  Louvenia ------ 3rd Dau Jabaz & Mary Ann Jones
                       Died 1851 (Marker broken)

Knight
  William L. ---- Feb 11, 1836 - Jan 18, 1878

Lee
  Dr. John
  Andrew -------- Jun 23, 1853 - May 29, 1914

  Lillian
  Quarles ------- Jan 5, 1854 - Jun 22, 1911

  Virginia Hannah
  Rogers -------- Wife of J. W. Lee
                      Mar 23, 1851 - May 4, 1893

Little
  A. J. --------- Died May 1844 Age 17

  Charles Henry - Son Seth & Elizabeth Little
                      May 7, 1854 - May 31, 1855

  Mrs. Eliza T. - Wife of Capt. J. J. Little
                      Died Nov 19, 1857
                      39 yrs 3 mo & 14 da

  Harriett S. --- Dau Seth & Nancy Little
                      Sep 11, 1835 - Dec 11, 1841

  Capt. J. J. --- Died Feb 22, 1872
                    Age 51 yrs 3 mo & 14 da

  Laura J. ------ Wife of W. G. Little Jr.
                    Dau J. L. & M. A. Hibbler
                    1838 - 1913

  Lucy P. ------- Wife of Dr. W. G. Little
                    Dau Dr. B. & M. A. Boykin
                    Oct 19, 1837 - Sep 1, 1869

  Margaret E. --- Dau Seth & Nancy Little
                    Jul 9, 1831 - Aug 6, 1846

  Martha Louise - Dau J. J. & E. T. Little
                    Apr 4, 1853 - Sep 22, 1853

Little (contd)

Mary E. ------- Dau J. J. Little of Warsaw,
                Ala. Died Nov 15, 1861
                Age 18 yr 7 mo & 4 da

Mary
Elizabeth ----- Wife of Seth S. Little
                Aug 30, 1843 - Jan 15, 1926

Nancy --------- Wife of Seth Little
                Oct 12, 1812 - Jul 22, 1865

Noah ---------- Oct 8, 1832 - Aug 2, 1899

Robert Seth --- Son W. G. & Laura J. Little
                Jul 24, 1864 - Sep 25, 1865

Sarah A. ------ Wife of J. J. Little
                Oct 14, 1833 - Jul 1, 1908

Seth ---------- Born in Edgecomb Co. N. C.
                Mar 30, 1807 - Jul 22, 1865

Seth S. ------- Apr 4, 1842 - Nov 29, 1879

Susan
Elizabeth ----- Wife of A. J. Little
                May 29, 1841 - Oct 18, 1899

Tempy --------- Wife of William Little
                Born in Greene Co. N. C.
                Oct 11, 1808 - Dec 5, 1872

W. W. --------- 1837 - 1869

William ------- Born in Edgecomb Co. N. C.
                Jan 5, 1805 - Sep 22, 1873

William G. ---- Born in Edgecomb Co. N. C.
                Dec 27, 1832 - Jul 24, 1879

William Gray -- Born in Edgecomb Co. N. C.
                Dec 19, 1828 - Jan 21, 1893
                He was a surgeon in the CSA
                Army

Willie Gray --- Dau W. G. & L. J. Little
                Jul 8, 1860 - Nov 22, 1861

Lyon
  Andrew -------- Born in Columbia Co. Ga.
                  Sep 8, 1801 - Mar 9, 1874

  Susan --------- Wife of Andrew Lyon
                  Born in Columbia Co. Ga.
                  1808 - Mar 21, 1877

Marsh
  Nannie W. ----- Dau A. D. & H. C. Rogers
                  Died Apr 18, 1880
                  Age 22 yrs 8 da

Meek
  Capt. James
  T. ------------ Jun 30, 1830 - Sep 1, 1866
                  A Confederate Soldier

  John McCaw
  Sr. ----------- Aug 6, 1855 - Dec 6, 1920

  Rosa Little --- Sep 4, 1862 - Oct 25, 1943

Moffitt
  Elihu --------- Sep 8, 1810 - Jul 13, 1840

Moore
  Susie Weston -- Wife of T. O. Moore
                  Jul 23, 1864 - Feb 28, 1900

  Thomas Oliver - Jul 1, 1856 - Oct 23, 1912

Morgan
  Mrs. Barbary -- Wife of Rev. John Morgan
                  Mar 15, 1810 - Nov 16, 1870

  Rev. John ----- Apr 1811 - Jun 7, 1871

Nash
  Caroline Foy -- Wife of Stephen E. Nash
                  Nov 3, 1833 - Dec 18, 1901

  Elmira J. ----- Dau S. E. & M. J. Nash
                  Feb 11, 1842 - Jun 4, 1865

  Ida M. -------- Dau S. E. & C. F. Nash
                  Nov 23, 1862 - Jul 21, 1866

Nash (contd)
James H. ------ Son S. E. & M. J. Nash
                Mar 8, 1844 - Jan 3, 1890

Stevonia E. --- Dau Stephen & Caroline Nash
                Dec 15, 1863 - Jul 3, 1919

Neal
Matilda Peebles
Mabry --------- Wife of Thomas P. Neel
                1854 - 1925

T. P. --------- Nov 22, 1847 - Apr 21, 1909

Oliver
Nannie
Speight ------- Died Oct 17, 1895
               A 50 yr 6 mo & 19 da

Robert Perrin - Sep 28, 1844 - Feb 10, 1905

Pearson
Ann W. -------- Apr 25, 1807 - Apr 26, 1879

Infant -------- Dau J. E. & Ann Pearson
                Born & Died Nov 1840

Joel E., M.D. - Sep 18, 1802 - May 24, 1868

Phillip
Edward -------- Son J. E. & Ann Pearson
                Apr 1, 1836 - Aug 1, 1841

Peebles
Dr. Jesse ----- Aug 15, 1826 - Jan 29, 1906

Pettit
Jane E. ------- Died Oct 14, 1905 Age 72

Lola C. ------- Jun 16, 1860 - Jan 13, 1875

Powell
Luella B. ----- Wife of R. W. Powell
                Oct 10, 1844 - Jul 25, 1873

Pratt
John W. ------- Nov 28, 1825 - Dec 18, 1871

Quarles
    Charles Mimms - Aug 10, 1852 - Feb 2, 1918
    Mrs. Frances -- Wife Capt. J. M. Quarles
                    Apr 11, 1831 - Jan 13, 1894
    John James ---- Son J. M. & F. D. Quarles
                    Mar 3, 1860 - Aug 27, 1863
    John M. ------- Died Jan 4, 1878
                    A 52 yr 3 mo 14 da
    Minnie
    Windham ------ Dec 25, 1862 - May 8, 1902
    Sallie Boykin - Jan 18, 1857 - Jul 6, 1863

Reid
    Reuben C. ----- Son of Robert & Priscilla Reid
                    Died Aug 24, 1849
                    10 yrs 7 mo 11 days
    Sarah A. A.
    L. ------------ Dau of Robert & Priscilla Reid
                    Died May 19, 1850
                    18 yrs 7 m 3 days
    Susan L. ------ Dau of Robert & Priscilla Reid
                    Died Oct 13, 1847

Ritter
    John ---------- Aug 8, 1802 - Aug 22, 1872
    Capt. Wade ---- Son of John Ritter
                    Jun 3, 1838 - Nov 23, 1871

Rogers
    Annie E. ------ Wife of C. M. A. Rogers
                    Mar 2, 1839 - Jul 18, 1895
    Asa D. -------- Died Feb 1, 1862 Age 45
    C. M. A. ------ Dec 25, 1837 - Jul 18, 1895
    Carrie Geiger - Wife of C. M. A. Rogers
                    Dec 20, 1846 - Aug 1, 1890

Rogers (contd)

Eliza Jane ---- Wife of C. M. A. Rogers
Dec 20, 1846 - Aug 8, 1885

James L. ------ Son Joseph & Tabitha Rogers
Dec 27, 1840 - Feb 27, 1859

James
Pinckney ------ 1859 - 1936

Jane Caroline - Consort of Redmond Rogers
Oct 4, 1822 - May 13, 1853

Joseph -------- Sep 1, 1809 - Dec 30, 1872

Lucy A. ------- Dau Redmond & Jane Rogers
Dec 12, 1839 - Nov 21, 1857

Margarette
Jane ---------- (No dates)

Martha Eliza -- Wife of Redmond Rogers
Born in Edgecomb Co. N. C.
Mar 17, 1819 - Mar 30, 1894

N. A. --------- Aug 31, 1818 - Oct 10, 1857

Sarah A. ------ Nov 25, 1812 - Jul 26, 1891
Wife of N. A. Rogers

Sophia Gray --- 1860 - 1943

Tabitha ------- Jul 11, 1817 - Jun 3, 1874

William ------- Son Joseph & Tabitha Rogers
Sep 29, 1845 - Nov 6, 1867

William Baker - Son N. A. & Sarah A. Rogers
Nov 25, 1851 - Jun 26, 1853

Scarborough
Martha J. ----- Jan 11, 1845 - Nov 6, 1868

Shaver
Caroline M. --- Wife Rev. O. H. Shaver
Born in Warren Co. Kentucky
Feb 13, 1820 - Apr 10, 1849

Simmons
David S. ------ Feb 27, 1833 - May 27, 1917

Speight
Edwin G. ------ Died Feb 15, 1863 Age 45

Stanton
Mrs. E. E. ---- Dau E. & E. Nash
             Died Sep 6, 1840 Age 27

Mrs. E. J. ---- Dau S. & S. Wilkerson
             Died Nov 21, 1849 Age 26

Mrs.
Elizabeth ----- Died Feb 15, 1843 Age 68

Elizabeth ----- Died Sep 13, 1844 Age 8

H. D. --------- Died Apr 15, 1856 Age 46

H. L. --------- Died May 16, 1863 Age 16

H. W. --------- Feb 16, 1841 - Feb 6, 1842

Henry G. ------ Whose remains still lie in some
               unknown spot at Lafayette, Ga.
               where he was killed in battle
               Jun 24, 1864 Age 19 yrs

James W. ------ Died Aug 23, 1840 Age 2

Mary Eugenia -- Wife of S. S. Stanton
               Died Sep 26, 1856
               Age 19 yrs & 6 mo

Mary Hardie --- Wife of S. S. Stanton
               Dau J. & M. C. Gordon
               Nov 28, 1835 - Oct 13, 1866

Mrs. Nancy ---- Died Mar 3, 1873 Age 68

R. W. J. ------ Died Apr 24, 1843 Age 35

Rebecca
Elbira -------- Dec 15, 1835 - Mar 12, 1926

Sarah E. ------ Died Aug 15, 1849 Age 2

338

Stanton (contd)
Warren G. ----- Born in Edgecomb Co. N. C.
                Sep 5, 1812 - Apr 22, 1886

Rev. Wilie J. - Died Oct 15, 1843 Age 68

William V. ---- Born in Edgecomb Co. N. C.
                Apr 1, 1818 - Sep 1, 1887

_?_ D. ----- Died Apr 1843 Age 44

Starnes
Agnes --------- Wife Francis L. Starnes
                Nov 29, 1854 - Oct 17, 1892

Lizzie Bell --- Wife of F. L. Starnes
                Sep 30, 1842 - Jul 27, 1875

Taylor
Eliza Amason -- Jun 16, 1854 - Mar 4, 1880

Dr. Samuel
William ------- Nov 5, 1846 - Oct 13, 1909

W. F. --------- May 15, 1829 - Jul 28, 1911
                A Confederate Soldier Age 82

Thigpen
Sophia -------- Died May 26, 1860 Age 27

Thompson
Samuel -------- Dec 7, 1829 - Jun 7, 1874

Sarah A. ------ Wife of Samuel Thompson
                Jun 7, 1830 - Sep 27, 1869

Tidwell
George -------- Son S. G. & E. Tidwell
                Apr 3, 1857 - Nov 10, 1867

Turner
Patience ------ Born in Wayne Co. N. C.
                Nov 18, 1779 - Feb 1, 1851

Weston
Elizabeth ----- Consort of J. M. Weston
                Jun 29, 1808 - Feb 1, 1858

Weston (contd)
G. L. --------- Wife of A. G. Weston
             Jun 4, 1839 - Mar 13, 1906

   Mary ---------- Consort of Robert Weston Sr.
             Jun 20, 1769 - Jan 11, 1845

   Robert Sr. ---- Aug 29, 1763 - Jul 1845
             A Soldier of the Revolution

   Sallie E.
   Rogers -------- Wife of William K. Weston
             Dec 11, 1847 - Jan 14, 1925

   William K. ---- Jun 21, 1844 - Nov 18, 1875

Whitaker
   Sarah H. ------ Wife of D. A. Whitaker
             D Oct 15, 1851   Age 54

White
   Mrs. Martha
   D. ------------ Feb 24, 1824 - Aug 18, 1865

   Miriam E. ----- Wife of Ben White
             Jan 25, 1822 - __?__
             (Marker broken)

Wilkinson
   D. C. --------- Apr 7, 1828 - May 23, 1851

   D. C. --------- Son Joseph & E. E. Wilkinson
             Jul 15, 1857 - May 31, 1859

   J. L. --------- Feb 5, 1826 - Oct 20, 1842

   Silas --------- Nov 21, 1803 - May 31, 1856

Windham
   Herbert
   Hargrove ------ Son J. I. & M. G. Windham
             Sep 1, 1864 - Feb 14, 1867

   James I. ------ Mar 14, 1824 - Dec 27, 1872

   Martha Ann ---- Aug 6, 1834 - Jan 19, 1856

Windham (contd)
  Mattie -------- Born in Franklin Co. Ala.
                    Feb 6, 1836 - Nov 1, 1878

  Sallie
  Estelle ------- Dau J. I. & M. G. Windham
                    Jul 31, 1860 - Aug 26, 1869

  Sarah --------- May 15, 1785 - Apr 7, 1856

  Walter -------- Son J. I. & M. G. Windham
                    Oct 3, 1861 - Oct 8, 1861

  Wiley --------- Mar 10, 1782 - Feb 11, 1842

Young
  Thomas Eugene - Jun 20, 1863 - Jul 20, 1933

SHANTY HILL CEMETERY
(Greene County)

From Gainesville, go north on State Highway 39 for a distance of approximately 4 8/10 miles. Turn northwest on a dirt road for a distance of approximately 2/10 miles, past a church, to a gate. The cemetery is approximately 1 mile beyond the gate in a deep woods.

Amason
  Edward D. ----- 7/7/1826 - 3/1/1863

Jolly
  Hannah -------- Born 1771 Died 5/21/1857

  Peter --------- Born 1775 Died 3/27/1841

Rogers
  Alexander A. -- 10/19/1804 - 6/25/1857

SHEARSON CEMETERY

From County Road 9, approximately 1/2 mile north of the Choctaw County line, turn west on the Charles Spur Road. After 1/10 mile, turn south on a dirt drive to the cemetery at approximately 1/3 mile on the west side of the road.

Allen

A. L. ---------- Aug 23, 1850 - Jan 13, 1933

Benjamin ------ Born 1787 Died 1870 Age 83

C. M. ---------- Jul 22, 1840 - Aug 13, 1898

E. Jane ------- Aug 12, 1841 - Feb 27, 1918

Enoch --------- Apr 28, 1825 - Feb 5, 1896

Hampton ------- Dec 3, 1829 - Apr 7, 1906

Hulda --------- Born 1791 Died Jan 31, 1874
               Age 83

J. F. ---------- May 13, 1860 - Oct 27, 1931

J. W. ---------- Hus of A. C.
               Sep 8, 1851 - Nov 5, 1885

Jane S. ------- Wife of Enoch
               Oct 16, 1818 - Apr 24, 1894

Mary Cornelia - Wife of Benjamin J. Allen
               Aug 20, 1844 - Dec 7, 1882

Mary J. ------- Wife of A. L.
               May 27, 1854 - Apr 4, 1896

N. A. ---------- Sep 16, 1845 - Aug 7, 1928

Richmond ------ Sep 1, 1818 - Oct 30, 1880

S. H. ---------- Nov 3, 1844 - Sep 27, 1899

S. J. ---------- Wife of C. M.
               Jan 22, 1840 - Aug 31, 1907

Sarah R. ------ Feb 25, 1814 - Jun 11, 1883

Allen (contd)
  Susan
  Elizabeth ----- Wife of Hampton Allen
                 Died Sep 23, 1922 Age 70

  William
  Nicholas ------ Son Richmond & Sarah R. Allen
                1846 - 1860

Bowers
  M. A. --------- Wife of W. E.
               Born in Lancaster District of
               S. Carolina
               Apr 23, 1829 - Sep 30, 1909

  W. E. --------- Born in Lancaster District of
               S. Carolina
               Jun 2, 1827 - Aug 24, 1883

Chapin
  Armenius ------ Died Aug 23, 1868 Age 20

  Hannah -------- Died Jul 19, 1874
                66 yrs 11 mo 2 days

Ford
  Harriet A. ---- Wife of W. L.
                Nov 14, 1849 - May 9, 1887

George
  Emma ---------- Wife of J. W.
                Jun 21, 1843 - Feb 14, 1916

  John W. ------- Jan 7, 18 ? - Jan 2, 1870

Gibbens
  J. Elridge ---- 1858 - 1944

Grace
  Elaine -------- Mar 30, 1948 - Apr 27, 1948

  John B. ------- Aug 14, 1860 - Aug 24, 1904

  Mary E. ------- Wife of John B.
                May 20, 1860 - Mar 31, 1897

  Mollie F. ----- Wife of John B.
                Jan 1, 1863 - Nov 1, 1916

Lewis
   Luther -------- May 7, 1864 - May 19, 1932

   Mittie -------- Wife Luther
                        Died Jul 7, 1899 Age 35

McCann
   Infant -------- Son Jesse & Mary McCann
                        (No dates)

   John G. ------- Born 1800

   Nancy Brock --- Wife John G.
                        1810 - 1890

   Susan --------- Dau John G. & Nancy
                        1833 - 1927

   William J. ---- Son John G. & Nancy B 1837

Pearson
   T. C. --------- Oct 22, 1848 - Nov 7, 1910

Poole
   Leonidas ------ Jan 27, 1828 - Sep 20, 1907

   Octavia ------- Oct 16, 1861 - Dec 8, 1882

Pratt
   S. G. --------- Died Mar 5, 1911 Age 74

   Sarah Ann ----- Dec 7, 1835 - Apr 4, 1915

   W. R. --------- Apr 27, 1858 - Aug 25, 1874

   William ------- Apr 5, 1813 - Aug 5, 1872

Stallworth
   Joseph P. ----- Hus M. J. ?
                        Nov 10, 1844 - Nov 6, 1885

Tew
   H. J. --------- Nov 10, 1857 - Oct 16, 1926

   Jane ---------- Age 82 yrs

   W. W. --------- Dec 7, 1853 - Jan 11, 1886

Wilkerson
  W. M. --------- May 15, 1860 - Jan 2, 1941

  Mrs. W. M. ---- Oct 4, 1858 - Sep 8, 1938

SHORTS BAPTIST CHURCH CEMETERY

Located on the north side of County Road 15, approximately 1/3 mile east of its intersection with State Highway 17.

Allen
  C. D. --------- 1860 - 1933

  Sallie P. ----- Wife of C. D.
               Aug 24, 1857 - Jul 15, 1934

Alvis
  J. H. --------- Feb 1861 - Mar 1908

  Susan V. ------ Apr 1861 - Mar 1908

Baskin
  Edith A. ------ Wife of J. E.
              Jun 25, 1835 - Oct 20, 1900

  James E. ------ Hus of Edith
              Mar 2, 1824 - Sep 24, 1903

Bennett
  G. H. --------- 1856 - 1927

Drinkard
  James C. ------ Feb 11, 1854 - Dec 6, 1926

  Sallie P. ----- Dec 18, 1858 - Sep 8, 1927

Fluker
  David Brooks -- Feb 22, 1849 - Nov 28, 1936

  Susan Frances - Aug 30, 1854 - Mar 4, 1937

McDonald
  Drury M. ------ Apr 8, 1860 - May 7, 1915

McDonald (contd)
  Jamima G. ----- Jan 29, 1835 - Mar 6, 1909

  M. W. --------- Apr 25, 1830 - Nov 8, 1909

  Moses Waldrop - Nov 25, 1864 - Jun 30, 1931

Meador
  R. L. Sr. ----- May 14, 1852 - Jun 14, 1935

  W. F. --------- Dec 9, 1856 - Jun 3, 1933

Sims
  Martha A. ----- Wife of W. F.
                  Oct 5, 1851 - Jul 2, 1934

  W. F. --------- Jun 27, 1843 - Feb 11, 1929

Smith
  Frances
  Grimes -------- Oct 15, 1852 - Mar 1, 1932

  William
  Joseph -------- Feb 19, 1854 - Dec 9, 1944

Ward
  Francis
  Marion -------- Dec 27, 1831 - Nov 5, 1906

  Minnie G. ----- Mar 31, 1862 - May 30, 1935

  Susie Ann ----- Wife of F. M.
                  Nov 9, 1843 - Oct 5, 1895

Whittle
  M. A. S. T.
  Godwing ------- Dau M. C. & Susan
                  Sep 9, 1857 - Jan 8, 1888

Woodward
  M. C. --------- Wife of Rev. T. B.
                  Jan 7, 1837 - Oct 12, 1915

  Maggie -------- Wife of C. O.
                  Feb 14, 1862 - May 30, 1935

  Martha C. ----- Jan 19, 1860 - Jan 23, 1953

Woodward (contd)
   Thomas B. ----- May 11, 1832 - Sep 12, 1895

Woolf
   Emily C. Pack - Wife of Erwin
                    Dec 9, 1827 - Nov 20, 1905

   Frances E. ---- Wife of W. R.
                 Dec 29, 1850 - Jan 7, 1930

   Jefferson
   Perry --------- Mar 1, 1849 - Aug 29, 1906

   Sallie
   Vaughn -------- Nov 7, 1850 - Oct 27, 1942

   William
   Reddin -------- Jun 27, 1847 - Jan 7, 1928

SIBLEY CEMETERY
(Destroyed)

Located approximately 200 yards northwest of the old Sibley home, which is approximately 2 miles northeast of the Sumter Farm & Stock Company lodge in Geiger.

Sibley
   S. B. --------- Feb 9, 1804 - Jan 25, 1876

SILOAM BAPTIST CHURCH CEMETERY

From Highway 17, approximately 4 miles south of York, turn south on County Road 9. At approximately 3/4 mile, turn west on Siloam Church Road. The church and cemetery are at 3/4 mile on the north side of the road.

Altman
   Henry A. ------ Died May 18, 1869
                   52 yr 5 mo & 18 days

Altman (contd)
   Mary M. ------- Dau J. W. & Sallie Altman
                   Apr 26, 1853 - Oct 18, 1856

Anderson
   John G. ------- (No dates)

Armstrong
   J. J. --------- Oct 17, 1855 - Apr 30, 1921

   Mary E. ------- May 3, 1858 - Mar 24, 1931

Banks
   J. H. --------- Feb 3, 1833 - Jan 26, 1887

Bates
   Margaret P. --- May 26, 1843 - Oct 15, 1890

Billups
   Emma ---------- Wife of Thomas M. Billups
                   Oct 21, 1804 - Dec 17, 1886

   Frances ------- Consort of Thomas M. Billups
                   Jr.
                   Mar 20, 1834 - Jul 17, 1852

   Martha A. ----- Dau Thomas & Amelia Billups
                   Jul 1, 1838 - 1847

   Thomas M. Sr. - May 16, 1783 - Jan 19, 1864

Brown
   Charlotte ----- Wife of Hiram Brown
                   Jan 1, 1818 - Nov 12, 1850

   Daniel H. ----- Aug 8, 1865 - Jun 26, 1940

   James D. ------ Jan 10, 1810 - Jan 29, 1874

   Maron F. ------ 1850 - 1931

   Virginia ------ Wife of F. M. Brown
                   Jan 17, 1847 - Feb 16, 1924

Daniel
  Sarah D. ------ Consort of Samuel D. Daniel
                  Jan 20, 1822 - Nov 25, 1850

Dearman
  Elisha -------- Oct 25, 1819 - May 28, 1882

  Eliza --------- Wife of E. Dearman
                  Oct 3, 1828 - Apr 14, 1890

  John A. ------- Feb 3, 1865 - Oct 23, 1928

  Narciss ------- Oct 14, 1853 - Mar 4, 1935

  T. A. --------- Apr 15, 1835 - Nov 19, 1880

  W. T. --------- Nov 13, 1850 - Apr 2, 1912

Franklin
  H. F. --------- Jan 10, 1838 - Oct 27, 1878

  Martha -------- Jan 13, 1837 - Oct 27, 1881

Gibbs
  Edwin
  Churchill ----- Feb 3, 1844 - Mar 30, 1874

Green
  Aba ----------- Born in Wake Co. N. Carolina
                  Dec 15, 1806 - Sep 5, 1867

  Conary
  Lucinda ------- Dau W. & C. A. Green
                  Jan 10, 1859 - Dec 5, 1860

  G. W. --------- Feb 18, 1837 - Nov 12, 1896

  John A. ------- Son Aba Green
                  Apr 6, 1850 - May 9, 1904

  Mary Ann ------ Wife of Aba Green
                  Born in Wake Co. N. Carolina
                  Jun 22, 1809 - Oct 4, 1879

  Ophelia E. ---- Wife of S. D. Green
                  Mar 16, 1850 - Dec 6, 1901

Green (contd)
Samuel D. ----- Son Aba Green
                 Oct 5, 1852 - Mar 3, 1939

Susan Walker -- Wife of John A. Green
                Apr 21, 1848 - Aug 31, 1912

Grimes
Thomas J. ----- 1854 - 1921

Halsell
Gabriel ------- (No dates)

Patience ------ Wife of Samuel Halsell
                Jan 24, 1796 - Oct 10, 1846

Hammond
Amelia B. ----- Consort of B. N. B. Hammond
                Oct 8, 1827 - Feb 27, 1850

Emaline ------- 1861 - 1948

Joe ----------- 1861 - 1926

Harris
Caroline ------ Jan 24, 1826 - Feb 15, 1890

J. M. --------- Jun 14, 1850 - Jul 31, 1926

John ---------- Feb 7, 1827 - Mar 18, 1883

M. S. --------- Wife of J. E. Harris
                Oct 11, 1858 - Jan 7, 1896

Martha S. ----- Wife of Samuel Harris
                Jan 7, 1862 - Sep 18, 1881

Mary E. ------- 1853 - 1931

Nettie
Franklin ------ 1860 - 1938

Penelope Ann -- Wife of Simon Harris
                Jan 1835 - Feb 28, 1918

Sam ----------- 1857 - 1942

Harris (contd)
  Simon --------- Born Chesterfield Dist. S. C.
                          Jan 31, 1836 - Jan 26, 1910

Hitt
  Austin -------- Jun 1, 1811 - Jun 18, 1853
                       Married Rebecca Hall
                       Nov 22, 1832

  Cordelia
  McDonald ------ Dec 29, 1861 - Apr 27, 1894

  Martha Bowers - Nov 7, 1862 - Oct 8, 1946

  Rebecca ------- Dau Austin & Rebecca Hitt
                      Nov 8, 1848 - Feb 19, 1874

  William Henry - Jul 29, 1860 - Jan 30, 1900

Holder
  Ellen V. Bean - 1855 - 1921

  John W. ------- Dec 26, 1860 - Apr 26, 1933

  Rebecca
  Bartlett ------ 1831 - 1872

  William James - 1834 - 1915

Holley
  Rachel -------- Jan 7, 1832 - Jan 28, 1905

Huff
  Ollie C. ------ Jun 1, 1863 - Feb 17, 1924

Jones
  Penny --------- (No dates)

  Rebecca ------- Mar 23, 1821 - Feb 21, 1893

  Riley --------- Feb 22, 1809 - May 8, 1882

Key
  Fannie -------- 1865 - 1953

  J. M. --------- 1855 - 1918

Land
Mabella S. ---- Jan 31, 1830 - May 27, 1882

McDonald
J. A. --------- Sep 15, 1843 - Mar 12, 1877

M. E. --------- Wife of R. T. McDonald
May 25, 1852 - Nov 4, 1870

Mary F. ------- Feb 18, 1852 - Aug 21, 1884

Robert T. ----- Feb 19, 1836 - Apr 12, 1913

S. C. --------- Wife of Robert T. McDonald
1846 - 1902

Miller
Emily W. ------ Wife of R. F. Miller
Mar 14, 1833 - Mar 31, 1922

Col. R. F. ---- Nov 9, 1819 - Aug 24, 1904

Sicly --------- Consort of Robert Miller
Dau Samuel & Patience Halsell
Jul 28, 1821 - Jun 29, 1852
Married Apr 29, 1841

Newton
Malissa ------- Oct 12, 1835 - Nov 27, 1851

Owen
Alfred -------- Born Laurens Dist. of S. C.
Mar 11, 1809 - May 14, 1869

Elizabeth ----- Jul 4, 1776 - Sep 1, 1854

Mrs. Mary M. -- Died May 30, 1905
Age 86 yrs & 4 mo

Parker
Marcus -------- Feb 29, 1824 - Jul 27, 1890

Sarah Eleanor - Wife of Marcus Parker
Apr 14, 1831 - May 24, 1902

Peters
Levi ---------- Apr 15, 1845 - Jul 7, 1892

Peters (contd)
  Mary E. ------- Jan 13, 1853 - Nov 9, 1926

Quimby
  Melissa
  Emeline ------- Sep 10, 1847 - May 20, 1892

Rawlins
  Susan --------- 1816 - 1832

Rushing
  Frances L. ---- Jul 19, 1843 - Nov 8, 1913

Sheffield
  A. ------------ Mar 20, 1851 - Apr 6, 1904

  Embly --------- Nov 4, 1831 - Sep 7, 1879

  L. ------------ Jun 18, 1826 - Sep 9, 1909

Shelton
  Add ----------- Jan 8, 1849 - Jun 17, 1927

  Nancy C. ------ Wife of L. C. Shelton
                  Aug 22, 1851 - Aug 10, 1915

Sims
  H. J. --------- Nov 10, 1817 - May 17, 1897

  S. A. --------- Feb 14, 1828 - Dec 15, 1881

Smith
  Alice F. ------ Jan 17, 1861 - Jan 20, 1936

Stallings
  Burrel -------- Sep 8, 1861 - Nov 21, 1891

  Drusilla ------ Jun 9, 1835 - Feb 26, 1904

  J. M. Sr. ----- Dec 11, 1834 - Apr 20, 1920

  J. T. --------- Died May 17, 1915 Age 57

  James M. ------ Aug 23, 1862 - Feb 24, 1939

  Mary F. ------- Wife of J. M. Stallings
                  Feb 10, 1838 - Dec 31, 1899

Stallings (contd)
Sarah Alice --- Wife of J. T. Stallings
 Died Jan 26, 1881 Age 33

William ------- 1822 - 1916

William H. ---- Son William & Drusilla
 Stallings
 Jun 9, 1858 - Dec 23, 1858

Stephens
A. M. --------- Wife of C. M. Stephens
 Nov 21, 1839 - Jan 8, 1891

Isabella ------ Wife of C. M. Stephens
 Feb 20, 1847 - Nov 18, 1917

Nancy
Elizabeth ----- Wife of W. M. Stephens
 Jan 31, 1856 - Mar 28, 1885

Tate
Elizabeth R. -- Feb 4, 1861 - May 13, 1948

J. H. --------- Feb 7, 1855 - May 10, 1930

Thorne
Robert Emily -- Feb 15, 1863 - Apr 27, 1952

Truelove
Elijah -------- Mar 1, 1831 - Jun 10, 1903

Elizabeth ----- Apr 18, 1836 - May 16, 1914

Jane ---------- Dau E. & E. Truelove
 (No dates) Age 5 yrs

Martin -------- Son E. & E. Truelove
 (No dates) Age 11 yrs

Sarah --------- Dau E. & E. Truelove
 (No dates) Age 1 yr

Tucker
Rilla E. ------ 1858 - 1910

Thomas J. ----- 1842 - 1914

Walker
  Bettie -------- Wife of James A. Walker
                  Jul 4, 1845 - Sep 27, 1913

  Evaline P. ---- Feb 22, 1832 - Feb 22, 1905

  F. M. --------- Jan 18, 1846 - Jan 16, 1928

  Florid R. ----- Jun 15, 1833 - Jul 24, 1908

  James A. ------ Sep 14, 1839 - Aug 5, 1900

  James A. ------ Dec 19, 1856 - Dec 5, 1937

  John Oliver --- Jul 15, 1859 - Oct 25, 1951

  Joseph F. ----- Jul 17, 1837 - Sep 14, 1857

  Lucy ---------- Wife of James Walker
                  Jun 12, 1858 - Jun 14, 1929

  Lucy K. ------- Wife of F. M. Walker
                  Jun 6, 1852 - Dec 4, 1932

  Mittie E. ----- Wife of W. H. Walker
                  Died Sep 19, 1900
                  36 yrs & 8 mo

  S. E. --------- Wife of W. H. Walker
                  Nov 1, 1849 - Feb 16, 1909

  W. H. --------- May 29, 1842 - Nov 13, 1914

Watkins
  Hester C. ----- Feb 24, 1840 - Feb 17, 1890

Weaver
  Hassie -------- 1863 - 1932

  John B. ------- 1861 - 1908

Woolf
  Frank Forrest - Jul 27, 1864 - Mar 13, 1938

SNEDECOR CEMETERY
(Greene County)

From Gainesville, proceed north on State Highway 39 for approximately 4 6/10 miles to a pasture gap on the east side of the road. The cemetery is approximately 500 yards east of the gap on a hill in a woods.

Boyd
    Rev. L. M. ---- Born in Newberry District of S. C. December 11, 1810 Died Marion Miss. December 12, 1870

    Mary E. ------- 1/24/1847 - 9/16/1850

    Sarah E. ------ Wife of Rev. L. M. Boyd 2/22/1818 - 8/26/1859

Campbell
    John ---------- 1/18/1815 - 3/17/1848

    Mary ---------- 7/6/1823 - 11/3/1842

Carnes
    Amanda -------- 1/27/1826 - 7/1/1841

    Henry C. ------ 8/31/1827 - May 1833

    John W. ------- (No dates) Age about 44

Collins
    Drucilla
    Eliza --------- Wife of Joseph Collins Dau Posey & Elizabeth Gordon 12/14/1814 - 7/19/1848

    Orlando ------- Son Joseph & D. E. Collins 2/17/1846 - 9/7/1846

    Posey G. ------ Son Joseph & D. E. Collins 12/21/1837 - 9/20/1841

Derryberry
    Georgia
    Pearson ------- Dau T. J. & C. W. Derryberry 7/18/1881 - 6/13/1882

Gordon
Adaline ------- Infant Dau Posey & Elizabeth
                Gordon (No dates)

Adelia H. ----- Wife of Thomas J. Gordon
                4/12/1829 - 6/4/1851

Elizabeth S. -- 11/14/1794 - 6/7/1837

Jefferson ----- 1/30/1808 - 2/27/1861

Jesse --------- 12/15/1891 - 2/24/1844

Jesse Sr. ----- 9/26/1767 - 8/21/1853

Lycurcus ------ Son William P. & Susan Gordon
                4/28/1839 - 7/24/1841

Olivia C. ----- 11/16/1829 - 1/27/1848

Posey --------- 9/25/1775 - 11/10/1830

Samuel W. ----- 2/8/1822 - 7/17/1842

Thomas H. ----- Born in South Carolina
                2/21/1804 - 4/13/1830

Jolly
Arnold -------- 7/24/1807 - 10/11/1876

Judith W. ----- Consort of Arnold Jolly
                2/17/1818 - 2/22/1870

Dr. M. A. ----- 8/4/1835 - 9/19/1880

Sallie B. ----- Wife of Dr. M. A. Jolly
                Died 7/22/1892 Age 45

Lanford
Bighard ------- Son of H. & E. B. Lanford
                (Broken, dates unreadable)

Pearson
David B. ------ A native of Tennessee
                Died 3/1/1873
                59 yrs & 10 months

Pearson (contd)
Eliza Ann ----- Consort of George C. Pearson
                Died 9/14/1836
                19 yrs 9 mo 14 days

George C. ----- 12/24/1809 - 1/8/1856

Rogers
Laura
Caledonia ----- Dau W. N. & N. M. Rogers
                9/11/1860 - 8/30/1868

Mary Ann ------ Dau W. N. & N. M. Rogers
                10/27/1861 - 12/7/1866

William N. ---- 9/2/1833 - 3/29/1870

Smith
C. ------------ (No dates)

D. W. W. ------ 2/28/1837 - 12/31/1861

Elizabeth W. -- Died 3/4/1839
               29 yrs 9 mo & 26 days

F. ------------ (No dates)

J. ------------ (No dates)

J. F. --------- 12/13/1826 - 2/6/1867

James H. ------ Died 1/4/1831
               39 yrs 1 mo & 2 days

Mary E. ------- Dau W. W. & S. S. Smith
               Died 1845

Rebecca
Frances ------- 12/3/1834 - 12/23/1932

S. A. --------- Dau J. F. & R. F. Smith
               2/29/1858 - 11/3/1859

Susan J. ------ Wife of William Smith
               9/20/1832 - 1/31/1858

William ------- Died 2/4/1843 Age 77

Smith (contd)
William R. T. - Son Wright W. & Sallie S. Smith
                1/17/1831 - 3/1/1859

Wright W. ----- 6/24/1804 - 11/2/1880

Snedecor
Eleanor ------- Born Greenbrier County,
                Virginia January 1, 1764
                Died Greene County, Alabama
                June 1847

F. P. --------- 1/2/1829 - 3/4/1884

Col. James ---- Born in Virginia
                9/15/1795 - 8/9/1842

Lucy ---------- Wife of F. P. Snedecor
                9/11/1836 - 10/27/1888

Sally --------- Relict of James Snedecor
                Born in Virginia 6/6/1795
                Died Mt Hebron, Ala. 7/3/1862

Stevenson
Mary Ann ------ 11/20/1811 - 8/10/1836

Tilman
Annie W. ------ Consort of Daniel W. Tilman
                Dau Jefferson & Mary C. Gordon
                Died 7/10/1854   20 y 6 m & 7 d

Infant -------- Son D. L. & Ann Tilman
                June 3, 1854

Walker
Jemerson ------ 3/19/1815 - 1/6/1857

William Henry - Son Jemerson & Zillia Walker
                6/22/1853 - 9/19/1854

Wood
William H. ---- 3/8/1837 - 12/29/1872

SOULS CHAPEL CEMETERY

From State Highway 17, approximately 1 1/2 miles south of Geiger, turn east on a dirt road. The cemetery is approximately 1 mile down this road on the north side of the road.

Allison
   Leodocia ------ 1800 - Mar 1, 1890

Ballard
   Frank --------- Nov 9, 1853 - Sep 25, 1923

   Mattie -------- Wife of Frank Ballard
                  Mar 23, 1853 - May 2, 1900

   Walter R. ----- 1859 - 1921

Campbell
   Robert Lee ---- 1853 - 1912

Cherry
   William J. ---- Jun 23, 1860 - Mar 10, 1919

Dawkins
   Dock ---------- (No dates)

   Ellen --------- (No dates)

   G. A. --------- Jun 25, 1836 - Nov 24, 1906

   John ---------- (No dates)

   Mrs. L. C. ---- Feb 14, 1843 - Oct 29, 1932

Eaves
   Nancy Ellen --- Mar 21, 1858 - Jun 2, 1918

Gilbert
   John W. ------- Died Aug 1, 1887
                  22 yr 5 mo 27 days

   William B. ---- Died Jan 26, 1882
                  19 yr 4 mo 29 days

Hailey
   Andrew
   Harrison ------ Jan 10, 1840 - Mar 28, 1912

Hailey (contd)
Keziah -------- Wife of A. H. Hailey
                Feb 13, 1838 - Feb 1, 1912

Hawkins
L. D. --------- Oct 25, 1817 - Aug 8, 1897

Sarah E. Ivy -- Apr 5, 1818 - Dec 18, 1909

Hutcherson
E. E. ---------- Wife of G. W. Hutcherson
                 Born Dec 8, 1846

G. W. ---------- Feb 2, 1837 - Dec 8, 1901

Ivy
Ben R. -------- May 13, 1850 - May 26, 1919

James S. ------ Son James B. & Sarah E. Ivy
                Feb 15, 1857 - Jul 8, 1903

Jesse C. ------ 1847 - 1924

Melvina W. ---- Dau James B. & Sarah E. Ivy
                Feb 20, 1842 - Mar 4, 1863

Sarah T. ------ Dau James B. & Sarah E. Ivy
                Feb 2, 1861 - Aug 12, 1862

McDaniel
Mary E. ------- Sep 6, 1823 - Jun 5, 1896

McKinley
Catherine J. -- Aug 10, 1837 - Nov 5, 1888

Daniel D. ----- Mar 17, 1843 - Apr 17, 1921

Nicholson
Abbie E. ------ Wife of M. A. Nicholson
                May 26, 1860 - Nov 10, 1895

George -------- Dec 30, 1863 - Jun 15, 1936

Jinnie -------- Mar 22, 1860 - Feb 10, 1940

Ogletree
Benjamin H. --- Hus Amelia J. Ogletree
                Aug 7, 1836 - Sep 3, 1897

Peel
    J. F. ---------- Aug 18, 1851 - Jul 23, 1909

    Lena Gilbert -- Aug 30, 1858 - Oct 7, 1943

Pinson
    Annie Bell
    Gilbert ------- Aug 23, 1857 - Mar 1, 1945

    Dr. H. -------- Jul 28, 1840 - Jan 8, 1919

Ramsey
    Emmett
    Templeton ----- Jan 9, 1861 - Nov 28, 1906

    Hattie Permilia
    Sibley -------- Sep 27, 1860 - Apr 16, 1938

    Moses F. ------ Pvt., 16th Regt., CSA
                    Oct 24, 1846 - Jul 12, 1920

Rodgers
    Aaron --------- Sep 17, 1855 - Oct 17, 1933

Secrest
    James L. ------ Co. C, Jeff Davis Legion, CSA
                    Dec 16, 1838 - Dec 9, 1885

Sibley
    Sarah R. ------ Wife of S. W. Sibley
                    Jul 18, 1844 - May 31, 1890

SPRATT CEMETERY

Located on a dirt road approximately 3/4 mile north of its intersection with State Highway 28, approximately 1 1/4 miles west of Interstates 20 and 59.

There are three infant graves at the foot of a large marker with the inscribed name SPRATT.

Spratt
    John B. ------- Son of R. D. & Lillis Spratt
                    1845

Spratt (contd)
   Mary ---------- Dau of R. D. & Lillis Spratt
                   1842 - 1845

   Walter -------- Son of R. D. & Lillis Spratt
                   (No dates)

ST JOHN CHURCH CEMETERY

From the intersection of State Highway 116 and County Road 85, approximately 1 2/10 miles west of Gainesville, go north on County Road 85 for approximately 5 1/2 miles to the church and cemetery on the east side of the road.

Crane
   Betsy --------- 1858 - 1925

Grain
   Dillie -------- Wife of James Grain
                   Feb 2, 1863 - Feb 24, 1898

Mobley
   Mandy --------- Died Apr 8, 1912   Age 68 yrs

Watkins
   Jane ---------- Dec 5, 1864 - Oct 11, 1937

Whitsett
   Jane ---------- Wife of Miler Whitsett
                   Feb 10, 1810 - Jan 7, 1896

ST JOHN'S CHURCH CEMETERY

From State Highway 17, approximately 13 1/2 miles south of York, turn east on County Road 15. At 1 1/10 miles, turn north on St John Road to the church and cemetery.

Brooks
   Calvin -------- Born 1860   Died 1919

Brooks (contd)
      Cellie -------- Born 1865 - Died 1916
Graham
      Alabama ------- Born 1852 Dec 27, 1917
      ? ------- Jul 15, 1859 - Mar 21, 1924
Ross
      Diana --------- Died Aug 16, 1913 Age 85
Ward
      Lizzie -------- Born Aug 10, 1853
                      Died Mar 30, 1915
      Rosener ------- Born 1850 Died Aug 20, 1914

SUMTERVILLE METHODIST CHURCH CEMETERY

From State Highway 17, 2 miles south of Emelle, turn east on County Road 20. At 4 1/10 miles, turn north on a dirt road. The cemetery is a few hundred feet down this road on the west side of the road, surrounded by a chain link fence.

Brown
      Cornelia G. --- Dau George A. & Sara B. Brown
                      Died Aug 15, 1858 Age 16
      Infant -------- Son G. A. & S. B. Brown
                      Died 1847
      Infant -------- Son G. A. & S. B. Brown
                      Died 1848
      Kate Henagan -- Wife of W. H. Brown
                      Born in Brownsville, S. C.
                      Mar 6, 1842 - Apr 16, 1867
      Mary Alice ---- Died Jan 11, 1847 4 yrs 1 mo
      Milton Dozier - Son G. A. & Sara B. Brown
                      Died Mar 14, 1861 2 yrs 10 mo
      William Henry - Oct 10, 1839 - Mar 22, 1913

Buford
  Edwin Dial ---- Son Thomas N. & Mary Dial
                  Buford Died Jul 14, 1837

  Mary Dial ----- Wife of Thomas N. Buford
                  D Jan 6, 1837
                  20 yrs 1 mo & 14 days

Davis
  Martha C. ----- Mar 30, 1834 - Apr 17, 1849

Dial
  David
  Montgomery ---- Died Sep 24, 1834 Age 49

  James --------- Son David & Jennett Dial
                  Jan 13, 1826 - Apr 28, 1860

  Jennett ------- Wife David M. Dial
                  Oct 1, 1783 - May 24, 1855

  William
  Montgomery ---- Son David M. & Jennett Dial
                  Died Oct 10, 1840
                  13 yrs 25 days

George
  Mary ---------- Wife of Basil George
                  Died Jul 6, 1837 Age 44

Godfrey
  Cornelia
  Ormond -------- Wife of W. E. Godfrey
                  Nov 6, 1859 - Dec 6, 1886

  E. B. --------- (No marker)

  Dr. James
  Myers --------- Sep 7, 1832 - Jan 20, 1890

  Lucy A. ------- Wife of Dr. J. M. Godfrey
                  Jul 13, 1834 - Mar 2, 1914

  W. E. --------- Son Dr. J. M. & Lucy Godfrey
                  Oct 14, 1856 - Jul 18, 1925

  William Sr. --- Revolutionary Soldier
                  (No dates)

Hodges
Sarah Melissa - Wife of J. G. Hodges
Jan 2, 1851 - Dec 18, 1889

Holland
John ---------- Born Prince George Co. Va.
Revolutionary Drummer Boy at 13
1766 - 1842

Hutchins
Celeste B. ---- Dau J. L. & Sara Hutchins
Died Jun 6, 1845   13 yr 12 da

Elizabeth ----- Wife of J. H. Hutchins
Died Apr 14, 1841   Age 43

Jesse H. ------ Son of Thomas H. Hutchins
Oct 11, 1810 - Aug 27, 1842

Ruth D. ------- Dau J. L. & Sara Hutchins
Died Jul 25, 1855   Age 12

Thomas H. ----- Aug 1763 - Nov 27, 1842

William ------- Son J. H. & Elizabeth Hutchins
Died Jul 28, 1835   Age 3

William P. ---- Son J. L. & Sara Hutchins
Died Sep 19, 1849   12 yrs 9 mo

Jackson
Elizabeth ----- Wife of Randle Jackson
Born in South Carolina
Apr 5, 1776 - Jun 15, 1854

Lt. J. T. ----- Son Jacinth & Prudence Jackson
Born in Barbour Co. Alabama
Feb 9, 1839
Wounded at Resaca, Ga.
May 15, 1864
Died at Atlanta Jun 1, 1864

Jacinth ------- Born in Brunswick Co. Va.
Oct 16, 1796 - Sep 5, 1869
Son of Randle Jackson

James C. ------ Son Jacinth & Prudence Jackson
Mar 29, 1815 - Aug 21, 1843

Jackson (contd)
  Prudence ------ Consort of Jacinth Jackson
                   Dec 20, 1797 - Oct 2, 1857

  Randle -------- Born in Brunswick Co. Va.
                  Oct 17, 1763 - Jul 17, 1839

  Sara E. ------- Dau Jacinth & Prudence Jackson
                 Feb 13, 1827 - Jul 8, 1844

Johnston
  Lucy Olivia --- Mar 12, 1842 - Dec 23, 1920

Knight
  Paul S. ------- Died Apr 8, 1843 Age 28

Massey
  Mrs. Emma A. -- Dau Lewis Brown
                 Mar 29, 1844 - Nov 23, 1888

Mayberry
  G. E. --------- Son G. W. & J. E. Mayberry
                 Died Dec 27, 1854 Age 10

McCain
  Adam Creed ---- Sep 6, 1859 - Jul 9, 1931

McDaniel
  Delila -------- Wife of Henry McDaniel
                 Apr 27, 1807 - Mar 10, 1876

  Elizabeth ----- Dau Henry & Delila McDaniel
                 Nov 28, 1841 - Jun 20, 1859

  Elizabeth C. -- Dau William & Penelope McDaniel
                 Died Mar 1842 Age 10

  George W. ----- Son Henry & Delila McDaniel
                 Mar 11, 1837 - Oct 9, 1965

  Henry --------- Died Oct 12, 1880 Age Abt 83

  Henry Clay ---- Son Henry & Delila McDaniel
                 Died Jul 26, 1844 Age 2 mo

  Hulda Ann ----- Dau Henry & Delila McDaniel
                 Dec 24, 1832 - Aug 19, 1858

McDaniel (contd)
James E. ------ Son Henry & Delila McDaniel
Jul 13, 1845 - Sep 22, 1846

John M. ------- Died Jul 7, 1882   Age 48

Margaret J. --- Dau Henry & Delila McDaniel
Jan 14, 1831 - Aug 11, 1860

Mary Knox ----- Wife of John M. McDaniel
Jul 29, 1845 - Mar 20, 1914

Pamelia ------- Wife of Henry McDaniel
Died Apr 19, 1884   Age Abt 42

Penelope ------ Wife of William McDaniel
Died 1874   Age 84

Rosa Knox ----- Died Jul 28, 1869
Dau John & Mary K. McDaniel

William ------- Died Mar 1835   Age 56

William
Harris -------- Son Henry & Delila McDaniel
Died Jun 30, 1842   Age 14

William
Henry --------- Son Henry & Delila McDaniel
Sep 9, 1847 - Jul 28, 1848

McKinsie
Edgar J. ------ Son John & Jane McKinsie
Dec 3, 1853 - Oct 11, 1857

Mitchell
(Twins) -------- Dau B. J. & Nancy Mitchell
B. & D. Jan 15, 1844

Nance
Mary Ann ------ Dau W. T. & Sarah Nance
Aug 16, 1847 - Aug 30, 1848

Nixon
Hester Ann ---- Wife of J. M. Nixon
Mar 21, 1824 - Sep 6, 1878

Ormond
    Thomas S.
      "Uncle Tom"   --- Born Green Co. N. C.
                        Jul 8, 1808 - Aug 31, 1868

Porter
    James Lemuel -- Son L. J. & M. M. Porter
                     Died Jul 26, 1857

    Sallie Bell --- Dau L. J. & M. M. Porter
                     (No dates)

Prince
    Sarah E. ------ Aug 17, 1837 - Mar 9, 1902

Richardson
    John Ruffin --- Born in Raleigh, N. C.
                     Feb 23, 1823 - Sep 16, 1900

    Sarah J. ------ Wife of J. R. Richardson
                     Nov 26, 1843 - Oct 21, 1908

Somers
    George -------- Died Jun 4, 1861   65 yrs 9 days

Watts
    Florence
      Godfrey ------- Wife of G. H. Watts
                       Aug 28, 1860 - Dec 29, 1889

Webb
    Infant -------- Dau John H. & Mary H. Webb
                     (No dates)

    John Parker --- Son John H. & Mary Webb
                     Died Mar 4, 1848 Age 6 mo

    Sara Ann ------ Dau John H. & Mary H. Webb
                     Died Apr 20, 1853 Age 16 mo

Wilson
    Mary McDaniel - Dau Henry & Delila McDaniel
                    Feb 12, 1850 - Feb 14, 1880

SWILLEY CEMETERY

Located deep in the woods in Section 16, Township 21 North, Range 1 West, a few hundred feet east of the end of the Swilley's Bend Road.

Fallon
Michael ------- Born Sep 29, 1808 in Kellybrook Co., Roscommon, Ireland
Died Nov 14, 1859

Swilley
Alice
Caledonia ----- Dau John & Mary A. Swilley
Jul 14, 1852 - Sep 26, 1853

John W. Sr. --- Jun 22, 1819 - Mar 26, 1870

Mary ---------- Dau John & Mary A. Swilley
Jan 25, 1854 - Apr 25, 1855

TATE CEMETERY

Located in the north one-half of Section 23, Township 17 North, Range 3 West, approximately 1/2 mile east of State Highway 17 and approximately 1/2 mile south of U. S. Highway 80.

Tate
Cornelia Ann -- Aug 28, 1832 - Oct 26, 1904

William ------- Born in North Carolina 1825
Died Mobile, Ala. Jun 6, 1862
While in service CSA

TAYLOR CEMETERY

From the intersection of County Roads 22 and 23 in Belmont, proceed west on County Road 22 for approximately 2 miles. The cemetery is on a high bank on the north side of the road.

McClelland
Nancy Ann ----- Wife of Jeremiah N. McClelland
Dau Sirus & Elizabeth Taylor
May 15, 1825 - May 31, 1857

McMillan
Clarinda M. --- Wife of H. McMillan
Aug 5, 1810 - Nov 6, 1860

Taylor
Cyrus --------- Died Jan 23, 1844
Age 27 yrs 9 mo 7 days

Elizabeth
Jane ---------- Dau of Sius & Elizabeth Taylor
Who departed this life
Sep 5, 1847 Age 25 yrs 4 mo

Martha Ann ---- Child of Sius & Clarinda Taylor
Departed this life Jan 25, 1845

Mary Ann ------ Dau of Sius & Clarinda M.
Taylor Who departed this life
Sep 25, 1846
In the 11th year of her age

Rufus --------- Child of Sius & Clarinda Taylor
Departed this life May 4, 1842

Sius ---------- Who departed this life
Oct 5, 1846
in the 59th year of his life

W. P. --------- Died Sep 18, 1840
Age 26 yrs 10 mo 3 days

TIDMORE CEMETERY

Located on the south bank of Cotohaga Creek, in Section 20, Township 16 North, Range 1 West, approximately 1 mile south of County Road 42 and approximately 1/2 mile south of the end of the Hazel Tidmore Road.

Tidmore
Anna O. ------- Oct 30, 1853 - Dec 24, 1903

TISDALE CEMETERY

Located approximately 200 yards east of the old Tisdale home in York, now the home of the Mason McLemores, on Rumley Road.

All of the markers in this cemetery have been destroyed. The following persons are known or believed to be buried there.

Boatman
Mrs. __?__ ---- Mother of Perry Boatman

Dodd
Mrs. __?__

Drew
Miss Jane

Miss Susan

Robnett
J. M. --------- Died Sep 28, 1881   Age 54

John Wilson --- Died Sep 4, 1881
Age 30 yrs 8 mo & 4 days

Tisdale
Alice --------- Died Aug 31, 1881
Age 25 yr 3mo & 23 days

TRAVIS CEMETERY

Located in the yard of the old Travis home, approximately 1 mile south of State Highway 28 and 1/2 mile east of the intersection of State Highway 28 and County Road 74.

Bell
    Edward -------- Died in the Battle of
                              Chickamauga (No dates)

    Richard Jr. --- (No dates)

Travis
    Amos ---------- (No dates)

    Elizabeth
    Coleman ------- Died Apr 26, 1896

    Ellen L. ------ Dau Enoch Travis
                        Dec 25, 1839 - Mar 3, 1843

    Enoch --------- Jul 9, 1797 - Mar 20, 1841

    Harriet ------- Dec 25, 1819 - Aug 23, 1843

    Wiley Coleman - Died 1916

This cemetery has been covered with a concrete slab. Markers have been broken off and removed. Only the Bell markers are intact.

WALLIS - MELLARD CEMETERY

From U. S. Highway 11, approximately 1 mile south of Livingston, turn west on County Road 12. The cemetery is approximately 4 2/10 miles down this road, approximately 25 yards north of the road in heavy overgrowth.

Asbury
    Elisha -------- Son E. A. & E. J. Asbury
                        Jan 16, 1843 - Sep 5, 1854

Mellard
   Elizabeth J. -- Consort of E. A. Mellard
                      Dau Seaborn & Elizabeth H. Mims
                      Departed this life Sep 15, 1852
                      Age 36 yrs 11 mo 26 days
                      Her last words were "I am gone.
                      Meet me in Heaven".

Wallis
   Frances ------- Dau W. A. & C. M. Wallis
                      Died Aug 11, 1849
                      Age 4 yrs 11 mo 4 days

WATKINS - TAYLOR CEMETERY

Located on the east side of County Road 85 in the S. W. Taylor Memorial Park, 2 miles south of the intersection of County Roads 34 and 85.

Taylor
   Narcissa ------ Dec 21, 1813 - Nov 11, 1881

   Samuel -------- Jun 13, 1802 - Aug 20, 1854

Watkins
   Levin --------- Mar 16, 1791 - Apr 28, 1865

   Mary Ann ------ Youngest Dau Levin & Sarah
                      Watkins who departed this life
                      on Jan 12, 1840 in her 18th
                      year

   Mrs. Sarah ---- Consort of Levin Watkins, Esq,
                      of Sumter County, Ala., who
                      departed this life on the 2nd
                      day of Sep 1842 in the 55th
                      year of age

WATSON CEMETERY

From the intersection of County Roads 22 and 23 at Belmont, proceed west on County Road 22 for approximately 2 8/10 miles. The cemetery is approximately 100 yards north of the road.

Watson
  John ---------- Born Jun 23, 1776
                  Died May 26, 1841

There are five unmarked crypts in this cemetery.

WATSON CEMETERY

From State Highway 17, approximately 2 1/2 miles south of Geiger, turn west on County Road 30. After 1 3/10 miles, turn south on the Jerusalem Church Road. After approximately 3 1/10 miles, turn south on a dirt road. The cemetery is 3/10 mile down this road on the left side.

Ashford
  Martha Jane --- Wife of William Ashford
                  Feb 8, 1829 - Aug 17, 1850

Watson
  Mattie B. ----- Wife of Tom Watson
                  Died Nov 22, 1872 Age 33

WATSON CEMETERY

From State Highway 17, approximately 2 1/2 miles south of Geiger, turn west on County Road 30. After 1 3/10 miles, turn south on the Jerusalem Church Road. After approximately 2 7/10 miles, turn south on the Nat Jones Road. The cemetery is approximately 4/10 mile down this road, several hundred yards to the right of the road.

Smoot
  Elijah -------- 1852 - 1941

WATT CEMETERY

From State Highway 17, approximately 1 7/10 miles north of Geiger, turn west on a dirt road. At approximately 2 miles, there is a set of gates on the north side of the road and a pasture road running north from the gates. The cemetery is approximately 1/2 mile up that road.

Aust
   Absalom ------- Nov 24, 1811 - Jan 19, 1863

   Mary Ann ------ Aug 7, 1828 - Sep 19, 1894

Jones
   Samuel L. ----- Mar 26, 1863 - Oct 21, 1922

WEIR CEMETERY

From State Highway 17, approximately 1/2 mile south of the Pickens County line, turn west on a dirt drive for approximately 1/4 mile to the old Weir homesite. The cemetery is approximately 1/4 mile west of the homesite.

There is an iron fence around the cemetery with the plaque, "Peter Weir - 1867. No markers.

WIDEMAN CEMETERY

From State Highway 17, approximately 11 1/2 miles south of York, turn east on County Road 42. At 3 3/10 miles, turn north on the Wideman Road. The cemetery is approximately 300 yards down this road on the east side of the road.

Luker
   Joseph E. ----- Jan 8, 1840 - Jan 5, 1904

   Mrs. S. E. ---- Wife of J. E. Luker
                   Feb 25, 1847 - Apr 17, 1903

Steinwinder
   Thomas G. ----- Dec 25, 1865 - Aug 11, 1933

Wideman
   Len ----------- 1826 - 1913

   Nancy J. ------ 1837 - 1908

   William E. ---- Jan 21, 1857 - Oct 3, 1933

WILLIAMS - GIBBS CEMETERY

From the intersection of State Highway 39 and County Road 24, approximately 12 1/2 miles north of Livingston, proceed south on Highway 39 for approximately 700 feet to a pasture gate on the east side of the road. The cemetery is approximately 2 miles down a pasture road from this gate.

Gibbs
   Ada ----------- Oct 5, 1862 - Aug 12, 1867

   Elizabeth ----- Wife of Jessie A. Gibbs
                  Jul 24, 1818 - Mar 12, 1897

   Estelle ------- Feb 14, 1853 - Apr 26, 1860

   Jessie -------- Dec 10, 1856 - Oct 7, 1865

   Jessie A. ----- Born in Virginia
                  Jan 22, 1814 - Jun 5, 1885

   Sabat S. ------ Dec 3, 1846 - __?__
                  (Marker broken)

   William Henry - Sep 20, 1840 - Jan 26, 1911

McKerall
   Fannie -------- Wife of P. G. McKerall
                  Sep 17, 1860 - Apr 2, 1888

Monette
   Callie -------- Wife T. F. Moore
                  Mar 11, 1850 - Jun 9, 1925

Monette (contd)
Fletch -------- Hus Callie Monette
                Oct 31, 1845 - Jul 11, 1895

Robinson
James F. ------ Oct 7, 1832 - Oct 24, 1916

Jennie A. ----- Aug 5, 1842 - Apr 22, 1924

Williams
Charles
Stokes -------- Jul 26, 1844 - Feb 21, 1930

David C. ------ 1817 - 1896

Eliza Gibbs --- Jan 21, 1859 - Mar 8, 1926

WINSTON CEMETERY

Located approximately 1/2 mile north of State Highway 116, on the south bank of Bodka Creek, approximately 5 1/2 miles west of Gainesville.

Chapman
Mary K. ------- Wife of Samuel Chapman
                Died Oct 20, 1841 Age 33

Gage
Billy --------- Son W. A. & S. O. W. Gage
                Jul 16, 1862 - Jan 31, 1867

Martha Hall --- Dau W. A. & S. O. W. Gage
                Jul 1, 1858 - Jul 3, 1861

Sallie O. ----- Wife of ?. S. Williams
                (Marker broken, no dates)

Sara Olive
Winston ------- Wife of W. A. Gage
                May 13, 1836 - Aug 17, 1861

Winston ------- Age 24 yrs (No dates)

__?__ --------- Olive's Babe (No dates)

Golsby
  Agnes Winston - Only Child of Governor John Anthony Winston (No dates)

  Anthony Winston ------- May 2, 1858 - Jul 1, 1859

  Belle Seawell - Died Oct 28, 1885 Age 23 yrs

  John Anthony Winston ------- Died Feb 12, 1889 Age 29 yrs

  Tommy Gray ---- Aug 12, 1864 - Oct 18, 1867

Gorman
  John E. ------- Died Sep 6, 1842
        Age 9 yrs 7 mo 7 days

Isbell
  George -------- (No dates)

  James --------- (No dates)

McMahon
  Gage Winston -- Wife of Carl McMahon
        1854 - 1936

Mitchell
  Sallie Gage --- Dau Daniel & Martha Mitchell
        Mar 1, 1863 - Nov 25, 1951

Morrison
  James --------- Born in Iredell Co. N. C.
        Aug 18, 1832 - Jul 26, 1856

Pettus
  Permelia V. --- (No dates)

Robinson
  Joseph A. ----- Born in Chesterfield Co. Va.
        Aug 1, 1812 - Sep 17, 1842

Winston
  A. A. --------- Son J. M. & R. V. Winston
        Died Jul 9, 1849
        Age 9 mo 5 days

  Ann ----------- Age 38 (Marker destroyed)

Winston (contd)

Ann Hall ------	Died Jan 29, 1848 Age 29
Anthony -------	Born in Buckingham Co. Va. Dec 5, 1782 - Sep 24, 1841
Charles Henry -	Aug 31, 1858 - Jun 22, 1924
Edwin H. ------	Son W. H. & M. E. Winston Apr 27, 1865 - Nov 9, 1865
Fleta Olive ---	Dau J. M. & R. V. Winston Died Oct 4, 1865 Age 6 yrs 11 mo
Henry P. ------	Son W. A. & S. A. Winston Mar 1, 1853 - Jul 10, 1865
Infant --------	Dau W. A. & S. A. Winston (No dates)
Irene ---------	Wife of Charles H. Oct 18, 1858 - Nov 7, 1898
Capt. James M. ------------	Born Jul 26, 1826 Married R. V. Brodnax Oct 4, 1845 Died Apr 4, 1905
John Anthony of Alabama ----	Sep 4, 1812 - Dec 21, 1871
Margaret A. ---	Wife of William O. Winston Dec 20, 1829 - Sep 29, 1911
Mary A. -------	(No dates)
Mary Agnes ----	Wife of John Anthony Winston (No dates)
Rebecca Virginia Brodnax -------	Wife of Capt. James M. Winston Died Apr 27, 1912
Sallie Ada ----	Dau William O. & Amanda Winston Sep 16, 1850 - Sep 8, 1857

Winston (contd)
  Sallie Ann ---- Born in Prince Edward Co. Va.
                  Mar 19, 1791 - Jul 24, 1843

  Sarah A. ------ Wife of W. H. Winston
                  Sep 13, 1821 - Dec 17, 1856

  Thompson ------ Son A. A. & S. J. Winston
                  Feb 15, 1851 - Jun 24, 1852

  Virginia H. --- Mar 12, 1847 - Apr 16, 1867

  W. O. --------- Apr 20, 1809 - May 28, 1894

  William M. ---- Jul 17, 1852 - Aug 27, 1882

(Unknown)
  Eleta --------- Sep 18, 1839 - Jun 9, 1856

WOODS - CAMERON CEMETERY

Located in the northeast corner of the intersection of U. S. Highway 80 and State Highway 17.

Woods
  Elisha -------- Husband of S. J. Woods
                  Jan 22, 1833 - Aug 25, 1898

  Sarah J. ------ Wife of Elisha Woods
                  May 15, 1848 - Jul 23, 1914

YORK MUNICIPAL CEMETERY

Located on Cemetery Avenue in York.

Alexander
  Helen
  McAlpin ------- May 16, 1858 - Oct 10, 1929

Allison
  Ann Virginia -- 1854 - 1929

Allison (contd)
    Bettie -------- Wife of C. H. Allison
                    Sep 30, 1856 - Dec 10, 1890

    C. H. --------- Feb 22, 1856 - Jun 26, 1909

    Evan Frank ---- Nov 28, 1865 - Jul 17, 1937

    John F. ------- Born Cabaras Co. N. C.
                    Feb 15, 1822 - Dec 26, 1897

    Mary E. ------- Born Montgomery Co. N. C.
                    Mar 4, 1833 - May 27, 1894

Altman
    E. S. "Betty" - Wife of W. A. Altman
                    Nov 17, 1863 - Jul 13, 1894

    John W. ------- Feb 27, 1819 - Feb 9, 1885

    N. G. --------- Oct 4, 1856 - Sep 14, 1906

    Roxie Curl ---- Wife of W. A. Altman
                    Sep 21, 1856 - Feb 5, 1890

    Sallie -------- Oct 26, 1827 - Jan 20, 1895

    William A. ---- Mar 9, 1846 - Jan 11, 1923

Bell
    John W. ------- Feb 28, 1819 - Mar 17, 1897

Bennett
    Willie G. ----- Dec 28, 1864 - Dec 27, 1943

Bordeaux
    Mary G. ------- Apr 11, 1860 - Dec 6, 1934

    Thomas D. ----- Born Lauderdale Co. Miss.
                    Oct 8, 1845 - Feb 15, 1891

Bowyer
    Emma Jane
    Morris -------- 1827 - 1915

Bragg
    B. K. --------- May 5, 1853 - Jul 4, 1903

Bragg (contd)
  J. R. --------- May 12, 1839 - Sep 16, 1913

  Martha E. ----- Wife of J. R. Bragg
                  Jun 16, 1840 - May 10, 1922

  Susan Knott --- Mar 5, 1850 - Dec 1, 1936

  W. T. --------- Sep 21, 1846 - Oct 17, 1916

Brown
  Mrs. M. E. ---- Mar 19, 1831 - Apr 6, 1909

Bush
  Penelope ------ Wife of Richard Bush
                  Jul 28, 1817 - Mar 10, 1894

  Richard ------- Nov 22, 1803 - Mar 6, 1880

Causey
  A. R. --------- Dec 17, 1865 - Feb 14, 1945

Clay
  Oliver Wright - Dec 10, 1864 - Nov 22, 1939

Cobb
  B. F. --------- 1842 - 1918

  F. M. --------- Mar 31, 1852 - Nov 26, 1925

  Mary B. ------- Wife of F. M. Cobb
                  Jul 26, 1854 - Jun 26, 1924

Cooper
  Francis M. ---- Mar 24, 1829 - Feb 10, 1887

  Mary Kimberly - Wife of Francis M. Cooper
                  Aug 30, 1835 - May 10, 1909

Curl
  Alonzo A. ----- 1856 - 1913

  Anna W. ------- 1860 - 1936

  Penelope C. --- Sep 19, 1829 - Jan 10, 1897

  Willis -------- Mar 10, 1820 - Feb 25, 1901

Curry
  Margaret
    Lorena -------- 1854 - 1946

Davis
  William M. ---- Jun 11, 1865 - Oct 22, 1929

Drummond
  Sallie J.
    Altman -------- Nov 23, 1848 - Jan 24, 1907
  W. W. --------- Feb 9, 1836 - Jul 22, 1896

Edmonds
  Alice F. ------ Feb 19, 1853 - Aug 12, 1940

  May Thorpe ---- Born in Matagorda, Texas
                  Apr 22, 1857 - Feb 25, 1942

  Nancy Madison
    Fluker -------- Wife of Dr. P. G. Edmonds
                    Born in Washington Co. Ala.
                    Aug 25, 1819 - Dec 25, 1900

  Phillip George
    M.D., D.D. ---- Born Lancaster Co. Va.
                    Apr 17, 1810 - Jul 10, 1878

  Phillip
    George -------- Feb 15, 1855 - Oct 5, 1922

  William ------- Dec 18, 1845 - Dec 24, 1920

Estes
  Alice F.
    Woodward ------ Wife of T. L. Estes
                    Dec 18, 1865 - May 4, 1928

  T. L. --------- Sep 24, 1854 - Jan 5, 1933

Falkenburry
  Francis M. ---- 1842 - 1900

  Mary C. ------- 1861 - 1951

Faskin
  Peter --------- Born in Aberdeen, Scotland
                    Jun 1, 1826 - Aug 18, 1903
                    Died at Bellamy, Alabama

Flowers
  Emma Olivia --- Mar 3, 1848 - Dec 15, 1931

  William James - May 1, 1841 - Mar 28, 1914

Fluker
  Louis H. ------ Jan 20, 1845 - Aug 6, 1922

  Nannie C. ----- Apr 4, 1846 - Aug 9, 1919

Gilder
  Annie Yeager -- Feb 7, 1863 - Aug 2, 1945

  Mary E. ------- Wife of Thaddeus Gilder
                Sep 30, 1827 - Sep 5, 1892

  Thaddeus ------ 1821 - 1903

  Dr. Thomas
  Jefferson ----- Feb 10, 1847 - Aug 17, 1905

Hagan
  Peter --------- Oct 22, 1838 - Jan 8, 1919

Hale
  Bettie Carr --- Wife of Dr. R. Hale
                Aug 12, 1861 - Sep 16, 1888

  J. A. --------- Jun 14, 1854 - Feb 28, 1912

  John Wesley --- 1846 - 1913, CSA

  Matilda Jane -- 1854 - 1893

  Dr. Robert
  Hadden -------- 1850 - 1931

Hawkins
  Joyce Gilder -- 1813 - 1895

Hightower
  C. D. J. Bush - Wife of Charles D. Hightower
                Jan 1, 1834 - Jun 8, 1902

Hightower (contd)
Charles D. ---- Feb 28, 1832 - Nov 27, 1873

Council Berry - Jun 4, 1861 - Jul 17, 1937

L. E. --------- Wife of R. B. Hightower
Apr 10, 1853 - Dec 23, 1894

Hill
Charles C. ---- 1832 - Aug 28, 1907
3rd Alabama Inf., CSA

David B. ------ 1857 - 1935

Meredith ------ Co. D, 46 Ga. Inf., CSA

Merinda E. ---- 1851 - 1935

Virginia E. --- 1844 - 1900

Holman
Frank --------- Mar 5, 1860 - Jun 21, 1928

Humphreys
William J. ---- Feb 3, 1865 - Jun 12, 1942

James
William H.,
M.D. ---------- 1828 - 1905

Killian
S. D. --------- Oct 30, 1845 - Jul 12, 1903

Sarah E. ------ Wife of S. D. Killian
Dec 21, 1846 - Oct 17, 1900

Knott
Miss Margaret
Elmira -------- Sep 18, 1852 - May 20, 1935

Lancaster
B. W. --------- Aug 28, 1854 - Jan 14, 1948

Eliza H. ------ Wife of B. W. Lancaster
Born in Perry County, Ala.
Nov 26, 1850 - Oct 5, 1894

L. A. --------- Mar 3, 1857 - Feb 3, 1931

Lancaster (contd)
  T. F. --------- Jul 4, 1852 - Jan 3, 1931

Landers
  Isabella ------ 1861 - 1923

  Sydney C. ----- 1862 - 1920

Long
  Elizabeth ----- Old brick crypt, now destroyed.
                  One of the first persons buried
                  in this cemetery.

  Mrs. Nancy ---- Aug 10, 1823 - Jun 4, 1902

Maggard
  D. H. --------- Dec 23, 1842 - Jan 23, 1905

  Mattie E. ----- Died Sep 5, 1910

Mathers
  Lula Barron --- Wife of J. A. Mathers
                  Born Nanafalia, Ala.
                  Jul 2, 1862 - Dec 25, 1899

Matthews
  James A. ------ Mar 31, 1858 - Jun 24, 1928

  Katherine
  Alice --------- Wife of J. A. Matthews
                  May 12, 1864 - Jul 19, 1937

Mayfield
  W. T. --------- 1857 - 1932

McAlpin
  Andrew
  Blanton ------- 1856 - 1930

  Arch ---------- Apr 17, 1841 - Mar 10, 1928

  Sarah J. ------ Wife of Arch McAlpin
                  Jan 16, 1856 - Dec 22, 1892

  William T. ---- Co. C, 4th Ala. Inf., CSA

McConnell
  Infant -------- Of John A. & Martha McConnell
                  (No dates)
  John A. ------- Jul 11, 1855 - Aug 28, 1883
  Joseph A. ----- Mar 6, 1852 - Mar 26, 1922
  M. G.---------- Wife J. A. McConnell
                  May 3, 1854 - Nov 18, 1881
  Martha J. ----- Wife of Dr. John A. McConnell
                  Nov 17, 1827 - Jan 23, 1892
  Mary E. ------- Wife J. A. McConnell
                  Nov 27, 1851 - Mar 11, 1910

McCorkle
  Elizabeth ----- Wife S. J. McCorkle
                  Jan 26, 1836 - Mar 10, 1896
  Joseph S. ----- May 4, 1864 - May 14, 1953
  Nona M. ------- Sep 10, 1865 - Feb 24, 1950
  S. J. --------- Nov 15, 1828 - Jun 19, 1913

McElroy
  Eloise -------- Aug 9, 1855 - Sep 25, 1935
  W. H. --------- Mar 5, 1853 - May 25, 1916

Mellown
  David E. ------ 1841 - 1911
  Mrs. Jane ----- May 4, 1816 - Jul 25, 1906
  Jennie Knott -- 1847 - 1943

Miller
  George
  Wideman ------- May 5, 1854 - May 22, 1909

Morris
  Mollie -------- Jul 8, 1843 - Feb 15, 1928

Peteet
  James M. ------ Apr 14, 1841 - Dec 24, 1910

Peteet (contd)
  Mary J. ------- Wife of J. M. Peteet
                    Nov 30, 1849 - Dec 15, 1898

Rainer
  William
  Robert -------- 1850 - 1934

Reid
  Julia
  Hightower ----- 1865 - 1951

Richards
  Frank G. ------ 1862 - 1939

  Susan Alvarez - 1864 - 1924

Rous
  George L. ----- Dec 8, 1862 - Nov 28, 1890

Royal
  Perrion
  Webster ------- Oct 8, 1855 - Apr 11, 1942

Rumley
  Bella --------- Wife of Fred Rumley
                  Dec 1, 1842 - Aug 1, 1900

  Fred ---------- Sep 15, 1844 - Mar 18, 1924

  Gertrude C. --- Apr 7, 1852 - Jan 5, 1927

  Infant -------- (No dates)

  William T. ---- Jan 30, 1850 - Feb 3, 1905

Sample
  Sallie E. ----- Sep 18, 1859 - Feb 1, 1947

Sims
  William Henry - 1858 - 1932

  Willie -------- 1860 - 1931

  __?__ J. M. --- 1861 - 1906

Smith
  A. C. --------- Jan 11, 1858 - Jul 3, 1921

Smith (contd)
Charlie
Newton -------- Dec 12, 1865 - Jun 22, 1907

Smitherman
Martha -------- Apr 13, 1846 - Sep 17, 1923

Stallworth
Mary J. ------- 1844 - 1918

Sturdivant
Jessie J. ----- 1857 - 1938

Nannie L. ----- 1860 - 1939

Taylor
Amanda -------- Died Dec 3, 1894 Age 40

William
Leonidas ------ Nov 7, 1861 - Mar 4, 1904

Thomas
Augusta ------- Jan 4, 1861 - May 8, 1943

Thompson
J. W. --------- Jul 19, 1849 - Oct 29, 1894

Martha Clay --- May 20, 1848 - Mar 26, 1927

Tidmore
M. M. --------- Dec 19, 1849 - Dec 29, 1927

Tucker
Annie Lyde ---- 1849 - 1946

Francis
Dillard ------- Nov 5, 1844 - Apr 5, 1923

Ungles
John ---------- 1846 - 1925

Warren
Elizabeth ----- Dec 13, 1860 - Sep 1, 1923

Wiggins
C. P. --------- Oct 17, 1857 - Jan 25, 1915

Wilkerson
  Martha J. ----- 1832 - 1895

Williams
  Fannie H. ----- Died 1928

  Fletcher B. --- Died 1936

Wise
  Florencia R. -- Nov 24, 1862 - Sep 14, 1938

  J. C. --------- Died Dec 13, 1913

Wood
  Alphondas L. -- Son M. & J. A. Wood
                  Born in Georgia
                  Dec 12, 1858 - Oct 19, 1889

  C. H. --------- 1858 - 1937

  Charles ------- Apr 2, 1865 - Jan 2, 1943

  Hester -------- Jun 5, 1860 - Jan 23, 1937

Wylie
  Oliver -------- Born Montgomery Co. N. C.
                  Nov 11, 1835 - Nov 4, 1890

YORK STATION CEMETERY
(Destroyed)

This cemetery was located on the west side of College Street in York, between Third and Fourth Avenues. Only one marker remains, in the garden of the house at the northwest corner of College Street and Third Avenue.

Geddie
  Elizabeth Jane

The following persons were probably buried here. The names were obtained from The Sumter County Register of Deaths, 1881 - 1892 by Jud Arrington, and partially verified by older residents of York.

Armstrong
  Andrew A. ----- Died Apr 2, 1881

Barr
  Susan
  Caldwell ------ Died Dec 3, 1881

Bloodworth
  J. R. --------- Died Jan 15, 1884   Age 73

Campbell
  Sam ----------- Died Jun 4, 1888   Age 68

Cole
  Mary ---------- Died Sep 9, 1882   Age 80

Davis
  Ann ----------- Died Apr 8, 1885   Age 35

Easley
  P. E. --------- Died Nov 1, 1887

Farrish
  Emma
  Elizabeth ----- Died Apr 7, 1881

  Rebecca Ann --- Died Apr 1, 1881

Flowers
  Richard
  Bennett ------- Died Jul 4, 1881

  Robert -------- Died Oct 24, 1887

  Samuel -------- Died Sep 9, 1882   Age 84

Garrison
  Elizabeth C. -- Died Jun 7, 1881

Gibbs
  Anna ---------- Died Aug 13, 1889

Giles
  James --------- Died Mar 20, 1888

Hale
  Mrs. E. C. ---- Born in Georgia
                  Died Sep 16, 1888

McAlpin
　William S. ---- Died Jan 21, 1885　Age 55

Peteet
　James Monroe -- Son J. M. & Mary J. Peteet
　　　　　　　　　Died Nov 1, 1878

Powell
　C. L. --------- Born in Texas
　　　　　　　　　Died Jun 30, 1889　Age 26

Praytor
　James
　Faulkner ------ Died Jan 31, 1882

Royal
　M. A. --------- Born in Georgia
　　　　　　　　　Died Feb 20, 1888　Age 71

Whitlow
　Stancel ------- Died Jul 6, 1886　Age 30

Witt
　Mary D. ------- Died Jul 15, 1887　Age 41

ZION BAPTIST CHURCH CEMETERY

From County Road 10, approximately 3 3/10 miles south of Cuba, turn south on County Road 5. After 5 miles, turn southeast on County Road 6. The cemetery is 6/10 mile down this road, across the road from the church.

Baskin
　Mary A. ------- Wife of John Baskin
　　　　　　　　　Feb 9, 1826 - Jan 24, 1890

Brunson
　Annie S. ------ Jan 20, 1862 - Mar 1, 1932

　Catharine E. -- Oct 4, 1834 - Feb 12, 1912

　G. E. --------- Feb 5, 1830 - Jul 4, 1917

Brunson (contd)
G. L.---------- G. E. & J. F.
Nov 8, 1858 - May 1, 1882

Geo. Melton --- Son T. M. & C. E.
Died Jan 13, 1856

Julia F. ------ Wife G. E.
Apr 19, 1836 - Nov 19, 1909

Kiziah -------- May 23, 1804 - Aug 3, 1836

S. M. --------- Feb 1. 1797 - Sep 11, 1854

Thomas K. ----- Aug 13, 1857 - Jan 14, 1935

Capt. Thomas
M. ------------ Jan 2, 1832 - Aug 23, 1891

W. A. --------- Son T. M.& C. E.
Sep 23, 1857 - Feb 18, 1881

Davidson
Isabella D. --- Wife J. R.
Dec 20, 1845 - Mar 27, 1924

Joseph R. ----- Apr 2, 1845 - May 17, 1920

Davis
Mattie K. ----- Wife S. E.
May 25, 1860 - Mar 10, 1931

S. E. --------- Mar 17, 1850 - Jun 30, 1911

Davison
W. H. --------- Jan 7, 1806 - Jul 25, 1884

Dawson
W. H. --------- Aug 15, 1814 - Mar 5, 1864

Ellis
John A. ------- Nov 16, 1848 - Mar 8, 1923

Mary Louise --- Dec 9, 1864 - Jan 5, 1932

James
Eliza McCann -- Wife Lytle
1857 - 1886

Jones
Dempsey J. ---- Jul 31, 1833 - Sep 3, 1912

    Helen M. ------ Dau Redding & Susan J.
Jan 12, 1845 - Sep 22, 1864

    Julia A. ------ Wife Dempsey J.
Mar 9, 1846 - Oct 1, 1874

    Susan Jane ---- Wife of Redding Jones
Jul 31, 1807 - May 28, 1895

Rainer
Zilpha H. ----- Died Jul 17, 1885

Ryan
Rev. John
King ---------- Nov 24, 1824 - Feb 24, 1888

    Mary P. ------- Mar 31, 1834 - Feb 15, 1926

Smith
Walter N. ----- Dec 3, 1864 - Jun 18, 1878

Watts
Elizabeth
Asbury -------- Aug 9, 1815 - Apr 29, 1905

    John R. ------- Jun 30, 1810 - Jun 1, 1883

    M. H. --------- May 28, 1838 - Dec 22, 1926

    W. H. --------- Aug 7, 1835 - Jul 14, 1918

Woodall
Amelia Ann ---- May 8, 1847 - 1851

    Eliza Jane ---- Mar 21, 1840 - May 28, 1845

    Frances
Brazillia ----- May 13, 1826 - Sep 19, 1846

    John Chamblis - Mar 1, 1852 - 1856

    Lillie -------- Jul 4, 1799 - Jul 28, 1855

    Mary Giles ---- Aug 11, 1807 - Dec 20, 1881

Woodall (contd)
Melissa ------- Born Apr 16, 1846

Sarah Amanda -- Mar 7, 1838 - Aug 15, 1851

Sarah
Elizabeth ----- Jul 21, 1843 - Dec 3, 1922

William A. ---- Apr 11, 1843 - Jul 31, 1917

ZION HILL METHODIST CHURCH CEMETERY

From State Highway 28, approximately 6 4/10 miles southeast of Livingston, turn east on County Road 22. The church and cemetery are approximately 1 6/10 miles down this road on the north side of the road.

Blackshear
Gale ---------- 1856 - Nov 27, 1922

Horn
Alise --------- Jul 10, 1862 - Jun 6, 1941

Josh ---------- 1854 - Oct 17, 1944

Scales
Frances ------- Nov 9, 1835 - Jul 3, 1896

Spencer
Mary ---------- 1853 - 1929

Spincer
Alex ---------- 1840 - 1925

Ella ---------- Feb 16, 1832 - Feb 3, 1925

William
Howard -------- 1852 - 1926

INDEX OF CEMETERIES

Arrington 105
Ballard 105
Belmont 106
Bethel 114
Bethlehem 122
Beulah 126
Blann 128
Boney 129
Boyd 134
Brashiers - Wall 139
Brewersville 139
Brown 147
Brown 148
Brown 149
Browning 150
Burton 150
Cagus 151
Campbell - Derby 153
Center Ridge 153
Central 156
Charcone 156
Chestnut Grove 157
Clay Memorial 160
Coats 168
Cokes Chapel 168
Coody 178
Croom 178
Curl 179
Davis 180
Denton 180
Dillard 180
Elizabeth 181
Elliott 183
Eskridge 184
Estes 184
Evans 185
Evington 185
Ezelle 185
Gainesville Odd Fellows 186
Gainesville Old 195
Garber 210
Gaston 212
Gaston Valley 213
Geiger 214
Giles 214

Giles - Neville 214
Graham - Peteet 217
Greenlees 218
Harris 218
Hatch 219
Haupt 220
Hawkins 221
Henagan 222
Hibbler 228
Hicks 228
Horn 229
Houston 229
Inge 229
Jamestown 230
Jarman 231
Jemison 231
Jenkins 232
Jones 232
Jones 233
King 233
Knox 233
Lacy 234
Lee 234
Lee Haven 235
Liberty 235
Little 239
Lockard 239
May 240
Mays 240
McCain 241
McElroy 242
McGrew - Hart 244
McInnis 245
Miller 247
Mims 248
Mt Gilead 248
Mt Herman New 249
Mt Herman Old 251
Mt Moriah 253
Mt Tabor 253
Myrtlewood 254
New Prospect 291
Old Providence 295
Old Side 297
O'Neal 307

INDEX OF CEMETERIES

Oxford 307
Parker 313
Parker 314
Pearce 315
Peavy 316
Phares 316
Potts 316
Rea 317
Reeds Chapel 317
Rhyne 319
Richardson 320
Rocky Mount 321
Rogers - Manderson 321
Seale 322
Shackelford 323
Shady Grove 324
Shanty Hill 340
Shearson 341
Shorts 344
Sibley 346
Siloam 346
Snedecor 355
Souls Chapel 359
Spratt 361

St John 362
St John's 362
Sumterville 363
Swilley 369
Tate 369
Taylor 370
Tidmore 371
Tisdale 371
Travis 372
Wallis - Mellard 372
Watkins - Taylor 373
Watson 374
Watson 374
Watson 374
Watt 375
Weir 375
Wideman 375
Williams - Gibbs 376
Winston 377
Woods - Cameron 380
York Municipal 380
York Station 390
Zion 392
Zion Hill 395

INDEX OF GRAVES

Abbott
  Alice Kennedy 222
Abrahams
  James 254
  James A. 254
  James Randolph 255
  Sarah T. Ward 255
Abrams
  George Thomas 324
  Georgianna Lee 195
  M. C. 324
Adams
  Elvira L.
    Ustick 255
  John W. 255
  John William 255
  Lockey H. 255
  Mary E. Jones 295
  Susan Ustick 255
  Talbot 295
  William F. L. 255
  William F. L.
    Jr. 255
Aiken
  Samuel J. 297
Alexander
  Caroline A. 195
  E. A. 157
  Eli E. 181
  Helen McAlpin 380
  Hezekiah 181
  Ibbie E. L. 181
  J. M. 157
  James Tytler 195
  Margaret Tytler 195
  Mary Jane 195
  Samuel Caldwell 181
  Shadrack Minnice 196
  Susie H. 181
  William Hiram 181
  William S. 181
Allen
  A. L. 341
  Belle S. 255
  Benjamin 341

Allen (contd)
  Benjamin J. 126
  C. D. 344
  C. M. 341
  Charles H. 255
  David C. 168
  E. Jane 341
  Emiline C. 168
  Enoch 341
  Frances S. 127
  Hampton 341
  Hulda 341
  J. F. 341
  J. W. 341
  Jane S. 341
  Mary Cornelia 341
  Mary J. 341
  N. A. 341
  Richmond 341
  S. H. 341
  S. J. 341
  Sallie P. 344
  Sarah R. 341
  Susan Elizabeth 342
  William Nicholas 342
Allford
  Margaret 324
  Mary 324
Allgood
  Altazana 230
  Blake Baker 230
  Darthula D. 230
  James William 230
  Sterling H. 230
  Sterling Henry 230
Allison
  Ann Virginia 380
  Bettie 381
  C. H. 381
  Evan Frank 381
  John F. 381
  Leodocia 359
  Mary E. 381
  William O. 181

Altman
 E. S. 381
 Henry A. 346
 John W. 381
 Mary M. 347
 N. G. 381
 Roxie Curl 381
 Sallie 381
 William A. 381
Alvis
 J. H. 344
 Susan V. 344
Amason
 Asa 297
 Edward D. 340
 Elbert 297
 Elizabeth 297
 Emalina 297
 Infant 298
 Lydia C. 255
 Margaret L. 298
 Nathan 298
 S. C. M. 255
 Sara 298
 Susan 298
 T. E. 324
 Van Buren 298
 William 298
Anderson
 Ann 129
 Hannah Wright 186
 John G. 347
 Josephus M. 222
 Mag 129
 Margaret Daniels 129
 Sarah 129
 Vincent 129
 William S. 129
Andrews
 H. H. 160
Armstrong
 Andrew A. 391
 J. J. 347
 Mary E. 347
Arnold
 Hettie H. 222
 J. W. 222

Arrington
 Andrew J. 222
 Carter 105
 Charles O. 255
 Daughter 105
 Edward 255
 Eugenia C. 256
 Helen Amelia 222
 Helen Ora 222
 Henry 256
 Infant 222
 James C. 256
 Joeanner 256
 Joseph 105, 256
 Joseph J. 222, 256
 Lucy B. 256
 Margaret G. 222
 Martha S. 106
 Mary 256
 Mary Eliza 256
 Mary F. America 256
 Mary Jackson 105
 Mary M. 256
 Patience Ann 256
 Robert 256
 Robert H. 256
 W. R. 256
 Willie Ann 256
Asbury
 Elisha 372
Ashford
 Martha Jane 374
Ashley
 Daniel 157
 Joe Lowe 157
 Milton 157
 Ollie 157
 W. R. 157
Aust
 Absalom 375
 Mary Ann 375
Autrey
 H. R. 222
Avery
 Joseph C. 186
Ayers
 Daniel 256

Babb
  Miner 213
Bailey
  Adelia 153
  Amanda 153
  H. L. 153
  J. W. 154
  Robert C. 154
Baker
  John Elmore 156
  Tempe 324
Baldwin
  Helen Vandegraff 257
Ballard
  Frank 359
  Hannah 105
  Mattie 359
  Walter R. 359
Bancroft
  J. 257
Banks
  J. H. 347
Bardwell
  Hiram Francis 257
Barker
  Benjamin 257
  Cordine H. 257
Barnard
  John 157
Barnes
  Bennett B. 325
  Harriett Ann 325
  J. W. 325
  James C. 325
  John R. 325
  Nancy A. 325
  Rebecca 325
  Rebecca Ann 325
  Robert A. 257
  Sallie W. 325
  Samuel Taylor 325
  Samuel W. 325
  ___?___ T. 325
Barnett
  Samuel A. 257
Barr
  Susan Caldwell 391

Barret
  Ann B. 196
  Caroline 196
  John S. 196
  Pattie Virginia 196
Barrow
  Mrs. F. E. 160
  John 160
Bartlett
  Emily Woolf 157
  Penelopie 248
  T. J. 248
Baskin
  Annie M. 127
  B. J. 178
  C. A. 178
  Edith A. 344
  James E. 344
  John 178
  John T. 178
  Margaret M. 178
  Mary A. 392
  Mary S. 178
  Nancy 178
  Nancy E. 178
  W. S. 127
Bates
  Annie L. 106
  Margaret P. 347
  Mary Speed 106
  Origin W. 106
Battle
  D. T. 257
  Ludie S. 257
  Mollie Kornegay 257
  Mrs. S. E. S. 257
  W. D. Jr. 257
  William D. 257
  Willie D. 257
Bayless
  Charles Sidney 298
Beach
  Erasmus Darwin 257
Beavers
  A. E. 242
  Elizabeth 242
  Ida 253
  Miss 253

Beavers (contd)
S. M. 242
Thomas W. 186
Thomas Walter 230
Beazley
Nancy 291
Bedwell
Albert M. 258
Beggs
Frank A. 181
Louisa V. H. 181
Martha Alexander 258
William 258
Bell
Caroline Amanda 325
Edward 372
Effie H. 186
Elizabeth
Goldsmith 298
James H. 325
Jane 151
Joe 151
John W. 381
L. C. 251
Lillian L. 186
Mattie D. Powell 258
Maurice 151
Patience Amanda 325
Richard Jr. 372
Sarah 325
Susan Rebecca 325
William Murphy 160
William R. 298
Bennett
B. Maria 196
G. H. 344
Katey 196
Mary 196
Willie G. 381
Bevill
Fannie L. 122
Beville
John Woodlif 139
Bickley
Margaret Alice 196
Thomas Jefferson 196
Billups
Emma 347

Billups (contd)
Frances 347
Martha A. 347
Thomas M. Sr. 347
Bingham
Mary 181
Samuel 181
Binns
Henrietta
Caroline 258
Martha Eleanor 258
Bishop
Sarah F. 160
Blackshear
Gale 395
Blacksher
David 106
Francis W. 106
Mary Bettie 106
Nancy 106
Sius 106
Uriah E. 106
William 106
Blackwell
Thomas J. 258
Blakeney
J. W. 139
Roberta E. 139
Temperance 106
Blakeny
Louisa 291
Blann
Antoinette 235
Eunice 128
Georgia 128
J. P. 128
Bliss
James 196
Jonathan 196
Laura 197
Lucretia
Leverett 197
Lucy M. 197
Mary Kidder 197
William L. 197
Blocker
Betty Robinson 214
George M. 215

Bloodworth
  J. R. 391
Blue
  Lucy 197
Boatman
  __?__, Mrs. 371
Boggs
  Louisa Ann 258
Boling
  William Ransom 139
Bolton
  Sarah E. 139
Bond
  Ivie J. 307
  Jacob J. 308
  James 308
  John W. 308
  Mary C. 308
  Mary E. 308
  Robert J. 308
  Susan F. 308
Boney
  Wimberk 129
Boone
  Ann 151
  David 151
  John C. 169
  M. E. 169
Bordeaux
  Mary G. 381
  Thomas D. 381
Bostic
  E. A. 326
  Garland 326
Boswell
  Bellzora 235
  Bill 235
  Jerusha 235
  Kommie C. 235
  Nancy C. 235
Bourdeaux
  Laura 218
  Laura Harris 218
  Mary Catherine 218
  Thomas Devane 218
Bowers
  M. A. 342
  W. E. 342

Bowyer
  Emma Jane Morris 381
Boyd
  Austin G. 134
  C. Virginia 134
  Clara Jane Powe 134
  Harriett Cadmus
    Moore 134
  Isarella
    Stephenson 258
  Jefferson 135
  Jennett 135
  John 135
  John James 135
  L. M. 355
  Mary E. 355
  Robert Clay 135
  Robert Jefferson 135
  Sallie E. 106
  Sarah E. 355
  Sarah M. Hudson 135
  Susan Davis 135
  William Ellery 135
Boyett
  Nancy 169
Boyette
  Ellen A. 298
  Locke 298
  Nancy 298
  Sarah I. 298
Boykin
  Benjamin 326
  Benjamin B. B. 326
  Edwin D. 326
  Martha 326
  Mary Gray 326
  Mary L. 326
  W. D. 326
Boynton
  (Unknown) 258
Brackett
  Anson 197
  Mary Chamberlin 197
Bradford
  James Thomas 258
  Jerusha L. 259
Bradshaw
  Elizabeth R. 186

Bradshaw (contd)
  James 186
  Janie 186
  John W. 259
  Lizzie 259
  R. T. 186
  Robert 186
  Thomas W. 186
Bragg
  B. K. 381
  J. R. 382
  Martha E. 382
  Mary E. 169
  Nancy 169
  Robert Braxton 169
  Sterling Parker 169
  Susan Knott 382
  W. T. 382
Branch
  Sarah Rebecca 259
Brashiers
  H. Tobitha 139
Breitling
  Otto G. 259
Brenneman
  Nannie R. 222
Brewer
  Eliza 160
  Eliza J. 291
  John R. 160
  Laura 160
  Louise 160
  Mary 292
  Mathew E. 160
  W. P. 292
  William 292
Brewster
  Dora Ann 235
  Emily Smith 235
Brock
  George William 259
Brockway
  A. E. 169
  Carrie L. 259
  Charles J. 259
  Martha E. 259
  Sallie M. 139

Bronaugh
  Andrew 245
Bronson
  Nancy 151
Brooks
  Calvin 362
  Cellie 363
Browder
  Annie Bass
    Garber 210
  James Chapron 210
Brown
  Ann 149
  Ann J. 157
  Arthur Godfrey 147
  B. F. Jr. 158
  B. F. Sr. 158
  B. T. 169
  Charlotte 347
  Cornelia G. 363
  Daniel H. 347
  Edwin J. 148
  Emma 149
  G. W. 317
  George A. 259
  Harrison 151
  Hiram 158
  Hunter M.
    Larkins 317
  Infant 181, 363
  James D. 347
  James P. 313
  Jere Chapman 187
  Jere H. 148
  Jim 149
  John C. 259
  John E. Jr. 147
  John Evender 147
  John Louis 259
  Julia A. 148
  Kate 169
  Kate Henagan 363
  Katie 151
  Laura 259
  Lemon 149
  Lula Godfrey 259
  Mrs. M. E. 382
  M. J. 248

Brown (contd)
  Maron F. 347
  Mary Alice 363
  Mary Jane 148
  Melissa 158
  Milton Dozier 363
  Nancy I. 158
  Narsis 158
  Patience 158
  Rolley 253
  Rosa Knox 259
  Sarah Godfrey 260
  T. F. 158
  Virginia 347
  W. S. 158
  William A. O. 295
  William Henry 363
Browning
  Elizabeth C. 150
  John Bailey 150
Brunson
  Annie S. 392
  Catharine E. 392
  G. E. 392
  G. L. 393
  George Melton 393
  Julia F. 393
  Kiziah 393
  S. M. 393
  Thomas K. 393
  Thomas M. 393
  W. A. 393
Bryant
  Atline 249
  Cherry Lane 298
  E. N. 299
  J. T. 197
  Mary L. 299
  Thomas 299
  William T. 299
Buford
  Edwin Dial 364
  Mary Dial 364
Bullock
  Charlie H. 260
  Susan F. 260
Buntin
  Martha A. A. P. 299

Bunyard
  I. B. 248
Burnett
  W. E. 122
Burton
  Absolem 150
  Absolem Farrah
    Jr. 151
  Amanda C. 251
  Jefferson C. 251
  John Wesley 156, 299
  Margaret Ann 151
  Nannie Amason
    Gregory 299
Burwell
  Margaret J. 114
  Mary Ann
    Frierson 114
  William Turnbull 115
Bush
  Mary E. 197
  Penelope 382
  Richard 382
  William H. 197
Butler
  Leonidas W. 260
  Sarah S. 240
Byrd
  Jessie 197
  Matilda 197
Cahoon
  Abigail 169
  Abisha N. 169
  Charlie B. 169
  David 169
  Edgar C. 169
  Fannie E. 169
  H. 169
  J. F. 170
  James H. 170
  Joseph C. 170
  Julia E. 170
  M. L. 170
  Meantha M. 170
  Mittie 170
  Thomas W. 170
  W. A. J. 170
  W. H. 170

Callaway
  Maggie Bryan 260
  Margaret
    Edmundson 260
  Robert Baker 260
Cameron
  Alice B. 326
  Kelly H. 326
  Major J. 326
  Nancy 251
  Nathaniel 251
Campbell
  Caroline 129
  Hugh 308
  John 355
  John A. 308
  John Smith 153
  Justina L. 153
  Katherine 308
  Lucy 151
  Mary 355
  Mattie 153
  Neal 308
  Robert Lee 359
  Robert M. 153
  Sam 391
Campbelle
  Georgia Garrette 308
Cannady
  Jimmie 170
  Maggie 170
  N. W. 170
  Naomi W. 170
  Siddie E. 170
Cannon
  S. A. 170
  T. B. 170
Carnes
  Amanda 355
  Henry C. 355
  John W. 355
Carney
  James R. 317
  Sara E. 317
  W. R. D. 317
Carpenter
  Annie Belle 326
  Joel Pearson 326

Carpenter (contd)
  Mamie K. 326
  Minnie H. 326
  Phillip N. 327
Carr
  A. J. 170
  Charlotte M. 215
  James P. 170
Carrigan
  George Theodore 181
  Infant 182
Carroll
  Katie 327
  Samuel J. 197
Casey
  J. T. 292
Cates
  B. R. 292
  J. W. 292
  Sallie A. 292
  William 292
Cathey
  Martin A. 222
  Susie Dial 222
Causey
  A. R. 382
Chapin
  Armenius 342
  Hannah 342
Chapman
  Adline 292
  Alta 260
  Mary Catherine 260
  Mary K. 377
  Mary Lucinda
    Newell 260
  Rebecca S. 260
  Reuben 260
Cherry
  Emma Eliza 129
  Jared W. 129
  Susan 129
  William J. 359
Chilcoat
  Martha Betty 260
Childe
  Amanda M. 187
  Mary H. 187

Childe (contd)
  W. H. 187
Chiles
  Jane Harper 260
  Samuel H. 260
  William Sidney 261
Cholmon
  Pink 292
Choutteau
  M. J. Gertrude 130
  Martha E. 130
Christian
  Elizabeth C. 197
  Lucretia 197
  Mary B. 197
  Mollie 198
  Thomas 197
  Turner C. 198
Christopher
  Kate Young 122
  William R. 122
Clanton
  Lucinda 327
  Martha Louise 327
  Mary Elizabeth 327
  Sylvia Jane 327
  Temperance 327
Clark
  A. V. 130
  Jack 261
  Jesse 240, 249
  Laura 241
  Sylvia 198
Clarke
  F. P. 123
  George A. 198
Clay
  Ella K. 171
  J. T. 308
  Mary 308
  Oliver Wright 382
  R. A. 161
  Robert P. 161
  Thadeus 161
Cleveland
  Lucy Adela 261
Coats
  Susan B. 107

Coats (contd)
  Tempie B. 107
Cobb
  B. F. 382
  F. M. 382
  Joysey S. 154
  Louisa C. 130
  Martha A. 251
  Mary 251
  Mary B. 382
  Tresa C. 251
Cobbs
  Bettie Gaines 261
  James 261
  Julia Boon 261
  Lucy Thom 261
  Maggie A. 261
  Margaret Lake 261
  Thomas 261
Cockrell
  Catherine 299
  Eleanor 261
  Eva Nash 261
  Hester Elizabeth
    Gulley 261
  Infant 261, 299
  James A. 299
  L. A. 261
  Louisa L. 299
  Mary S. 299
  Millicent 299
  Minna 262
  Nathan 299
  Susan Spratt 262
  William Joseph 299
  __?__ Jamie 261
  __?__ Lily Belle 261
Cole
  Mary 391
Coleman
  Allison 140
  Emma S. 262
  Jesse Bell 262
  Mary I. 215
  Robert 140
  Samuel Cruse 140
  Sarah Kynerd 262
  Susadele McCary 140

Coleman (contd)
  Susan R. 323
  Wiley T. 215
  William H. 140
  William H. Jr. 323
Colgin
  Margaret A. 107
  Mary Ann 198
  Mary E. L.
    Neville 198
  Sallie Elyson 198
Collier
  Permelia 223
Collins
  Drucilla Eliza 355
  Hiram C. 107
  Orlando 355
  Posey G. 355
Conner
  Aggie 151
Cook
  Chauncy 262
  J. M. 262
Cooke
  Katie G. 187
  Susan Reavis 187
  Turner R. 187
Cooper
  Agnes 107
  Francis M. 382
  John 107
  Mary Kimberly 382
  William Frank 262
  __?__ 152
Copeland
  Nathan 262
Core
  A. C. 152
Cornick
  Mary 262
Cospey
  J. M. 250
Cowin
  Cornelia C. 262
Crane
  Betsy 362
Cravens
  Margaret E. 262

Crenshaw
  Frances 262
  Mary H. 262
  Thomas A. 263
  __?__ 263
Crews
  Clara M. Cahoon 171
  O. L. 171
Criswell
  Elijah 327
Crocker
  Jane T. 140
  John W. 140
Croom
  Bryan 178
  Evelyn 179
  James Bryan 179
  James Richard 179
  Nicholas P. 179
  Richard 179
  Richard Bryan 179
  Winifred B. 179
Crow
  Walter Elmer 187
Culpepper
  Alfred Mickens 235
  Ambrose 236
  Asenath 128
  Caroline C. 236
  Emma G. 236
  George Clarence 128
  Hardin 236
  James 236
  John J. 236
  John L. 236
  Julia Ellis 236
  Karon J. 236
  M. A. 236
  Mary 236
  Mary A. 236
  Mary Ann 236
  Matthew 236
  Nancy J. 236
  Rubin 236
  Thomasetta 236
  Willie Ann 236
Cunningham
  Evelyn 263

Cunningham (contd)
  Tully R. 263
  William 263
Curl
  Alonzo A. 382
  Anna W. 382
  Infant 179
  Jefferson Davis 179
  Penelope C. 382
  Sarah Ann 179
  Willis 382
Curry
  Margaret Lorena 383
  Martha 219
  Theodore 158
Cusack
  Martha L. 140
Dabbs
  Sarah 198
Daily
  Etta 263
Dainwood
  George W. 263
  George William 263
  Lilburn 263
  Lydia Weir 263
  Matilda Baldwin
    Ustick 263
Dallas
  Eliza 107
Daly
  Maria 263
  Martha C. 263
Dancy
  Edwin C. 327
Dandridge
  J. N. 198
Daniel
  Alice A. 156
  Arthur 327
  George H. 327
  James T. 115
  Marcus C. 327
  Peninah 327
  Sarah D. 348
  Thomas 327
  William 327

Daniels
  Asenath
    Florentine 161
  William Seth 161
Dank
  Gregory 152
Danner
  E. G. 135
  Elizabeth Boyd 135
  Hugh G. 135
  Jacob Getson 135
  Robert G. 180
  Robert Getson 136
  Susan Emmer 180
  Thomas G. 136
Darden
  Clemmons 328
  John P. 161
Davenport
  Cora 136
  Thomas 136
David
  Bettie 223
  E. C. 223
  John J. 223
Davidson
  Augustus
    Cleveland 263
  Elizabeth Keene 263
  Grandmother 161
  Ida Sanders 140
  Isabella D. 393
  J. D. 161
  Joseph R. 393
Davis
  Mrs. A. C. 158
  Ann 391
  Bessie Bell 308
  Hannah 198
  Headley 136
  Hugh 264
  Lela Ada 308
  Martha C. 364
  Mary A. 136
  Mary J. Dial 136
  Mattie K. 393
  S. E. 393
  Thomas C. 308

Davis (contd)
　William M. 383
　William R. 180
Davison
　W. H. 393
Dawkins
　Dock 359
　Ellen 359
　G. A. 359
　John 359
　Mrs. L. C. 359
Dawson
　John A. 123
　W. H. 393
Dean
　Catherine 171
Dearman
　Anjelico 249
　Elisha 348
　Eliza 348
　John A. 348
　Mally 249
　Narciss 348
　Sarah C. 249
　T. A. 348
　T. L. 249
　W. T. 348
DeLoach
　Alfred B. 264
　Etheldra C. 264
　Susan Thornton 264
　W. R. 264
Derby
　A. J. 153
　Elizabeth
　　Campbell 153
Derryberry
　Celestia Jolly 187
　Georgia Pearson 355
　Thomas Jacob 187
Desha
　Eleanor 264
　Euphemia 264
Dewitt
　Mary A. 251
Dial
　Catherine G. 136
　David Montgomery 364

Dial (contd)
　Ella Campbell 136
　Emma 115
　George H. 136
　Jacobus Jeremiah 136
　James 136, 364
　James P. 136
　Jennett 364
　Jo 136
　John 251
　Maggie Eakins 137
　Mary Etta 137
　Mary F. 251
　Mattie A. 223
　Robert Jefferson 137
　William
　　Montgomery 364
　William Woodward 115
　Willie A. 223
Dickinson
　Caroline 247
　Martha P. 247
Dill
　J. F. 127
　Martha 127
Dillard
　Edward W. 187
　Eliza 180
　John J. 180
　Watson W. 180
Dillon
　R. G. 215
　William E. 215
Dimick
　Clara L. 187
　George Hamilton 187
　Nelson T. 187
Dixon
　James J. 300
　Mattie A. 300
Dodd
　Mrs. __?__ 371
Dodson
　Elizabeth 264
　Ernest Clark 264
　Juliett T. 264
　Robert Wesley 264

Dorough
  Emma Ann 317
  Fannie Blann 128
  George F. 128
  James W. 317
Doss
  Elizabeth
    Grizzle 198
Dotti
  Maria Soberling 264
Dove
  Catharine C. 309
  John 309
  L. J. 309
  M. J. 309
Dozier
  Mollie 115
  Slater 115
Drake
  Josephene 152
Drew
  Jane 371
  Susan 371
Drinkard
  Alice E. 123
  Emma A. 123
  F. M. 123
  H. A. 123
  James C. 344
  Nancy 123
  Sallie P. 344
  Washington 123
Droll
  J. F. 209
Drummond
  Amanda E. 115
  Sallie J. Altman 383
  W. W. 383
Dubose
  Mary V. 123
Dukes
  J. S. 171
Duncan
  Matilda
    Elizabeth 220
Dunning
  Robert Wiley 198
  Sallie Ann 198

Durr
  Ida 149
Dyer
  P. S. 328
Easley
  P. E. 391
Eason
  Ann W. 300
  Elizabeth M. 300
  Henry 300
  John Mitchell 264
  John Thomas 300
  Joseph Addison 264
  M. L. G. 264
  William H. 300
  Winifred W. 300
Eaton
  H. F. 187
  T. 188
Eaves
  Nancy Ellen 359
Edmonds
  Alice F. 383
  May Thorpe 383
  Nancy Madison
    Fluker 383
  Phillip George 383
  William 383
Edmundson
  James 328
Edwards
  Alonzo Jones 264
  Narcissa
    Hansford 264
Elliott
  Calvin Andrew 156
  Elizabeth Jane 183
  John Knox 183
  John Luther 183
  William
    Melangthon 183
Ellis
  E. 328
  Fannie M. 198
  Gray 199
  John A. 393
  Mary Louise 393

Ellis (contd)
  Octavia
    Josephine 223
Embree
  Infant 199
  Mary Elizabeth 199
Ennis
  Annie E. 265
  Robert
    Washington 265
Epes
  James Vernon 245
  John W. 300
  Mamie 300
  Martha J. 300
  Richard J. 300
Eskridge
  J. H. Pettigrew 184
  Lemuel 184
  S. 184
Estes
  Alice F.
    Woodward 383
  R. A. 184
  Susian 184
  T. L. 383
Estill
  Samuel H. 140
Estis
  Caldwell 107
Etheridge
  J. T. 292
  Martha J. 292
Evans
  A. P. 185, 265
  Abner 107
  Frederick P. 265
  Joe Helen 265
  Myrtle 328
  Paul Emmet 265
Everett
  W. G. J. 265
Evington
  Caroline L. 185
Ezell
  Anna 171
  J. C. 171
  Viola Shurley 171

Ezelle
  Calvin 154
  Delia E. 185
  John 185
  Johnnie 154
  Margaret T. 185
  Sammie 154
  Sarah F. 154
Falconer
  Mary H. 140
Falkenburry
  Francis M. 383
  Mary C. 383
Fallon
  Michael 369
Farrish
  Emma Elizabeth 391
  Rebecca Ann 391
Faskin
  Peter 384
Faulkner
  James Davis 300
Faust
  John E. 265
Fawcett
  Lyle B. 199
  Robert B. 199
Fellows
  Delphine 265
  G. B. 265
  H. D. 265
  Hortense Parrent 265
Ferrell
  Henry I. 328
Few
  Alma A. 328
Fields
  Frank P. 188
Fincher
  J. 233
Fitzpatrick
  Isabella A. 223
  Thomas F. 223
Flamme
  Freeda Mary 188
  John P. 188
Fleming
  Emma J. 115

Fleming (contd)
  Infant 115
  James H. 115
  Margaret C. 115
  Mary 115
  Mary B. 115
  Robert H. 115
  William 115
  William H. 116
Flowers
  Annie Cadwell 107
  E. M. 171
  Emma Oliver 384
  Goodman 315
  H. G. 171
  Joseph E. 171
  Margaret Lee 315
  Richard Bennett 391
  Robert 391
  Robert B. 107
  Samuel 391
  Sophronia 171
  William James 384
Fluker
  David Brooks 344
  Emmie K. 265
  George M. 265
  Isabella 244
  Louis H. 384
  Nannie C. 384
  Susan Frances 344
Foard
  Francis 265
Folsom
  Squire 130
Fontaine
  Infant 123
  J. H. L. 123
  Sarah A. 123
Ford
  Harriet A. 342
Forman
  Catherine 247
Forster
  Laura Brown 265
Fortner
  A. D. 265
  Gilford J. 130

Fortner (contd)
  Mrs. L. A. 266
  Lucinda B. 130
  Richard N. 130
Foster
  Mary Mobley 199
Foushee
  J. M. 123
Foy
  Davis 300
  Eliza T. 301
  Lemuel 301
  Mary 301
  Nancie 301
  Patrick 301
  Robert Emmet 301
  Sarah K. 301
  T. T. 301
  Terrance 301
Franklin
  H. F. 348
  Martha 348
Frazier
  A. E. 154
  Theodore 154
Freeman
  Martha 301
  Thomas W. 241
Frittenden
  James J. 209
Frost
  Ezekial 199
  M. D. 199
  N. S. 199
Fulford
  Channie 152
Fulton
  Annie G. 116
  Edwin Kerr 116
  Elizabeth Dial 116
  Elizabeth K. 116
  Franklin W. 116
  Infant 116
  James Harvey 116
  James Henry 116
  Mary Bell 328
  Mary Elizabeth 116
  Mary M. 116

Fulton (contd)
  Nena Montgomery 116
  Paul 328
  William Frierson 116
Gage
  Billy 377
  Martha Hall 377
  Olive Winston 266
  Sallie O. 377
  Sara Olive
    Winston 377
  Winston 377
  _?_ 377
Gaines
  F. 154
  Fannie 266
  Susan Frances 266
Garber
  Alexander
    Menzies 210
  Anna Maria
    Rhodes 210
  Eugene Rhodes 210
  James Rhodes 210
  Joseph Baldwin 210
  Juliet Elizabeth 210
  William Coleman 211
Garden
  Phila S. 242
Gardner
  Melvina Sledge 266
Garland
  Narcissus Jane 140
Garrison
  Elizabeth C. 391
  James V. 161
  L. Catherine 161
Gast
  Edward Harrison 188
  Ellen Sharon 188
  Madden 188
  Pierre Du 188
  Thomas 188
  William 188
Gaston
  William H. 107
Gates
  Eddie 188

Gatewood
  G. H. 140
Gattis
  Susan E. S. 230
Gay
  Benjamin 328
  Delphia 328
  Mittie L. 328
  Wallace 328
  Willie J. 328
Geddie
  Elizabeth Jane 390
Gee
  Betty Isaacs 266
  Paul J. 266
Geiger
  A. 328
  Carolinus 214
  John W. 214
  William Henry 328
Gentry
  J. W. 329
George
  Emma 342
  John W. 342
  Mary 364
Gere
  Augusta Marshall
    Croom 171
Gholson
  Mary Elizabeth 156
Gibbens
  J. Elrdige 342
  Winfield Scott 188
Gibbins
  M. A. 292
Gibbs
  Ada 376
  Anna 391
  Anne Frances 266
  Edwin Churchill 348
  Elizabeth 376
  Estelle 376
  H. T. 188
  Jessie 376
  Jessie A. 376
  Mattie Scott 188
  Sabat S. 376

Gibbs (contd)
  William Henry 376
Gibson
  Abbie 140
  Sarah Ella 140
  William 140
  William A. 245
Gilbert
  John W. 359
  William B. 359
Gilder
  Annie Yeager 384
  Mary E. 384
  Thaddeus 384
  Thomas Jefferson 384
Giles
  Jacob 215
  James 391
  John Hiram 214
  Maria F. 215
  Martha Sarah 214
  Nancy A. 215
  Sarah Moore 214
  Simmons H. 215
Gill
  Mrs. M. M. 199
  William H. 199
Gillespie
  Adele 107
  Marian 107
  Mary McRee 107
Gillis
  Anna R. 309
  John M. 309
Gilmore
  Child 212
  J. N. 171
  James 212
  Jane 212
  Nathaniel G. 212
  Willie Ann
    Eskridge 212
Godfrey
  Cornelia Ormond 364
  Dozier 223
  Dozier Elizabeth 223
  E. B. 364
  Harriet P. 223

Godfrey (contd)
  James Myers 364
  John D. 223
  Julia Augusta 329
  Lucy A. 364
  Mary E. 223
  W. E. 364
  William 223
  William Sr. 364
Golsby
  Agnes Winston 378
  Anthony Winston 378
  Belle Seawell 378
  John Anthony
    Winston 378
  Tommy Gray 378
Goodin
  Lucy A. 161
Goodwyn
  Eliza W. 236
  James W. 237
  Thomas H. 237
Gordon
  Adaline 356
  Adelia H. 356
  Cornelius 154
  Elizabeth S. 356
  Ella Wrenn 301
  Georgia 301
  Ira Pearsall 318
  James I. 318
  Jefferson 356
  Jesse 356
  Jesse Sr. 356
  Lycurcus 356
  Mary 318
  Mary C. Larkins 318
  Mary S. 318
  Olivia C. 356
  Posey 356
  Samuel W. 356
  Thomas H. 356
  T. P. 301
Gorman
  John E. 378
Gould
  Bettie Beebe 266

Gowdey
  George Clarence 266
Grace
  Elaine 342
  John B. 342
  Mary E. 342
  Mollie F. 342
Grady
  James Robert 141
  M. A. 141
  M. L. 141
  Mollie Ann
    Rushing 141
  P. M. 141
  Rebecca 141
Graham
  Alabama 363
  Harriet 217
  Joseph 141
  Onita 329
  Mrs. S. M. 217
  __?__ 363
Grain
  Dillie 362
Grant
  Alice E. 152
  F. Virginia 152
  Frank T. 250
  Green W. 218
  Helen Neville 215
  Silas 152
  Susan 250
  Thomas 250
Grantham
  Fannie 154
Gray
  Nancy Berton 199
Grayson
  J. Y. 108
  Ralph W. 108
Green
  Aba 348
  Conary Lucinda 348
  G. W. 348
  John A. 348
  Mary Ann 348
  Ophelia E. 348
  Rolly 231

Green (contd)
  Samuel D. 349
  Susan Walker 349
Greene
  Daniel 313
  Mattie Floyd 313
  Pamelia Ann 313
  Sue 313
Greenlee
  Hugh 199
  Hugh Washington 224
  Katie Coblentz 224
  Lily May 224
  Mary Elizabeth 199
Greenlees
  John 218
  Joseph 218
Greer
  Martha A. 245
Gregory
  J. J. 244
  Sarah A. 251
  William J. 301
Grice
  Charity 117
  John 301
  Mary Simms 302
Griffin
  Anderson 199
  Dandridge G. 200
  Edward 200
  Eliza Jane 200
  George 200
  J. E. 200
  James 319
  Mary 200
Grimes
  George 127
  I. C. 161
  Martha 161
  Martha Ann 127
  Thomas J. 349
Grove
  Augustus George 329
  Augustus J. 329
  Clarence 329
  Frank M. 329
  Julian 329

416

Grove (contd)
  Lu Hill 329
  Mary E. 329
  Peninnah F. 329
  Zoubie Rogers 329
Guard
  A. J. 200
  Mary A. 200
Gulley
  Cemantha C. 141
  Ellen Bell Lee 141
  Ezekial Slocum 141
  Woodson Slocum 141
Hadden
  David Louis 108
  Isaac 117
  Martha B. 117
  Robert Wilson 117
  Sophia Elizabeth 108
  Stella 108
Hagan
  Peter 384
Hagood
  R. J. 302
Haguewood
  Callie I. 309
Hailey
  Andrew Harrison 359
  Keziah 360
Hainesworth
  J. L. 266
Hair
  Elizabeth W. 266
  James 266
  Martha A. A. 266
  Martha W. 266
  Robert A. 267
  William A. 267
Hale
  Amanda Jane 302
  Bettie Carr 384
  David M. 117
  Mrs. E. C. 391
  Elizabeth 302
  Harvey Stewart 267
  J. A. 384
  John Wesley 384
  Joseph Warren 182

Hale (contd)
  Malinda Frances 302
  Margaret
    Alexander 182
  Mary Ann 267
  Mary Catherine 182
  Mary E. 182
  Mary Emma 182
  Mary Isabella 171
  Matilda Jane 384
  Robert Hadden 384
  William Frank 182
Hall
  Mrs. Archa 172
  Archibald 172
  Beatrice 161
  Caloway 237
  Edward 161
  Elnora 161
  Evan P. 172
  Grandma 161
  Jimmie 173
  Marcellis 161
  Simon 172
  Susan 172
Halsell
  Eliza 329
  Ella A. 329
  Gabriel 349
  J. A. 329
  J. R. 329
  Mrs. M. A. 330
  Patience 349
  Sallie Bess 330
  Sparta L. 330
  W. M. Sr. 330
  William Sr. 330
Hammond
  Amelia B. 349
  Emaline 349
  Joe 349
Hand
  Martha Ann 141
  O. C. 141
  Sallie J. 141
  Samuel Patton 141
  Wayne Thomas 142

Handley
  J. H. 150
  Schararrissa
    Browning 150
Hardge
  Simon 254
Hardin
  Elmie 237
  J. M. Sr. 237
  Jessie Columbus 237
  Joseph Y. 237
  Julia E. 237
  Lauizer 237
  Martha A. 237
  Mary Culpepper 237
  Simeon C. 237
  Spinks 237
  Tiny 237
Hare
  John 330
  Josephine 156
  Martha H. 330
  Mary J. 156
  Sarah Ellen 156
Harper
  C. C. 108
  Daniel Y. 130
  J. W. 108
  Julia Wilder 309
  R. S. 108
  Sophia 108
  William J. 108
  Wyatt 108
  Wyatt Judson 108
  Z. C. 108
Harrell
  John S. 309
  L. R. 309
Harrington
  Elbert 123
  Rosa 127
Harris
  Augustin H. 189
  Caroline 349
  Dora O. 200
  Edwin Percy 189
  Ella F. 148
  Eva 267

Harris (contd)
  Gertrude 267
  H. H. 267
  Henry C. 267
  Infant 148
  Irene 267
  J. M. 349
  Jacob P. 237
  John 349
  John Ellis 162
  Lizzie 267
  M. S. 349
  M. W. 189
  Martha S. 349
  Mary Catherine 172
  Mary E. 189, 349
  Mary S. 267
  Nettie Franklin 349
  Norlet T. 267
  Park McClelland 267
  Penelope Ann 349
  R. M. 267
  Richard 219
  Robert 267
  Sam 349
  Sam B. 267
  Simon 350
  Susan 250
  Willie 267
  Y. W. 189
Harrison
  Harriet 200
Harry
  Francis Marion 251
Hart
  J. N. 244
  Mary 244
Hartsfield
  James M. 108
Harwood
  Mary Scott Gray 189
  Robert Ellyson 189
  Ruffin Gray 189
  Samuel B. 189
Hatch
  Ann 219
  Catherine E. 219
  Lemuel B. 219

Hatch (contd)
  Noble 219
  William A. 219
Haupt
  Infant 220
  Lewis 220
  Matilda 220
  Matilda Dale 220
  Sebastin 220
Hawkins
  Alice B.
    Scarborough 292
  Ann Caroline 221
  D. B. 267
  Elizabeth W. 221
  John T. 221
  Joyce Gilder 384
  L. D. 360
  Martha A. 221
  Sarah E. Ivy 360
  Susan M. 221
  Thomas Hewitt 221
  W. H. 221
Hearne
  Henry Alexander 162
  Mattie Martha 162
Henagan
  Ann 245
  Darby 292
  Effie M. 245
  James M. 268
  Julia A. 246
  Kate Brown 268
  Kate L. 292
Henderson
  Charlotte C. 108
  Lewis 108
  Lewis W. 108
  Mary E. 268
  Nathan 250
  Obedience 109
  Sarah J. 109
  Thomas 268
  William E. 109
Hendricks
  Clarra 302
Henning
  George 200

Henry
  James 250
Henson
  Lida Patton 142
  Lyda P. 142
Herd
  Eleanor 182
Herndon
  John Minor 189
  Lucy Chew 189
Herr
  Ben F. 268
  Ernest 268
Hibbler
  Charlie 228
  Eliza Watkins 200
  Frances A. 228
  Infant 228
  Martha Blount 330
  Martha N. 228
  Martha S. 228
  Robert 200
  Sarah Jane 228
  William 228
  William H. 228
Hicks
  William 228
High
  J. W. 302
  Mrs. T. A. 302
  William R. 302
Hightower
  C. D. J. Bush 384
  Charles D. 385
  Council Berry 385
  L. E. 385
Hill
  Charles C. 385
  David B. 385
  Elizabeth 200
  Emma 189
  James Twyman 268
  Kate 189
  Meredith 385
  Merinda E. 385
  Robert 200
  Sallie Roberts 189
  Virginia E. 385

Hillyer
  Agnes Carr 172
Hilman
  Emma R. 246
  Jezreel P. 246
  Joseph J. 246
  Joshua W. 246
  Judson J. 109
  Mary Jane 246
  Nimrod 246
Hinson
  Elizabeth D.
    Dorough 318
Hitt
  Austin 350
  Cordelia
    McDonald 350
  Martha Bowers 350
  Martha Jane 249
  Rebecca 350
  Robert Clark 249
  William Henry 350
Hodges
  C. C. 117
  Infant 117
  Sarah Melissa 365
Hodgins
  Merrit 220
Hoit
  Elizabeth Hair 268
  Hamilton Hair 268
  Isiah D. 268
  Mary E.
    Scarborough 293
  Zane M. 268
Holcomb
  A. H. 302
Holder
  Ellen V. Bean 350
  John W. 350
  Rebecca Bartlett 350
  William James 350
Holland
  John 365
Holley
  Rachel 350
  W. G. 182

Hollis
  Emily A. 302
Holloway
  Infant 302
  Melvin W. 302
Holman
  Frank 385
Holmes
  Fannie M. 162
  James H. 172
  Thomas N. 172
  Tommie 172
Holt
  LeRoy 117
Holyfield
  Daniel 109
Honeycutt
  Emma P. 162
  Z. W. 162
Hooks
  Coster 268
  E. W. 268
  Margaret Adeline 268
Hopkins
  Elizabeth W. 268
  Julia B. 269
  Kate E. 269
  William W. 269
Hopper
  Eli Hugh 137
  J. D. M. 137
  James A. 137
  Jim 137
  John 137
  Maggie Dial 137
  Sarah Elizabeth 137
  Sarah P. 137
  William T. 137
  Willie Ann 137
Horn
  Alise 395
  Curtis Drury 142
  E. M. J. 142
  Elizabeth A.
    Massey 189
  Iredell H. 190
  Isaac Mc. 142
  Isaac W. 142

Horn (contd)
  John Lee 142
  Josh 395
  Mary S. 123
  Nancy A. 190
  Thomas A. 142
Horton
  Elizabeth 109
  Frances S. A. 109
  Margaret Ann 109
  Stephen 109
Houston
  Almira S. 330
  Caroline 250
  Davis Caldwell 229
  Florence May 269
  Hamilton 230
  J. Sanford 269
  Joe Clint 269
  John 230
  John Clinton 269
  John J. 330
  Lizzie 269
  M. C. 269
  Martha L. 269
  Mollie G. 269
  S. A. 269
  Sallie M. 269
  Virginia 269
  W. A. 269
Hudson
  Sarah B. 246
Huff
  Ollie C. 350
  Sue 162
Hughes
  H. H. 201
Hull
  Adah W. 269
Humphreys
  William J. 385
Hunnicut
  Fannie Elizabeth
    Halsell 330
  John A. 330
Hunster
  Eliza A. 158
  Mary E. 158

Hunter
  Anna J. 269
  Boanerges Clay 270
  Ella Lake 270
  James Howlett 270
  Mary Elizabeth 270
  Robert L. 270
  Thomas 293
Hurlbert
  Emma F. 162
Husband
  Louis 162
  Mary E. 162
Hutcherson
  E. E. 360
  G. W. 360
Hutchins
  Celeste B. 365
  Elizabeth 365
  James L. 190
  Jesse H. 365
  Ruth D. 365
  Sarah R. 190
  Thomas H. 365
  William 365
  William P. 365
Hutchinson
  Virginia
    Richardson 270
Hutton
  Anderson 201
  Ann 201
  Emmett Calhoun 201
Hyatt
  Devereaux M. 270
Idle
  Almeda 162
Inge
  John 229
Isabell
  George 378
  James 378
Ivy
  Ben 270
  Ben R. 360
  James S. 360
  Jesse C. 360
  Melvina W. 360

Ivy (contd)
  Sarah T. 360
Jackson
  Charlotte 293
  Eliza M. 270
  Elizabeth 365
  Henry M. 190
  Isephena A. E. 303
  J. T. 365
  Jacinth 365
  James 190
  James B. 270
  James C. 365
  John 270
  John R. 303
  Louisa 293
  Lucy Barret
    Reavis 201
  Mary A. 303
  Mary Jacqualine 303
  Mollie B. 270
  Prudence 366
  Randle 366
  Rebecca Wrenn 303
  Sara E. 366
  Thomas Klugh 201
  Will D. 303
James
  Edward Payton 318
  Eliza McCann 393
  Lytle E. 162
  William H. 385
Jarman
  Hunter Gordon 270
  Mary 231
  Peter Bryant 270
  Thomas Sr. 231
  William Thomas 162
Jemison
  Harriet P. 231
  J. S. 232
  Jane 270
  Jane E. 232
  John Steel 270
  Joseph 232
  Robert 232
  William H. 232
  ___?___ 271

Jenkins
  Annie Andrews 130
  Infants 330
  J. T. 330
  Jane L. 271
  Jennett L. 232
  Joseph W. 271
  Leroy 271
  Louvenia 331
  Susan 130
  Thomas Leonidas 130
Jeter
  Sarah M. 201
Johnson
  Elizabeth 230
  Henry 230
  John M. 123
  Lewis 142
  S. A. 254
Johnston
  Eliza A. 124
  Ella 201
  Emily H. 271
  John S. 271
  Lucy Olivia 366
  Margaret V. 271
  Mattie M. 271
  Nathan 124
  Persis M. 124
  Thomas A. 271
Jolly
  Arnold 356
  Hannah 340
  Judith W. 356
  M. A. 356
  Peter 340
  Sallie B. 356
Jones
  Addison Ward 215
  Alexander P. 232
  Benjamin A. 215
  Benjamin A. Jr. 215
  D. Bestor 271
  Dempsey J. 394
  Frederick
    Houston 271
  Gabriel 232
  Harden L. 271

Jones (contd)
  Helen M. 394
  Isaac Hull 224
  James W. 230
  John D. 172
  John Wootten 201
  Julia A. 394
  Maria A. 215
  Martha Ann 233
  Mary Esther 271
  Mary Hutchinson 271
  Penny 350
  Rebecca 350
  Redding H. 172
  Riley 350
  Rollie 232
  Samuel L. 375
  Sarah J. 172
  South West 201
  Susan Jane 394
  Victoria 232
  W. A. C. 271
  William H. 271
  William Henry 295
  Zechariah 232
Jowers
  Ellen 172
  W. M. 172
Joyner
  Mary Etta Cherry 130
  William Bert 131
Kay
  Dora 252
Kelley
  Phamie B. 124
Kelly
  Julis 254
Kemble
  Sarah J. 201
Kenard
  John M. 271
Kendall
  Abigail W. 117
Kennard
  Amanda 272
  Bettie 272
  James P. 272
  Minerva Ann 272

Kennard (contd)
  Missouri
    Phillips 272
  Nancy D. 272
  Sally J. 272
  Smith O. 272
Kennedy
  Catharine Lowery 224
  Franklin 246
  George Earnest 224
  Harriett A. 303
  John 303
  Margaret 219
  Sallie A. 246
  Sallie J. 224
  Vernal Hardy 224
  Willie B. 224
Kennon
  Marielou 131
  S. Evans 131
Kent
  E. H. 131
  Martha Anderson 131
  Nancy Ann 252
  Sarah Winn 252
Kerr
  Daniel W. 215
  Edward Taylor 117
  Frances
    Elizabeth 117
  James D. 117
  John L. 117
  Laura D. 117
  Mary Elizabeth
    Williams 118
  Mary J. D. 118
  Peggy M. Jones 216
  Sarah D. 118
  Telemachus 118
  W. W. 118
  William 118
Key
  Fannie 350
  J. M. 350
  Parks Oliver 137
Killen
  Amaranth M. 313
  Aramenta 229

Killen (contd)
    Infant 229
    Mary 229
Killian
    S. D. 385
    Sarah E. 385
King
    Sallie T. 233
Kinnard
    Calvin 272
    Michael
        Claiborne 272
Kirkland
    Elizabeth 131
Knight
    B. F. 249
    Joseph 303
    L. A. 157
    Mary A. 249
    Paul S. 366
    William L. 331
Knott
    Margaret Elmira 385
    Virgie Portis 318
Knox
    Frank M. 201
    J. M. 309
    John 233
    John Clementine 234
    Maggie 201
    Mary Jane 234
Kornegay
    Daniel 211
    Elizabeth B. 211
    George 211
    Robert 211
Kring
    Bettie G. 201
    E. N. 201
Lacy
    Caroline M. 131
    Elisha 131
    Mart 216
    Martha 131
    Martha Lela 237
    Mary 234
    Mary Ann 303
    Nicholas 234

Lacy (contd)
    W. A. 131
    William 237
Lake
    Ella 272
    Joseph Henry 272
    Joseph J. 272
    Margaret Gains 272
    N. Scales 273
    Sarah Lane 273
Lamberson
    J. L. 273
Lammers
    Betty G. 293
    Delia 293
Lancaster
    Agnes C. 252
    Albert 184
    Albert Jr. 273
    B. W. 385
    Ben 273
    Ben F. 309
    Eliza H. 385
    Elizabeth 273
    J. A. 309
    James Edwin 252
    Joseph 184
    L. A. 385
    Laura J. 309
    Lucy A. 252
    Martha Jane 273
    Nancy Caroline 162
    Sally 273
    Sarah M. 253
    T. F. 386
    Talitha Ann
        Elizabeth 253
Land
    Mabella S. 351
Landers
    Isabella 386
    Sydney C. 386
Lanford
    Bighard 356
    John B. 201
    Maria Adeline
        Rogers 202

423

Larkin
  Abram 142
  Irene 142
  Mary S. Elliott 142
  Sophie Henson 142
  William 142
  William Robert 142
Larkins
  Elizabeth
    Pearsall 318
Lavender
  Infant 118
  Jane 118
  Margaret 241
  Sarah A. 118
Lawhon
  Annie H. 273
  Infant 273
  John 273
Lawler
  M. E. 224
  Sarah J. 109
Lawrence
  William Haywood 273
Lawson
  Alex 212
Leard
  James O. 252
  Louvenia 252
Lee
  Adeline 234
  Bettie J. 224
  Catherine
    Rebecca 142
  Daniel W. 143
  Elizabeth Helen 143
  Frank 273
  Ida John Corine 143
  J B. 224
  J. W. W. 224
  James M. 143
  Jennie Lee 224
  John Andrew 331
  John R. 143
  John William 190
  Lillian Quarles 331
  Mrs. M. P. 315
  Mamie E. 143

Lee (contd)
  Mary Eliza 143
  Mary Elizabeth 143
  Susan 143
  Thomas J. 224
  Virginia Hannah
    Rogers 331
  William 143
Leitch
  H. B. 293
  Sarah Catherine 293
Leverett
  H. B. 273
Lewis
  Aurelia Axtell 202
  Eliza Webster 202
  Laura Aurelia 202
  Lewellyn Sr. 303
  Luther 343
  Martha C. 162
  Mary Russell 202
  Mattie G. 202
  Mittie 343
  Moses 202
  Moses Boardman 202
  Rachel 303
  S. A. 163
  Sallie Martin 202
  Warner H. 163
  William Garrett 225
  William M. 202
Lide
  Hugh James 149
  Hugh S. 273
  Infant 149
  Jere Brown 149
  Lillian 149
  Sumter 149
Liggett
  Annie Crutcher 163
Lipscomb
  G. W. 225
  J. E. 225
  M. G. 225
  Mary M. R. 225
  Willie A.
    Ogletree 225

425

Little
  A. J. 331
  Ben B. 274
  Blake 274
  Charles Henry 331
  Eliza T. 331
  H. Emmett 274
  Harriett S. 331
  J. J. 331
  James Hibbler 274
  Laura J. 331
  Lucy P. 331
  Manie 274
  Margaret E. 331
  Margaret L. 239
  Martha Louise 331
  Mary E. 239, 332
  Mary Elizabeth 332
  Nancy 332
  Noah 332
  Robert Seth 332
  Mrs. S. B. 274
  Sarah A. 332
  Seth 332
  Seth S. 332
  Susan 274
  Susan Elizabeth 332
  Tempy 332
  W. W. 332
  William 332
  William G. 332
  William Gray 332
  Willie Gray 274, 332
Lockard
  Amanda F. 274
  Caroline 239
  Gertrude Alice 274
  John 239
  Lucinda Adeline 274
  Nancy L. 239
  Nancy Stewart 239
  Robert F. 239
  Sarah A. 239
  T. E. 274
  William 274
  William J. 239
London
  Laura 118
Long
  Alice M. Eaton 190
  Annie Horn 190
  Donna Julia 190
  Elizabeth 386
  Henderson W. 202
  Henry D. 190
  Julia Jackson 190
  Nancy 386
  Pricilla
    Dickinson 202
  Richard B. 202
  Thomas M. 190
Lott
  Henrietta T. 274
Love
  Ida K. 225
  Marion V. 163
  Mary A. 163
Lowe
  Baker M. 209
  Catherine 274
Lowry
  Florence G. 225
  George W. 225
  Joseph J. 225
  Margaret A. 225
  Prudence H. 225
  Robert H. 225
  Vernal 225
  Vernal L. 225
Luke
  Marion 274
  Mary E. 274
Luker
  Joseph E. 375
  S. E. 375
Lummus
  Elizabeth Ann 318
  James Wesley 163
  Loueasa 318
  Lula S. 163
  William A. 173, 318
Lunceford
  Benjamin F. 131
  Harriett
    Caroline 131
  Herbert Lee 131

Lunceford (contd)
  J. W. 131
  Muhulda J. 132
  S. C. 132
Lynn
  Agnes Lancaster 163
  Ella 252
  James 252
  M. W. 252
Lyon
  Andrew 333
  Susan 333
Mager
  Emile 163
  Lottie Brewster 163
Maggard
  Con 315
  D. H. 386
  Joseph A. J. 275
  Mattie E. 386
Makin
  Mary Alice 275
Manasco
  Phoebe Hill 203
Maniece
  Thomas Oden 203
Marks
  Levi 124
  Selena 124
Marsh
  Darius 318
  Nannie W. 333
Marshall
  Elizabeth Brooks 173
  Matthew A. 173
  Mattie H. Rogers 203
Martin
  Ann E. 143
  J. A. 173
  Mary E. 128
  Simeon P. 128
  William H. 143
Mason
  Ann 275
  Ben 173
  George 275
  Mary H. 173
  Matilda 150

Mason (contd)
  Robert 275
  Robert Saunders 275
  Sarah A. 275
  Sophia Slaughter 275
  Thomas 173
Massangale
  Robert Allen 132
Massey
  Emma A. 366
Masters
  Jennie 173
  Joseph B. 173
Math(?)
  Fannie 253
Mathers
  Lula Barron 386
Mathews
  Lou 128
  William B. 128
Matthews
  Irene Torry 143
  James A. 386
  John 168
  Katherine Alice 386
  Penelope V. 144
Maury
  Alexander C. 275
May
  Ann 240
  Ben 303
  Benjamin A. 163
  Catharen Louisa 240
  Elizabeth 109
  Florence P. 225
  Frank 240
  Green 241
  James 225
  Jefferson 293
  Marsaline 293
  Mary 240
  Nannie Foy 304
  Sally 293
  Sam 254
  Sarah A. 173
  Susan 254
Mayberry
  G. E. 366

Maye
  Andrew W. 293
Mayfield
  W. T. 386
McAboy
  Milalia 152
McAllister
  William 109
McAlpin
  Andrew Blanton 386
  Arch 386
  Jennie 163
  John F. 158
  Robert A. 158
  Sarah B. 158
  Sarah J. 386
  William S. 392
  William T. 386
McCain
  Adam 241
  Adam Creed 366
  Adam S. 241
  Clarence M. 275
  Elizabeth 241
  Ella Key 137
  Frances Lou
    Hodges 275
  George W. 137
  Isabella M. 275
  Lelia Marion 241
  W. J. 275
McCall
  Fannie 254
McCann
  Amanda L. 238
  Hugh 238
  Infant 343
  John G. 343
  Nancy Brock 343
  Susan 343
  William J. 343
McCarroll
  Belle 144
McCarty
  Joseph W. 144
McClamroch
  Albert S. 163

McClelland
  Nancy Ann 370
McClendon
  Ezekiel 304
McConico
  Eliza 275
McConnell
  Infant 387
  John A. 118, 387
  Joseph A. 387
  M. G. 387
  Martha J. 387
  Mary E. 387
McConnico
  Bettie Ann 276
  C. S. 276
  Garner M. 276
  Jacqueline S. 276
  Maggie Jane 276
  Zora Jane 276
McCorkle
  Elizabeth 387
  Joseph 118
  Joseph S. 387
  Nona M. 387
  S. J. 387
  Thomas J. 118
  Violet 118
  W. F. 118
McCown
  Charlotte 313
McCrory
  Ida Frances
    Folsom 132
  James Bird 132
McCurdy
  Oliver Moore 109
McDaniel
  C. C. 124
  Carrie C. 124
  Cynthia Ann 163
  Delila 366
  Eli 163
  Elizabeth 366
  Elizabeth C. 366
  George W. 366
  Henry 366
  Henry Clay 366

McDaniel (contd)
  Hulda Ann 366
  James E. 367
  John M. 367
  Maggie A. Baskin 163
  Margaret J. 367
  Mary E. 360
  Mary Knox 367
  Pamelia 367
  Penelope 367
  Rosa Knox 367
  William 367
  William Gray 164
  William Harris 367
  William Henry 367
McDonald
  Ann M. 158
  Daniel A. 182
  Daniel B. 182
  Drury M. 344
  George W. 158
  J. A. 351
  James 276
  James H. 144
  Jamima G. 345
  John H. 158
  Louisa M. 182
  M. E. 351
  M. W. 345
  Malcolm Boyd 276
  Martha A. 182, 276
  Mary F. 351
  Mattie 159
  Moses Waldrop 345
  Robert T. 351
  S. C. 159, 351
  William 159
  __?__ 276
McDow
  Jane 118
  Martha C. 118
  Mary A. 119
  W. L. 119
McDowell
  Ann Marshall 220
  Anna 220
  Baby Brother 220
  Joseph Sebastin 220

McDowell (contd)
  Marshall 220
  William H. 220
McElroy
  A. P. 242
  Andrew J. 242
  Anna E. 242
  Annie 152
  Aseneth E. 242
  E. M. 242
  Eloise 387
  G. W. 242
  I. R. 242
  Isaac R. 242
  J. J. 242
  Jasper Newton 242
  Jesse W. 242
  Lula Wilder 309
  M. E. 242
  Mariah 242
  Mary Sybil 309
  Matilda T. 243
  Miss 253
  Nancy 243
  Sallie 243
  Sarah Elizabeth 243
  Son 243
  Spate 152
  Thad C. 310
  W. H. 387
McGehee
  Cora Etheridge 293
McGowen
  Annie Ward 164
  J. C. 252
  Nancy 252
  R. J. 252
  Thomas Pinckney 164
  Virginia N. 164
  William E. 164
  William F. 252
  William R. 164
McGrew
  Clark 245
  Infant 245
  William
    Patterson 245

McHelm
  R. Melville 276
McInnis
  Julia Ann 246
  Malcolm 246
  Malcolm E. 246
  Robert H. 247
McKerall
  Fannie 376
McKinley
  Catherine J. 360
  Daniel D. 360
McKinney
  John 203
  Julia 203
McKinsie
  Edgar J. 367
McKnight
  F. H. 276
  Margaret Sprott 276
  Susan A. 276
  William Thomas 276
McLean
  Eliza H. 293
  Emma 294
  Lewis A. 294
  Mary O. 294
  Peter 294
McMahon
  A. W. 190
  Carl W. 203
  E. R. C. 190
  Gage Winston 378
  John J. 203
  Kate 203
  Mattie 191
  Mollie 203
  R. G. 191
McMillan
  A. G. 144
  Clarinda M. 370
  Dora 144
  F. G. 144
  Kate G. 144
McMillon
  Anna B. 144
  Daniel 144
  Drury 144

McMillon (contd)
  Elizabeth 144
  Isaac N. 144
  Preston N. 144
McMurry
  Millie Culpepper 238
McNeil
  D. L. 310
McRae
  Martha H. 276
  W. B. 277
  William P. 277
  Willie 277
McRee
  Eliza G. 109
  William 109
McSween
  Benjamin
    Franklin 322
  Daniel 322
McTurk
  Isabella 191
Meador
  Job 110
  Mary V. 132
  R. A. 164
  R. L. Sr. 345
  Rebecca M. 132
  W. F. 345
Meek
  James T. 333
  John McCaw Sr. 333
  Rosa Little 333
Megereson
  Frank 241
Mellard
  Elizabeth J. 373
Mellen
  George Frederick 277
  Henry Levi 277
  Mary Briscoe
    Baldwin 277
  S. S. 277
  Susan H. 277
Mellown
  David E. 387
  Jane 387
  Jennie Knott 387

Mellown (contd)
  Julia Hagins 173
Melton
  Bartlett 110
  Bascomb 110
  C. C. 110
  Ella Thomas 110
  Mary 110
  William 110
Meredith
  Ann Eliza 191
  Reuben Anderson 191
Metcalf
  Jacob R. 191
Miller
  Charles Brooks 277
  Charlie G. 310
  Emily W. 351
  Ezekiel 164
  George Wideman 387
  Gilbert L. 164
  John Francis 248
  Louisa J. 164
  Malissa 164
  Maria F. 310
  Owen Pigford 310
  R. F. 351
  Sicly 351
  Thomas J. 310
  William E. 248
  Willie A. 310
Mims
  Elizabeth
    Hubbard 248
  Seabourn 248
Mitchell
  Annie P. 277
  Arbrette 164
  B. F. 119
  Benjamin George 226
  Benjamin James 119
  Benjamin L. 164
  D. W. 277
  Daniel 191
  David A. 173
  Edwin L. 277
  Elizabeth Lowry 226
  Franklin Lowry 226

Mitchell (contd)
  James 191
  James A. 277
  Jessie Nichols 277
  John Montgomery 226
  Martha Augustus 191
  Mary E. 173
  Nancy 313
  Preston Augustus 277
  Sallie Gage 378
  Twins 367
  William H. 173
Mobley
  Green B. 203
  Henrietta 203
  Mandy 362
  N. B. 203
  Savilla 203
Modawell
  Alice Eloise 173
Moffitt
  Elihu 333
Monett
  Samuel 278
Monette
  Callie 376
  Fletch 377
Moore
  A. E. 278
  Aaron 278
  Amanda E. 278
  Eliza 119
  Elizabeth C. 119
  James A. 119
  Jemima 191
  Josiah 278
  Lula 310
  Mittie T. Reavis 203
  S. Evlyn 119
  Susie Weston 333
  Thomas 119
  Thomas J. H. 119
  Thomas Oliver 333
  W. H. 278
  Wesley 250
  William F. 278
  William H. 119

431

Mooring
  J. A. 191
  John Scott 191
  Lizzie LeRoy 191
  Martha A. 191
  Theodocia
    Hainsworth 278
Morgan
  Barbary 333
  Isabel 110
  John 333
  Phalby T. 310
  Thomas J. 310
Morris
  Betty S. 204
  George 144
  Harriet 144
  Mollie 387
Morrison
  James 378
Morse
  Henry 204
  Mary Ina 204
Mosley
  Susan 174
Muncrief
  Frances M. 110
  Sampson B. 110
  Sophia 110
Mundy
  Emma Tate 174
  H. J. 159
  J. A. 159
  Mary E. 159
  W. A. 159
Murley
  Anne 278
  D. S. M. 278
  J. S. M. 278
  Mary Alice 278
  S. W. M. 278
  W. A. 278
Murray
  Belle Lee 144
  Belle Trott 278
  Robert Lewis 278
  William L. 156

Myers
  Ann 278
  Asbury 226
  Bettie L. 119
  Infant 304
  James Asbury 226
  James G. 226
  James W. 304
  Martha 226
  Samuel W. 304
  Tom 278
  Wilson G. Jr. 304
Nairne
  John Wiley 295
  Mary G. 296
Nance
  Averrila 192
  James Walter 192
  Mary Ann 367
  Sarah 192
  William 192
  William H. 192
Nash
  Caroline Foy 333
  Cora 279
  Elmira J. 333
  Ida M. 333
  James H. 334
  Joe T. 279
  Lampedo 279
  P. G. 279
  Paulina 279
  Stevonia E. 334
Neal
  Matilda Peebles
    Mabry 334
  T. P. 334
Neelly
  Mary Elizabeth 132
Neilson
  Eugenie Amason 279
Nelson
  F. J. W. 192
  Phillip Meade 279
  __?__ 174
Nevill
  Lizzie L. 119
  Mary 120

Neville
  A. L. 216
  Amelia 216
  Andrew L. 216
  Maria Cross
    Giles 216
  Martha
    Washington 216
  Mary Russell 216
  Mattie E. Massey 216
  Nancy J. 216
  Robert S. 216
  Sallie Blocker 216
  Sarah H. Spencer 216
  Shepard Spencer 216
  William 216
  William Hervey 216
  William Hervey
    Jr. 217
Newman
  Frank 279
Newton
  Malissa 351
  Mary C. 132
  Richard 132
Nichols
  Annie M. 279
  W. J. 279
  William Sanders 279
Nicholson
  Abbie E. 360
  Cherry 250
  G. T. 154
  George 360
  Henry 250
  Jinnie 360
  Joseph 314
  Mrs. S. E.
    Gordon 319
Nix
  Mrs. M. L. 182
Nixon
  Alice Boyd 138
  Hester Ann 367
  J. W. 138
Norville
  Hardy W. 279
  Hardynia Kate 279

Norville (contd)
  John H. 279
  Jordon Short 279
  Mary Ann Hodges 279
Norwood
  James K. 280
Nowles
  Sarah A. M. 280
Nuffer
  C. B. 110
Ogletree
  Amelia J. 226
  Benjamin H. 360
Oliver
  Eliza Perrin 296
  Francis Howe 296
  Freeman Goode 296
  Lewellyn 296
  Lewellyn Jr. 296
  Nannie Speight 334
  Robert Perrin 334
  Sallie G. 296
  ___?___ 296
O'Neal
  E. A. B. 204
  Emily
    McCallister 307
O'Neil
  Addie E. 192
Ormond
  Cherry Ella 304
  John Fletcher 304
  Thomas S. 368
Oswalt
  Minor C. 204
  Nancy Sanford 204
  Robert M. 204
Owen
  Alfred 351
  Elizabeth 351
  Mary M. 351
Owens
  Emily Permilla
    Ashley 159
  Francis 159
  Mary Lavina 132
Paash
  Sophia E. 192

Pankey
  Elizabeth 310
  J. B. 310
  Sara Miller 310
Parham
  John C. 204
  Lena Winston 204
  Matilda 304
  Matthew 304
  Nancy 304
  Sallie Whitsett 204
Park
  Irene H. 280
Parker
  Adamant 313
  Agnes Stewart 314
  Annie 132
  Armsted Burt 120
  Arthur
    Theophilus 192
  E. J. 180
  Elizabeth P. 280
  Ellen 240
  Infant 314
  James 314
  James H. 132
  James Lake 280
  Lucy Harper 314
  Marcus 351
  Mary 314
  Mary Ann 110
  Mary M. 280
  Mary W. 314
  Osceola 314
  Robert Murphree 315
  Sarah Eleanor 351
  Socrates 280
  Tennie Letcher 280
  Virginia Stewart 315
Parks
  Reubin A. 192
Parrent
  Cornelia Ann 280
  Ellen M. 280
  James L. 280
  Mary Caroline 280
  Preston Nash 280

Parrish
  Elizabeth 133
  S. P. 133
Pate
  Ida 174
  Martha 247
  Samuel R. 247
Patterson
  James D. 226
  John William 204
  Nannie P. 204
Patton
  Alice B. 144
  D. U. 145
  Eliza 145
  Ella McMillan 145
  Joseph 145
  Joseph B. 145
  Nancy 235
  Wayne C. 110
  Willie A.
    Beville 145
Pearce
  W. E. Sr. 315
Pearson
  Ann W. 334
  Cordelia F. 217
  David B. 356
  Eliza Ann 357
  George C. 357
  Infant 334
  Isaac F. 204
  Joel E. 334
  Phillip Edward 334
  Sarah 204
  T. C. 343
  W. E. 217
Peavy
  L. D. 316
Peebles
  Jesse 334
Peel
  J. F. 361
  Lena Gilbert 361
Pendergrass
  A. H. 159
  Hattie O. 159
  John H. 182

Pennington
  A. 124
  E. J. 124
  Margaret 124
  R. A. 124
Perkins
  John 280
Perrin
  Elizabeth S. 296
  Mary Florida Lacy
    Jones 217
  Sarah C. 296
  T. U. 217
  William A. 217
Perry
  Ann 314
  John C. 110
Peteet
  Anderson 218
  Aseneth
    Clementine 212
  James M. 387
  James Monroe 392
  Mary J. 388
Peters
  Levi 351
  Mary E. 352
Peterson
  Bill 250
Pettigrew
  Louise Eskridge 226
  Sarah Isadors 164
  Wallace H. 164
  William
    Beauregard 226
Pettit
  Jane E. 334
  Lola C. 334
Pettus
  Permelia V. 378
Petty
  L. B. 280
Phares
  Bolivar 316
  Cornelia E. 316
  Diana 316
  Elizabeth 316
  John G. 316

Phares (contd)
  Mary G. 110
Phelps
  George R. 205
  Walter Helen 243
  William F. 243
Phillips
  Adam E. 280
  Alice J. 164
  Annie E. 182
  Elizabeth D. 247
  Ellen Cobbs 281
  Florence M. 226
  Henry Jackson 111
  Infant Son 247
  John 226
  John T. 281
  L. W. 164
  Margaret
    Lawrence 227
  Martha Elizabeth 111
  Martha G. 227
  Mary E. 164
  Thomas A. 182
Pickens
  Fannie West 281
  William King 281
Pierce
  Eliza Ann 165
  H. C. 165
  Joe 165
  Rosie L. 165
  William F. 165
Pigford
  Emma S. 310
  Owen 310
  S. M. 310
  W. H. 310
Pinson
  Annie Bell
    Gilbert 361
  H. 361
Pond
  Annie 127
Poole
  Catherine J. 165
  Leonidas 343
  Octavia 343

Poole (contd)
  Theodoria 165
  Viola 165
Pope
  George L. 211
Porter
  Frederick 294
  James Lemuel 368
  Sallie Bell 368
Portis
  Benjamin Person 319
  Howard W. 319
  Susan Jane 319
Posey
  Eleanor 281
Post
  Agmon 192
  Azubah Chapman 192
Potts
  Anna McCarta 316
  __?__ry 316
Powe
  Allen C. 138
Powell
  C. L. 392
  E. A. Jr. 281
  Elizabeth Ann 174
  Luella B. 334
  Penelope 111
  Temperence 111
Powers
  Julia T. 145
Pratt
  Derius Edward 174
  Elizabeth P. 174
  George A. 174
  John W. 334
  Maude Callaway 281
  S. G. 343
  Sallie Boland 174
  Sarah Ann 343
  W. R. 343
  William 343
Praytor
  Hugh Boyd 148
  James Faulkner 392
  Mary Jane
    Stewart 148

Praytor (contd)
  Middleton A. 281
Prestwood
  Austin 138
  John 138
  Mary 138
  Mary Eleanor
    Powe 138
Price
  E. G. 281
Prince
  Richard 247
  Sarah E. 368
Pruitt
  Dewitt A. 281
  Leanora 227
Purser
  Charles 174
  Sarah Ann 174
Quarles
  Charles Mimms 335
  Frances 335
  Garrett Minor 281
  John James 335
  John M. 335
  Minnie Windham 335
  Sallie Boykin 335
Quimby
  Melissa Emeline 352
Radcliffe
  Frank 176
  Minnie A. 174
Ragsdale
  Hiram C. 192
Rainer
  Charles F. 238
  George W. 165
  Margaret A. 165
  W. J. 238
  William Robert 388
  Zilpha H. 394
Rambo
  Jincy 193
  Mary J. 193
Ramsay
  Alexander H. 120
  J. Reid 120
  James Wrenn 120

Ramsay (contd)
  Sarah I. 120
Ramsey
  Ella D. 133
  Emmett Templeton 361
  Hattie Permilia
    Sibley 361
  Moses F. 361
  Nancy Graves
    Yancy 133
  William R. 133
Randall
  Clara B. 281
  Newton 281
Rast
  David Irvin 281
  Ellen Ustick 281
Ratican
  Michael 282
Rawlins
  Susan 352
Rea
  Hilliard W. 317
  Mary 317
Read
  Rhoda 221
Reavis
  Mary B. 205
  Robert E. 193
  Turner 205
Reed
  John Harvey 149
  Miss 253
Reid
  Amanda 150
  Julia Hightower 388
  Reuben C. 335
  Sarah A. A. L. 335
  Susan L. 335
Rencher
  Elizabeth Jane 111
Renfroe
  Mary M. 304
  Molly E. 304
Rew
  Elizabeth W. 165
  Margaret 174
  Mattie K. 174

Rew (contd)
  R. H. 174
  Robert Y. 165
  W. B. 175
Reynolds
  Alfred C. 282
  Ella B. 282
  Jefferson
    Lavernia 294
Rhaly
  Bryant J. 310
  Margaret 311
Rhodes
  Charles E. 211
  Constance L. 211
  E. M. 211
  James 211
Rhyne
  Jabez A. 319
  John E. 319
  Mary H. 319
  Sarah A. 319
Richards
  Frank G. 388
  Susan Alvarez 388
Richardson
  A. W. 304
  Almeta E. 305
  Arch T. 305
  Bryant 320
  F. W. 320
  Freeman 232
  George A. 320
  Infant 320
  John H. 305
  John Ruffin 368
  Mary Emma 305
  Sallie T. 305
  Sarah J. 368
  Una Ray 320
  Uny 320
  W. H. 133
  __?__ 320
Richie
  Jabes C. 227
Rigdon
  Lexena Elizabeth 138

Riley
  William 120
Ritter
  John 335
  Wade 335
Rix
  Charles 120
  Eleanor Porter 120
  Frank Underwood 120
  Frederick Dial 120
  Harry Spence 120
  Rebecca 120
Roan
  G. T. 282
Roberts
  Baker L. 205
  Jack 175
  Lucy C. 205
  Nancy Ann 175
Robertson
  A. Mc. 121
  Ida Lee 205
  John H. 305
  Maria E. 205
  Virginia 205
  William Francis 205
Robinson
  B. R. 238
  Eliza M. 282
  James B. 217
  James D. 124
  James F. 377
  James L. 124
  Jennie A. 377
  Joseph A. 378
  Laura K. 217
  Mary E. 124
  Sarah C. 238
Robnett
  J. M. 371
  John Wilson 371
Rodgers
  Aaron 361
  Mossie C. 124
  W. E. 124
Rogers
  Alexander A. 340
  Annie E. 335

Rogers (contd)
  Asa D. 335
  C. M. A. 335
  Carrie Geiger 335
  Eliza Jane 336
  Eugenia A. 321
  James L. 336
  James Pinckney 336
  Jane Caroline 336
  John Aduston 193
  Joseph 336
  Laura Caledonia 357
  Lucy A. 336
  Margarette Jane 336
  Martha Eliza 336
  Mary Ann 357
  N. A. 336
  R. T. 322
  Sarah A. 336
  Sophia Gray 336
  Tabitha 336
  William 336
  William Baker 336
  William N. 357
Ross
  Diana 363
Rothrock
  George T. 240
Rous
  George L. 388
Royal
  M. A. 392
  Perrion Webster 388
Rumley
  Bella 388
  Elizabeth Tolson 175
  Fred 388
  Gertrude C. 388
  Infant 388
  Martin 175
  William T. 388
Rushing
  America E. 111
  Anzo Taylor 111
  Christopher C. 111
  Elizabeth 111
  Frances L. 352
  Franklin Pierce 111

Rushing (contd)
  George C. 111
  J. K. P. 145
  J. M. 111
  J. P. 145
  James M. 111
  John P. 145
  Leonidas 111
  Lorenzo 111,112
  Marshall B. 112
  Mary 112
  Mary Lee 112
  Shepherd 112
  Susan 112
  Susannah 112
  W. R. 145
  Mrs. W. R. 145
  Winston 112
Russell
  David Moor 205
  E. E. R. 296
  Elizabeth Reed 296
  Grandma 165
  Mary Bliss 205
  Mary Flint 205
  Walter W. 205
Rutherford
  James S. 154
  Mary Ann 154
Ryan
  John King 394
  Mary P. 394
Salmon
  William Thomas 183
Sample
  David E. 321
  Elizabeth 321
  R. T. 321
  Sallie E. 388
  Sarah 321
  W. N. 321
Sanders
  A. J. 252
  Edward C. 193
  Elizabeth J. 206
  John T. 127
  Maggie B. 282
  Moses M. 121

Sanders (contd)
  Rosey M. 206
  Thomas J. 206
  William 193
Sanford
  Joseph L. 294
Saunders
  Ellen J.
    Wedgeworth 227
  Sophia 282
Savage
  James 282
Sawls
  Ella J. 227
Scales
  Constantine
    Perkins 112
  Frances 395
  Harden L. 145
  Joseph P. 145
  Laura C. 145
  Martha Elizabeth 282
  Nancy Patton 145
  Thomas A. 145
  Uriah E. 145
  William A. 145
Scarborough
  A. R. 294
  Andrew Greer 294
  Annie 294
  James T. 294
  Lama A. 294
  Martha J. 336
  Nancy 294
  Ruth Greer 294
  William T. 294
Scarbrough
  William H. 282
Scott
  Eln ? 206
  John B. 193
  Kate W. 193
  Rebecca 175
Scruggs
  Etta Elizabeth
    Houston 282
  Fannie Lowe 282
  Infant 283

Scruggs (contd)
  J. L. 283
  James Whitehead 283
  Joseph Oglesby 283
  Malvine T. 283
  Tempie M. 283
Seale
  A. L. 146
  B. B. 146
  Bettie Currie
    Thetford 146
  Bluford 322
  Carter H. 322
  Elizabeth 322
  Frances M. 322
  Malinda F.
    McMillan 146
  Martha 168
  Mary Culpepper 322
  Mary E. Lockard 322
  R. L. 323
  Thomas F. 323
  William C. 323
Secrest
  James L. 361
Seely
  Caroline M. 283
  James D. 283
Seibert
  Elizabeth 112
  J. Nickel 112
  John 112
  William 112
Sewell
  Sue 305
Shackelford
  Infant 323
  James T. 323
  Jane 323
  Kerran Ann 324
  R. D. 254
  R. D. Jr. 324
  Richard D. 324
  Thomas G. 324
Shamburger
  Emma R. 165
  James Andrews 319
  Sarah Portis 319

Shamburger (contd)
  William B. 165
Shaver
  Caroline M. 336
Shaw
  Annie T. Glass 165
  Cynthia Alice
    Lewis 165
  E. M. 243
  Eastern 243
  Emeline R. 243
  Frances
    Elizabeth 243
  Marthie A. 243
  Orson 243
  R. W. 243
  Sarah Cornelia 243
  W. O. 243
  William Uriah 165
Shea
  Eliza Jane 157
  John 157
Shearer
  Ellen 283
  William Kirby 283
Sheffield
  A. 352
  Embly 352
  L. 352
Shelby
  J. T. 159
  Martha N. 183
  Mattie E. 311
  Nancy Jane 154
  S. N. 311
  William L. 154
Sheldon
  Mary W. 175
Shelton
  A. J. 159
  Add 352
  Elizabeth 159
  Huston Taylor 159
  J. K. P. 159
  Mary L. McDaniel 166
  Nancy C. 352
  R. J. 283
  Rachel C. 159

Shelton (contd)
  Robert R. 160
Sherard
  Alfred D. 283
  John H. 283
  Solon L. 283
Shurley
  America 175
  Dora 212
  Glemma 212
  Mariah E. 175
  Richard D. 175
  Sarah A. 175
  Sarah E. 212
  Thomas 175
Sibley
  S. B. 346
  Sarah R. 361
Silliman
  Alice Gibbs 311
  C. U. 121
  Jennie Mitchell 121
  Lizzie T. 311
  Mary A. 311
  S. M. 311
  William A. 311
  William C. 311
Simmons
  David S. 337
  James A. 155
  Susan A. 155
Simms
  Ben F. 305
  Harriett 305
  Henry H. 305
  John T. 305
  Leroy 305
  Leroy L. 305
  Mary Leslie 305
  William T. 305
Simpson
  Mat 254
Sims
  Aline J. 283
  H. J. 352
  Martha A. 345
  S. A. 352
  W. A. 283

Sims (contd)
  W. F. 345
  William Henry 388
  Willie 388
  __?__ J. M. 388
Sledge
  Annie H. 284
  Edward Simmons 284
Smith
  A. C. 388
  Addison
    Gillespie 284
  Adella M. 112
  Albert Henry 193
  Alice 206
  Alice F. 352
  Ann Berlin 206
  C. 357
  Charles C. 206
  Charlie B. 113
  Charlie Newton 389
  Cornelia E.
    Houston 284
  D. W. W. 357
  E. W. 284
  Elizabeth W. 357
  F. 357
  Florence D. 284
  Frances Grimes 345
  Harriet Harris 193
  Helen E. Cusack 284
  Isaac 206
  J. 357
  J. F. 357
  James H. 357
  James M. 311
  John D. 284
  John T. 284
  John W. 113
  John W. Jr. 113
  Joseph A. 284
  Josephine 113
  Lela Haupt 221
  Lena Hadden 284
  Louisa Ann 193
  Lucy B. 121
  M. S. 254
  Maggie J. 227

Smith (contd)
  Margaret Scott 113
  Martha E. 284
  Martha T. 113
  Mary 206
  Mary E. 357
  Mary Phifer 284
  Meliss Ann
    Henderson 206
  Ottaway E. 206
  P. 206
  Rebecca Frances 357
  Robert H. 311
  S. A. 357
  S. A. E. 285
  Sally Ann 285
  Samuel 285
  Sarah Ramsay 285
  Stephen N. 285
  Stephen Uriah 285
  Sterling S. 121
  Susan J. 357
  Susan T. 285
  Thomas B. 285
  Thomas W. 206
  W. W. 227
  Walter K. 285
  Walter N. 394
  William 357
  William Joseph 345
  William R. T. 358
  William Wiley 238
  Wright W. 358
Smitherman
  Martha 389
Smithline
  Charles 193
Smoot
  Elijah 374
Snedecor
  Eleanor 358
  F. P. 358
  James 358
  Lucy 358
  Sally 358
Snow
  Hamilton Post 193
  Kate Amelia 193

Snow (contd)
  Leveret 193
  Maria Esther 193
  Willie Atwater 194
Somers
  George 368
Soule
  Abigail 194
  Fannie 194
  John M. 194
Speed
  Dixie T. 146
  Elizabeth 113
  James B. 113
  James Franklin 175
  James R. 113
  John B. 175
  Margaret Jane 175
  Martha Ann 175
  Martha Carr 175
  S. E. 146
  Wager O. 176
Speight
  Edwin G. 337
Spencer
  Elizabeth B. 296
  Hannah P. 296
  Mary 395
  Shepherd 297
  Shepherd Jr. 297
  Susan E. 297
Spidle
  Elizabeth 113
  John M. 113
  Robert L. 113
  Sallie E. 113
Spincer
  Alex 395
  Ella 395
Spratt
  James P. 285
  John B. 361
  Lillis Barnett 285
  Mary 362
  Mattie A. Beggs 285
  Robert Barnett 285
  Robert D. 285
  Walter 362

Sprott
　John 285
　Leonora Brockway 286
　Mary 286
　Mary A. V. 286
　Robert 183
　Samuel Henry 286
Stabler
　Mary M. Portis 319
Stallings
　Burrel 352
　Drusilla 352
　J. M. Sr. 352
　J. T. 352
　James M. 352
　Mary F. 352
　Sarah Alice 353
　William 353
　William H. 353
Stallworth
　Joseph P. 343
　Mary J. 389
　Mattie Lynn 166
　__?__ 166
Stanton
　Mrs. E. E. 337
　Mrs. E. J. 337
　Elizabeth 337
　H. D. 337
　H. L. 337
　H. W. 337
　Henry G. 337
　James W. 337
　Joseph H. 206
　Mary Eugenia 337
　Mary Hardie 337
　Nancy 337
　R. W. J. 337
　Rebecca Elbira 337
　Sarah E. 337
　Warren G. 338
　Wilie J. 338
　William V. 338
　__?__ D. 338
Staples
　Elizabeth A. 286
Starnes
　Agnes 338

Starnes (contd)
　Lizzie Bell 338
Steavens
　H. H. 249
Steele
　Eliza Ann 206
　Theophilus 206
Steiner
　Kate 125
Steinwinder
　Thomas G. 376
Stephens
　A. M. 353
　Angeline 166
　Daniel Calvin 166
　Eliza Jane 166
　Elizabeth 249
　Isabella 353
　John H. 286
　Nancy Elizabeth 353
　Penelope R. 286
　W. H. 166
Stevenson
　Drucilla
　　Elizabeth 176
　Humphrey 176
　Mary Ann 358
Stewart
　Calvin L. 311
　Christina 311
　Emma L. 315
　John Monroe 315
　Julia Brown 148
　Norman 311
　Samuel A. 194
Stillings
　James N. 286
Stillman
　Carrie Fraser 194
　Fannie R.
　　Collins 194
　Martha Hammond 194
　Mary 194
　Sallie Dudley 194
Stone
　George W. 230
　Lizzie 231

Strutton
  Nancy Seale 323
Stuart
  Bettie 194
  J. T. 217
  John B. 217
  Martha A. 194
  Mary E. 217
Sturdivant
  Jessie J. 389
  Martha Troup 286
  Mary Ann 166
  Nannie L. 389
Sullivan
  Cornelia 294
  Helen Terrell 295
  James M. 295
Swain
  Anna E. 311
  J. H. 311
  J. N. 311
  J. T. 166
  L. A. 312
  Mary A. 312
  Mary V. 312
  N. E. J. 166
  Robert D. 312
  William S. 312
Swan
  Tency 286
Swilley
  Alice Caledonia 369
  John W. Sr. 369
  Mary 369
Talbot
  Edmund 295
  Rhoda 295
  Sophia C. 295
  W. H. 295
Tankersley
  Eva Luvenia 286
  Robert 286
  Sarah F. H. 286
Tartt
  A. B. 306
  Annie M. 286
  Cadmus E. 231
  Emily L. 306

Tartt (contd)
  James 306
  Martha Lela 121
  Martha M. 231
  Mary C. 306
  Nannie A. 231
  Thomas Morrison 287
Tate
  Anne E. 127
  Cornelia Ann 369
  Elizabeth 166
  Elizabeth R. 353
  Emma J. 160
  George W. 127
  J. E. 166
  J. H. 353
  James T. 160
  Mattie J.
    Sanders 127
  R. H. 127
  Sarah Gray 176
  William 369
Taylor
  Amanda 389
  Cyrus 370
  Dock Mills 113
  Eliza Amason 338
  Elizabeth Jane 370
  John W. 125
  Madison B. 113
  Martha Ann 370
  Mary Ann 370
  Narcissa 373
  Octavia L. 113
  Rufus 370
  Samuel 373
  Samuel William 338
  Sius 370
  W. F. 338
  W. P. 370
  William Leonidas 389
Tew
  H. J. 343
  James A. 176
  Jane 343
  W. W. 343
Thetford
  J. W. 320

Thigpen
  Sophia 338
Thom
  Margaret 287
Thomas
  Augusta 389
  Catina A. 133
  Edward 312
  Mary E. 312
  Narcissa F. 133
  Pollie Fulton 121
  William Maurice 133
Thompson
  Angelina S. 287
  Bassett Henry 166
  Felix Gibson 287
  Harvey P. 138
  J. W. 389
  James Harvey 287
  Mack 166
  Martha Clay 389
  Rufus K. 287
  Samuel 338
  Sarah A. 338
Thorn
  Rebecca 176
Thorne
  Robert Emily 353
  T. L. 249
Thornton
  Ellen Thom 287
  Henry Randolph 287
  Hortense
    Randolph 287
  Lucy Cobbs 287
  Maria A. 287
  Reuben Thom 287
  Seth B. 287
  Seth Brett 287
Tidmore
  Anna O. 371
  M. M. 389
Tidwell
  George 338
Tillman
  Sallie 221
  William H. 125

Tilman
  Annie W. 358
  Infant 358
Tims
  W. R. 238
Tisdale
  Alice 371
  J. W. 288
  Malcolm Henagan 288
Tolbert
  Mary Ellen 207
  Rhoda 207
Torry
  G. W. 146
  Kate M. 146
  M. Hadden 146
Townsend
  Mary 127
Travis
  Amos 372
  Elizabeth
    Coleman 372
  Ellen L. 372
  Enoch 372
  Harriet 372
  Jesse Cobb 288
  Rosa S. 288
  Wiley Coleman 372
Treadaway
  Ann Elizabeth 133
  Hollam A. 166
  Virginia M. 166
Trigg
  William S. 288
Trott
  David H. 288
  David H. Jr. 288
  John J. 288
  Margaret Ann 288
Truelove
  Elijah 353
  Elijah L. 166
  Elizabeth 353
  Jane 353
  Martin 353
  Sarah 353
Tucker
  Annie Lyde 389

Tucker (contd)
  Francis Dilard 389
  Howard 312
  Infant 312
  Janie Gillis 312
  Rilla E. 353
  Thomas J. 353
Tureman
  F. S. 288
  Matilda H. 195
  Sallie McGrew 288
  Zack 288
Turk
  Etta 288
  S. B. 288
Turner
  Alice 146
  Ann Alexander 207
  Ann M. 146
  C. K. 209
  D. L. 146
  Elizabeth 138
  Elizabeth
    Gillespie 146
  John S. 146
  Mattie A. 146
  Patience 338
  W. F. 146
  ___?___ 146
Turrentine
  Joshua Lucy 195
Tutt
  Ada V. 113
  Artelia 114
  Clara B. 114
  James Beazley 114
  James S. 114
  James V. 114
  Laurie L. 114
Twilley
  W. R. 312
Tymes
  W. H. 125
Tytler
  S. J. 207
Underwood
  Adelaide
    Randolph 121

Underwood (contd)
  Emma 121
  Infant 121, 227
  L. V. 121
  Mallie 288
Ungles
  John 389
(Unknown)
  Eleta 380
Upchurch
  Abel James 167
Ustick
  John G. 288
  Lydia Farand 288
  William King 289
Vail
  Dade Portis 176
  Sarah H. D. 176
  Sarah Olivia 176
Vandegraff
  Agnetta 207
  Juliette E. 207
  Juliette Ewing 207
  Samuel B. 207
  William J. 207
Vary
  Elbert M. 289
  John F. Jr. 289
Vaughan
  Edward C. 289
Vaughn
  A. L. 167
  C. C. 167
  Elizabeth 167
  M. A. 167
  Mary S. 233
Verell
  Mary 289
Vise
  Jane Flowers 114
Voss
  H. Otto 289
  W. H. A. 289
Wabbington
  Ed 254
Waddell
  Frances Ann 167
  James A. 167

Walker
  Bettie 354
  Evaline P. 354
  F. M. 354
  Florid R. 354
  James A. 354
  Jemerson 358
  John Oliver 354
  Joseph F. 354
  Lewis 167
  Lucy 354
  Lucy K. 354
  Maggie Stewart 312
  Matilda 167
  Mittie E. 354
  S. E. 354
  W. H. 354
  William Henry 358
Wall
  Elizaann 139
Wallace
  Eliza R. 176
  Emmer L. 167
  James 289
  Josephus 176
  T. B. 167
Waller
  Arthur T. 208
  B. 207
  Bettie B. 208
  Cary A. 208
  Corbin B. 208
  John W. 208
  Leon P. 208
  Logan 208
  Lucy 208
  Lucy W. 208
  Mary B. 208
  Samuel 208
Wallis
  Frances 373
Walston
  Maggie T. 147
Walton
  J. T. 176
  James F. 289
  LeVert F. 186
  Louise H. 176

Walton (contd)
  R. J. 176
  Rachel Laura 176
Ward
  A. E. 186
  A. Tommie 177
  Ann 289
  Ann M. 177
  David S. 167
  Francis Marion 345
  H. B. 177
  Hattie C. 177
  James W. 177
  Jane Margaret 289
  Laura R. 177
  Lizzie 363
  Minnie G. 345
  Mollie D. 167
  Mollie H. 177
  Rosener 363
  Solomon 177
  Susan L. 323
  Susie Ann 345
  Wallace M. 177
  Will 213, 250
Warren
  Elizabeth 389
Washington
  Benjamin L. 297
  Bettie 208
  Bettie A. 297
  Robert 208
  Robert W. 297
Watkins
  Hester C. 354
  Jane 362
  Levin 373
  Mary Ann 373
  Sarah 373
Watson
  Alabama W. 208
  Alice 212
  Elizabeth 244
  Harriett A. 213
  Hattie E. 208
  John 374
  Mattie B. 374

Watts
  Elizabeth Asbury 394
  Florence Godfrey 368
  John R. 394
  M. H. 394
  Martha Elizabeth 238
  W. H. 394
Weaver
  Hassie 354
  John B. 354
Webb
  Archibald C. 244
  C. H. 244
  Infant 368
  John Parker 368
  S. A. 244
  Sallie V. 167
  Sarah A. 125
  Sarah Ann 368
  V. P. 244
  William B. 244
Weir
  Peter 375
Welch
  L. S. 177
Weller
  Erin H. 221
  William H. 221
Wessenburg
  Maggie Kornegay 211
  William W. 211
Westbrook
  C. F. 167
  J. C. 167
  Mary E. 168
Westcott
  Georgie E. 177
  Georgie E. Preston 177
  Joseph Edwin 177
  Mollie E. 177
Weston
  Elizabeth 338
  G. L. 339
  Mary 339
  Robert Sr. 339
  Sallie E. Rogers 339
  William K. 339

Wetmore
  Laura Ledelle 289
  Richmond Pearson 289
Wheeling
  Esther 121
  William 121
Whitaker
  Sarah H. 339
White
  Addie Brown 149
  Ben 152
  D. P. 155
  Daniel O. 289
  David Campbell 149
  Drucilla C. 155
  George Sydney 213
  James 133
  John M. 208
  Luther L. 155
  Manervie 152
  Martha D. 339
  Mary 152
  Mary Ann 208
  Mary E. 213
  Miner 213
  Miriam E. 339
  Pleasant 213
Whitehead
  Jonathan 125
  Lemuel F. 290
  Mary E. 290
  Redding 290
  Tempee 125
Whitely
  C. H. 247
Whitfield
  James George 179
  Jane 324
  Susan Croom 179
Whitlow
  Stancel 392
Whitney
  David S. 208
Whitsett
  Jane 362
  John C. 208
  John G. 208
  Laura Bliss 208

Whitsett (contd)
    Martha B. 208
    Martha Lucretia 209
    W. J. 209
Whittle
    M. A. S. T.
        Godwing 345
Wiatt
    Henry H. 147
    John F. 168
    Josephine Mason 168
    Mary C. 147
    William C. 147
Wideman
    Henry 168
    Infant 125
    Len 376
    Nancy J. 376
    William E. 376
    Zeola Yeager 125
Wiggins
    C. P. 389
Wilder
    R. B. 312
    Robert N. 312
    Sarah O. 312
    W. H. 312
Wilkerson
    Amanda Thrash 125
    G. N. 125
    Martha J. 390
    W. M. 344
    Mrs. W. M. 344
Wilkinson
    D. C. 339
    J. L. 339
    Silas 339
William
    Howard 395
Williams
    Albert A. 227
    Charles Stokes 377
    David C. 377
    Eliza Gibbs 377
    Fannie H. 390
    Fletcher B. 390
    George W. 290
    Henry J. 155

Williams (contd)
    J. J. 160
    Johnson C. 290
    Maggie W. 183
    Margaret A. 155
    N. A. 155
    R. J. 155
    Sarah H. 290
    W.P. 155
    Z. R. 249
Williamses
    Edward 219
Williamson
    Eliza 241
    James F. 147
    Lena Harris 195
    Molly P. 147
    S. E. 147
    Squire 241
    Susan D. 195
    Virginia B. 195
Willingham
    Carrie Powers 133
    Phillip 133
Willis
    J. P. 227
    Martha Culpepper 238
    Sallie Elizabeth 227
Wilson
    Alex 290
    Boyd H. 209
    Fannie 306
    George W. 290
    George Westley 290
    Henderson Matilda
        Malinda 306
    Infant 290
    Isaac R. 306
    James Cobbs 290
    Jane Olivia 290
    Louiza 152
    Martha O. 306
    Mary McDaniel 368
    Mary Rebecca 290
    Matilda Ann 306
    Mollie U. 306
    Penninah 306
    R. D. 290

Wimberly
 Andrew Jackson 114
 Cora Landrum 114
 Emma J. 147
 S. A. 147
Wimbish
 L. J. 290
Windham
 Herbert Hargrove 339
 James I. 339
 Martha Ann 339
 Mattie 340
 Sallie Estelle 340
 Sarah 340
 Walter 340
 Wiley 340
Winningham
 J. H. 177
 Nancy E. 178
Winston
 A. A. 378
 Ann 378
 Ann Hall 379
 Anthony 379
 Charles Henry 379
 Edwin H. 379
 Fleta Olive 379
 Henry P. 379
 Infant 379
 Irene 379
 James M. 379
 John Anthony 379
 Margaret A. 379
 Mary A. 379
 Mary Agnes 379
 Rebecca Virginia
  Brodnax 379
 Sallie Ada 379
 Sallie Ann 380
 Sarah A. 380
 Thompson 380
 Virginia H. 380
 W. O. 380
 William M. 380
Wise
 Florencia R. 390
 J. C. 390

Witt
 Mary D. 392
 Monan 291
Wood
 Alphondas L. 390
 C. H. 390
 Charles 390
 Hester 390
 William H. 358
Woodall
 Amelia Ann 394
 Eliza Jane 394
 Frances
  Brazillia 394
 John Chamblis 394
 Lillie 394
 Mary Giles 394
 Melissa 395
 Sarah Amanda 395
 Sarah Elizabeth 395
 William A. 395
Woodard
 Felix Hamilton 121
Woods
 Elisha 380
 Sarah J. 380
Woodward
 Carolina 321
 Cora 321
 Joseph G. 321
 Julius E. 321
 L. A. 250
 M. C. 345
 Maggie 345
 Martha 125
 Martha C. 345
 Pricilla 213
 Sarah E. 321
 Thomas B. 346
Woolf
 Emily C. Pack 346
 Frances E. 346
 Frank Forrest 354
 Jefferson Perry 346
 Sallie Vaughn 346
 Sarah 160
 William Reddin 346

Wooten
  Joseph Richard 291
  Mary Martha
    Malvina 291
Wrenn
  Arthur McD. 122
  Catherine W.
    Cockrell 306
  Elias H. 306
  Elias N. 122
  Eliza P. 122
  George M. 122
  Infant 307
  J. Walter 122
  James 122
  James T. 307
  Josiah 122
  Josiah H. 307
  Margaret J. 122
  Mary E. 122
  Mary Frances
    Templeton 122
  Nancy Elizabeth 147
  Nannie E.
    Cockrell 307
  Rixie Richardson 307
  Samantha A. 134
Wright
  Angeline 155
  Armelia 155
  Daniel L. 155
  Ida Coleman 291
  James W. 155
  John L. 155
  Samuel Inge 291
  Sarah DeV. 291
  W. A. 209
Wyatt
  John 254
Wylie
  Oliver 390
Yarbrough
  Alfred 134
  Ambrose 238
  Joseph 238
  Mary 134
  Mary Ann 134
  Neil Smith 134

Yeager
  John C. 125
  M. B. 125
  Mary E. Johnston 125
  Medora D. 126
Young
  Allen A. 126
  Alzira 126
  F. J. 126
  Fannie W. 126
  J. M. 126
  Lizzie G. 126
  Margaret 126
  Narcisa P. 126
  O. C. 178
  Robert 126
  Robert A. 126
  Thomas Eugene 340
  W. W. 126
  William Robert 126

www.ingramcontent.com/pod-product-compliance
Lightning Source LLC
Chambersburg PA
CBHW071222230426
43668CB00011B/1272